The Brownings' Correspondence

Volume 1
September 1809 – December 1826
Letters 1 – 244

EBB as a Baby

The Brownings' Correspondence

Edited by

PHILIP KELLEY & RONALD HUDSON

Volume 1

———

September 1809 – December 1826

Letters 1 – 244

Wedgestone Press

The editorial work on this volume was made possible in part by a grant from the National Endowment for the Humanities, an independent federal agency.

The plates for this volume were made possible by a subvention from the John Simon Guggenheim Memorial Foundation.

Published and Distributed by
Wedgestone Press
P.O. Box 175
Winfield, KS 67156

Library of Congress Cataloging in Publication Data

Browning, Robert, 1812–1889.
    The Brownings' correspondence.

    Correspondence written by and to Robert and Elizabeth Barrett Browning.
        Includes index.
        Contents: v. 1. September 1809–December 1826, letters 1–244.
        1. Browning, Robert, 1812–1889—Correspondence.
2. Browning, Elizabeth Barrett, 1806–1861—Correspondence.
3. Poets, English—19th century—Biography.   I. Browning, Elizabeth Barrett, 1806–1861.   II. Kelley, Philip.
III. Hudson, Ronald.   IV. Title.
    PR4231.A43   1984   821'.8 [B]   84–5287
    ISBN 0–911459–09–X

Manufactured in the United States of America.

A Request

The editors invite all users of this edition to convey any additions or corrections by writing to them through the publisher.

Contents

[v]

Illustrations

[vii]

Acknowledgements

THE DEBTS WE HAVE INCURRED in collecting and editing the Brownings' correspondence are virtually without number—and as the volumes are issued in the ensuing years, the count will increase immeasurably. Additional acknowledgements will be listed in our final volume.

The initial source of inspiration of this edition can be traced to the late A.J. Armstrong, Chairman of the English Department at Baylor University during forty years. Fifty years ago he publicly expressed the need for a collected edition of the poets' correspondence (*Baylor Bulletin*, 1934). Although Dr. Armstrong had the vision, it was too soon after Browning's death for anyone to pursue constructively such a comprehensive publication. Dr. Armstrong's energy was channelled into teaching, and creating a unique study centre on Baylor's campus which would foster a climate for future editorial endeavours. Here in the Browning Room (later greatly expanded into the present Armstrong Browning Library) he gathered all published sources relating to the Brownings, and collected original documents that form the nucleus of this edition.

It was the late Mary Maxwell Armstrong who transferred her husband's vision to the present editors. Mrs. Armstrong succeeded her husband as director of the Armstrong Browning Library and in that capacity fostered in us an interest in the poets. Her examples of energy and determination have since been a constant inspiration.

Our deepest gratitude goes to the owners of the letters, individuals and institutions, who have allowed us to publish them. Full details of these owners are given in the List of Collections at the end of each volume.

Readers will see the extent of our indebtedness to thirteen libraries where much of our research was conducted, and we are pleased to record our gratitude both to the libraries and the persons who facilitated our labours: the Armstrong Browning Library, Baylor University (especially Jack W. Herring, Betty A. Coley, Rita S. Humphrey, Nancy B. Dobbins, Veva B. Wood and the late Sue Moore); Balliol College, Oxford (especially E.V. Quinn and the late John Bryson); The Henry W. and Albert A. Berg Collection, New York Public Library, Astor, Lenox and Tilden

Foundations (especially Lola L. Szladits and the late John Gordan); The Fitzwilliam Museum, Cambridge (especially Phyllis M. Giles and Paul Woudhuysen); The Henry E. Huntington Library (especially Jean F. Preston, Mary Robertson and Sara S. Hodson); The Pierpont Morgan Library (especially C.A. Ryskamp and Herbert Cahoon); The Carl H. Pforzheimer Library (especially Donald H. Reiman and Mihai H. Handrea); St. Marylebone Central Library (especially A.J.D. Stonebridge and Ann Saunders); The Browning Collection, Denison Library, Scripps College (especially Judy Harvey Sahak); The Harry Ransom Humanities Research Center, University of Texas (especially John P. Chalmers, Ellen S. Dunlap and Cathy Henderson); Alexander H. Turnbull Library (especially Gillian M. Ryan and Patricia A. Sargison); The English Poetry Collection, Wellesley College (especially Hannah D. French, Eleanor L. Nicholes, Eleanor A. Gustafson and Anne Anninger); and The Beinecke Library, Yale University (especially Marjorie Wynne).

We would here like to record our great indebtedness to Edward R. Moulton-Barrett who has given every possible assistance and encouragement. Having allowed us unrestricted access to his collection of family papers, through his intervention we met other members of the family: John Altham, Mary V. Altham, R.J.L. Altham, the late Roger Curry, Anthony Moulton-Barrett, the late Edward F. Moulton-Barrett, the late Edward S. Moulton-Barrett, Gordon E. Moulton-Barrett, Kenneth A. Moulton-Barrett, Myrtle Moulton-Barrett and Ronald A. Moulton-Barrett. All these received us with kindness, and gave permission to publish material in their possession, for which we record our thanks.

Collectors everywhere have been generous and helpful. From these, five must be singled out for special thanks: Michael C. Meredith, Richard Little Purdy, Gordon N. Ray, John M. Schiff, and R.H. Taylor.

Many others have contributed to this edition. We wish to record our gratitude for various services and favours to: Elaine Baly, Joan Barenholtz, Warner Barnes, Anne Biss, Walter Blanco, Roy E. Bolton, Michael Case, Elizabeth Chellis, Nancy N. Coffin, Morton N. Cohen, Norman Colbeck, Nora Collings, Rosalie Glynn Grylls (Lady Mander), Edward F. Guiliano, Gordon S. Haight, N. John Hall, Peter N. Heydon, Eleanor Hoag, David J. Holmes, Park Honan, Emily Blanchard Hope, T.S. Hope, Jr., Nicholas Horne, Ian Jack, Velma Prince Kelley, Warren R. Kelley, William D. Kelley, Peter Kinnear, Rena Kleefeld, Gretchen H. Lainson, Hal Lainson, Cecil Y. Lang, Mark Samuels Lasner, Edward C. McAleer, Thomas McBeth, Thomas K. Myer, Winifred A. Myers, Robert Nikirk, Anelle O'Neil, Donald Owen, Frank Paluka, William S. Peterson, Willard B. Pope, Meredith B. Raymond, Margaret Reynolds, Barbara Rosenbaum,

R.E.B. Sawyer (of Chas. J. Sawyer, booksellers), Margaret Smith, Jim Speer, Mary Rose Sullivan, Karen Summers, G. Thomas Tanselle, Richard Townsend, Alexander D. Wainwright, Jack Wernette, Margaret Wernette, and Fred J. Wippich.

Formal acknowledgements are given to the American Council of Learned Societies, the American Philosophical Society, the John Simon Guggenheim Memorial Foundation, the National Endowment for the Humanities, and The Carl and Lily Pforzheimer Foundation, for funds without which this work could not have been carried forward.

We are grateful for permission to quote from letters with a provenance to Sotheby's Moulton-Barrett Sale, 7 June 1937, copyright of which was transferred by John Murray, now in the holdings of: Armstrong Browning Library, Baylor University; The Henry W. and Albert A. Berg Collection, The New York Public Library, Astor, Lenox, and Tilden Foundations; British Library; The Pierpont Morgan Library; The Harry Ransom Humanities Research Center, University of Texas; and The Beinecke Rare Book and Manuscript Library, Yale University.

Grateful acknowledgements go to those cited in the lists of illustrations for this and subsequent volumes. Thanks to them we can augment the correspondence with a wealth of portraits and other pictorial items.

In conclusion, grateful thanks are given to John Murray, for permission to quote from the works of the Brownings protected by his copyright.

Cue Titles, Abbreviations & Symbols

ABL	Armstrong Browning Library, Baylor University, Waco, Texas
Altham	Mary V. Altham, Babbacombe, England
Altham, R.J.L.	R.J.L. Altham, London
Berg	The Henry W. & Albert A. Berg Collection, The New York Public Library, Astor, Lenox and Tilden Foundations
B-GB	*Letters of the Brownings to George Barrett*, ed. Paul Landis (Urbana, 1958
Bibliotheca Bodmeriana	Bibliotheca Bodmeriana, Cologny-Geneva, Switzerland
BIS	*Browning Institute Studies*, (New York, 1973–)
BL	British Library, London
Browning Collections	*The Browning Collections. Catalogue of Oil Paintings Drawings & Prints; Autograph Letters and Manuscripts, Books ... the Property of R.W. Barrett Browning, Esq.* (London, 1913). Reprinted in Munby, *Sale Catalogues*, VI (1972), 1–192
Checklist	*The Brownings' Correspondence: A Checklist*, comps. Philip Kelley and Ronald Hudson (New York and Winfield, Kansas, 1978)
Collings	Nora Collings, Borough Green, England
Diary	*Diary by E.B.B.: The Unpublished Diary of Elizabeth Barrett Barrett, 1831–1832*, eds. Philip Kelley and Ronald Hudson (Athens, Ohio, 1969)
DNB	*Dictionary of National Biography*
EBB	Elizabeth Barrett Barrett / Elizabeth Barrett Browning
ERM-B	Edward R. Moulton-Barrett, Platt, England
GM-B	Gordon Moulton-Barrett, Miami, Florida
Hereford	County Council of Hereford and Worcester, Records Office, Hereford
Huntington	The Henry E. Huntington Library, San Marino, California
HUP	*Elizabeth Barrett Browning. Hitherto Unpublished Poems and Stories*, ed. H. Buxton Forman, 2 vols. (Boston, 1914)

[xv]

Marks	Jeannette Marks, *The Family of the Barrett* (New York, 1938)
MM-B	Myrtle Moulton-Barrett, Ringwood, England
Morgan	The Pierpont Morgan Library, New York
MPL	*Patrologiæ Cursus Completus . . . Series Latina*, ed. Jacques Paul Migne (Paris, 1844–65)
OED	*Oxford English Dictionary*
PG-C	Philip Graham-Clarke, Abergavenny, Wales
"Poems by EBB"	Notebook in the hands of EBB and Mary Moulton-Barrett entitled "Poems by Elizabeth B. Barrett," now in the Berg Collection (see *Reconstruction*, D1419)
"Poems by EBB II"	Collection of EBB's compositions in the hand of Mary Moulton-Barrett, now in the Berg Collection (see *Reconstruction*, D1420)
RAM-B	Ronald A. Moulton-Barrett, Aberdeenshire, Scotland
RB	Robert Browning
Reconstruction	*The Browning Collections: A Reconstruction*, comps. Philip Kelley and Betty A. Coley (London, New York, Waco, Texas and Winfield, Kansas, 1984)
SBHC	*Studies in Browning and His Circle* (Waco, Texas, 1973–)
Scripps	Browning Collection, The Ella Strong Denison Library, Scripps College, Claremont, California
SD	Supporting Document. A checklist of contemporary supporting documents appears in this and subsequent volumes. Appendix II to this volume contains SD1–SD577
Tayler	Mrs. H.M. Tayler, London
Texas	The Harry Ransom Humanities Research Center, University of Texas, Austin, Texas
Tragi-Comedy	Maisie Ward, *The Tragi-Comedy of Pen Browning* (New York, 1972)
UCLA	Special Collections, University of California, Los Angeles, California
Wellesley	Wellesley College Library, The English Poetry Collection, Wellesley, Massachusetts
[ ]	Square brackets indicate material inserted by editors
⟨ ⟩	Angle brackets denote some irregularity in the manuscript. The absence of a note indicates that the information within the brackets is a conjectural reconstruction caused by seal tear, holes or physical deterioration of the manuscript
⟨. . .⟩	Angle brackets enclosing ellipsis show an actual omission caused by a defect or physical irregularity in the manuscript. Except in the case of text lost

through seal tears, holes, etc., the nature of the irregularity is indicated by a note. This symbol appears on a line by itself if lost text exceeds half a line

⟨★★★⟩   Angle brackets enclosing triple stars indicate the lack of a beginning or end of a letter

| | Vertical bars are used before and after a word which, though not physically obliterated, is a word of uncertain transcription

. . .   Ellipses indicate omissions from quoted material in notes and supporting documents, but in the actual texts of the Brownings' correspondence they merely reproduce the writers' style of punctuation

Introduction

THE AIM OF THIS EDITION is twofold: to provide accurate and complete transcriptions of all known letters written by and to Robert and Elizabeth Barrett Browning, and to complement them with consistent annotations. When the last volume is completed, we feel that literary historians, critics, biographers—as well as casual readers—will share our firm belief that this collection is one of the most important of all Victorian literary correspondences.

History of the Project

The first public notice of our intention to publish this edition appeared in 1963—*Victorian Poetry*, 1, 238–239. Much preparatory work had already gone into the project prior to this announcement. The initial interest, nurtured by the late Mary Maxwell Armstrong, Director of the Armstrong Browning Library (1954–59), Baylor University, was focussed on compiling a census of all Browning correspondence. As each letter was located, a file was established to record the following data: 1) date; 2) address from which the letter was written; 3) addressee; 4) source of information; 5) prior publishing history; and 6) location of the original document. Some of this information was gathered as early as 1957.

In only a very few cases were we able to record all this information at one time. Many of the letters were undated; the addressee was often just "a dear friend"; prior publications were often embedded in obscure periodicals or editions of Victorian memoirs; and, because of their commercial value, original manuscripts were constantly changing hands before finally reaching a permanent collection. An earlier publication, *Robert Browning: A Bibliography*, eds. Broughton, Northup and Pearsall (Ithaca, New York, 1953), had listed almost 1,900 letters written by RB. It was indispensable in the initial stage of our project, but no such tool existed for EBB's letters.

Much of the concentrated research prior to the 1963 announcement was conducted in London, a few blocks from 50 Wimpole Street in the Borough of St. Marylebone, which has one of the best public libraries in

England. Its staff located and requested through inter-library loan over a thousand volumes of Victorian belles-lettres, from which references to the Brownings and their correspondence were gleaned. Hundreds of letters were written to libraries in Great Britain, the United States and the Continent, surveying their holdings for original letters of the poets. At the end of 1960 over 4,000 entries had been logged and it seemed that the census was nearing completion.

Unexpectedly, an acquaintance was struck with Edward R. Moulton-Barrett, great-grandson of Elizabeth Barrett Browning's brother Alfred. He showed considerable interest in our undertaking and proved invaluable both as a source of unrecorded family history, and in securing introductions to various relations whom he thought might possess additional material for our study. Mr. Moulton-Barrett's own collection of family papers, none of which had ever previously been made available for research or public scrutiny, was so extensive that it took eight months to compile a catalogue of its contents. (These papers are included in the Checklist of Supporting Documents, commencing with Appendix II of this volume.)

With few exceptions, up to this time (1960) the census reflected manuscripts in major public institutions or in well-known private collections. It seemed logical that many letters and items of Browningiana must exist in out-of-the-way locations elsewhere. We were concerned that letters, particularly in the hands of descendants of original recipients, were likely to remain inaccessible and uncatalogued unless a means of publicizing the census could be found, providing an avenue through which owners could contact us.

It was also a concern that no practical steps were being taken by Browning enthusiasts to commemorate the centenary of the death of Elizabeth Barrett Browning—29 June 1961. Thus was born a plan to link the need for wider awareness of the census to an exhibition of manuscripts, first editions, portraits and other memorabilia, suitably displayed to commemorate the forthcoming centenary.

The St. Marylebone Central Library readily agreed to sponsor and mount the exhibition. Mr. Moulton-Barrett gave his enthusiastic support by lending material for display. Queen Elizabeth II graciously lent Victoria's copy of a rare edition of *Sonnets from the Portuguese* and agreed to our quoting unpublished passages from Victoria's diary about *Aurora Leigh*. The British Library lent one of its rarest books, the only known copy remaining in England of EBB's *The Battle of Marathon*, and the National Portrait Gallery supplied the Field Talfourd portraits of the poets. From Wellesley College, some of the original love letters were flown to London, to be displayed with the original marriage certificate and wedding rings. The appeal for suitable items to include, made to the general public, met with overwhelming response. Eventually 144 items were selected, a catalogue of which was compiled. The event opened on 31 May 1961. It was well covered by the press, and so well attended that its duration was extended a month past the originally announced closing of 8 July.

The primary benefit ensuing was that it led to numerous new items of Browningiana being reported from throughout the English-speaking world, most in private hands. Indirectly the exhibition led to grants being awarded by the American Philosophical Society and the John Simon Guggenheim Memorial Foundation which enabled us to record this newly-reported material. The grants also enabled us to spend three months in the stacks of the British Library recording information from the catalogues of auctioneers and book dealers. The funding also allowed us to add to our files a seventh category—photocopies or transcripts of the correspondence, greatly needed to assign chronology to undated letters.

As the material was processed, we became conscious of the significance of the new discoveries, and the implications contained therein. As our files began taking on the character of the nucleus of a much-needed publication of the correspondence, we elected to set aside the census and to concentrate on an edition of the full text of the letters. At the time of our 1963 announcement we had located some 8,000 letters and optimistically estimated that the project would "result in a twenty-volume edition of the letters, taking some fifteen years to complete. The first volume should appear in six to eight years." We neglected to preface our statement with some form of qualifying phrase as "Subject to funding . . ."!

With the hope of securing institutional funding for the publication, in 1964 our files and base of operation were relocated from England to the United States. Unfortunately the enormity of the undertaking has proved to be the major obstacle preventing our finding a single underwriting agent. To date it remains primarily sustained by private funds. Our commitment to edit the edition did not lessen, but by necessity it became secondary to our careers in the world of publishing. Our focus on Browning studies was concentrated on smaller projects, as time permitted.

One project involved editing an earlier discovery. On 29 June 1961, exactly one hundred years after the death of Elizabeth Barrett Browning, Kenneth A. Moulton-Barrett, on the intercession of his cousin Edward, had produced a manuscript, bound in a paper wrapper and annotated in the hand of Robert Browning "Diary by E.B.B." In 1965, ownership of the document changed hands when it was acquired by the Berg Collection of the New York Public Library. With permission, we proceeded to edit the manuscript, and it was subsequently published by Ohio University Press in April 1969. Second grants from both the American Philosophical Society and the Guggenheim Foundation followed shortly thereafter.

Soon after the diary's release we became involved in another Browning project—only this time it was not related to a publication. In October 1969, we received a telephone call from Congressman W.R. Poage's office, asking if we knew that "the Brownings' abode in Florence, Italy, was going to be destroyed." The Armstrong Browning Library, in Poage's district, had been unsuccessful in an attempt to preserve Casa Guidi, and the Congressman's staff was notifying anyone with Browning interests. Visiting Italy later in the month, we learned that the rooms had been sold and were to be converted into commercial offices. However, there was a clause in the contract to the effect that, if a plan were forthcoming by midnight, 20 March 1970, by which the Brownings' rooms could be preserved as a memorial to the poets, the sale could be cancelled. We reported our findings to the New York Browning Society and the group initiated a fund-raising campaign. For the next two years much of our energy was devoted to helping the society successfully raise the sum necessary to preserve Casa Guidi. In 1971, title to the rooms was vested in the Browning Institute, a group with an international membership, formed for this purpose.

The interest caused by the publication of EBB's diary, and the popular news coverage about the securing of Casa Guidi, resulted in new and startling reports of original correspondence. This was all duly recorded.

By 1973, ten years after our announcement, notable technological advances were being made in computer and word processing equipment. As we worked daily in the printing industry, we foresaw a time when the collected edition would make use of these developments. As an interim aid to Browning scholarship, we reverted to the census project and published *The Brownings' Correspondence: A Checklist* (New York and Winfield, Kansas, 1978).

This publication produced various ramifications. Again new letters were uncovered or reported, now recorded in five supplements in *Browning Institute Studies*. It also succeeded in providing us with full access to several collections where admission had previously been restricted. Most important, however, is the role the *Checklist* played in a text-editing grant being awarded by the National Endowment for the Humanities. This 1979–81 grant enabled us to finalize editorial work—taking full advantage of technological advances in word processing and photo-typesetting computers—on the letters covering the years 1809–41.

Now, twenty-one years after our first public notice of this work, we offer the initial volume, confident that the delay, while frustrating, has been beneficial. We are cognizant of the current critical attention being given to the Brownings and the rumblings for new biographies and annotated texts. None can be more aware of the fact that, if such studies are to be anywhere near definitive, they will be gravely hampered until the publication of this edition is well advanced. As we go to press we have records of approximately 10,500 documents, and others continue to appear with regularity. We can foresee that, when complete, this edition may include as many as 12,000 letters and fill forty volumes. Time has taught us to be circumspect in projecting a date for its completion. We simply state that the volumes will be forthcoming and as timely as possible within the framework of available funds. As they do appear, we look forward to their acting as a basis for a balanced evaluation of the Brownings, both in their lives and their works.

A first glance by one who wishes to study the letters of the Brownings would suggest that there is an embarrassment of riches. Starting with S.R. Townshend Mayer's edition of EBB's letters to R.H. Horne (1877), numerous volumes of the correspondence have appeared. Other letters are embedded in articles, critical studies, and biographies. The superficial indications of plenitude are, however, misleading. Despite the published volumes of letters to individual correspondents, some of them splendidly edited, there are only three general collections of the correspondence, and each of these suffers from editorial deficiencies. Moreover, fewer than a third of all known letters have appeared in print. Many that were published some time ago suffered extensive excisions to avoid embarrassment to persons still living or unfavourable mention of individuals only recently dead.

One criticism of this project, although uncommon, is that the Brownings are not worthy of a collected edition. From our position, having studied the whole of the correspondence in manuscript, we disagree. While some social notes are of marginal interest, they are by word count a small fraction of the whole output. A large collection of letters is more than the sum of its parts, and it often happens that a trivial note that would hardly seem to merit publication proves to be the missing piece in a jigsaw puzzle which would otherwise defy the most pertinacious scholar.

Other critics state that it is sufficient to have the original letters available in libraries. Even if an individual could travel from Tokyo to Leningrad and master the handwritings, one-third of the manuscripts are in private hands and not automatically accessible. Admittedly, the scope of this publication is staggering. Various alternatives and shortcuts have been suggested from its conception. It is our firm belief that no substitute for a conventionally published edition of the Brownings' collected correspondence will adequately serve the needs of scholars.

Some readers will undoubtedly question the inclusion of so much juvenilia. While not attempting to endow this material with any significant literary value, we do feel strongly that it all adds to the picture of EBB as the prized daughter of an affluent family, and gives biographical perspective both to her and those around her.

We do not feel it is appropriate to attempt, in this first volume, any critical evaluation of the complete corpus of the Brownings' correspondence. We do intend to venture such an analysis in the final volume, when readers will have all the letters available in print and will be better able to weigh our comments.

For those readers who are interested in locations of originals or in the past publishing history of the correspondence, or who wish to study the scope of forthcoming volumes, we refer them to our earlier work, *The Brownings' Correspondence: A Checklist*, and its ongoing supplements, published periodically in *Browning Institute Studies*.

To help establish a general overview of this collected edition it is useful to have a basic knowledge of each poet's early background, to know the development of their general and joint correspondences and have their views on its preservation and publication, all of which has direct bearing on the material available for this edition.

Generally speaking, the preservation of letters is always influenced by the fame of their writer. That we have earlier and more letters of EBB, directed outside the family circle, is largely due to her determination to reach "the beacon of fame" (see p. 352). This influence can also explain why we have later letters written by Tennyson and Landor to their fellow-poets, but lack those penned by EBB's sisters.

RB and His Background

Robert Browning was born in Southampton Street, Camberwell, 7 May 1812, the first child of Robert and Sarah Anna (*née* Wiedemann) Browning. His paternal ancestry was firmly planted in rural Dorset, where his forebears lived at or near Woodyates. Among the first to leave this setting was Robert Browning, grandfather of the poet. With the sponsorship of the local Dorset lord, the fourth Earl of Shaftesbury, he received a clerk's appointment in the Bank of England in 1769. He was later promoted to First Clerk of the Bank-Stock division, a position he held until his retirement in 1821. In 1778 he married Margaret Tittle and they settled at Battersea where their first child, Robert Browning, father of the poet, was born in 1782. Two years later the family removed to Camberwell. A few years later Reuben, a great-uncle of the poet, also settled in the immediate area and played a key role in the development of his nephew, RB's father.

RB's maternal ancestry can be traced to Dundee, Scotland, where his mother, Sarah Anna Wiedemann, was born at Sea-Gate House in 1772. Her grandfather, William Wiedemann, often referred to as German, was probably a Dutchman who had immigrated to Scotland. Prior to 1806, sometime after the death of her father (a mariner, also named William) and possibly that of her mother, she moved to England. She settled with or near her sister, who had married a Camberwell brewer, William Silverthorne.

Browning's father, after an aborted attempt at working on the West Indies plantations belonging to the Tittle family, took up a career as a clerk at the Bank of England in 1803. His father's influence no doubt contributed to this appointment, as it did in securing positions in the house of Rothschild for sons William and Reuben. After the death of Margaret Tittle Browning, her husband remarried and eventually settled in Islington, but her son remained at Camberwell where he met and married Sarah Anna Wiedemann, 19 February 1811.

They settled in a modest cottage and proceeded to raise a family, the poet and his sister Sarianna, born 1814. Influenced by his father, Browning developed artistic and literary abilities very early in life. From his mother, he absorbed an interest in music, and was much influenced by her intense religious devotion.

Amidst this scene of domestic tranquillity, with extended family members living near at hand, the emphasis on written communications seems to have been slight. However, letters that were exchanged, from the poet's earliest days, were carefully preserved. These were found among RB Senior's effects upon his death in Paris in 1866. They were stored in a trunk, along with copies of *Pauline*, at 19 Warwick Crescent. RB's early letters, written during his trip to Russia (1834), and his two visits to Italy (1838 and 1844), are assumed to have been in the collection. Unfortunately, in 1887, RB spent over a week destroying much of the contents of this trunk. As a result, records of RB's early life are very sparse.

We do know that RB spent very little time away from his family except for his three trips abroad. Prior to his marriage, RB and his family lived in modest circumstances in the London suburbs of either Camberwell or New Cross. These homes were overflowing with his father's books and graced by his mother's much-admired gardens. At New Cross, RB's study, "the little writing room of mine," was on the top floor, traditionally thought once to have been the secret chapel of a Roman Catholic family.

On the whole, it is apparent that RB's need and inclination to write letters were limited. Also, one must bear in mind the high cost of postage. Most family members and friends would be addressed in person, and written messages to friends in London were primarily perfunctory. Exceptions are RB's letters written to male companions abroad: Alfred Domett, Joseph Arnould and Amédée de Ripert-Monclar. Simply put, letter writing was not a major occupation for RB. Only in his letters to EBB did he consistently apply himself to the role of all-encompassing correspondent.

EBB and Her Background

Elizabeth Barrett Moulton-Barrett was born at Coxhoe Hall, County Durham, 6 March 1806, at seven in the evening. The first-born of Edward and Mary (*née* Graham-Clarke) Moulton-Barrett, she was privately baptized three days later by a family friend, the Rev. William Lewis Rham, Rector of Fersfield in Norfolk. Both her paternal and maternal families enjoyed great prominence and wealth and had a long-established relationship, primarily in matters of business.

The Barrett fortunes reached their apogee during the lifetime of Edward Barrett (1734–98), EBB's paternal great-grandfather, builder and owner of Cinnamon Hill Estate, Jamaica, whose only surviving child, Elizabeth, had married Charles Moulton. At his expressed desire, his heirs, his daughter's two surviving children, Edward and Samuel, assumed in 1798 the Barrett name and coat-of-arms, thus creating a new family name—Moulton-Barrett.[1] It was John Graham-Clarke, EBB's grandfather, who acted as intermediary for Edward of Cinnamon Hill and secured permission from the King for the change (see SD23, Appendix II).

Troubles overtook the Barrett empire not long after the 1798 death of Edward of Cinnamon Hill. These stemmed from family conflicts and from questionable management under absentee ownership, plus such factors as poor crops, low sugar prices, and unsettled world conditions.

Judith Barrett, Edward's widow, remarried when she was sixty to Michael White Lee, a much younger man. He was "a gay Captain and forsook her." Judith left Jamaica and settled at Bristol, England. It is unclear whether she settled there to be near her daughter, Elizabeth Moulton, or the daughter went to Bristol to be with her mother, but they resided there and at nearby Clifton until Judith's death and her burial in Bristol Cathedral, 1804. During the succeeding years Elizabeth Moulton and her companion, Mary Trepsack, moved frequently, taking leases of residences in or near London.

Edward Moulton-Barrett and his brother, both born in Jamaica, had travelled "home" to England in 1792 to commence their formal education.

---

1. However, Edward and Samuel stylized the usage as Edward M. Barrett and Samuel M. Barrett, the full name appearing only on legal documents. From the earliest, Elizabeth signed her works and letters E.B. Barrett or E.B.B. The only recorded instances where she gave her signature in full as Elizabeth Barrett Moulton-Barrett were on her marriage certificate and register (see *Reconstruction*, H598 and 599). It was only after EBB's death that her brothers and their children began to use the double-barrelled name. RB explains this appellation in a letter to George Murray Smith, 19 July 1889: "The name should be—Elizabeth Barrett Browning—if referring to later years,—Elizabeth Barrett Moulton-Barrett, if to earlier. Her name *was* as I gave it—her Father having added the second name to his own surname—so that the two were borne and discarded together."

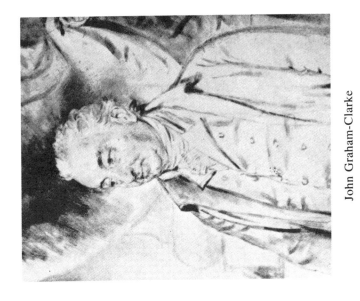

John Graham-Clarke

Arabella Graham-Clarke

Kenton Lodge

Fenham Hall

Coxhoe Hall

Edward never returned to Jamaica. There is confusion about the brothers' early years in England. Apparently they did not spend much time with their mother, but were away at school or being tutored privately. Records indicate that they were frequent guests, during holidays, of the Graham-Clarke family at Newcastle-upon-Tyne.

Edward attended prestigious Harrow school, but his length of time there is not certain. Family legend has it that he was soon withdrawn by his mother after having been severely beaten by an older boy for letting some toast burn.[2] Records show that he entered Trinity College, Cambridge, in 1801, and studied under a famous tutor, Thomas Jones, known for his strong stand against slavery. One of Edward's close student associates at Cambridge was John Kenyon, whose linkages with the families of EBB and RB are incredibly complex. Kenyon, like Edward Moulton-Barrett, had been born in Jamaica of a wealthy plantation family. His family was related to the Barretts and had close business ties with RB's Tittle forebears. Prior to knowing Edward Moulton-Barrett at Cambridge, Kenyon had been a schoolmate of RB's father at Bristol.

While at Cambridge, Edward declared his love for Mary, eldest daughter of John Graham-Clarke. By all accounts she was a beautiful and gentle girl, being described thus by her mother at this time: "With cheeks whose blushes baffle Flora's paint. / Sweet girl thus blessed with every Native grace / While days succeeding yet new graces bring / Still may your mind grow lovely as your face / With both may every season prove a spring!" (SD43).

At first there was opposition to the match on the part of Edward's guardian, James Scarlett, possibly because of his ward's youth—he was nineteen. But becoming acquainted with Mary, twenty-four, Scarlett eventually gave in. He reportedly said, "I hold out no longer—she is far too good for him." They were married 14 May 1805.

After a honeymoon in the south of England, Edward took his bride to Coxhoe Hall which he had leased. It was a comfortable carriage drive from his wife's family home, Kenton Lodge, near Newcastle. Frequent guests at this mansion included members of Mary's large family, Edward's mother, his brother Samuel, Mary Trepsack, and numerous cousins from both sides of the family.

Edward Moulton-Barrett did not come of age until 1806, and his brother Samuel not until 1808. Until then, control of their business affairs was in the hands of their guardian James Scarlett, later (1835) first Lord Abinger, considered by many to be the most brilliant lawyer of his time. Born in Jamaica himself, Scarlett went to England for schooling in the year Edward was born (1785). On-site management of his wards' Jamaican

2. See RB's "Prefatory Note" to *Poetical Works of Elizabeth Barrett Browning* (London, 1890), I, vii–viii.

estates had to be left to other persons. Edward's estates were run by his uncle Robert Moulton, brother of his father, Charles.

Correspondence between Scarlett and Edward indicates great dissatisfaction with Robert Moulton. He was, among other things, apparently seeking to divert some of Edward's funds and property to Charles Moulton. Management of the estates was eventually transferred to James Scarlett's brother Philip, but this involved much difficulty. On 13 December 1805, James Scarlett wrote to Edward (SD44) as follows: "My brother is proceeding in Chancery to compel your Uncle to give up the Estates, but all legal measures are slow, whereas *force & fraud* are prompt & choose their own time." By the end of 1806, the year in which Edward came of age, James Scarlett was writing to him (SD65) about Philip's "administration of your Estates as trustee."

On 1 October 1811 (SD150), James Scarlett sent Edward some interesting and important comments about his past relations with Robert Moulton. Two of his letters to Moulton, written long before, had surfaced, and he was afraid of the impression they might make when and if Edward saw them. He wrote in part: "As R M & I were upon the most intimate terms & as I had at one time as warm an attachment to him as I ever had for any body, I cannot doubt but that there are many things in my letters to him that were never meant for any other eyes and I own I am a good deal surprized that any motive of any kind should induce R M to submit to any other eyes correspondence that was rendered sacred by the friendship & unreserved confidence that existed between us. ... The struggle which it cost me to have my opinion shaken about him (and it did cause me more grief than any other event of my life) is a pledge of my sincerity when I say that I should feel the greatest obligation to any one who would convince me that I am now under an error about him & that he still merits all the attachment & devotion which I once felt for him. It will be a painful task to me, but I shall nevertheless if either you or Sam require it, think it my duty to communicate to you the grounds on which my present opinion rests."

EBB was born as Robert Moulton was being replaced because of the mismanagement of her father's estates. Edward Moulton-Barrett, greatly in debt "owing to extreme prodigality," and the generally poor state of West Indies affairs, was forced to enter into an agreement with the London firm of Boddington and Sharpe. They advanced him sums for his personal expenses against future crops. He cut back severely in his own life-style, parting "with many of my horses and their attendants." He returned or did not take delivery of coaches he had ordered. In denying his father a loan he wrote, "as you know, my grandfather left no provision for wife or younger children nor will they have any thing but what they get from me, you will not blame me for my resolution when I tell you Mary is again in the family way" (SD70).

From references in the correspondence of Edward Moulton-Barrett at this time, we note his interest in the welfare of slaves on his Jamaican plantations. On 4 January 1807 (SD67) he wrote to Philip Scarlett, answering two letters which apparently reported earlier mistreatment of the slaves. He said: "From four preceeding letters of yours I was prepared to hear the poor Negroes had been badly dealth [sic] with; it gives me great concern that any dependants of mind [sic] should suffer any species of cruelty. I now feel happy they are under your Protection, for I am sure they will be well taken care of and made to bear no unnecessary hardship."

On 1 August 1807 Edward wrote to Philip Scarlett (SD79) as follows, concerning the birth of his first son, Edward, EBB's beloved Bro: "I have the satisfaction of informing you that I was blessed on the 26th June last with a Son he and his Mother are doing well, the Negroes ought I think to have a holiday and some money distributed among the Principals. You will however do as you please."

There is no evidence of any such celebration for the birth of Edward's first daughter, EBB herself, in the previous year. Baby daughters seemingly were not highly regarded. On 2 October 1810, Mary Trepsack wrote a letter (SD144) which mentioned the birth of EBB's sister Mary (who died a few years later). She said: "Mary has another Girl to the great disappointment of every one."

Miss Trepsack's letter was written to Elizabeth Barrett Williams, a person with a strange and important role in the overall Barrett story. Her father was Henry Waite, member of still another influential Jamaican family, and she was a niece of Judith Barrett, EBB's great-grandmother. Elizabeth married Martin Williams and by him had two children. Later— as a widow—she became intimate with Judith's son, her cousin Samuel Barrett, brother of EBB's paternal grandmother. They had four sons "without benefit of clergy." Samuel died in 1794 at age 29, but Elizabeth continued as a respected family figure until her own death in England in 1834. An 1820 letter (no. 113) written by EBB's brother Edward, while attending school in London, mentions a visit to Mrs. Williams' house.

Among the four sons of Samuel Barrett and Elizabeth Williams was Richard Barrett, who became one of the most prominent Jamaicans of his time. Though not of legitimate birth, he was in effect a first cousin of EBB's father. Born in 1789, he inherited a substantial amount of Barrett property in Jamaica. He was trained in England for the legal profession, but returned to Jamaica shortly after coming of age in 1810. Besides gaining a reputation as an astute businessman and successful planter, he was an editor, judge, and legislator. Serving numerous terms in Jamaica's House of Assembly, he was three times elected Speaker.

Humane toward his own slaves, Richard Barrett recognized the evils of slavery, but still viewed it as necessary for Jamaica's economic survival. In 1833 he was chosen by his fellow colonists to appear before the British House of Commons and argue for continuation of slavery in the colonies. Reportedly he defended his cause with "phenomenal ability," but the Parliament nevertheless voted for abolition.

Indications are that Richard Barrett was capable of great charm—as well as ruthlessness—but he was no friend of the Moulton-Barretts, EBB's branch of the family. He was with the branch of cousins, collectively known as the Goodin Barretts, who engaged in a long and costly legal dispute with Edward Moulton-Barrett and his brother Sam. Involving the ownership of slaves and stock in Jamaica, it continued for more than a quarter of a century, and eventually was to cause severe financial reverses for Edward and Samuel Moulton-Barrett.

In an 1842 letter to her close friend Mary Russell Mitford, EBB wrote of Richard Barrett as "a cousin of ours, between whom and us there was *no* love . . . a man of talent and violence and some malice, who did what he could, at one time, to trample poor Papa down."

In the early 1800's, "poor Papa" and other people involved in West Indies plantation affairs faced a wide array of problems. For one thing, Britain's Parliament in 1807 passed a law abolishing the colonial slave trade (though not slavery itself). After 1 March 1808, no additional slaves could be brought into the British possessions. This meant that the planters, in order to maintain their supply of slaves, had to devote added attention to raising them on the colonial estates.

Then there were the low sugar prices, already noted, stemming in part at least from the Napoleonic Wars and their interruption of trade. In a letter to Edward Moulton-Barrett dated 15 October 1806 (SD60), James Scarlett wrote: "It is certain that since your grandfather's death in 1798 Sugars have sold very low—for the 7 years preceding they were very high." He also warns against the danger of bad crop years.

Other perils arose, though sometimes as clouds with silver linings. On 4 January 1807 (SD67) Edward wrote to Philip Scarlett: "I cannot say I am sorry to inform you that I lost 270 Hogs heads of Sugar in the storm for had they arrived they would not have fetched so much as what they were insured at."

In any case, Edward felt that he was under severe pressure during this period. On 29 March 1807 (SD73) he wrote to Philip Scarlett: ". . . I am really poor and setting up house and various other expenses and

Edward Barrett

Edward Moulton-Barrett

Samuel Moulton-Barrett

Edward Moulton-Barrett

Mary Moulton-Barrett

Samuel Moulton-Barrett

Edward Moulton-Barrett

Edward Moulton-Barrett

really the state of West Indian affairs do not tempt one much to lay out money in Jamaica." On 4 October 1807 (SD84), writing again to Philip Scarlett, he said: "You give a lamentable account of the Prospects for next year. I however hope for the best. We really have pressed on us, an accumulation of misfortunes, the times never were so bad. The only consolatory ray that dawns on us is they cannot be worse."

Another problem, dating from around the time of his marriage, is mentioned by Edward in a letter to Philip Scarlett, 30 November 1807 (SD89). "I am sorry to say I must beg you will send no more sugars to Mr. Clarke's,—he has not for the last two years settled our account ... it is an unpleasant business and has given me great uneasiness." This situation with his wife's father continued for some time and was probably one of the underlying causes for Edward's decision to move his family south. Three days after the birth of Bro, in June 1807, James Scarlett reported (SD76) that an estate, Bedwell Park, Hertfordshire, was on the market. By February 1808 Edward had given his landlord notice that he was quitting Coxhoe Hall. That autumn he was at Mickleham, where his mother had taken a house, and soon he set up his own household at North End, Hammersmith, while he scouted for a permanent residence.

The Hope End estate, where Edward and his family eventually settled, is mentioned by name in a letter which Mary Moulton-Barrett wrote to her mother on 12 May 1809 (SD123). Apparently tired of uncertainty over where they were to locate, she said: "I well know, that it will be a satisfaction to all parties, when Edward gets happily settled in a place to his wishes." Mary, her parents and Scarlett hoped Edward would settle his family in Yorkshire, near Samuel and the Graham-Clarkes.

The first letter of this collected edition was written from Ledbury in September 1809 by Edward to his infant daughter Elizabeth, after an inspection of the Hope End Estate. Soon afterwards it was purchased from Lady Tempest, wife of Sir Henry Vane Tempest, who lived near Coxhoe Hall. (We are later to hear of this previous owner when EBB says in letter 389 to Hugh Stuart Boyd that her ghost is reportedly haunting the Hope End neighbourhood.) The Estate consisted of 475 acres, including park land with deer, surrounded by hills covered with timber. The name, Hope End, signified "a closed valley."

Edward began almost at once to erect, from Turkish-style designs by Loudon (see *Reconstruction*, H87), a new mansion having minarets with solid concrete walls and cast-iron tops, windows over fireplaces, and other innovations. The original house, a brick-built Georgian mansion, was converted into stables, separated from the main house by a courtyard containing a clock tower. The grounds contained two ponds, converted from an existing stream, a cascade and kiosk, a grotto, a summer cottage, and an ice-house, and there was a subterranean passage leading from the house to the gardens. (The most comprehensive description of the estate is contained in the Sale Catalogue; see *Reconstruction*, M246 and volume 2, Appendix III.) Construction was in progress well into 1815 and the richly decorated drawing-room took a total of seven years to complete. EBB's rooms were at the very top of the house. One, originally designed as a bedroom, was turned by her father into a pleasant sitting room.[3] Her bedroom was on the opposite side of the passage.

An 1824 guide to Ledbury directed the traveller to "Hope End, the residence of E.M. Barrett, Esq.; this house is the only specimen of Turkish architecture in the kingdom. Hope End is placed in a situation enchantingly sweet; the grounds are decorated with the exquisite taste for which their owner is remarkable."

Mary Moulton-Barrett took great pride in her children's accomplishments—especially those of EBB and Bro—and spent many hours laboriously copying their poems and other literary endeavours. Undoubtedly their efforts were helped along by her own writing talents. While she did not write professionally, she expressed her thoughts and feelings very capably in long and chatty personal letters, and a journal (SD235) which she kept during an 1815 trip to France shows her as a keen observer and commentator. From comments in EBB's childhood writings, we know that her mother showed careful concern for the children's schooling, at home on the Hope End estate. It appears also that she played a sort of game with EBB, serving as "publisher" for some of the latter's juvenilia.

In time, twelve children were born to Edward and Mary Moulton-Barrett, eight of whom were born at Hope End. As their family grew, Edward and Mary became involved in local politics and the activities of county life. But the power base upon which their life-style depended was slowly dissolving. Edward's visits to London, to attend to West Indies affairs became more frequent. In the midst of this development, Edward received a staggering blow: the death of his wife, 7 October 1828. How much she was aware of his financial difficulties is unclear, but due to her ill health and the general uncertainty, Edward probably didn't convey

---

3. EBB had a similar room at Wimpole Street. In 1839, when she was in Torquay, her father urged Septimus to use it for his studies: "And do you, a sensible fellow, really suppose that if you cannot study with perseverance & attention in Ba's little Room, that any place can be found, where you may find these requisites, without which no advantages offered can compensate. ... By the bye, in what snug nook has our Ba obtained all the vast learning & wisdom she possesses—hard work & determined perseverance were her nooks. Few Professors that she could not dumbfound. Keep her view & you will go point blank to Helicon's Stream, my boy" (SD1071).

the true scope of the situation. Four years after her death, creditors foreclosed and the Hope End Mansion and park lands were lost. Edward was able to keep the valuable woodlands for the rest of his life. In August 1832 he moved his family from Hope End to rented houses—first in Sidmouth, then Gloucester Place, London. Miss Mitford, writing to Lady Dacre, 3 July 1836 (SD804), sums up EBB's history to that time.

> . . . I knew that you would be charmed with Miss Barrett's book. Did I tell you her story? Ten years ago she was living with her father at a fine place amongst the Malvern Hills, the eldest of ten [sic] children. He was then a man of £15,000 a year. A cousin came to him & showed him a will dated 60 years before under which he claimed £75,000. Mr. Barrett, who had never heard of the claim showed the will to a lawyer who advised him to dispute it.– He did so; & after the cause had been driven from court to court it has been given against him with enormous costs & interest, so that his place in Herefordshire is sold, & he is living to use his own expression "a broken down man" in London. Of course the poverty is only comparative—people who live in Gloucester Place are probably what I should call rich—still with ten children coming into life the change is of course great; & the mother being dead, & the father utterly dispirited, my lovely young friend has been living in the middle of gaiety in a seclusion the most absolute—seeing nobody but the old scholar to whom the "Prometheus" is inscribed, & chiefly occupied in teaching her little brothers Greek–

In 1838, Edward took a leasehold on 50 Wimpole Street and the furniture and books from Hope End were uncrated and a permanent home established.

The Moulton-Barrett and Graham-Clarke families were extremely mobile, with large extended family ties in England, Ireland, the Continent and the West Indies. EBB aptly described her family to Miss Mitford— "We, you know, number our cousins after the tribes of Israel." Communicating by writing, which they could afford, was considered the norm. While there seems to have been little conscious effort to preserve family letters, circumstances have led to many of them being preserved. Succeeding generations of the Moulton-Barretts have been great caretakers of family documents and letters.

An immense amount of rich documentation for EBB's childhood exists, probably without parallel in English literary history. The letters between young EBB and her sisters, brothers, and parents (which fall within our publication) constitute only a small part of the enormous Moulton-Barrett archives, for the most part still in family hands. For the early years, the secondary material rivals the primary material in bulk, and while not a literary correspondence, merits attention for its social commentary. It places EBB's father in a different light from that traditionally held and casts Mary Moulton-Barrett as the prime motivator in EBB's early creative development.

Throughout her life, EBB had a natural propensity, later encouraged by her illness and forced isolation, for carrying on extended correspondence with a few friends. By the time she commenced her correspondence with Browning, she had penned four major series of letters—those to H.S. Boyd, R.H. Horne, Julia Martin and Mary Russell Mitford.

The Poets in Italy

After their marriage, the Brownings conducted their correspondence in much the same manner: Browning primarily wrote perfunctory letters in order to accomplish a particular purpose—except possibly those to his family—while EBB continued her established correspondences, adding to her recipients family members (most noticeably Henrietta, Arabella, and Sarianna Browning), Fanny Haworth, Isa Blagden and Anna Jameson.

From Florence, EBB wrote to her sister Arabella, 10–11 May 1848: "Any papers of mine, letters, &c left in Wimpole St. (and there was a deal box full, which came from Hope End besides the green box) these things I beg you to take care of for me—and we will make a bonfire of many of them when we meet." Arabella took her charge faithfully (it is doubtful that any bonfire took place) and gathered up all the documents into the deal box—a large narrow black coach box (see *Reconstruction*, H539.1). Many of these items were claimed by EBB on her visits to England, and were taken to Florence. Upon EBB's death, RB sorted through the papers and several bear his dockets, dated during the month after her death. These he had crated, placed in storage, and eventually shipped to London and 19 Warwick Crescent.

The Poets' Attitude Towards Publication

Numerous references in EBB's letters indirectly indicate that she fully expected her letters to be collected and published. In writing to RB in February 1846, she said: "I, for my part, value letters . . . as the most vital part of biography." When in her late letters EBB objected to being "anatomized" by the public, it was on the grounds that she was not yet dead.

RB's attitude was quite the opposite. He was fiercely resolved, almost to the point of mania, that access to his personal life be denied. As he grew older, he advanced his own views as being also those of his wife. He determined that as long as he lived, biographers would not see any document in his possession and thereby give rise to unwanted publicity. It is worth quoting at length his views, as set forth in his letter to his brother-in-law, George Moulton-Barrett, 2 May 1882, on numerous appeals for biographical details of EBB.

... The applications have generally been for a publication of the Letters I may possess or have a control over—or at least for leave to inspect them for the sake of what biographical information they might contain. I have once, by declaring I would prosecute by law, hindered a man's proceedings who *had obtained all the letters to Mr Boyd*, and was soliciting, on the strength of that acquisition, letters in all the quarters he guessed likely.[4] The only instance in which I departed from my rule was that of Horne—who, poor, old and pitiable, saw a golden resource in the publication of the correspondence which began and, in the main, ended before I knew the writer. ... We are all of one mind here, I, you,—no doubt, the Brothers,—and assuredly the One whose feelings we know and respect. Now, I possess hundreds of letters—besides those addressed to me,—those to the Martins, Miss Mitford, Mr Boyd, Chorley, Kenyon, Miss Blagden—and others: and moreover am promised the reversion of other collections when their owners die. ... While I live, I can play the part of guardian effectually enough—but I must soon resolve on the steps necessary to be taken when I live no longer—and I complete my seventieth year next Sunday. I shall soon have to pass in a very superficial review all these letters, just inspecting so much of them (and a mere dip into each will suffice) as to ascertain what should be destroyed, what preserved as containing nothing to hurt the living or the dead: it is an immense sacrifice—but one that must be made, and I shall not for a moment consider anything but what I know would be the desire of my wife in the matter. So much for my part of the duty. There is however a danger which I apprehend, and cannot be responsible for. The letters to Arabel were deposited in security somewhere: I suppose that the copyright of them belongs to me—so that, if by any accident publication was attempted, I could prevent it: but if I am off the scene, if you, and the Brothers, in due time follow me, *who* is to be the keeper of what must inevitably be the most intimate and complete disclosure of precisely those secrets which we unite in wishing to remain secret forever? Are the young people likely to be interested in this as we are, or certain to be as able to withstand literary cajoleries ... as I have been and shall be? The same danger is to be apprehended from any publicity given to the letters to Henrietta—which I am altogether powerless concerning: as indeed I probably am in the case of the letters now in question. So, dear George, I do all in my limited power by bringing, once for all, this state of things under your notice. There will not be found in the whole of the correspondence one untrue, ungenerous word, I *know*— but plenty of sad communication which has long ago served its purpose and should be forgotten. Unfortunately the unscrupulous hunger for old scandals is on the increase—and as the glory of that most wonderful of women is far from at the full—I cannot help many forebodings— which you share with me, I know.

4. In 1863, two years after EBB's death, George Stampe's proposal to publish EBB's letters to Boyd was withdrawn after RB threatened to obtain an injunction against him. Earlier, in 1830 and 1835, E.H. Barker's proposals to publish these letters were turned down by EBB. Upon Boyd's death the letters fell into the hands of Mary Ann Smith, youngest daughter and biographer of Dr. Adam Clarke. EBB asked her to return them, but she declined. RB successfully claimed them from Mrs. Smith's son some years later.

In a letter to the same brother-in-law, 5 November 1887, RB reintroduces the topic:

> ... let me repeat—for probably the last time—how much it is on my
> mind that, when I am no longer here to prevent it, some use will be
> made of the correspondence not in my power: *all in my power* is safe,
> and will ever remain so: and I shall enjoin on Pen, with whom will
> remain the property allowed by law in the manuscript letters—*not* in
> the writings themselves, but in the publication of them,—to hinder
> this by every possible means. The letters to the sisters,—of which I
> never read one line, but their contents are sufficiently within my
> knowledge,—these unfortunately contain besides the inevitable allu-
> sions to domestic matters, all the imaginary spiritualistic experiences
> by which the unsuspecting and utterly truthful nature of Ba was abused:
> she was duped by a woman through whose impostures one more versed
> in worldly craft and falsehood would have clearly seen at once,—and
> the discovery of this came too late to prevent disclosures which will
> never be properly accounted for by the careless and spiteful public,
> only glad to be amused by the aberrations of a soul so immeasurably
> superior in general intelligence to their own. I have done all I can
> do,—you have naturally influence where I am helpess, and so I leave
> the matter—with grave forebodings.

George Moulton-Barrett clearly did not totally share his brother-in-law's views. Unknown to RB, Arabel's letters were in his care and he took no steps to destroy or suppress them. Nor did he intercede with Henrietta's husband, who had already, in 1875, laboriously copied out a much-edited version of the letters to Henrietta, omitting all references he considered too personal.[5] In his preface (unpublished) he clearly stated that it was his wife's wish that the letters to herself be printed.

George apparently wrote to RB suggesting that he should edit a selection of EBB's letters. The poet's response is illuminating in that it provides a measure of justification in presenting this edition of unexpurgated correspondence. He wrote, 21 January 1889:

> ... I am greatly obliged by the loan of the letters and piece of poetry,
> which I return with truest thanks. I feel deeply indeed the interest
> which attaches itself to the merest scrap of that beloved handwriting,
> and am perfectly aware of a very general desire on the part of the
> Public to possess such a collection of letters as you suggest might be
> made,—and some collection of what may be procurable will be one
> day made, I have no doubt, when matter over which I lose control
> becomes, by accident or otherwise, the property of the collector. But
> there seem to me insuperable obstacles to my taking on myself such
> an office: not so much,—strange as that might appear,—from the
> repugnance of the writer to any publicity of the kind, as from certain
> unfortunate circumstances connected with the case. I could disregard

5. Surtees' transcripts were used by Leonard Huxley in his *Elizabeth Barrett Brown-ing: Letters to her Sister, 1846–1859* (London, 1929). Over a third of the original text was excised by Henrietta's husband. The full text of these letters will appear in this edition.

perhaps a feeling caused simply by the modesty and avoidance of notoriety which were conspicuous in the writer, and which I have on occasion been forced to withstand: but the difficulty is that if once a beginning is made there will be no power of stopping there: we cannot pick and choose what portions of a life may be illustrated and what left obscure—and it is precisely upon what is so left that the public curiosity would be exercised. I could perhaps see my way to presenting just so much of the correspondence as merely relates to literature, politics, theology, description of persons and things: but if once matters of a personal and more intimate nature were ventured upon, every endeavour would be made—eventually—to supply the gaps: and, you will believe me, it is not for my own memory, once safe out of this gossip-loving and scandal-hungry world, that I am at all apprehensive. Two years ago, I spent more than a week in destroying my own letters to my family,—from my earliest days up to the death of my father they had all been preserved. But I possess hundreds of letters of the most interesting kind—addressed to Mr Boyd, Mrs Martin, Miss Mitford, Mrs Jameson, and others—which I could not bring myself to do away with,—whatever may be the ultimate disposition of them. As for the letters to myself,—and for months before our marriage I received one daily,—these which are so immeasurably superior to any compositions of the kind I have any experience of,—would glorify the privileged receiver beyond any imaginable crown in the world or out of it—but I cannot, any more than Timon, "cut my heart in sums—tell out my blood." Notwithstanding all this, my dear George, you may be assured that the responsibility attending my ownership of letters and other documents is never absent from my thoughts, and I remain open to any conviction which may result from circumstances that have not as yet taken place. The unhappy letters which concern spiritualism I wish with all my heart could be eliminated from those out of my hands, and burnt forthwith—as they ought to be.

We must be thankful that RB's earlier thoughts of destroying portions of EBB's letters were not carried out. EBB's habit of interweaving topics in her letters would have made this exceedingly difficult. In the end, Browning couldn't bring himself to destroy any of her manuscripts—even those letters that touched on spiritualism. This does not keep us from lamenting his act of annihilation of his own letters, which act accounts in part for the imbalance of letters in early volumes of their collected correspondence.[6] Those readers whose primary interest is in RB must bear with the fact that RB himself is to be blamed for being initially

6. One other factor influencing the extent of EBB's correspondence vis-à-vis RB's is the cost of sending letters prior to the introduction of the Penny Post in 1840. Postage was then assessed on the basis of the number of sheets used, a second sheet doubling the rate charged—and even a single sheet, if weighing over an ounce, was charged at four times the basic rate. Although the Moulton-Barretts always attempted to evade postal charges by the use of the post-free franking privilege extended to members of Parliament (Samuel Moulton-Barrett, during his term as an M.P., and their neighbour Lord Eastnor being especially helpful in this respect), or by sending local letters by the hand of servants or carters, they were never deterred by the high cost of postage when the charges could not be avoided.

overshadowed. Their patience will be amply rewarded by our decision to include both poets' letters, as EBB's communications during their marriage abound with biographical information about him.

RB's clearing-out of papers in 1887 probably wasn't as wholesale as has been reported or imagined. It seems to have been directed mainly toward his own letters to his parents and sister. (There exist in EBB's correspondence to Sarianna numerous letters with portions extended in the throat of the envelope, which bears the address in RB's hand. It may be assumed in these cases that a letter from Browning was originally enclosed.) Browning possibly destroyed more letters addressed jointly to himself and EBB, but again seemingly those from family members, personal in nature, and not letters from public figures. Presumably among the casualties were Pen's letters to his father and the countless letters written to EBB by her sisters. Only one such letter survives, written by Henrietta, returned to the sender as misdirected, and still preserved by her family. It is illuminating in that its length and topics covered emulate EBB's letters to her.

RB refrained from destroying his own correspondence with Isa Blagden, and of course with EBB. Strangely, he did not destroy the letters written to himself by Julia Wedgwood. The 1887 culling of the correspondence seems to be the only such instance—the number of letters addressed to him after 1887 is appreciably greater.

Disposition of RB's Estate

In April 1891, after RB's death, his accumulated books, manuscripts and letters were crated and sent to Venice where his sister Sarianna had elected to live with her nephew. Although RB apparently did communicate to his son and sister his views on privacy, a decade after his death both were assisting Frederic G. Kenyon in making the selection for his two-volume edition of EBB's letters (1897), and later they aided Reginald Smith (Smith, Elder & Co.) in publishing the love letters (1899).

In 1912, upon the death of Pen Browning, all the letters that RB had collected, and those added by Pen himself, became the property of Pen's widow, Fannie, and sixteen first cousins on his mother's side. For the most part the letters were located at Pen's estate near Florence, La Torre all'Antella. Most correspondence was removed immediately by Marchesa Peruzzi (Edith Story) and Fannie to the Marchesa's home on Via Maggio. Fannie returned some of Pen's letters to their authors—Frederic G. Kenyon and Reginald Smith are two cases in point. Many letters to the poet, probably late letters, she took upon herself to destroy.[7] After it had

---

7. Fannie Browning wrote to T.J. Wise, 1 November 1933, "At the time of the Sale in 1913 seeing the futility or advisability of so many *too* many letters being kept, I destroyed hundreds. Only of course *not* The Poet's own" (MS at Rutgers University).

been determined that Pen had died effectively intestate, the administrators of his estate ordered his effects to be sold. Fannie and the Marchesa Peruzzi were required to give up the letters in their care to an agent from Sotheby's. They were offered for sale on the second day of a six-day sale, May 1913.

However, it is known that Fannie did not surrender all the items. She removed some of the enclosures from the love letters—these have since turned up. She deposited in the Library of Congress a sizeable collection of letters addressed to the poet. She also retained the letter EBB left (enclosed in her letter to her brother George) addressed to her father and announcing her departure from Wimpole Street. It and seven subsequent unopened letters were returned to RB with "a very violent and unsparing letter," in response to an appeal for reconciliation during the Brownings' 1851 visit to London.

On 22 May 1913, T.J. Wise wrote to Fannie:

> My mind is full of the memory of those 8 tiny letters, all but one still unopened, sent by the broken-hearted—or *half* broken-hearted— daughter to the sternest of parents. The one I read was painful in the extreme, but the whole correspondence . . . *must* be preserved intact. Pray do not think me ungrateful or unkind if I beg you to allow me to acquire these precious letters, should you ever be able to see your way to do so. I should, you know, regard them as a sacred trust.

Col. Edward A. Moulton-Barrett, chief administrator of Pen's estate, was adamant that Fannie surrender these highly personal letters to his family, and, at the end of May 1913, he successfully forced her to give them up. He deposited them into the care of his solicitor and distant cousin Henry P. Surtees.

Again we quote from a letter of T.J. Wise to Fannie, 4 June 1913:

> I can quite understand that the Barrett family should wish to destroy these letters from Elizabeth to her father. But the same reason that prompts *them* to wish for the destruction of the letters prompts *us* to wish for their safe and careful preservation. They will justify, more than anything else possibly can, the action taken by Elizabeth & Robert Browning,—an action which the position adopted by her father rendered inevitable and right. I do hope your lawyer will support you in this matter. It seems to me that if you have given up the letters as a portion of Pen's estate, that the same reason would render it illegal for the Barrett's to have them destroyed. Your lawyer should, I imagine, claim their sale, & I should be only too glad to purchase them at any fit and proper valuation. . . . I have destroyed your letter, as you instructed me to do.

As late as 1920, Wise was still trying to obtain these letters. They remained with Surtees until 1924, when by mutual consent of Moulton-Barrett family members they were sent to Lt.-Col. Harry Peyton Moulton-Barrett, titular head of the family.

On 20 February 1924 he acknowledged to Surtees their receipt and stated: "The letters have been burned by me in the presence of a witness." However, sometime prior to his death in 1936 he made an inventory of his possessions, with a cryptic entry: "2. Desk containing (destroyed) letters together with several sketches and obituary notice of EBB." There can be little doubt that these were the letters which EBB wrote to her father. A desk, incorporating in its structure a concealed drawer, and believed by Lt.-Col. Moulton-Barrett's son to be the one referred to, was sold at a provincial public auction in October 1945. Unfortunately, the transaction was done by proxy, without a search of the contents. The purchaser, a furniture dealer, cannot recall to whom the desk was resold.

Unlocated Collections

In the catalogue of EBB's centenary exhibition it was noted that four major collections of letters remained unlocated—those addressed to Isa Blagden and Sarianna Browning by EBB and letters addressed to Mrs. FitzGerald and Mrs. Sutherland Orr (sister of Sir Frederick Leighton) by RB. Within a few years of the exhibition three of the collections surfaced. Only those letters written to Mrs. Sutherland Orr remain elusive. As they have never appeared at auction, one must assume that, if she didn't destroy them, they are still in the hands of family descendants we have been unable to locate.

Another missing collection—about 130 letters from H.S. Boyd to EBB—was offered for sale by C.H. Last, bookseller in Bromley, England, around 1927. All attempts to locate them have failed, as have efforts to find the Robert Browning/Julia Wedgwood correspondence. These 65 letters were edited in 1937 by Richard Curle, but the unreliability of this edition is apparent by comparison with facsimiles provided in the volume.

As Browning foresaw, letters became available in the ensuing years, posing problems of what to print and what to exclude. Imagination often did more harm in conjecturing the excisions than the full passage could possibly have done. At this distance of time, there is no question of the benefit to be derived from printing the entire extant correspondence in full—the "gossip-loving and scandal-hungry world" is still with us, but the truth will be available for those who seek it diligently.

Editorial Approach and Principles

Over the years we have had to face a large array of technical editorial decisions, most of them growing out of the sheer bulk of the correspondence. We are often made aware that the only decision that hasn't been redefined is the original aim to present all extant letters written to the

Brownings as well as those written by them. Our definition of "letter" embraces written communications intended for delivery to the addressee, even when the form used is verse, as in birthday odes.

When the manuscript of a letter has been located our transcription is based on the original or a photocopy thereof. We include letters from four other sources: manuscript copy in the hand of a second party; unpublished typed copy, manuscript of which is missing; previously published text of which the manuscript has since disappeared; auction or dealer catalogues, if a direct quotation has been printed. If our transcript is not from the original manuscript, our source is reproduced faithfully; we have corrected only obvious errors although it is probable that a previous editor altered spelling and punctuation.

Following is a detailed description of our editorial principles.

1. The letters are arranged in chronological order.

2. Each letter is assigned a number; point numbers are used if the letter is a late entry. This number, used for cross references, appears first in the letter's heading.

3. The name of the sender(s) and the name of the addressee(s) are also presented in the heading. Square brackets are not used here to indicate editorial conjecture. Any questionable attributions are noted.

4. Our primary aim is to present the letter text in the form in which the writer intended it to be read; therefore text that has been altered by the author is given only in its final reading; text cancelled or obliterated by the author is not restored.

5. Text that has been altered or obliterated by a second hand is restored when possible. If we are unable to reconstruct the passage the nature and extent of the alteration or obliteration are indicated in a note.

6. We reproduce as many of the author's individual characteristics as possible within the parameters allowed by the source and the rules of typography. Variant spellings and errors are copied exactly, and only those lapses which seem most likely to be interpreted as misprints are noted by the conventional [sic]. Thus easily understood irregularities, such as a word or even a name spelled differently in the same letter, or the substitution of you for your, are left as given, unless the context requires a comment. In foreign words, accents are reproduced as written, and missing accents have not been supplied.

7. Words that were unintentionally duplicated are omitted without comment.

8. Interpolations are included in the body of the text without caret or comment.

9. Passages where quotation marks are repeated at the beginning of each line are adapted to current usage by omitting the repetitious markings.

10. Words and phrases underlined once or twice in the original manuscript are represented respectively by italics and small capital letters; if underlining occurs more than twice it is represented in small capital letters with a note.

11. Greek passages are rendered in modern forms, old-style orthography and ligatures not being retained. No italicizing occurs in Greek passages. The writer's underscoring has been reproduced *as* underscoring if it is for emphasis of certain syllables and accents.

12. Not reproduced are underscorings in addresses, dates and signatures.

13. Words missing due to holes, seal tears, or deterioration of the manuscript are treated as follows: if enough of a partial word remains to suggest the full word, the balance is supplied in angle brackets. Wholly conjectural words are given in angle brackets, preceded by a question mark if the reading is uncertain. Where there is no sound basis for conjecture, missing words or phrases are represented by ellipses within angle brackets.

14. The transfer of an author's punctuation (which usually conforms to no consistent system) into typography is the most complex problem with which we were confronted. We have endeavoured to be faithful to the original in our interpretation, but have added paragraph divisions in a few cases to avoid unclear run-ons. Also, the writers' variable-length dashes have had to be standardized.

15. Superior letters have been retained. The period below has also been retained; dashes below have been converted to periods.

16. Ampersands, abbreviations and contractions have been retained, including EBB's habitual placing of the apostrophe between two parts of the word rather than over the omitted letter(s).

17. The writing locale is given at top right, although the writer may have included this information elsewhere in the letter. If a letter was written from several places, the succeeding place(s) appear only in the text. The location is supplied in square brackets when no place is given in the manuscript. If it is preceded by a question mark, this indicates a questionable editorial conjecture.

18. The date of writing also appears at top right, although the writer sometimes gives this information elsewhere in the letter. If a letter was

written over several days, inclusive dates are given in square brackets without comment, although the succeeding dates often appear as well in the text. Dates based on postmarks or dockets are given in square brackets, preceded by the word *Postmark* or *Docket*. With these exceptions, any dating contained within square brackets indicates editorial conjecture explained in a note. Any element of doubt is indicated by the use of a question mark within the square brackets, the doubt extending from the question mark to the closing square bracket. Thus, [16 March] [?1854] would indicate that we are confident of the 16th March dating, although conjectured, but that the year is open to question. Letters that we have been unable to date exactly are placed at their earliest possible dates.

19. The complimentary close is separated from the letter except when so informal as to be considered part of the text.

20. Conclusions of letters, and postcripts, often appear in margins, on envelopes and occasionally are cross-written. In this edition all text is presented in its proper sequence without reference to its physical placement, unless this has a bearing on the message.

21. The following information appears after each letter:

   a. Address of recipient, if given by the writer.

   b. Docket or endorsement added by the addressee, or a contemporary.

   c. Previous published text, usually the most accessible.

   d. Derivation of the text. Letters from original manuscripts are indicated by *Manuscript* preceding the name of the present holder. If the manuscript is held in more than one location, the citations appear in alphabetical order and thus do not correspond to the portions of the manuscript. Letters based on previous publications are indicated by *Text* preceding the citation. Other derivations are indicated by *Source* preceding the citation.

22. Notes are numbered sequentially for each letter. We endeavour to identify every person mentioned, though, inevitably, some of the minor personalities have defied our efforts. Because of the repetitive nature of many of these references, we are able to identify each person only once, unless a subsequent mention requires additional clarification. To assist the reader in refreshing his memory, the index indicates the principal identifying note(s) for persons and places mentioned frequently. We have also attempted to amplify places, events, quotations and statements that seem in need of elucidation. Textual irregularities are also clarified.

In addition to the letters, each volume will contain a list of cue-titles, abbreviations and symbols; a chronology; biographical sketches of principal figures; a checklist of supporting documents; a list of absent letters; a list of collections; a list of correspondents; and a comprehensive index. The final volume of the edition will be devoted to a fusion of all previous indices.

During the course of this work, we intend to reproduce all available likenesses of RB and EBB, each to appear chronologically in its appropriate volume.

Letters that surface after publication of the relevant volume, or are unavailable to us now, will be issued in a supplementary volume at the completion of the project.

Chronology

1805 14 May: Marriage of EBB's parents, Edward Moulton-Barrett and Mary Graham-Clarke, at Gosforth Church, Northumberland, by the Rev. John Fenwick

1806 6 March: EBB born at Coxhoe Hall, Co. Durham, which had been leased by her father.

9 March: EBB privately baptized by the Rev. William Lewis Rham, Rector of Fersfield, Norfolk, a family friend.

28 May: Edward Moulton-Barrett attained his majority.

1807 26 June: Edward Moulton-Barrett ("Bro") born at Coxhoe Hall.

1808 10 February: EBB and Bro publicly baptized at Kelloe Church, Co. Durham.

ca. late autumn: EBB's father removes his family south to London.

1809 March: Henrietta Moulton-Barrett born at 10 Upper Berkeley Street, London. Baptized privately at Baker Street Chapel.

ca. April: EBB's father took accommodations for his family at North End, Hammersmith.

September: EBB with her family at Mickleham, Surrey, home of her grandmother, Elizabeth Moulton.

ca. November: Hope End Estate, nr. Ledbury, Herefordshire acquired by EBB's father. Mortgage held by James Scarlett— released ca. February 1814.

1810 March: Arabella Graham-Clarke (grandmother) and Arabella Graham-Clarke (aunt) visit Hope End.

ca. 15 July: EBB's first extant letter, to Elizabeth Moulton. The Barretts go to the sea a week later.

September: Improvements at Hope End in progress: new mansion under construction from designs by Loudon; existing Georgian mansion converted into stables.

16 September: Mary Moulton-Barrett born at Hope End.

October: Elizabeth Moulton and Mary Trepsack visit Hope End.

13 November: Henrietta and Mary publicly baptized at Colwall, nr. Hope End.

1811 19 February: Marriage of RB's parents, RB, Sr. and Sarah Anna Wiedemann, in Camberwell, near London.

[xlv]

March: The Barretts in Cheltenham with Elizabeth Moulton and Mary Trepsack.

December: EBB's family at 351 High Street, Cheltenham.

1812 13 January: Samuel Moulton-Barrett born at Cheltenham.

30 January: Frances Graham-Clarke marries Thomas Butler, afterwards 8th Baronet, of Cloughgrenan.

April: The Barretts return to Hope End.

7 May: RB born at Southampton St., Camberwell.

14 June: RB baptized by the Rev. George Clayton, Parish of St. Giles, Camberwell.

1813 4 July: Arabella Moulton-Barrett born at Hope End.

14 August: Samuel and Arabella baptized at Colwall.

1814 Construction projects completed at Hope End.

7 January: Sarianna Browning, sister of RB, born at Camberwell.

March: EBB writes poetical work, "On the Cruelty of Forcement to Man."

16 March: Mary Moulton-Barrett, sister of EBB, dies. Buried in Ledbury Parish Church.

10 April: Sarianna baptized by the Rev. George Clayton, Parish of St. Giles, Camberwell.

June: EBB at Carlton Hall, Yorkshire, seat of her Uncle Sam; excursion to Matlock, Derbyshire.

June–September: EBB at Fenham Hall, Newcastle-upon-Tyne, home of her maternal grandparents.

28 December: Charles John Moulton-Barrett born at Hope End.

1815 18 June: Battle of Waterloo.

ca. October: The Barretts go to Baker St., London, Elizabeth Moulton's residence.

17 October: EBB and parents leave London for Paris (Hotel de Rivoli) via Rochester, Dover, Calais and Boulogne.

26 November: The Barretts return to London.

1816 January: The Barretts return to Hope End.

15 July: George Goodin Moulton-Barrett born at Hope End.

28 October: Charles John and George Goodin baptized by Rev. Hoskins, Colwall.

1817 Decoration and other improvements at Hope End completed.

ca. May: EBB and family at Albion Place, Ramsgate. Daniel McSwiney and Madame Gordin engaged to tutor Barrett children. EBB commences work on *The Battle of Marathon*.

ca. September: The Barretts, except for Arabella and her nurse Minny, return to Hope End.

December: Graham-Clarke family members visit Hope End.

1818 27 July: Henry Moulton-Barrett born at Hope End.

7 August: John Graham-Clarke, EBB's maternal grandfather, dies at Newcastle-upon-Tyne.

September: EBB visits Cheltenham.

1819 4 May: EBB writes her "First Greek Ode."

24 May: Princess Victoria born.

ca. June–July: EBB and family visit Worthing, where Arabella and Minny had removed from Ramsgate in May.

19 July: Charles Moulton, EBB's paternal grandfather, dies in Jamaica aged 61.

December: Graham-Clarke family members visit Hope End.

1820 29 January: George III dies. George IV ascends the throne.

March: EBB and family visit Elizabeth Moulton, 62 Baker Street, London. Arabella Graham-Clarke (grandmother) and Arabella Graham-Clarke (aunt) also in London. When the Barretts return to Hope End, Bro remains with his grandmother, prior to entering Charterhouse in the ninth form.

6 March: probably as a present for her 14th birthday, 50 copies of EBB's first book, *The Battle of Marathon*, privately printed.

10 March: Samuel Moulton-Barrett, EBB's uncle, elected to Parliament, representing Richmond, Yorkshire.

20 May: Alfred Price Moulton-Barrett born at Hope End.

October: Arabella and Minny return to Hope End, after 3½ years' absence.

December: James Graham-Clarke, EBB's uncle, visits Hope End.

1821 April: EBB, Henrietta and Arabella ill. EBB's sisters recover but she grows progressively worse.

May: EBB first appears publicly as a poet when her "Stanzas, Excited by Some Reflections on the Present State of Greece," are published in *The New Monthly Magazine*, Second Series, I, 523.

ca. June: EBB and Henrietta contract measles.

June: EBB sent to Spa Hotel, Gloucester, for medical treatment. At least one member of her family is with her throughout her stay.

July: "Thoughts Awakened by Contemplating a Piece of the Palm Which Grows on the Summit of the Acropolis at Athens," published in *The New Monthly Magazine*, Second Series, II, 59.

18 October: Jane Graham-Clarke, EBB's aunt, marries Robert Hedley.

1822 Samuel Moulton-Barrett, EBB's brother, enters Charterhouse in the twelfth form.

11 February: Septimus James Moulton-Barrett born at Hope End.

ca. May: EBB returns to Hope End.

13 June: Charlotte Graham-Clarke marries the Rev. Richard Pierce Butler.

19 August: Henry, Alfred and Septimus baptized at Colwall.

1823 20 March: At Gloucester, Samuel Moulton-Barrett, EBB's uncle, marries Mary Clementina, daughter of the late Rev. Henry Cay-Adams, of Painswick.

ca. June: EBB and family settle in Boulogne for an extended stay.

1824 ca. January: The Barretts return to England.

11 April: Octavius Butler Moulton-Barrett born at Hope End.

13 June: Samuel Barrett dies at Gloucester, leaving the Moulton-Barretts vulnerable to a claim by Richard Barrett (Sam's brother and principal heir) involving ownership of slaves and stock. Later in the year, Richard Barrett's lawsuit results in a ruling against the Moulton-Barretts. The slaves are formally delivered over to Richard Barrett as receiver. The Moulton-Barretts appeal the decision.

30 June: EBB's "Stanzas on the Death of Lord Byron" are published in the London *Globe and Traveller*.

July–August: EBB and Henrietta visit the Graham-Clarkes at 8 Cambray Street, Cheltenham.

1825 July: EBB and Henrietta go to their paternal grandmother at Hastings, 1 Kentish Buildings, then 2 Paragon Place, for a stay of 11 months.

July–August: Mary Moulton-Barrett visits her sisters in Ireland, accompanied by daughter Arabella.

November: EBB's unidentified lines on "Judah" apparently published in unidentified paper.

19 November: EBB's "The Rose and Zephyr" published in *The Literary Gazette, and Journal of the Belles Lettres*.

1826 Edward Moulton-Barrett, EBB's brother, leaves Charterhouse, having advanced to the third form.

RB leaves the school of Rev. Thomas Martin Ready at Peckham. His education at this establishment, probably for six years, was augmented by his father's instructions. He was also tutored privately in French and Italian. He studied music under John Relfe, Musician-in-Ordinary to the King and a pupil of the Abbé Vogler. During this period RB is profoundly influenced by Shelley; this lasts for several years and leads to periods of atheism and vegetarianism.

25 March: EBB's *An Essay on Mind with Other Poems*, underwritten by Mary Trepsack, published by James Duncan, London.

6 May: EBB's "Irregular Stanzas" published in *The Literary Gazette, and Journal of the Belles Lettres*.

ca. June: EBB and Henrietta leave Hastings and return to Hope End.

October: EBB and Henrietta visit Foxley, seat of Uvedale Price.

November: EBB spends several days at Eastnor Castle, neighbouring estate of Lord Somers.

The Brownings' Correspondence

Volume 1
September 1809 – December 1826
Letters 1 – 244

1. EDWARD MOULTON-BARRETT (FATHER) TO EBB

Ledbury
Tuesday Evening [5 September 1809][1]

My Dear Puss

I sit down to perform my promise of writing you. I will endeavour to inform you of the whole of our actions since I parted from you; I got to Town safe, and Lockhead and myself dined with Sam, not your Sam,[2] at whose Hotel I slept, the next morning We went to North End,[3] where I prepared myself for my journey; We got that night, namely Saturday, to Woodstock, and the following to Malvern Town, which I meant to have been our head quarters, but we found our accommodations so very indifferent that we determined to remove them to Ledbury, to which place we took Hope-End in our way, and went on that Day nearly round the Estate, after being completely fagged, we set off for Ledbury to a very comfortable Inn; This Morn^g we again went to Hope-End and compleated our tour of it, besides looking thro' the center of the Estate and examining the Cottages; We shall go tomorrow to inspect the Timber &c– The more I see of the Property the more I like it and the more I think I shall have it in my power to make yourself, Brother & Sister & dear Mamma happy.[4] There is no fruit whatever this year in the Garden, but should we be fortunate enough to be here next year no doubt we shall have abundance[.] I cant say when I shall have it in my power to return but hope at the expiration of a couple of Days m⟨ore⟩ to be on my way back, that is ha⟨ppily⟩ as it may happen. I shall expect [to] see you well without any symtoms of that lurking Cough, and Buff as rosy as ever. My Best love to Mamma tell her, I believe I shall write her before my return also kiss the two other Pusses for me & Grandmamma, and love to Bell & Trep—not forgetting Junius–

My Paper adminishes [sic] me

I am, my Dear Ba[5]
Y^r truely affectionate and happy Papa
E M Barrett

Tell that cut-throat Buff that I shall expect him, on my return to repeat Goosy, Goosy Gander &c as well as usual–

Address, on integral page: Miss E. Barrett / Mrs Moulton's / Mickleham / near Leatherhead / Surrey–
Docket, in Mary Moulton-Barrett's hand: First letter from her dearest Papa– September 6th 1809 To happy Ba!– Given as the greatest of treasures into dear Grandmammas care. To be returned when her little pet is old enough to feel all the values of the best & most affectionate of Fathers.
Publication: None traced.
Manuscript: British Library.

[1]

1. Dated on basis of docket and of Edward Moulton-Barrett's heading "Tuesday Evening." EBB eventually wrapped this letter in a cover sheet along with letter 322 and labelled the sheet: "From my beloved Papa." The second letter deals with the death of EBB's mother. On the inside of the cover sheet, EBB wrote: "One of these letters was addressed & given to '*happy Ba*'—the other letter, to miserable & bereaved Ba! The writer of one of these letters, the beloved writer, subscribes himself 'your truly affectionate & happy EMB'– The writer of the other, 'your attached, however afflicted EMB.' And yet the same person wrote both letters, & with the same affection, & to the same correspondant. Oh God! not *our* will! but *thy* will! Have mercy, oh God—remembering that we are dust! Comfort us oh comforter! Do we not need comfort!"

2. Edward Moulton-Barrett had been staying at his mother's home at Mickleham, had left there on 1 September, and was writing back to report on his progress. The people remaining there, and mentioned in this letter, included: EBB herself; EBB's mother, Mary Moulton-Barrett; EBB's brother Edward (referred to as Buff) and sister Henrietta; Edward Moulton-Barrett's mother, Elizabeth Moulton (Grandmamma); her companion Mary Trepsack (Trep); her male servant Junius; and Arabella Graham-Clarke (Bell), EBB's maternal aunt. Lockhead was a distant cousin by marriage. The Sam with whom they dined was Samuel Barrett, Edward Moulton-Barrett's first cousin, and "your Sam" was Edward Moulton-Barrett's brother.

3. North End, Hammersmith, was where Edward Moulton-Barrett had taken a house after moving south from Coxhoe Hall, and it was his base while looking for a suitable country estate. His father, Charles Moulton (d. 1819), also lived in the neighbourhood.

4. He did eventually buy the property, and the family moved there a few months after the writing of this letter.

5. There has been much speculation regarding the derivation and pronunciation of this name, by which EBB was known throughout her life. Presumably, one should accept EBB's own explanation of its origin as being the correct one; in verse VII of her poem "The Pet-Name" (published in *The Seraphim, and Other Poems*, 1838) she wrote:

> "My brother gave that name to me
> When we were children twain,
> When names acquired baptismally
> Were hard to utter, as to see
> That life had any pain."

EBB also said, in a letter to Robert Browning (9 September 1845): "I am never called anything else ... proving as Mr. Kenyon says, that I am just 'half a Ba–by'—no more nor less:—and in fact the name has that precise definition." This derivation led to the suggestion that the name was pronounced "Bay," but the written evidence points to "Baa": a birthday ode (letter 124) rhymes "Ba" with "spar," and a riddle propounded by Hugh Stuart Boyd (see letters 367 and 368) suggested that EBB's family were like sheep, always saying "Baa." Even more conclusive, in our view, is an 1831 inscription in *Viger's Greek Idioms*, which EBB signed with the Hebrew character beth and the subscript denoting that it was followed by a long "a" (*Reconstruction*, A2390).

---

2. ELIZABETH MOULTON TO EBB

[Mickleham]
[6 March 1810][1]

I flatter myself my beloved Elizabeth will be pleased to have a Letter from GrdMama, who has taken the pen my dear Good Girl to congratulate you on your entrance into your fifth year– May each succeeding one find you as happy as no doubt, you are now—& be to your parents all that their fond Hearts can wish—also dear Henrietta, whose Birth day was on Sunday; you must give her a dozen Kisses for Trip, & myself. I have been some time anxious to write to you, (but put it off till this day,) to say how delighted I am at the accounts I have had of you– I hear you can read very prettily indeed, & very fond of your Books; that you mind whatever Papa, & Mama, says to you, in short, that you are a darling good Girl; which makes GrdMama love you, if possible, more than ever– You must give our Love to dear Bro,^{2} & tell him we expect to hear that He is grown fond of his Book; talk to him my dear Ba, & tell him what pleasure it will give his friends when he can read– Dunces are always laugh^d at, & I know you w^d not wish to see him one—as you can read so well yourself, you sh^d endeavour to prevail on him to let you teach him ——

Junius^3 at Dinner this day poured out a Bumper of Wine to each of us, & said we must drink dear Miss Barretts Health– He had one himself, & on taking it to his lips, wish'd you very good, Dear Miss, I *wish her, very, very happy* ——

Give My Love & Kiss to Mama, thank her for her Letter—two Kisses to Bum^4 for herself, & *present*: tell her I shall value them for her sake—the verses will also be not less priz'd for being the production of the varmint young Man —— I cannot say anything of their Merits, or demerits, as M^r. Lockhead has not yet made his appearance– I look for his arrival with no small impatience, as he will be able to tell me a great deal about you ——

Love & Kiss dear Papa, tell him Parish set off last Week to Portsmouth much recoverd, took out nine young Men with him for Mr Scarlett^5– ——

Ask Papa if he had any news from Jamaica by this last pacquet– If Doctor Scarlett^6 is restord to health

Mickleham is not so pretty as when you were here, the Ground is now all coverd with Snow —— Trep Kisses & wishes you all happiness– God Bless you my precious Child

prays Yours ever affectionate GrdMama
EM–

Publication: None traced.
Manuscript: Pierpont Morgan Library.

1. Dated by the reference to EBB's birthday and her entrance into her fifth year (1810).
2. "Bro" became the nickname of EBB's brother Edward, superseding Buff.
3. Junius, who is thought to have been born in slavery in Jamaica, was a member of Mrs. Moulton's household until her death, after which he remained with Samuel Moulton-Barrett, EBB's uncle.

4. "Bum" and "Bummy," as well as "Bell," were nicknames of Arabella Graham-Clarke, EBB's maternal aunt.

5. Portsmouth was frequently used as the port of embarkation for Jamaica. A letter from Henry Waite Plummer to Leonard Parkinson on 21 February 1805 (SD42, Appendix II) shows that a carpenter by the name of Parrish was employed at the Moulton-Barretts' Cinnamon Hill estate in Jamaica.

The Mr. Scarlett to whom he was journeying would have been either James Scarlett (later Lord Abinger) or his brother Philip, both of whom had holdings in Jamaica. James, however, was an absentee landlord, so the reference here is assumed to be to Philip, who, in addition to his own interests, was at this time acting as agent for Edward Moulton-Barrett, another absentee landlord.

6. Dr. Robert Scarlett, younger brother of James and Philip. In a letter to Edward Moulton-Barrett of 17 February 1810 (SD132), James Scarlett wrote: "My brother Robert I hear was ill with a fever when the packet sailed, out of danger, but not able to write."

---

3. EBB TO ELIZABETH MOULTON

[?Hope End]
[ca. 15 July 1810][1]

My dear Grandmama:

I love you very much. we are going to the sea on Monday week, we are all very sorry you are gone away, you had better come with us to the sea, we all send you kisses, your dear Ba Elizabeth Barrett, love to Trepsack & Forst.[2]

Address, on integral page: Mrs Moulton.
Docket, on scrap of paper, in Elizabeth Moulton's hand: for My Beloved Ba–
Publication: None traced.
Manuscript: Pierpont Morgan Library.

1. Dated by Elizabeth Moulton's reply (letter 4).
2. Probably Frost, a female domestic in Elizabeth Moulton's household.

---

4. ELIZABETH MOULTON TO EBB

[?Mickleham]
July 18th —— [1810][1]

This Morning post brought me a Letter very prettily written indeed for a little Girl of four Years old, so pleas'd am I, that I cou'd not let the day pass without writing a few lines, to thank my Beloved Child for her attention & expressions of Love, which I most sensibly feel– I am so proud of my Letter that it shall be put in a very careful place, till my Darling pet grows up, then I will shew it to you, & together, talk over the delight you took in writing, & the raptures I experienced in reading your first performance– Tell Papa & Mama to give you as many Kisses as I have bestowd on it, which I assure D[ea]^r Ba are not a few; say to Papa it made me doubly happy, putting me in mind of the time I receivd his first Letter, which I still have, & will give you as a Keepsake when I come to *see you*[2]—— Ask Bro when I am to have a Letter from him, I hope he is a good Boy, & attends to his Book– He will never be a Man till he does——

Trepsack sends you many Kisses & is quite pleasd at your improvement, Kisses also to Bro, Henrietta—let Mama know that you are to plead my excuse, I intended this day writing to her but cou'd not resist the pleasure I felt to let you know how good I thought you– tell her she must not stand upon ceremony, as she must always have a great deal to say about *you, Bro & Henrietta*– tell Papa he too shall hear from me before long– at present I am quite taken up with the Letter from my dear little Girl of four years old, & can think, & talk, of nothing else——. *Junius* says *God Bless* little Miss, I always knew she was very good, & am quite pleasd to see her write so well—— I suppose you will receive this in the Morn^g—when all the family are assembled at Breakfast. You must go to each of them, & in a very pretty manner present Trepsack & Grdmama best Love– *tell Bum* next time Mama writes, she must Send the Dutchess of Northumberland's Seal, as I want the impression, Kiss dear Grandmama Clarke[3] for me & ask her if she is not delighted with a little Girl of our acquaintance[.] My best affections with many Kisses attend

My dearest Ba
from yours truly attach^d
EM——

Publication: None traced.
Manuscript: Pierpont Morgan Library.

1. Writer mentions EBB's being four years old, the age she reached in March 1810.
2. This letter has been preserved (see SD21).
3. Arabella Graham-Clarke, EBB's maternal grandmother, who apparently was visiting Hope End at this time. It was through her (*née* Altham) that the Graham-Clarkes, and EBB herself, traced their descent from King Edward I (*A Portfolio of Royal Descents*, London, 1902).

5. ELIZABETH MOULTON TO EBB

[?London]
[ca. September 1810][1]

I have just a few minutes to write to my Dearest Ba—to thank her for thinking of me & writing by dear Papa– there was one *word* in your

Letter extremely well written– I kiss'd it very often—but I w^d rather have welcom'd my dear little girl herself & was in hopes Papa w^d have brought you with him——

We thank you for your kind invitation & will do ourselves the pleasure of paying your little Ladyship a visit very soon——

I was quite rejoicd to see dear Papa look so well– Grdpapa Clarke^2 is also in good health– He loves Ba very much, because you are so very good– Kiss dear Bro & Henrietta Mama & Charlotte^3 for us——

Trip joins me in Love——

God Bless you my Beloved Elizabeth——

EM—

Address, on integral page: My dearest mad[am] Ba.
Docket, below address, in EBB's hand: Dear Grandmama.
Publication: None traced.
Manuscript: Pierpont Morgan Library.

1. This was written after Elizabeth Moulton's reply (letter 4) to EBB's very first letter, but it was apparently written before the 16 September 1810 birth of EBB's sister Mary, who is not mentioned. An intended visit to Hope End is mentioned, and Mary Trepsack wrote to Elizabeth Barrett Williams on 2 October 1810 that she and Elizabeth Moulton were there (see SD144).

2. John Graham-Clarke (1736–1818), EBB's maternal grandfather.

3. Charlotte (Lotte) Graham-Clarke, EBB's maternal aunt.

6. ELIZABETH MOULTON TO EBB

[?London]
[ca. September 1810]^1

My dearest Elizabeth

On Wednesday we leave here for Hope End; I shall be rejoic'd to see your little Face once more; also Bro & Henrietta– Now my sweet child will you be glad to see Grandmama & Trip– tell Mama her chair leaves Town Tomorrow—she gave a wrong direction. Morgan & Sanders—16 Catherine St Strand—the other articles I have——

Remember us affectionately to Dr Papa & Mama, Charloote [*sic*], Bro—Henrietta–

God Bless my dear Ba

EM——

Publication: None traced.
Manuscript: Pierpont Morgan Library.

1. Dated from the fact that this letter seems to follow very shortly after Elizabeth Moulton's previous letter (no. 5) mentioning a planned visit to Hope End.

Architectural Designs for Hope End Mansion

My dearest Grandmama,

I am afraid you have thought me, a very naughty child not to have thanked you sooner for the beautiful work box, you were so kind as to send me, I love it very much for your sake, I cannot tell you how much. I wish to see you, dear Grandpapa, Bum, & all of you, if we cannot go to Fenham, you must come here. I send you a little sketch, kisses & love to all, Your namsake is very pretty, I am your most affec. child
Elizabeth Barrett

Letter 10

7. ELIZABETH MOULTON TO EBB

[?London]
[ca. May 1811][1]

How truly happy I feel in taking up my pen to thank my dear little Girl for her nice Letter, to say, that I think her very much improved in her writing—which makes G^{d}Mama most happy indeed—*sombody* whisperd to her, how good *her dear Ba* continued to be, which was the reason of her sending the Tippet——

D[ea]^r Sam is a great deal better he w^d not stay with us till he was quite strong, but ran away this mor^{ng}; Mr Bent is gone with him as far as Eaton, where he means to sleep– Sam[2] comes in a week, & says if he possibly can, he will go to Cheltenham to see his dear little pets, all of whom He loves very dearly——

I am sorry to hear papa, & Harry,[3] are so naughty,—you must give them your opinion about drinking the waters, the good it will do them, tell Papa, it will take away his Headache altogether—Harry, that it will prevent her *taking Physic* from Mr *Bridges*; all this I hope will in time, induce them to comply with your wishes; we are pleasd to hear Mama's Stockings fit her, give our best Love, & thank her for the few lines she sent in your Letter, & trust when we hear again that she has had no return of Headache——

when you walk out, you must call at the Shoe Makers & scold him for not sending our Boot, & Shoe, & give our Love to Mrs Appleton & Mrs Waite,[4] & hope they are better——

Kisses to Mama, Charlotte, Bro, Harry, & Mary[5] from both of us. GrdMamas best Affections Attend her Dearest Girl Ever

EM—

Handsome Sam[6] has just paid us a visit the first time of his going out— He is much improved in good looks, & talks of going to the North in a few days—— Love to dear Papa

Docket, on scrap of paper, in Elizabeth Moulton's hand: for My Beloved Ba.
Publication: None traced.
Manuscript: Pierpont Morgan Library.

1. Dated by a reference in a letter from Elizabeth Barrett Williams to her youngest son, George Goodin Barrett, 1 April 1811 (SD146): "Your Aunt M[oulton] & Trip remains at Cheltenham with Edwards Family, but I hope to see them in Town soon." Elizabeth Moulton's letter seems to have been written immediately after the return to London.
2. The Sam mentioned twice in this paragraph is Samuel Moulton-Barrett, EBB's uncle.
3. One of Henrietta's early nicknames.
4. Mrs. Appleton and Mrs. Waite cannot be identified with any certainty. Probably they were friends with Jamaican backgrounds, as there was a firm named Watson & Appleton in Montego Bay, and the family of Waite had connections by marriage with the Barrett family.

5. EBB's sister, Mary Barrett Moulton-Barrett, who died in infancy.
6. Samuel Barrett, eldest son of Elizabeth Barrett Williams. In the letter referred to in note 1, she writes that Sam "has been very ill but is now on the recovery, he is confined to the House and will be so for sometime longer."

---

8. ELIZABETH MOULTON TO EBB

[?London]
[ca. May 1812][1]

My Beloved Ba!

You must think Grdmama very Idle not to answer your two affectionate Letters; you w^d not have been so long without hearing from me, had I been able to hold a pen, it is only within the last fortnight that I began to get better & I know my good little Girl will be glad to hear I am *now* QUITE well, & anxiously looking every day for a Letter to say, my own dear *Ba* is coming to see me– We shall have a nice little Girl for you to play with—|Pool| Scarlett[2] will spend her Holidays here & then go to Cheltenham with us——

Kiss all your Children for me– I hope Harry continues to be a good Girl & has learnt all the prayers you were so kind to make her repeat every Sunday mor^{ng}——

I had two ⟨or⟩ three Letters from *your Sam* since we wrote last to Cheltenham– He sends Loves & Kisses to all his pets– *You* must give his Love to Papa & Mama & say Uncle Sam begs they will not take it unkind his not writing to them– He had nothing worth sending them in a Letter—but *He* will make his excuse himself in July—as he expects to be in England very early in that month– *He* has been Ill & confind to the House—the Duke of Leinster, his Brother Ld Wm Fitzgerald, & a Mr Howard,[3] were his constant attendants– He says, directly the weather becomes more fair,; I shall leave Palermo & accompany the Duke & his Brother round the Island, then proceed to Malta, then to England– He says I must tell his dear Ba you will have a Letter from him by the next pacquet & if he can get a safe conveyance he will send you a Maltese chain——

Say something very pretty to Aunt Fanny[4] for Trepsack, & Grdmama, tell her how very sorry we are that we cannot see her before she leaves England, & we wish her very very happy– Love to dear Papa & Mama & Ta[5] for both of us– Kiss your dear little *Sam* for us——

Ever My Sweet Ba
Your Affectionate Grdmama
EM——

tell Papa to ask Mr Lockhead for Treps papers that he has as they are much wanted

Publication: None traced.
Manuscript: Pierpont Morgan Library.

1. Letter was apparently being sent to Cheltenham, where EBB's brother Sam had been born on 13 January 1812. He is mentioned, but sister Arabella, born 4 July 1813, is not. Assuming that the year was 1812, an earlier month than July is indicated by reference to uncle Sam's plans.
2. Not identified, but presumably a young member of James Scarlett's family.
3. Augustus Frederick Fitzgerald, third Duke of Leinster (1791–1874) and his brother, Lord William Charles Fitzgerald (1793–1864). Mr. Howard has not been identified.
4. Frances Butler (*née* Graham-Clarke), EBB's maternal aunt. She had married Thomas Butler on 30 January, and was about to leave for his estate in Ireland.
5. Another family name for Henrietta.

---

9. EBB TO MARY MOULTON-BARRETT

[Hope End]
August 31.[s]t [1812]^1

My dear Mama
    I love you very much: & I hope you love me: I hope you like kinnersley;^2 we have been very good, Bro has just told me how England is bounded & has done it very well. tell dear Papa the Rusians has beat the french killd 18.000 men & taken 14000 prisners. Bro & Hen meo & Sam joins with me in love to Papa & you & John^3
                                                                    your dear
                                                                    Ba

Address, on integral page: Mrs Barrett / kinnersley castle / Hereford.
Publication: None traced.
Manuscript: British Library.

1. Dated by reference to the war between Russia and France. It was, however, the Russians who were defeated at Smolensk, 17 August 1812.
2. Kinnersley Castle, Hereford home of Leonard Parkinson, who had been, among other things, a dealer in slaves with George Goodin Barrett, EBB's father's late uncle.
3. John Altham Graham-Clarke, EBB's maternal uncle, had married Leonard Parkinson's daughter, Mary, on 18 January 1812. They made Kinnersley their home.

---

10. EBB TO ARABELLA GRAHAM-CLARKE (GRANDMOTHER)

[Hope End]
[3 March 1814]^1

My dearest Grandmama,
    I am afraid you have thought me, a very naughty child not to have

thanked you sooner for the beautiful workbox, you were so kind as to send me, I love it very much for your sake; I cannot tell you how much. I wish to see you, dear Grandpapa, Bum, & all of you; if we cannot go to Fenham,[2] you must come here. I send you a little sketch,[3] kisses & love to all, Your namsake[4] is very pretty, I am your most affec.[te] Child

Elizabeth Barrett

Address, on integral page, in Mary Moulton-Barrett's hand: M[rs] Graham Clarke / Fenham House / Newcastle [on] Tyne.
Publication: None traced.
Manuscript: Edward R. Moulton-Barrett.

    1. Dated by Mary Moulton-Barrett's covering letter (SD183)
    2. The Graham-Clarke estate near Newcastle. Although Mary Moulton-Barrett addressed her letter to "Fenham House," the obituary notice of EBB's grandfather and subsequent printed references, all speak of "Fenham Hall." The façade is illustrated facing p. xxvii.
    3. Landscape drawing on page with letter.
    4. Arabella, EBB's sister, born the previous July.

---

11. EDWARD MOULTON-BARRETT (FATHER) TO EBB

[Hope End]
[Docket: 24 April 1814]

To the dear Child, whose offering this day has contributed so much to the gratification of her Papa, who views in it not alone the Germs of ⟨Geni⟩us[1] but the assurance that the Love of Virtue has taken such ea[r]ly Root in her mind. A Ten Shilling Note is sent for dear Ba to give pleasure to herself in adding to the comforts of others—[2]

EMB.

Address, on integral page: Miss Barrett / Poet-Laureat of / Hope-End—
Docket, above address, in Mary Moulton-Barrett's hand: April 24[th] 1814 Keep this dear note as long as you live, my darling Ba! MB.
Publication: None traced.
Manuscript: British Library.

    1. Ink blot.
    2. EBB wrote of this note in her "Glimpses into My Own Life and Literary Character" (see Appendix III, part 2): "In my sixth year for some lines on virtue which I had penned with great care I received from Papa a ten shilling note enclosed in a letter which was addrest to the *Poet Laureat of Hope End*; I mention this because I received much more pleasure from the word *Poet* than from the ten shilling note— I did not understand the meaning of the word laureat but it being explained to me by my dearest Mama, the idea first presented itself to me of celebrating our birthdays by my verse." (In return for his honorarium, the Poet Laureate was expected to celebrate in verse the sovereign's birthday and other occasions of national rejoicing.) As EBB's first known birthday ode was given to her mother on 1 May 1814, this appears to corroborate the docket, but EBB was then in her ninth year, not in her sixth as stated in "Glimpses into My Own Life." The lines on virtue are probably those printed in *HUP*, I, 33 (*Reconstruction*, D23).

EBB holding Samuel, with Edward, Henrietta and Mary Moulton-Barrett

12. EBB TO EDWARD MOULTON-BARRETT (FATHER)

[Hope End]

To my dearest Papa 27th April 1814

Sweet Parent! dear to me as kind
Who sowed the very bottom of my mind,
And raised the very inmost of my heart,
To taste the sweets of Nature, you impart!

I hope you will let us drink tea with you & have your fiddle tonight–
Your dear child Elizabeth.

an answer to the Nursery–

Publication: HUP, I, 36 (from copy in Mary Moulton-Barrett's hand, Huntington Library).
Source: EBB's fair copy in "Poems by EBB," Berg Collection.

---

13. EBB TO MARY MOULTON-BARRETT

[Hope End]

Sent to Mama on 1st May: 1814.[1]

T'was dark—the tempest blew aloud,
And light'ning flashed from every cloud,
A wretched Mother, fondly pressed,
Her infant Babies to her breast;
These were stern winters lonely prize,
They shut—they closed poor little eyes.
They died, contented in their Mothers arms
No houses near—nor little farms!
The restless leaves were hushed, in yonder wood
No mortal lived—no cottage stood!
This wretched mother's gone into her wat'ry grave,
No man can pass—no man can save!
The waters shook, as there she fell,
The chilling tempest blew farewell!–

Publication: HUP, I, 38–39 (from copy in Mary Moulton-Barrett's hand, Huntington Library).
Source: EBB's fair copy in "Poems by EBB," Berg Collection.

1. Her thirty-third birthday.

14. EBB TO HENRIETTA MOULTON-BARRETT

[Hope End]

An Epistle to Henrietta—14ᵗʰ May 1814

Thy gentle smile displays thy virtues sweet,
Altho' dear Addles[1] far to [sic] much you eat,
But now you have a horrid cold,
And in a ugly night cap you are rolled,
Which spoils the nat'ral beauty of your face,
Where dimples play in every cunning place;
I wish you would so nicely run,
And then we would have merry fun,
But o'er the fire you poking sit,
As if for nothing you were fit.
Our little lamb is very well,
Oh come into our pretty cell!
Indeed I hope you'll soon get better,
And I am dearest Henrietta,
Your very dear Elizabeth Barrett,
Compared to you, a chatting parot [sic].

Publication: HUP, I, 42–43 (from copy in Mary Moulton-Barrett's hand, Huntington
   Library).
Source: EBB's fair copy in "Poems by EBB," Berg Collection.

   1. The term "addled," which describes a spoiled egg, can also mean "confused"
(*OED*). Apparently Henrietta sometimes became confused, and one of her family names
was "Hen," and hens lay eggs. Through this somewhat addled chain of thought, she
acquired the nickname "Addles."

---

15. EBB TO EDWARD MOULTON-BARRETT (FATHER)

[Hope End]
28 May [1814][1]

Addressed to dearest Papa on His birthday upon the recovery of little
Arabella, from a dangerous illness

Oh! come my Muse, this twenty eighth of May,
Come let us celebrate this happy day!
Whilst I my humble lines rehearse.
The nightingale and linnet's sing the verse,

When Death's pale hand o'er Baby spread,
The pillow raised her little head,
Her face was white, her pulse beat low,
From every eye sad tears did flow,
But God to her his angel sent,
To make her well on mercy bent,
Stern Deaths driven by the angel chace [*sic*],
And Health comes suffering to replace,
So blest thy birthday Parent dear,
And blessed be thy birthday every year!

Publication: HUP, I, 44 (from copy in Mary Moulton-Barrett's hand, Huntington Library).
Source: EBB's fair copy in "Poems by EBB," Berg Collection.

1. Dated by Mary Moulton-Barrett in "Poems by EBB II." Also appears in chronological order in "Poems by EBB." This celebrated the 29th birthday of EBB's father.

16. EBB TO SAMUEL MOULTON-BARRETT (UNCLE)

Carlton[1]
16th June 1814

To her Uncle Sam, with her poetry—

Dear Sam, accept my humble lay,
How dear to me, I need not say,
And when from Carlton I am gone,
I'll never cease, thy love to mourn.
At childhood's age, these faults forgive,
When I am older, if I live,
I'll offer better verse to thee,
Who's been so very kind to me:

Publication: HUP, I, 48 (from copy in Mary Moulton-Barrett's hand, Huntington Library).
Source: EBB's fair copy in "Poems by EBB," Berg Collection.

1. Estate in Yorkshire near Richmond, about 7 miles S. of Darlington, purchased by EBB's uncle Sam soon after he attained his majority in 1808, and retained by him until he went to Jamaica in 1827. Samuel Moulton-Barrett represented Richmond in Parliament from 10 March 1820 to February 1828.

17. EBB TO EDWARD MOULTON-BARRETT (FATHER)

Fehnam
August 22ᵈ 1814

An Epistle to my dearest Papa in London

As in the shady shrubbery I sit
With insects buzzing round my head
I call my Muse her silence now to quit
And my few thoughts to thee in Verse are led.

For absent is my Parent dear
I wish he would to Fenham come
For dull it makes the house appear
When thou art fled, when thou art gone

Happily we went to the play
"Revenge" excited our delight
When Young in Zanga¹ on Thursday
Kept sleep away, tho' by lamp light.

It was a Tragedy so deep
And Ba and Bro so much amused
We could not then have fallen asleep
Leonora only we abused.²

There's Mʳ Butler³ stole two pound
From off Bum's painted table
And then he beat her fairly round
As long as he was able.

So Mʳ Sheriff,⁴ if you please
Send Constables to take him
To put this party more at ease,
For he's the rogue who plagues them.

Now they are all gone to dinner
Alone I'm left to write to thee
For I should think myself a sinner
Had any thing such charms for me.

My love to Grandmama I send
And love to Trepsack too,
My kindest thoughts them e'er attend,
But best of loves to you!——

Publication: HUP, I, 53–55 (from copy in Mary Moulton-Barrett's hand, Huntington
  Library).
Source: Copy in Mary Moulton-Barrett's hand in "Poems by EBB," Berg Collection.

1. *The Revenge*, a tragedy featuring a captive Moor named Zanga, was written by Edward Young (1683–1765) in 1721.
2. Copy includes footnote: "The part of Leonora badly performed." Leonora was the heroine of Young's play.
3. Thomas Butler married Frances Graham-Clarke in 1812.
4. A reference to EBB's father's current position as High Sheriff of Herefordshire.

---

18. EBB TO MARY MOULTON-BARRETT

Fenham
Sep.[r] 1st 1814

My dearest Mama:
    Pray do not let us say our lessons today, but longer ones instead, tomorrow– I made these lines this Morning–[1]
Your very Affec[te] Child
E.B.B.

Send back the pencil with your answer to n[o] 5.–

Publication: None traced.
Source: Copy in Mary Moulton-Barrett's hand in "Poems by EBB," Berg Collection.

1. Letter accompanies two quatrains commencing "Fair and chrystal is the Spring," also in "Poems by EBB," published in *HUP*, I, 56, from a copy in her mother's hand at Huntington.

---

19. EBB TO MARY MOULTON-BARRETT

[Hope End]
[October 1814][1]

Madam
    I request you to accept this little story[2] for 3[s] & if you would buy this yourself & write copys to be sold for the public. I am Madam your most obedient humble Servant
Elizabeth Barrett

    You owe me 8[d] for other things

Publication: HUP, I, 62 (from copy in Mary Moulton-Barrett's hand, Armstrong Browning Library).
Manuscript: Berg Collection.

1. In "Poems by EBB," Mary Moulton-Barrett dated a copy of this item "Oct.[r] 1814."
2. Letter accompanies an original story titled "Sebastian or the lost Child a Tale of other Times" (*HUP*, I, 62–65).

20. EBB TO MARY MOULTON-BARRETT

[Hope End]
[October 1814][1]

Madam
It would give me great pleasure if you would dispose of this[2] as you did the other
I am Madam
Your most obedient humble servant
Elizabeth B. Barrett

Publication: HUP, I, 68 (from copy in Mary Moulton-Barrett's hand, Armstrong Browning Library).
Manuscript: Berg Collection.

1. In "Poems by EBB," this entry, though undated, appears between two entries dated October 1814. EBB assigned a numeral "1" to the first of those two entries (letter 19) and a numeral "3" to this one. Whatever may have been numbered "2" is not accounted for.
2. Letter accompanies an original story titled "The Way to humble Pride" (*HUP*, I, 68–71).

---

21. EBB TO ARABELLA GRAHAM-CLARKE (GRANDMOTHER)

Hope End
Jan.[ry] 9 1815

My dearest Grandmama,
Thank you a thousand times for your sweet letter it was indeed quite delightful– I must tell you the news that past since I left you all. As we were in our beds I heard a noise so I cald to Bro & he thought it was only my fun But he cald to Rosa[1] when she came the watter was all runing down the wall so Papa & Grandmama Moulton & dearest Jane[2] came up stairs & she was obliged to go in Grandmamas room Bro & Henrietta in Janes, & Sam in Little Babys[3] who is very well– My Doll is not broken yet But Grandmama Brought me a beautyfut [*sic*] one & then at Christmas she gave me another little one which has some nice clothes & a pretty fur cap & a cloth coat nightgown & night cap &[c]– Dearest Mama is better & the sweet little Baby indeed all of us. I was very sory that dearest Bum went to Ireland without coming here. whenever I hear the dogs bark it puts me inmind [*sic*] of Button[4]—who I am sory to hear has almost lost his tricks[.] I hope you will soon come here as we will certainly go abroad in the Spring[5] good bye dearest Grandmama & believe me your ever affec[ate] Child
Elizabeth B Barrett

I send the books we brought from Fenham[.] I hope Grandpapas leg is well—
Papas respectful complemints & Grandmamas Love & Janes regards to all of you—

Address, on integral page: Mrs Graham Clarke / Fenham / Newcas[t]le on Tyne.
Publication: None traced.
Manuscript: Edward R. Moulton-Barrett.

1. In the course of a discussion on names in a letter to Mary Russell Mitford dated 15 January 1840, EBB wrote: "was there not a 'stern unbending Rosalinda Theodora Mary' . . . who officiated as nurse when I lived in a nursery?" A letter of 25 October 1815 (SD236) from Mary Moulton-Barrett to her mother shows that Rosa accompanied EBB and her parents to Paris in the autumn of 1815.
2. Jane Graham-Clarke, EBB's maternal aunt.
3. Charles John Moulton-Barrett, born 28 December 1814.
4. A pug dog in the Fenham household. EBB wrote an unpublished verse "To the Memory of Sir William Button" in September 1817. "Poems by EBB," Berg Collection, contains a copy in the hand of Mary Moulton-Barrett (see *Reconstruction*, D1047–48).
5. Edward Moulton-Barrett had a plan to take his whole family to France for an extended stay. This did not develop. Instead, EBB and her parents made a brief visit to Paris in the autumn.

---

22. EBB TO SAMUEL MOULTON-BARRETT (BROTHER)

[Hope End]

To little Sam on his birth day Jany. 13th 1815[1]

Oh Come fair Muse, Oh raise thy fondest strain
Come let us hear thy plaintive Voice again
Now haste, & Celebrate this jovial day
Throw out our merry strains, let's jump & play.
Three years have flown now o'er thy glossy head,
Three years! And Ah! how quickly have they fled.
The fourth—be early wise, and truly good,
Ask of thy bounteous Maker, sense & food
Accept sweet Sam, these wishes on thy birth,
From her, who loves thee well, as any on the Earth;
A Brothers[2] sent—Most sweetly to beguile
And cheer thy birth day, with his infant smile
O welcome little Babe; I welcome thee
And trust thou'lt some time give thy love to me!
May we live happy in each others love
And bless our Parents 'till we rise above!
Here pause my Muse! here hush thy golden lyre
For Currant wine[3] must quench celestial fire!

Publication: HUP, I, 80–81 (from copy in Mary Moulton-Barrett's hand, Huntington Library).
Source: Copy in Mary Moulton-Barrett's hand, Edward R. Moulton-Barrett.

1. His third birthday.
2. A reference to Charles John Moulton-Barrett, born 28 December 1814.
3. In a footnote to both her copies, Mary Moulton-Barrett describes currant wine as "A Customary birth day treat."

---

23. EBB TO MARY MOULTON-BARRETT

[Hope End]

On the first of May. Mama's birth day—1815.[1]

Come Oh my Muse, Sing of the first of May
Kind Heaven to me a precious boon has given
For Earth was blest with thee on this fair day
And when death comes, thou'lt rise to smiling Heav'n
Accept this pledge of love my dear Mama
And cheer my verses with a bounteous smile
Aurora sings in her triumphal car
And Natures Music does the hour beguile.

Publication: HUP, I, 86 (from copy in Mary Moulton-Barrett's hand, Huntington Library).
Source: Copy in Mary Moulton-Barrett's hand in "Poems by EBB," Berg Collection.

1. Her 34th birthday.

---

24. EBB TO EDWARD MOULTON-BARRETT (FATHER)

Hope End
during the improvements there
On Papa's birth day
May 28.th 1815.[1]—

Hail dear Papa! I hail thy natal day
The Muses speak, my hidden thoughts of love
That love is more than e'en the Muse can say
That love, shall reign, untill we rise above:

Sweet Philomel[2] enchants the listening grove
While musics warblings twitter in her throat
By murmuring streams, mute silence roves
Echo scarce dares repeat the Heavenly note:

'Tis thus these hills declare their bounteous Sire
As on thy birth, to thee, His gifts they pay
Sweet Philomella tends the tuneful choir
And all is joy to see this happy day.

On thy fair birth the meadows smile
How brightly on this day, the prospects rise!
May they, all painful care beguile
And humble Sorrow as it flies!

The smile of hope illumes thy Soul
Amidst these vales, where Philomel doth sing,
Where beauty reigns without control,
Through out His works, God's praises ring!

These polished walls, raised by y^r tasteful hand,
These smiling shrubs, these tangled walks & hills;
These rising rocks,—hewn by your active band
And drooping flow'rets washed by murmuring rills:

These waters by your hand are taught to glide
And wild ducks strain their soaring wing
Far on the limpid wave they ride
While sweets the gathering zephyrs fling—

An useful farm, now owns thy generous sway
And oxen fatten fast at thy command
A pleasure comes with each untasted day
Thou reap'st the fruit—& nurstles [*sic*] all thy land.

Long may'st thou live, as on this happy day ·
Amidst thy smiling little Family
And may we grateful, e'er thy cares repay
And play about the shilling gallery!—

And may we ever, bless this smiling home,
And live united, by a tender love,
Secluded from that world, where vices roam,
Then hand in hand, proceed to God above!—

                 Your most affec^{te} child
                 Elizabeth B. Barrett.

Publication: HUP, I, 88–90 (from copy in Mary Moulton-Barrett's hand, Armstrong Browning Library).
Source: Copy in Mary Moulton-Barrett's hand in "Poems by EBB," Berg Collection.

1. His 30th birthday.
2. Poetic name for the nightingale.

25. EBB TO MARY MOULTON-BARRETT

[Hope End]
[14 August 1815]¹

Dear Mama
    Take this for my sake

I am
Elizth Barrett

an answer—

Address, on integral page: excuse the writing / Mrs Barrett / Hope End.
Publication: HUP, I, 93 (from copy in Mary Moulton-Barrett's hand, Huntington Library).
Manuscript: Berg Collection.

1. This note follows a short essay which begins: "Where can happiness be found?" (*HUP,* I, 92–93). It is dated in Mary Moulton-Barrett's hand.

---

26. EBB TO ARABELLA GRAHAM-CLARKE (AUNT)

London Baker S[t]reet
Decr 26 [1815]¹

My dearest Bum
    I hope you do not think it is unkind that I do not write to you, as I wrote two letters to you about three months ago; but *you* did not answer them, so I did not write any more. I have got a watch, I dare say you know I have, but *now* I wear it, I had only got it about three days, and it went to the watchmaker to be mended.
    My dearest Bum, you do not *know* how happy I was in Paris!, the Louvre is the most magnificent thing in the world I am sure; we were (that is to say Mama and me, for Papa and *Mr Matt Wyat* were looking over curiosty shops); I dare say you will stare when I say Mr Matt Wyat went only *once* into the Louvre, and a painter!² Mama and I went many times into that beautiful place. From Jardin des plants I have taken a lesson of gardening, it was I am sure two *yards,* and *French* yards, deep in that most beautiful black flower soil; my dear Bum I have found nothing like England, & Ireland, for you are there; you do not know how much I love you, indeed my love is more than I can express. However far—we may be sepreated [*sic*], either in the gulph of life, or of death, my love shall triumph over it, and shall never be constrained, and I shall ever remain affectionately
Yours
Elizth B. Barrett

Kindest love to dearest Fanny to my Uncle, and to Richard and love little unknown.[3]
[Continued by EBB's mother] This Elegant Scratch you will I know be glad to have, & therefore it goes, bad & ill written as it is– She shews it me while George[4] waits for it– I am very very anxious & uneasy to hear from you[.] I hope my letter reached you, dispatched as soon as we returned from France– I shall write very soon—— Dec.[r] 26. Happy happy Christmas to all.

Address, in Mary Moulton-Barrett's hand, on integral page: Miss Graham Clarke / Cohamon / New Town Barry / Wexford.
Publication: None traced.
Manuscript: Berg Collection.

1. Dated by EBB's visit to Paris, 17 October to 17 November 1815. EBB's notes on this trip were published in *HUP*, I, 165–173.
2. Possibly the painter Matthew Cotes Wyatt (1777–1862), whose works were exhibited at the Royal Academy, 1803–14.
3. This sentence refers to Thomas Butler (1783–1861), his wife Frances (*née* Graham-Clarke), their eldest son, Richard Pierce, born 4 March 1813, and their third child, Arabella Sarah, born 27 May 1815.
4. Probably George Butler, a younger brother of Thomas.

27. EBB & HENRIETTA MOULTON-BARRETT TO MARY MOULTON-BARRETT

[Hope End]
[ca. 1816][1]

My dearest and kind Mama
As I know you will not refuse a request that is reasonable I venture to adress you remember that we have a great many things to do tomorrow to alter my poetry to get flowers to write my verses and so has Hen—so Pray dear Mama do excuse us our Music tomorrow and believe us your affec[te] children

Eliz[th] & Henrietta

Address, on integral page: To our kind / Mama an answer / to the nursery.
Publication: None traced.
Manuscript: Berg Collection.

1. Letter is all in EBB's handwriting, upon which conjectural dating is based.

28. EBB TO HENRIETTA MOULTON-BARRETT

To dearest Henrietta
On her birthday
Hope End March 4th 1816[1]

Come forth my Muse, from the dark shades of night,
Haste to illume the lyre, with cheering light;
Thy penance ended, on this joyous day,
Arouse from silence, and invoke our play;
And thou, awaker of the new tuned lyre,
'Tis thou, who breath'st afresh celestial fire;
Oh Henrietta! may, to thee be given,
Fair Truth and Virtue, riches ta'en from Heaven;
May they subdue all trials that await,
And shed their lustre on thy happy fate;
Long may this little circle smiling meet,
In love and joy this happy day to greet!

Elizabeth Barrett.

Address, on integral page: To Henr[ietta] / at Breakfast / With wish[es] for her good / app[etite].
Publication: HUP, I, 99 (from copy in Mary Moulton-Barrett's hand, University of Texas).
Manuscript: Berg Collection.

1. Her seventh birthday.

29. EBB TO EDWARD MOULTON-BARRETT (FATHER)

Hope End
May 28.th 1816

To My Dearest Papa
On His Birthday[1]

Oh brilliant glory, I invoke not thee
Nor soar to please save by simplicity
Wrapt in its truth, my Parent kind I see
Then come my Muse, with joy I call for thee
From bowers of bliss!—Come strike Apollo's lyre
Mingle sweet blessings with celestial fire!

Hail Father dear! Who taught me virtuous truth
Who guidst me, thro' the thorny way of youth;
Oh say my Muse!—interpret in thy song
The praise of him who chides me when I'm wrong
Whose judgement gentle, kind applause does give
Wins grateful love, while Memory shall live
Thy birth is welcomed by thy childrens smiles
This day so dear, their every care beguiles
And Oh may o'er thy head, Gods blessing wave
Long years of joy conduct thee to the grave!

But ah! my loves beyond the Muses art—
She cannot paint the feelings of my heart
Then go sweet poetry, go lovely spell
My Muse, and Parent dear, *both* fare ye well!–

EBB.

Publication: HUP, I, 101–102.
Source: Copy in Mary Moulton-Barrett's hand, Scripps College and University of Texas.

1. His 31st birthday. At the end of the ode, Mary Moulton-Barrett noted that EBB also gave her father a nosegay of flowers (comprised mainly of heart's-ease, *viola tricolor*), accompanied by this verse: "Accept my gift! for loves sweet couch is flowers / By Nature's hand, strewn o'er lifes fragrant bowers, / May *heart's ease* which thy child can give / Shed peace for thee, while thou shalt live!–" (See *Reconstruction*, D4.)
It is also recorded that, at the same time, EBB gave her father a letter in Latin, "the first ever attempted," with the following written on the back: "May flowery gales, which waft this pledge of love / Breathing affection from a heart Sincere / To thee my fond attachment prove / My love and verse accept, O Parent dear!–" (See *Reconstruction*, D520.)

---

30. EBB TO MARY MOULTON-BARRETT

[Hope End]
June 1816

Excuse me my Arithmetic, dear Mama; in a hurry yours——[1]

Publication: None traced.
Source: Copy in Mary Moulton-Barrett's hand in "Poems by EBB," Berg Collection.

1. This note follows a short unpublished essay which begins: "In one of the hottest Evenings," also in "Poems by EBB."

31. EBB TO EDWARD MOULTON-BARRETT (BROTHER)

To My Dearest Brother Edward
(On His Birthday)
Hope End, June 26, 1816[1]

Hail Brother dear! and hail this cherished day
Which on my life bestowed a gift so bright,
With joyful haste, I tune the lyre so gay
To praise thy virtues with sincere delight.

Then come blest Truth, accompany my Song,
And let not flattery mingle in my verse,
For generous feelings to thy heart belong
And kindness, which love's lay may well rehearse.

But ne'er did powerful Rome spread more dismay
Than tattered book of harmless Latin dead,
Let fun conduct thee thro' this happy day—
Tomorrow, may Minerva shield thy head!

Text: HUP, I, 108.

1. His ninth birthday. According to Buxton Forman, this poem was preceded on the same page by a brief composition in French, which is printed—with translation—in *HUP*, I, 106–107.

---

32. EBB TO ELIZABETH MOULTON

Hope End
July 17th 1816

I dedicate this little volume[1] to her whose smile ever cheers my endeavours to please, to her who shines an ornament to her sex, and all around her– To her, my dearest Grandmama,[2] these pages are inscribed, with the greatest gratitude and esteem by her

affectionate child
Elizabeth B Barrett

Publication: None traced.
Manuscript: Armstrong Browning Library.

1. Unpublished manuscript entitled "Julia or Virtue / a novel" (also at ABL).
2. Elizabeth Moulton is deduced to be the recipient because the following letter (no. 33) by EBB went to her other (maternal) grandmother. If both letters were to the same person, the manuscript mentioned here probably would have been mentioned in both.

---

33. EBB TO ARABELLA GRAHAM-CLARKE (GRANDMOTHER)

[Hope End]
July 27th 1816

My dearest Grandmama
    I am very glad to tell you, dear Mama is getting [on] quite nicely, she can walk a *little* now, and the sweet little Boy improves every day,[1] Indeed we want nothing to complete, our happiness, but to have the pleasing gratification of seeing you, dearest Grandpapa, Charlotte, and Jenny, not forgetting Lawson, & Smith,[2] &^c, as you know I wish for *Bum*, Fanny, &^c I need not say *Not forgetting* over again–. Oh but I must tell you, we have got grapes, now but remember not ripe, and we have pineapples, also, Oh what am I thinking of! Mr Somebody, or Mrs Somebody, gave them to us, But really the grapes are ours– Oh dearest Grandmama, Hope End is so beautiful, Nature here displays all her art, the ivy that droops upon the ground, she fastens up to some majestic tree, without the aid of nails, or ⟨an⟩ active gardener– We have played at a new game lately, we have each been Queen, or King of some country, or island, for example I and Arabella are the empresses of the Hyeres, Bro and Henrietta are the emperor and empress of Italy, Storm is the Prince of Rome, and Sam is Emperor of Oberon– Pray dear Granny, beg Grandpapa Charlotte, and Jane to be on my side, for we sometimes have Battles, the other day Henrietta and I fought, I conquered, took her prisoner and tied her to the leg of the table; And pray ask Lawson and, Smith, to be on their *pet* Sams side, Hoping this and loving you all very much, I am.
Always
Affectionately
Your child
EB, otherwise, Signed,
Empress of the Hyeres

An answer as quick as time will permit
"Time" alias *distance.*
    Pray tell Sunny James[3] we send him a thousand kisses Pray ask *him* to be on my side–
    We have heard the melancholy news from Garryhunden of Miss Butlers death[4] and are anxiously expecting a letter to hear how long it will prevent their coming: You must excuse this bad writing for I have been romping in the hay till I am quite tired & not likely to appear to advanta⟨ge e⟩ither on paper or on my legs:

Publication: B-GB, pp. 335–337.
Manuscript: Pierpont Morgan Library.

1. George Goodin Moulton-Barrett, born 15 July.
2. Jenny was EBB's aunt Jane; Lawson and Smith were Graham-Clarke servants.
3. James Graham-Clarke, EBB's maternal uncle.
4. We have been unable to identify this member of the Butler family; very probably she was a sister-in-law of EBB's aunt, Frances Butler.

---

34. EBB TO EDWARD MOULTON-BARRETT (FATHER) & MARY MOULTON-BARRETT

[Hope End]
Sept. 1816

To Mama & Papa.
An Answer if you please.–

I hail thee sweet Affection, loves abode
The true and safest path to Virtues God!
Then Parents hail, both dear, both always kind,
Who rear with care, my ever grateful mind,
But pleasures golden beak, molests the store,
Of Truth,—which love w^d add to, daily more,
And as a hen that guards her chickens dear
Shrinks at the sight of the grim giant Fear
Sees a huge hawk with pouncing talons rise
And bear her offspring to the vaulted skies;
Yet grant a *little* favor, Parents dear
Tho' your refusal, I must greatly fear,[1]
But if a hungry chicken wants to eat
The hen throws victuals close before its feet.
Then let me to the Music Meeting go
The pleasure it would give me none can know;
If you are troubled for my nights repose,
Half of Bells bed is open to my woes,
I pray you grant what I have asked of you
So cheered with hope, I fondly bid Adieu!–

Publication: HUP, I, 105–106 (from copy in Mary Moulton-Barrett's hand, Wellesley College).
Source: Copy in Mary Moulton-Barrett's hand in "Poems by EBB," Berg Collection.

1. The source used for the *HUP* text bore the notation "The petition refused."

Modified Architectural Sketches for Hope End Mansion

Samuel Moulton-Barrett

Carlton Hall

35. EBB TO SAMUEL MOULTON-BARRETT (UNCLE)

[Hope End]
[ca. December 1816][1]

My dearest Sam

Strong as were the words of your letter, they were felt with double force coming from one who I love so dearly; I never thought you ever suspected me of an untruth, which that word "invent" implies, (as I wish to be sincere); I hope the shining prospect of a Venetian chain would not in the least induce me to implore your forgiveness more earnestly, than I do now, for I own I was wrong, nor can I justify myself, But it is I may truly say, my intention to avoid for the future, those direful enemies bad pens, and dark evenings; indeed I am afraid you could not read my thanks to you for the beautiful vinegar box, and earrings, which are the admiration of every body, and for which I do not know how to thank you; I have finished "Telemaque,"[2] and have read one, or two of Racines[3] plays, which I like very much, I have a great curiosity to know your opinion of Southey,[4] as every one here declares against him allowing him very few beauties, and thinking him unintelligable; for my part I must say he is one of my favorite poets; do you not think some parts of "Thalaba" "The curse of Kehama" &c are very beautiful, and "Roderic"[5] particularly so? Bum is the only person who agreed with me, indeed she only read "Thalaba," but she thought it both beautiful, and descriptive, I wish you would recommend to me an entertaining book, to read as I am quite at a loss for one; Are the "Persian Tales"[6] worth reading? I have begun Latin, and I have gotten as far in the Grammar as "Propria quæ maribus";[7] I do not like it at all, I think it is twice as difficult as French, but I suppose like many stupid things, it is very useful. Poor Bro I believe, has not much more taste for it than I have, but he is now so far advanced in it, as to translate the Latin Bible; he has not yet gone to school Papa cannot yet determine where to send him to. Funny Sam is very well, and amuses us more than anything else in the house by his odd tricks, and strange gestures; he is always ready to confess the micheif [*sic*] he does, and truth makes every thing that is expected from him yet; he does his lessons every day for one hour with dearest Mama, and would like to ride every day too if he had permission, but Moses[8] is not often disengaged for him to ride on; he always takes charge of your letters, which he treasures up with great care. We have some pretty rabbits, one is milkwhite, with red eyes, the other is black and white; The other night one of them got into the rack, and the horse bit its tail off, but it is quite well now; I have also got a little goldfinch, which sings beautifully, and a hen and chickens which I rear'd myself, and who fly [to my] shoulder, and eat out of my hand; Indeed we should be quite happy if we had you here, I hope [you] do not mean to stay another year abroad? I can assure you, funny Sam has not forgot you, he is quite delighted with his ten shillings, which he says he means to give to the poor people; the money you sent us has done a great [deal] of good by giving clothes to the poor people, and we hope it will do still more as we intend to have a soup shop, for which they pay a penny a quart.– Papa has made us the handsome present of the quarter of an ox, which will help us greatly.–

Hope End is very much improved and is much alterd, indeed I do not think you will know it again, I am sorry to say nobody has seen our poor Quails since they were let out, I am afraid they are all dead. I do not know whether I am to write to you in French or in English, but I am inclined to hope that you will forgive me writing this in English as I wish to be clear in the expression of the regret I experience from your being angry with me; pray write soon that I may be assured of your forgiveness.– I hope you will have a merry Christmas The grey poney is now very quiet and carries Bro on her back very often Sam told me to tell Monnies[9] that he was to come back very soon; Papa, Mama, Bro, Henrietta Sam Arabella, Storm and the little Baby, send their love to you and a thousand kisses, and

I am

Your ever affectionate, & repentant child,
Elizabeth B Barrett.

Publication: None traced.
Manuscript: Berg Collection.

1. December dating conjectured from mention of Christmas. The year 1816 derives from the mention of EBB's beginning to learn Latin, as her first recorded writing of Latin was in May 1816 (see letter 29, note 1). The year is confirmed by the reference to "the little Baby," George, born 15 July 1816.

2. *Les Aventures de Télémaque* (1699), a didactic romance by François de Salignac de la Mothe-Fénelon (1651–1715).

3. Jean Racine (1639–99), French dramatist, author of *Andromaque* and *Phèdre*.

4. Robert Southey (1774–1843), the Poet Laureate.

5. *Thalaba the Destroyer* (1800), *The Curse of Kehama* (1810), and *Roderick, The Last of the Goths* (1814).

6. *The Thousand and One Days: Persian Tales* (1783).

7. "Pertaining to the sea."

8. A Shetland pony, great favourite of the children at Hope End. EBB wrote in an undated prose essay (see Appendix III, part 5): "Her poney, Moses, had a tail longer by nine times than the patriarch's beard . . . a black poney with a ragged mane."

9. Apparently somebody travelling with Samuel Moulton-Barrett. He may have been employed in the household, as Mary Moulton-Barrett, writing to Storm while he was staying in London with his uncle and grandmother in 1821 (SD372), said: "How kind Monies has been to shew you so many pretty things."

36. EBB TO CHARLES JOHN MOULTON-BARRETT

To dearest Storm
On his birthday
Hope End December 28th 1816[1]

My Muse come forth and touch the Heavenly lyre
Breathe the wild accent of celestial fire
Let rosy gladness celebrate this day
Let joy oer Winters gloom a vivid spark display
And thou the sweet inspirer of my lay
May Virtues choicest gifts beguile thy destined way!
May the great scource [*sic*] of good preserve thy life
And keep thy Virtue ever free from strife!
Then from Minervas lore lets haste away
And think of nought but gladness & of play.

Elizabeth Barrett.

Address, on integral page: To dearest Storm / on his birthday.
Publication: HUP, I, 124 (from copy in Mary-Moulton Barrett's hand, MS unlocated).
Manuscript: Berg Collection.

1. His second birthday.

---

37. EBB TO MARY MOULTON-BARRETT

Hope End
[1817][1]

Toujours tres chere Maman
Avec beaucoup de joie Je vous addresse pour vous dis les bon nouvelles que J'ai parlé Francois un semaine demain pour recompense Je voudrais (s'il vous plait) d'etre nourice du petit George pour un jour et pour fais tout que les Nourices fassent[.] Je sais que vous dissez "Oh vous o[u]blierez tout votre lecons pa[r]ticularment votre *Musique*" mais Je vous assure que Je ne veux rien oublie car je fais tous les autres jours beaucoup plus d'attention car Je me souviens que vous m'avez dit q'un jour d'attention se valent deux de parssesse[.] Si vous voulait me donner la recompense que Je souhaite vous faites votre chere enfant bien hereuse.

Elizabeth

P.S.
Rosa mettoit sa nom à cette lettre pour montrer que J'ai gagner ma recompense[.][2]

Address, on integral page: A Ma / chere Mama.
Publication: None traced.
Manuscript: British Library.

Translation: Always very dear Mama / With much joy I send you the good news that I have spoken French for a week tomorrow. As a reward I would like (if you please) to be the nurse of little George for a day and to do all that Nurses do. I know that you will say "Oh you will forget all your lessons particularly your Music" but I assure you that I don't want to forget anything because I have been studying very hard these past days because I remember that you said to me that one day of hard work is worth two of idleness. If you want to give me the reward I wish for you will make your dear child very happy. / Elizabeth / P.S. Rosa added her name to this letter to show that I have earned my reward.

1. Having returned from Paris late in 1815, EBB probably began studying French early in the following year (the earliest reference to her writing French being in June 1816—see letter 31, note 1). She continued her study of the language at Ramsgate during the summer of 1817 with a tutor, Mme. Gordin. The handwriting is of this period, and "little George" had been born in July 1816.
2. This and the following letters in French contain many errors of spelling and syntax, attesting to EBB's imperfect command of the language. We avoid the repeated use of "[*sic*]" to underscore her amateur efforts.
   In some places, her errors are compounded by a lack of clarity in the handwriting, adding to the difficulties of transcription and translation. The English version given above, and the translations offered for subsequent French letters, are the best we can achieve, but total accuracy cannot be guaranteed.

---

38. EBB TO MARY MOULTON-BARRETT

[Hope End]
[1817][1]

Ma chere Maman

   Oh comme Je vous aime et Je souhaite beaucoup de vous resemblée. J'espere que vous ne disez pas oh il y a toujours les mepris dans les ecrits d'Elizabete mais J'espere que vous disez bien fait ma chere ce n'est pas toujours que vous ecrivez si mal– Je vous prie Maman donnez moi une jolie livre pour m'amusante ce soir[.] Ma tête à ête mieux ce soir mais c'est tres lourd[.] Je vous envoyé une tres bonne baiser et Deiu vous benit Ma chere Maman [(]bonne comme mon ceour[)] adieu

Elizabete de Barrett

Address, on integral page: Mrs Barrett / Hope End.
Publication: None traced.
Manuscript: Berg Collection.

Translation: My dear Mama / Oh how I love you and I wish much to be like you. I hope that you do not say oh there are always mistakes in Elizabeth's notes but I hope that you say well done my dear you do not always write so badly. I beg you Mama give me a nice book to amuse myself with this evening. My head has been better this evening but it is very heavy. I send you a very good kiss and God bless you my dear Mama (good like my heart) goodbye. / Elizabeth Barrett.

1. Dating assumptions the same as for letter 37.

---

39. EBB TO MARY MOULTON-BARRETT

[Hope End]
[1817][1]

Ma chere Maman

Vous nous faites bien de plaisir si vous voulez que J'ecris à Miss Money pour la demander lui et sa sœur[2] de venir demeurer avec nous et Me[r]credi et Vendredi– Vous savez Je crois comme nous serons heureux si vous nous accordorez notre demande D'urgence. Mama imaginez que vous etiez petite—en effet Je pense que vous n'auriez pas le cœur de nous refuser– Envoyez votre reponse Je vous conjure tout de suite et envoyez aussi le tome 2 de Waverly[3] – Je vous plaids beaucoup beaucoup– Comment amusez vous ces gens la? Pour moi Je vais me mettre au lit et de toute mon cœur Je vous assure– Morpheus est le roi ce soir et J'espere qu'il le sera tous les soirs de ma vie[.] Comme Je vais etre heureuse

Oh adieu
votre enfant
Ba

Pour l'amour de nous Maman envoyez nous votre reponse vite tres vite– vite–

Address, on integral page: M[rs] Barrett / given by the / post man / Impatience / to the care of success.
Publication: None traced.
Manuscript: British Library.

Translation: My dear Mama, / You will give us much pleasure if you want me to write to Miss Money to ask her and her sister[2] to come to stay with us from Wednesday to Friday. You know I believe that we will be happy if you will grant us this request urgently. Mama, imagine yourself little—really I think you won't have the heart to refuse us. Send your answer right away I beg you and send also the second volume of Waverly.[3] I feel very very sorry for you. How do you keep all these people entertained? For myself I will go to bed and with all my heart, I assure you. Morpheus is king tonight and I hope he will be every night of my life. How happy I'm going to be / Oh, goodbye / your child / Ba / For love of us, Mama, send your answer quickly, very quickly, quickly.

1. Dating assumptions the same as for letter 37.
2. The sisters Ellenor and Mary Money, daughters of the Rev. Kyrle Ernle Money, Vicar of Much Marcle, 8 miles S.W. of Hope End.
3. Walter Scott's *Waverley, or 'Tis Sixty Years Since* (3 vols., 1814). The volume mentioned here is in the editors' possession (*Reconstruction*, A2047).

40. EBB TO MARY MOULTON-BARRETT

[Hope End]
[ca. 1817][1]

Ma fort chere Maman

Excusez moi Je n'aime pas du tout Maneuvring[2] elle n'est pas à ma gout[.] J'avoue que c'est Mademoiselle Edgeworth encore mais ce n'est plus l'auteur de Patronage en effet ou est Caroline ou est Rosamonde– Elles sont mal suplié par la POLICISER[3] la sotte– J'en conviens que M[r] Palmer e[s]t un caractere charmant c'est un rayon de la vertu qui brille meme pres des fous et des policisers–[3] M[rs] Beaumont a une ame fort et elevée mais non pas au dessus de la flatterie de l' Hypocrisé non pas au dessus de Maneuvring– cette ame fort est toujours employée dans les machinations secrets cette ame n'est elevée que pour l'ambition mais non pas pour l'ambition noble de servir son patrie ni meme pour l'honneur et la gloire—non c'est un ambition servile pour gagner le rang pour gagner les richesses—ses talents ne sont employes que pour cela– pardonnez moi ma chere Maman si Je ne crois pas qu il y a beaucoup des policisers[3] aujourdhui pardonnez moi si Je vous dis que Maneuvring n'est pas a mon gout——

Je vous en prie ne penser pas que J'aime les nouvelles parcequ' ils y sont—mais parceque les nouvelles (excepte celle-la) que vous me choisirez me font toujours plaisir– Ne pensez pas Je vous prie car Je sais que vous le croie que J'aime toutes les caractères sans demandant la cause ne le croyez pas– L' Histoire de la Grèce n'est pas encore ne pouvez vous m'envoyez quelque autre livre– ne pensez pas que Je prendrai un gout pour les nouvelles—elles ne servent que de me faire reprendre les livres d'etude avec plus de joie– quand vous m'envoyez la livre Je vous prie ne dites pas le moindre mot de leur caracteres car Je me plais beaucoup de les decouvrir

Ma chere Maman Je reste toujours
Votre fille qui vous aime à jamais ——

Postscript

Je benis "Cent fois les bas malpropres qui ont ète la cause de mes plaisirs en effet J'en conviens que de tous les maux il vient du bon" —— [4]

Address, on integral page: Mrs Barrett / Hope End.
Publication: None traced.
Manuscript: Berg Collection.

Translation: My very dear Mama / Excuse me, I do not at all like Manœuvring,[2] it is not to my taste. I recognize that it is still Miss Edgeworth, but it is no longer the author of Patronage in reality—where is Caroline, where is Rosamond? They are badly made up for by the silly woman schemer. I agree that Mr. Palmer is a charming character, he is a ray of virtue that shines even near crazy people and schemers. Mrs. Beaumont has a strong and elevated spirit, but not above the flattery of Hypocrisy, not above Manœuvring—that strong spirit is always used in secret machinations, that spirit is lifted only by ambition, but not by the noble ambition of serving her country nor even for honour and glory—no, it is a servile ambition for gaining rank, for gaining wealth—her talents are employed only for that. Pardon me my dear Mama if I do not believe that there are many schemers today, pardon me if I tell you that Manœuvring is not to my liking.

I beg you not to think that I like the novels because they are there—but because (except that one) the novels you choose for me always give me pleasure. Do not think [that] I beg you, for I know that you believe I love all the characters without seeking the reason, do not think it. Can you not send me some other book besides The History of Greece—don't think that I shall take a liking for novels—they serve only to make me take up study-books with more gladness. When you send me the book I beg you say not the least word of its characters because I greatly enjoy finding them out. / My dear Mama I remain always / Your daughter who loves you for ever—— / Postscript / I bless "a hundred times the dirty stockings that have been the cause of my pleasures, truly I admit that from all evil something good comes."

1. Dating assumptions the same as for letter 37.
2. "Manœuvring" was first published in *Tales of a Fashionable Life* (1809), by Maria Edgeworth (1767–1849). Following references are to her novel *Patronage* (1814) and to characters in the two works: Mr. Palmer and Mrs. Beaumont in the former; Caroline and Rosamonde in the latter.
3. This is an obsolete English word, not a French one, used by Mrs. Edgeworth in "Manœuvring," meaning an intriguer or schemer.
4. This letter is written in pencil, which compounds the problems mentioned in letter 37, note 2.

---

41. EBB TO MARY MOULTON-BARRETT

[?Hope End]
[ca. 1817][1]

Ma chere chere Mama

Oui J'en conviens que Caroline[2] est la perfection[.] J'avoue qu'elle n'est pas former tout-a-fait d'etre heroine– Non elle à trop de sens d'esprit–

Le petit nombre de nouvelles que J'ai lue m'assurent de ce pensé— pour exemple Rob Roy—l'ame elevée et sublime de Diana Vernon nous frappe l'admiration et la seule maitresse de nos coeurs elle oublie les devoirs de femme en le caractere d'homme elle est une heroine Caroline ne l'est pas—elle voulait remplir le caractere qu'elle portait la douleur en oubliant ses plaisirs pour ses parents m'a plue beaucoup mais quand Lady Jane est malade quand elle s'empresse de secourir son amie alors Caroline est ellememe. Je vous assure ma chere Maman que J'en fus plus frappée que de presque toute cette ouvrage– Quelle belle caractère est cette Madame Hungerford en verité J'en suis charmée[3]–⟨★ ★ ★⟩

Publication: None traced.
Manuscript: Berg Collection.

Translation: My dear dear Mama / Yes I agree that Caroline[2] is perfection. I admit that she is not entirely made to be a heroine. No, she has too much sense of mind.

The few novels I have read confirm this thought—for example, [in] Rob Roy—the lofty and noble soul of Diana Vernon strikes us with admiration and, the only mistress of our hearts, she forgets womanly duties in the personality of a man; she is a heroine, Caroline is not—[when] she chooses to fill the character she sustains [with] grief for her parents, forgetting her pleasures, it pleased me greatly, but when Lady Jane is ill, when she hastens to help her friend, then she is Caroline herself. I assure you, my dear Mama, that I was impressed by nearly the whole of this work. What a beautiful character is that Madame Hungerford—truly, I was charmed by her—

    1. Dating assumptions the same as for letter 37.
    2. In this letter, EBB continues her comments on Mrs. Edgeworth's characters, Caroline in *Patronage*, Lady Jane Granville and Mrs. Hungerford in *Manœuvring*. She also speaks of Diana Vernon in Scott's *Rob Roy* (1817).
    3. See letter 37, note 2.

---

42. EBB, EDWARD & HENRIETTA MOULTON-BARRETT TO MARY MOULTON-BARRETT

[Hope End]
[ca. 1817][1]

Lov[l]iest of all lovly Beings whose eyes like the rays of the Sun bring comfort wherever they deign to glance

We thy children[2] rival of Venus beg and beseech thee by Juno Jupiter Minerva Mars The nine Muses and all the Gods immortal or Demi-Gods to give ear to us and not to cast away our Prayer as Joves Consort did that of Troy– This request is as follows–

That as we are now in the golden age and have parted from inexorable Jupiter show yourself as Saturn and do not refuse us the boon to have a little supper among ourselves the three Graces a few saussuages will crown us with joy like that Jove himself would impart by giving us one shake of that ambrosial head indeed (begging his Majesty's pardon) we would be still more at the |summit| of bliss as we should not be terrified out of our wits niether should we be almost knocked out of our seats by the same inexorable monarch niether should we if displeased be kicked down to Tartarus[3] to help the miscreant to roll up a stone to the top of the hill–[4] In consideration of this you will not We are certain refuse us this priveledge

If so or not we shall always I hope remain as the Stygian flood always loved certainly always loving you–   EBB
                                       EMB. HBB

    How many kisses more I know not

Address, on integral page: Mrs Barrett / Hope End—
Publication: None traced.
Manuscript: Berg Collection

1. Conjectural dating based on handwriting and style of expression.
2. Entire letter, including signatures, appears to be in hand of EBB. The other initials represent Edward Moulton-Barrett and Henrietta Moulton-Barrett. On page 4, across fold from address, three wax seals appear. Left to right, they are labelled "Henrietta," "Bro," and "Ba."
3. The infernal regions of mythology.
4. The punishment of Sisyphus was to roll a huge stone up a hill; as it constantly rolled down again, his task was everlasting.

43. HENRIETTA MOULTON-BARRETT TO EBB

[Hope End]
[ca. 1817][1]

My dearest Ba

I would be very much obliged to you if you would write to dear Mama and ask her if she would let me have the little room which I askd her [for] before. Pray excuse this bad writen, but now I must End, so farewell.

I am Your afec[te]
Henrietta

Address, on integral page: Miss Barrett / Hope End.
Publication: None traced.
Manuscript: Mary V. Altham.

1. Conjectural dating based on handwriting.

44. EBB TO HENRIETTA MOULTON-BARRETT

To my dearest Henrietta
On her birthday
Hope End March 4th 1817[1]

My Muse with joy come forth and breathe the sacred fire
With joy unceasing strike the Heaven born lyre
And thou my Sister dear the Muses strain
To paint thy virtues would I—but in vain
Spring and affection gladly meet this day
Sacred to happiness and noisy play
Thy dimpled cheeks be clad with dancing smiles
And thy sweet birth be spread with laughing wiles

Then may a hand divine defend thy feeble yout⟨h⟩
And keep thy spotless soul for Virtue and for Truth

———————

Your affec^{te} Sister
Elizth Barrett.

———————

Address, on integral page: To my dearest Henrietta / Eating her good Breakfast / On her
birthday.
Publication: None traced.
Manuscript: Berg Collection.

1. Her eighth birthday.

———————————————

45. ELIZABETH MOULTON TO EBB

[?London]
[ca. May 1817][1]

Thanks My Beloved Ba for your kind and charming Letter, it was read
over two or three times– I have sent you six slips to wear under your
frocks, you are now too big to go without them & they will also keep
you *warm*—if they are too long or want any other *alteration* Dr Mama
will let *Maddox*[2] do them for you also two frocks one for Harry, 7
India Handkerchiefs for Dr Papa, My Love to him tell him I hope he
does not expose himself to this damp Weather if he does he may depend
his pains will be as violent as ever– Our sweet Storm is ever in my
thoughts, Dr George Goodin & himself must be a charming pair; the
latter must now run all about, I sh^d think begin to talk—pray how
comes on BRO[3] & Sam– You my Sweet Ba dont say a word about your
Musick—Harry I know is fond of it & therefore must in time play well,
she is a dear good Girl.——
     Your friend Trip is now writing you, you must write her & explain
what you want, & you will have it——
     Now My darling Child you must allow me to say I think you are
too BIG to attempt fighting with Bro, He might give you an *unlucky*
Blow on your NECK which might be serious to you. He is strong &
powerful– I have seen him very rude & boisterous to you & Harry He is
now a big Boy fit only to associate with Boys, NOT GIRLS– Give my
Love to him & all our dear Pets Kiss & Love Storm, George Goodin for
me– Trip joins me in Love to dear Mama, Papa–
                              Dearest Ba—
                                   your truly affectionate Gr^dMama
                              EM–

Address, on integral page: Miss Barrett.
Publication: B-GB, pp. 337–338.
Manuscript: Pierpont Morgan Library.

1. Dated by reference to EBB's brother George Goodin Moulton-Barrett, who was born on 15 July 1816.
2. Mary Maddox, who acted as dressmaker and seamstress for the Moulton-Barretts. She was the subject of a poem by EBB, published in *HUP,* I, 128.
3. Underscored three times.

---

46. EBB TO MARY MOULTON-BARRETT

To my dearest Mama
on her birthday
Hope End May 1st 1817[1]

From the wide Heavens Aurora bends her flight,
Her rosy finger opes the gates of light,
Apollo's ensigns grace the spotless sky,
And Natures robes bespeak simplicity;
Then hail dear Herald of the Summers train,
Thy smile lifts Winter from the grateful plain:
Peace and religion unto the[e] are prest
And virtue ever riegns [*sic*] within thy breast:
And oh may we thy anxious cares repay,
Close followers of thy step in truths fair way:
In hope of Heavens delic[i]ous joys to rest,
To be for ever good, for ever blest.

Elizabeth Barrett.

Address, on integral page: Mrs Barrett / Hope End / Herefordshire.
Publication: None traced.
Manuscript: Berg Collection.

1. Her 36th birthday.

---

47. EBB TO MME. GORDIN

[Ramsgate]
[ca. July 1817][1]

Ma chere Dame
    Il faut que Je vous adresse ma premiere lettre pour vous dire que mon petit Frère le plus jeune vient de se baigner aujourdhui et quand il

est sorti tout mouillé de l'eau il avoit tout l'air d'enfant Cupidon. Il faut que Je continue ma lettre aujourdhui et quoique Je n' aie pas beaucoup de nouvelles à vous donner Je voudrais bien pouvoir employer le peu de temps qui me reste avant les neuf heures à vous écrire– le maitre de danse vient aujourdhui ma soeur en est bien joyeuse mais moi J'en suis bien fachée parceque Je n'aime pas du tout la danse. Maman a dit qu elle iroit dans la journée faire un tour de promenade sur le rivage et J'aurais envie de l'accompagner—mais je pense qu'il voudroit mieux m'occuper à lire et à apprendre le Français et les autres langues qui m'occupent dans ce moment car la litérature me donne des plaisirs que rien ne pourrait egaler, et Je suis bien sûre que Je continuerais toujours à lire et d'aimer l'instruction plus que la musique ou la dan⟨se⟩² ou toute autre chose de telle façon que se soit[.] J'espere aussi qu'en poursuivant assez des études celles qui sont de mon goût je serai encore en état de assurer bonheur à venir me flatte[.] Madame que vous pardonnerez aux défauts que J'ai fait ici à cause du peu de temps que J'ai l'avantage de votre instruction et Je sens déjà que j'ai beaucoup profité même dans le peu de leçons que vous m'avez données

soyez sûre que Je serai toujours
la vôtre
Elizabeth Barrett

Publication: None traced.
Manuscript: Yale University.

Translation: My dear Lady / I must send you my first letter to tell you that my little Brother, the youngest, has bathed today and when he came out all soaked with water he had quite the look of an infant Cupid. I must continue my letter today and although I have not much news to give you I would much like to be able to use the little time which remains to me before nine o'clock to write to you. The dancing master comes today, my sister is so very happy about it but I am very annoyed because I do not like dancing at all. Mama said that she will go during the day for a walk on the beach and I would have liked to accompany her—but I think that it would be better to occupy myself with reading and learning French and the other languages which occupy me at this moment because literature gives me pleasures that nothing could equal, and I am very sure that I shall always continue to read and to love learning better than music or dancing or any other thing of the kind that I know. I hope also that in pursuing enough the studies which are to my taste I shall at least be in a position to assure happiness and pride in myself. Madam, may you pardon the mistakes I have made here because of the little time that I have had the advantage of your teaching and I already feel that I have profited much even in the few lessons that you have given me. / Be sure that I will always be / yours / Elizabeth Barrett

1. Written while EBB was at Ramsgate in the summer of 1817. Here she had a French tutor, Mme. Gordin, and was expected to write at least one letter in French each week. Letters written at this time, apparently as exercises, are heavily corrected in another hand, presumably that of Mme. Gordin.

2. Ink blot.

48. EBB TO CHARLES JOHN MOULTON-BARRETT[1]

[Ramsgate]
[ca. July 1817][2]

Mon cher petit Frère Tandis que vous vous promenerez dans la place d'Albion et que vous vous amuserez à jouer dans les bocages et parmi les fleurs variées de ce jardin je me ferai un devoir de vous écrire et ce sera pour vous témoigner combien mon affection pour vous est sincère et pour vous assurer du veritable desir que j'ai pour votre bon-heur– croyez à la vérité de mes sentimens et personne ne vous souhaite plus de bonheur que moi[.] Je vous dirai que tant que vous serez jeune laissez faire la jeunesse[;] elle ne vous fera pas de mal mais quand vous serez plus agé donnez à la lecture tout le temps que vous pourrez et soyez toujours de bonne foi[;] en faisant ainsi vous ferez le bonheur de votre Père et celui de votre mère comme aussi de vos amis et de votre très chère soeur

EBB

Address, on integral page: Ma chère Dame.[3]
Publication: None traced.
Manuscript: Berg Collection.

Translation: My dear little Brother / While you will be strolling in Albion Place and you will be amusing yourself by playing in the groves and among the varied flowers of this garden, I will make it a duty to write to you and this will prove to you how much my affection for you is sincere, and assure you of the true desire I have for your happiness. Believe in the truth of my feelings and know that nobody wishes you more happiness than I. I will say to you that as long as you are young, let youth be itself; it will do you no harm, but as you get older, give all the time you can to reading and be always of good faith; by doing this you will make your Father happy and also your mother, your friends and your very dear sister / EBB

    1. The identity of the recipient is conjectured to be Charles John, who was three years old at this time, based on the salutation and content. It could, however, have been written to George, whom EBB mentioned in the previous letter.
    2. Dated by reference to Albion Place, Ramsgate, where EBB and other family members were staying at this time.
    3. Heavily-corrected draft, submitted for Mme. Gordin's approval.

---

49. EBB TO MARY MOULTON-BARRETT

[Ramsgate]
[July 1817][1]

Dedication to Mrs Barrett

To her from whom I have derived the little knowledge I possess I dedicate these lines,[2] with a full assurance, that she will forgive the

failings with which they are so abundantly sown, and recieve them as a
pledge of the sincere affection

of her grateful child
Elizabeth Barrett

Publication: Books at Iowa, 4 (1966), 19.
Manuscript: University of Iowa.

  1. Mary Moulton-Barrett wrote this date on EBB's manuscript. She also wrote
"Ramsgate July 1817." on her own copy in "Poems by EBB," Berg Collection.
  2. Poem, "The sorrows of the Muses," published with her letter.

---

50. EBB TO SAMUEL MOULTON-BARRETT (UNCLE)

[Ramsgate]
[ca. July 1817][1]

Mon chér Sam
    Quoique c'est pour longtemps que Je ne vous aie ecrit Je n'ai pas
cependant oubliée la bonté touchante de votre lettre, qui developa
neanmoins plus fortement que jamais, les couleurs frappans de ma
faute qui agrandit à proportion, que vous vouliez l'ecraser⟨.⟩[2] Je trouve
que Ramsgate est bien agréable, car c'est une change delicieuse de
Londres, des maisons fumantes, à l'air pur d'ici, des places noires, aux
montagnes champêtres; enfin la ville est comme une nuit sombre et
longue mais quand vous venez ici, c'est comme le jour naissant qui vous
donne la nouvelle vie; mais Je sens que quand Je revienne à Hope End,
que le Pan puissant embellit, et où tous les divinités pastorales font leur
demeure, ce seroit comme les champs Elysées, mais Je serois bien plus
heureuse, si Je pus errer avec vous sur les montagnes sublime de la
Suisse, où la beauté se reunit à l'affreuse, et où tout vous fait penser
aux géans enormes, qui combatirent avec Jupiter le Pere des Dieux; si
J'y etois, Je me croirois aux cieux, mais comme la nuit attend toujours
le jour, et comme le Paradis est un resemblance, quoique humble, du ciel
il faut être content dans aucun situation, ou la Providence nous place–J'ai
ici une Dame, qui s'appelle Madame Gordin, une Francaise, et qui
m'apprend sa langue; elle vient ici deux fois par jour, et maman est bien
contente d'elle. Bro a un Maître de Latin,[3] et il m'apprend la Grec aussi,
et J'aime ce langue beaucoup, parceque quand Je sois plus ageé, Je puis
lire Platois, et tous les grands auteurs de la Grece. Je m'etonne que vous
ne voulez pas voyager en Gréce, où peut on tirer plus d'instruction, ou
plus de plaisir, que des monumens brisées, que sont les tombeaux des
plus grands peuples de l'univers? Je vous prie, allez à Athens, où
dem[e]urent les Muses—ne pensez vous pas que la Grece portoit les arts,

EBB as a Child

EBB Aged 12

les sciences, même la vertu au plus grand perfection qu'on les a jamais
porte[—]ne pensez vous pas, que la gloire de ce royaume a effacer celle
de Rome? Soyez en sure,—ecrivez moi tout de suite, Je vous en prie, et

Je suis votre enfant
tres affectioneé
EBB[4]

Publication: None traced.
Manuscript: Berg Collection.

Translation: My dear Sam / Although I have not written to you for a long time, I have not
however forgotten the touching kindness of your letter, which nevertheless brings out more
strongly than ever, the striking complexion of my mistake which grows in proportion as
you seek to squash it.[2] I find Ramsgate very agreeable, as it is a delightful change from
London, from smoky houses to the pure air here, from dark places to rural hills; in short
the city is like a dark and long night but when you come here, it is like the dawning day
which gives you new life; but I feel that when I return to Hope End, which mighty Pan
beautifies, and where all the pastoral gods make their dwelling, it will be like the Elysian
fields, but I would be happier if I could wander with you over the sublime mountains of
Switzerland, where beauty joins with the fearful, and where everything reminds you of the
enormous giants who fought with Jupiter the Father of the Gods; if I were there, I would
believe myself in heaven, but as night always follows day, and as Paradise is a likeness,
however humble, of Heaven, it is necessary to be content in whatever situation where
Providence places us. I have here a Lady, named Madame Gordin, a Frenchwoman, who
is teaching me her language; she comes here twice a day, and mama is well pleased with
her. Bro has a Latin Master,[3] and he is teaching me Greek also, and I like the language
very much, because when I am older, I will be able to read Plato, and all the great authors
of Greece. I am astonished that you do not want to visit Greece, where can one receive so
much learning, or so much pleasure, than from the broken monuments, that are the tombs
of the greatest people of the universe? I beg you, go to Athens, where the Muses live—don't
you think that Greece sustains the arts, sciences, even virtue to greater perfection than
anyone ever has—don't you think, that the glory of this realm eclipsed that of Rome? Be
sure of it,—write to me soon, I beg you, and / I am your very affectionate child / EBB.

1. Dated by the reference to Ramsgate, which EBB visited in the summer of 1817, and
by the mention of her beginning the study of Greek.
2. See letter 35.
3. Daniel McSwiney, dates unknown, was Irish by birth.
4. See letter 37, note 2.

51. EBB TO LORD SOMERS[1]

[?Hope End]
[ca. September 1817][2]

My Lord /

I will not presume to hold forth my opinion in comparison to that
of the unknown tho obvious able author of the pamphlet in answer to
your Lordships[3]

— — — —

Whose name is recorded without blemish and who is adored by Virtue as the brightest gem of Truth. His disinterested justice procured him many laurels he perfered [sic] the interest of his country to his own. ⟨. . .⟩[4] Your lordship ought to thank Providence that this follower of virtue glided thro life unconsciouse [sic] of the conduct of his successor Alas the Knowledge of futurity would [have] forced from him a sigh in the midst of his glories and would have enbittered [sic] his latter years of peace which flowed from the fountain of his Justice.

> Heaven from all creatures hides the book of fate
> All but the page prescribed the present state
> From brutes what men from men what spirits know
> Or who would suffer being here below?

————————

> Oh blindness to the future kindly given
> That each may fill the circle marked by Heaven[5]

And now my Lord you will permit me to observe the difference of these ages & those that are past if it be for ever God alone knows to his almighty hand we must commit the fate of liberty with that of Great Britain

> What future bliss He gives not us to know
> But gives that hope to be our blessing now[6]

But as I do not take up my pen to grieve the unaccessible but always wise ways of Providence I will proceed with my original subject of defending the ancient constitution that sacred star which is now pillaged of its rays to satisfy the interests of the Ministers was signed by King John but afterwards carried to the greatest glory by Elizabeth when Oliver Cromwell led it to the utmost verge of perfection while this beam of happiness was still in existance England persevered in her spirit her inhabitants still kept themselves together beneath a load of afflictions without money and incapable of gaining an honest livelihood But want of provisions was amply compensated by the blessed knowledge that they were still free Hard indeed must have been the heart to tear from them their only consolation their balm in their sorrows and their glory in victory But tho England is thus laid destitute on the dust in spite of all the *laudable* exersions [sic] of your Lordship & the Ministers there is still a spark unquenched which enables us to despise our Tyrants & to drop the silent tear of gratitude to Sir F. Burdet[7] and to those who have bent their exertions for the recovery of our lost liberty tho their endeavours have proved vain they do no less merit our grateful and sincere thanks But I do not wish to sound in your ears praises which your Lordship does not aim at possessing neither will [I] endeavour to revenge our fallen liberties for we are already revenged and your Lordship is the only instrument of the ceaseless shame which now polutes your name if your lordship would percieve the reason of this sentance I shall give it in the plain & direct words of truth you were always considered as one of the mightiest supporters of the constitution As an independant man who had an oppinion of his own & who studied nought but to be on the side of truth & of liberty How greatly were we decieved! Lord Sidmouth[8] & the Ministers operated powerful changes indeed changes which we could not have believed magic to effect– We beheld with surprise your Lordship still pretending to be guided by liberty, tho' in the Eyes of Europe a confirmed Tory, and for what I blush to relate:—to be made lord leuftenant [*sic*] of the county of Hereford, allowing room for the recurring prospect of an Earldom. —— [9]

And now my lord I believe I have done with this subject & tho I do not dive deep into politics yet I have said enough to convince your lordship that I may truely sign myself

Your lordships most obedient humble servent
The Friend of liberty

Publication: None traced.
Source: EBB's draft copy, with corrections in Mary Moulton-Barrett's hand, Armstrong Browning Library.

1. The recipient is deduced from the mention of the Lord Lieutenancy of Hereford, and other internal references.

John Somers Cocks, 2nd Baron Somers (1760–1841), lived with his family at Eastnor Castle, some 3 miles S.E. of Hope End.

2. Lord Somers had been appointed to the honorific post of Lord Lieutenant of Herefordshire in August 1817. This draft protest almost certainly refers to the introduction in February 1817 of a parliamentary bill to suspend the Habeas Corpus Act, one of the cornerstones of an Englishman's liberty. A series of riots in various parts of the country had led to the appointment of a secret committee of the House of Lords, which determined that "a traitorous correspondence existed in the metropolis, for the purpose of overthrowing the established government." The proposed bill ensued, and it became law in March 1817, after much heated debate in both houses of Parliament.

3. Lord Somers had published in 1817 *A Defence of the Constitution of Great Britain and Ireland*, directed against the concepts of annual parliaments and universal suffrage. His stand on these issues was unpopular with some of his neighbours. A letter from James Martin to Edward Moulton-Barrett (30 January 1818, SD 278) speaks of the latter's opposition to Somers' nominees for the parliamentary election, and congratulates him "for having dared to oppose yourself to the will & mandate of the potent Baron of Eastnor." The same letter mentions "the wretched Pamphlet which he has written & published against the most usefull & necessary of all political Reforms" and says it betrays "the weakness of his head & the selfishness of his heart."

4. The words "he passed this life" are written here and crossed out.

5. Pope's *An Essay on Man* (1733–34), Epistle I, lines 77–80 and 85–86, slightly misquoted.

6. *Ibid.*, lines 93–94, slightly misquoted.

7. Sir Francis Burdett (1770–1844) spoke against the bill, "believing that an attempt was made to create alarm . . . as a ground for measures which would prevent the people from demanding their rights."

8. Henry Addington, Viscount Sidmouth (1757–1844) was the Government spokesman who introduced the bill in the House of Lords on 24 February 1817, declaring that the malcontents had "parliamentary reform in their mouths, but rebellion and revolution in their hearts."

9. The "recurring prospect of an Earldom" was realized in 1821, when Lord Somers was created Earl Somers and Viscount Eastnor.

52. EBB TO JAMES GRAHAM-CLARKE

Hope End
Sep: 20.th 1817

My dear James:

I am indeed astonished to hear h⟨ow⟩[1] ill you have treated the Muse; she has just threat⟨ened⟩ to leave you, if you continue your conduct. I therefore think it is but friendly to warn you of the precipice, which, unknown to yourself, you are on the brink of: it puts me in mind of the manner they catch elephants in, who when they tumble into the pit prepared for them bewail in vain their fallen majesty– Believe me, you do not only incur the displeasure of the Muse, but that also of Apollo, who is now sharpening his fiery darts to put you to confession; the Cyclops do not take your part for I believe they are now forging thunder bolts to revenge the Imperial Master of the lyre– Nay, his anger may pursue you soon—to the door of the |Fen|[2] house in spite of the scent which is I suppose still governing JC– most likely Hermes will furnish him (as Ulysses) with the herb Moly,[3] with this difference, that instead of repulsing the enchantments of Circe, it should vanquish the tyrant of the nose– I now beg you my dear James to open your desk & to beg pardon of the Nine Sisters whom you have so seriously offended. It is indeed an insult to sacrifice Minerva ⟨a⟩t the suit of Momus,[4] whose inexorable decrees are exorbitant upon men, who still persevere to kiss their chains because they are of gold——

E.B.

Publication: None traced.
Source: Copy in Mary Moulton-Barrett's hand, Berg Collection.

1. Ink blot.
2. Handwriting unclear; possibly a reference to Fenham Hall.
3. The mythical antidote to Circe's sorceries.
4. The son of Nox. He was driven out of heaven for his carping criticisms of the gods.

53. EBB TO EDWARD MOULTON-BARRETT (FATHER)

[Hope End]
[ca. November 1817][1]

My very dear Papa

We recieved your welcome letter last night if you had been witness of the burst of joy which ensued on the arrival of the papers you could have guessed how much we love you at present it is impossible– Hope End in spite of the romantic prospects which environ it in spite of the beauty of beholding Nature wrapt in her bridal robe which we have at present IS dull and IS lonely[;] the sun rolls over our heads—no Papa is here to greet us with his hospitable smile– The moon shakes off her yoke— No whig to enlighten our fire side hours with history of the election– Yet Yet Yet—inexorable Fate can no prayer however urgent separate (as Hanibal softened with vinegar the Alps)[2] can no prayer separate the links of that chain that holds the lord of Hope End away from his manor– We hope so and we exist upon those hopes– M^r McSwiney says you are a real Stoic I trust stoicism does not prevent you from loving us– Mathews set off the day after we recieved your letter for "The Hill" but I understand he behaved in a very ungallant manner for he commenced his journey without waiting for the company of Aurora[3]– But I must not be partial perhaps it might be the Goddesses fault for laying it [sic] bed too late or perhaps I might take that blame off her shoulders by assuring you she had a bad cold or a headache and why not so– Homer (whose word ought to be taken) affirms Cytherea was wounded by Diomede[s] at the siege of Troy and Jove threatened Minerva with the pains of Tartarus for giving the Greeks assistance[4] —nay Jove himself according to the mythologists was distracted with such "infernal pains" in the head he was obliged to trouble Vulcan to cleave it open[5] then under such instances I think we can do no less that [sic] to excuse the rosy fingered inocent Goddess of the small crime of laziness—

I have been reading Lord Byrons Corsair &^c how foolish I have been not to read them before they did not entertain me much as I have perused the extracts and the reviews on them– Malgré[6] this however I think many of the passages exquisitely beautiful the parting of Conrad and Medora & the intercesory between the hero and Gulnare are in my humble opinion two of the MOST beautiful– Tell Babes you know I DO love her & DID ALWAYS—tell her also I have gotten a few nice story books for her or if she is more learned SERMONS *travels & History–* I am afraid I have transgressed much beyond the bounds alloted to me—

and after having sent as many Kisses as you can give to my beloved and kind Grandmama and Treps I remain your

ever most affectionate & loving Daughter—

Elizth Barrett—

Publication: None traced.
Manuscript: British Library.

1. Dated by the reference to Daniel McSwiney, who began tutoring Bro and EBB in 1817, and by the mention of "Babes" (their sister Arabella). This letter was probably written after EBB's return to Hope End from her 1817 visit to Ramsgate, where Arabella remained until May 1819, after which she was taken to Worthing.
2. Livy, XXI, 37.
3. i.e., too early to carry EBB's letter. Mathews has not been identified, but might have been the cabinet maker of that name in Ledbury. He was obviously used in some general capacity by the Hope End household.
4. *Iliad*, bks. V and VIII.
5. According to legend, Minerva sprang from the head of Jove when Vulcan split it open with his axe.
6. "In spite of."

54. ARABELLA MOULTON-BARRETT &
MARY ROBINSON[1] TO EBB

[Both letters in the hand of Mary Robinson]   [Ramsgate]
[20 November 1817][2]

My Dearest Ba I thank you for your Propper Letter I often read it and think of you I am delighted to hear you have got so many nice chickens I Should have Liked to have seen your play very much I hope dearest Ba you will write me another Letter as I like to read them so much I wish you were here to bathe With me The sea is so very Pretty You would Like It very much Give my best Love to Dear Papa and Mama and All Bros & Sist

Your affett A Barrett.

My Dear Miss Barrett I know you will be very happy to receive this Letter from D⟨ea⟩r baby I am happy to Say She is ve⟨ry fin⟩e and would like very muc⟨h to be goin⟩g with you She i⟨s s⟩o merry and Lo⟨ok⟩s So well you would be delighted to see her. Tell your Dear Mamma her face is much better her Arm Improves but very Slowly. It is much Less but Still is Stiff in the Joint She has not the Least Pain in it and uses It very well but cannot touch her Shoulder with it, her health is very good She eats and Sleeps Well Mr Snowden offten sees her And Says She improves very much Ask your Mama If She would Like for Mr Snowden to write to her his Opinion.

My Dearest Ba I am happy to hear you Are so Merry and Good I should have been delighted to have seen you perform In the Play. I understand your Little Georg⟨e⟩ Is grown quite A Beauty And Sweet Little Storm How I should Like to see them We have Beautiful Weather here– Ramsgate Looked very Gloomy yesterday on Account of the Princess Charlottes Funnerl [*sic*] All the Shops and houses Shut Upp and every body in deep Mourning the Flags hoisted half mast high and the Bells Tould all the day– I hope my Dear We will see you soon If We dont Pray dont forget your ever

Attached Minny

Address, on integral page: Miss Barrett / By favor of Major Fance.[3]
Publication: None traced.
Manuscript: Edward R. Moulton-Barrett.

1. Mary Robinson ("Minny") had joined the household as nurse to Arabella. She later became housekeeper at Hope End, a position she maintained in all subsequent Moulton-Barrett residences. She died in the early 1860's at Arabella's London home, after a long illness.
2. Dated by the reference to Princess Charlotte's funeral, which took place at Windsor on 19 November 1817, the Princess having died in childbirth on 6 November. She was Heiress Presumptive to the throne, hence the following lines from an incomplete poem by EBB (*Reconstruction*, D670): "Oh Charlotte hope of Britains sea girt isle / And is the lovly spirit, robed in bliss / For ever ever winged away its flight?"
3. The Fances were Hope End neighbours.

55. EBB TO CHARLES JOHN MOULTON-BARRETT

To dearest Charles John
On his birthday– Hope End December 28th 1817[1]
With wishes for his prosperity–

Oh child beloved, Affections Muse
Shall welcome thee with kindred mirth
Nor shall her hallowed breath refuse
⟨To⟩[2] hail dear Stormy at his birth.

Neptune joy for thou hast borne
Our little treasure—tho' opprest
He made of thee a grievous mourn
And feared thy Ministers blue vest[3]

Let the mighty Thunderer
Who the highest takes his place
⟨Turn⟩ him from the tracks of war
And give the nod before thy ⟨sweet face.⟩

_____

May Pluto from the eternal seat
Dupe to none tho deep their wiles
Suffer at sweet joys intreat
His iron brow relax in smiles.

_____

Sister Fates whose magic song
Gives to lifes whole course a limit
Slowly draw this thread along
⟨Whi⟩ch winds both grace and virtue in it

_____

Powers above with Heavenly mirth
⟨Wit⟩h sparkling nectar crown the bowl
And drink to Storm at Stormy's birth
⟨T⟩hat years around his head may roll

_____

Dear child accept a Sisters lay
An anxious Sisters pledge of love
May joy urge on the hours this day
⟨And⟩ lifes whole course as happy prove

_____

E B Barrett

Publication: None traced.
Manuscript: Berg Collection.

  1. His third birthday.
  2. Manuscript shows excessive wear. Reconstruction made by comparison with Mary Moulton-Barrett's copy in "Poems by EBB."
  3. The copy in the hand of EBB's mother carried a footnote explaining this line as follows: "The bathing Women at Ramsgate, objects of alarm this year to the hero of these verses." It was the function of these women (called dippers) to stand at the foot of the steps of the bathing machine, ready to seize and immerse reluctant bathers.

56. EBB TO MARY MOULTON-BARRETT

[Hope End]
[ca. 1818][1]

Mama will you come and here me my lessons tomorrow I will come at three o'clock–

Address, on integral page: Postpaid [imitating postal authorities] / Mrs Barrett / Sam / Hope End.
Publication: None traced.
Manuscript: Berg Collection.

1. Mary Moulton-Barrett used address page for listing various 1817 household expenses. One entry reads: "Common Candles & Soap for 1817 £53.13.9." Included on page with EBB's note are brief greetings in the hands of Henrietta Moulton-Barrett and Edward Moulton-Barrett (brother).

---

57. EBB, EDWARD, HENRIETTA & SAMUEL MOULTON-BARRETT TO MARY MOULTON-BARRETT

[Hope End]
[ca. 1818][1]

My dear old Lady
     With the hope of succeeding in this our favorite project we beg you not to disdain the bad paper & worse pen which combine with us to beg you by every thing which you hold m⟨os⟩t[2] dear to endeavour to l⟨e⟩nd us those ever wise counsels which we prize so much to try, to get that old rogue Papa to let us FIX a day to go to Kinnersley[.] The pleasure it can give us no one can know—indeed it is past human comprehension. Do you not think dearest mam it would be a good way to write a nice funny letter to him, he is in a very good humour indeed whatever you think tell us pray write directly and stick it in one of the stones at the entrance to the cavern[3] if you are out of doors pray come in for one instant and scratch one line remember in every word of assent there is a healing balm if you are in the house send it to our *lodge*[.] Do you think it will be a good way to tell Edward to speak to Papa of it af⟨ter⟩ dinner—for Heavens ⟨sake⟩ Mama be quick w⟨e'll be⟩ almost dead in the ⟨mean⟩time we remain ⟨your⟩ ever dutiful & Lovi⟨ng⟩ Sons & Daughters

Sam Barrett
Henrietta Barre⟨tt⟩
Edward Barret⟨t⟩
Elizabeth Bar⟨rett⟩

Address, on integral page: Mʳˢ Barrett / Hope End.
Publication: None traced.
Manuscript: Berg Collection.

1. Conjectured dating based on handwriting. The letter is all in EBB's hand, except the other children's signatures.
2. Ink blot.
3. The grotto at Hope End.

---

58. EBB, EDWARD, HENRIETTA & SAMUEL MOULTON-BARRETT TO EDWARD MOULTON-BARRETT (FATHER)

[Hope End]
[ca. 1818][1]

My dear old Gentleman

I hope you will make the best use of your spectacles and your good humour to read this you require both.– With the most sanguine expectations your answer is expected—by four people who have need of your consent to crown them with joy say inexorable monarch of Hope End can no intreaties mortal or immortal prevail upon you to command the crested chariot to be linked to the four high mettled steeds to bear us to Kinnersly[.] Remember the hearts of oaks are not far distant it is the *sejour*[2] of Whigs where Ministers are buried in *oblivion*[.] Do not knit your brows your glass eyes may tumble off– This is not the thought of a moment it is not a seed droped in the midle of Winter from which we can derive no advantage it is an April flower who dares to raise his beautiful head to meet the rays of the sun in scratching this note I have wished to compare you to Phebus[3] throw out then your benignant beams and do not turn away your head among the black clouds & leave our poor flower to the mercy of killing frosts– with PHEBES[4] consent we have penned this her healing showers has contributed not a little to strenghten [*sic*] our hopes we have desired long for you to put the SIGNET on them it will be to us "the stamp of Fate". Now then compleat our Happiness fix the day for HER coronation let it not be long a few days & that bliss will partly be withered[.] How many hours of disapointment will follow[.] With the sincere hope your countenance will not be ruffled with a frown (for it spoils the natural beauty of your face) we must close this epistle– Hasten to answer it propitiously let it be soon every minute seems a day every day a month & every month a year with the hope the I hope not flattering hope we must remain with the greatest love

The suitors of Hope and of your smiles

Elizabeth B Barrett
Edward Barrett
Henrietta Barrett
Sam Barrett

Address, on integral page: E M Barrett Esq.ʳ / Hope End / Ledbury.
Publication: SBHC, 9 (Fall, 1981), 23.
Manuscript: Berg Collection.

1. Apparently their mother, in response to the preceding letter, advised the children to send this appeal to their father. EBB wrote the text, and the three others added their signatures.
2. "Abode."
3. Phœbus or Apollo, the sun god.
4. Phœbe or Diana, goddess of the moon.

---

59. EBB TO HENRIETTA MOULTON-BARRETT

[Hope End]
[ca. 1818][1]

Ma chere Soeur– Je suis bien facheé de ce Que vous soyez tombeé de l'escalier et qu'à present voilà estropiée[.] Il faut esperer que ce ne sera rien et que bientot vous allez être guerie et quoique vous soyez privée du plaisir de vous promener au jardin vous pourez toujours vous y asseoir et comme cela vous aurez tout de meme l'avantage de prendre l'air[.] Maman a dit que nous irions faire un petit tour sur l'eau dans un bateau[.] J'espère que vous ma chère Henriette vous irez aussi car ce sera une récréation fort agréable et avec cela on n'aura pas besoin de se lasser à marcher[;] il fait beau temps aujourdhui et tout y est favorable[.] Je ne vous ecris pas davantage en attendant cette petite partie de plaisir[;] demain nous en parlerons encore– Je vous souhaite le bon jour une bonne sante et beaucoup de plaisir[.] C'est dans l'espoir de vous voir jouir des agrémen⟨ts⟩[2] de cette journeé que Je me felicite d'être du nombre de ceux que ce propos y a assiste– Je suis votre soeur qui vous aime toujours[3]

EB

Publication: None traced.
Manuscript: Berg Collection.

Translation: My dear Sister– I am quite upset at your falling down stairs and that you are now crippled. One must hope that it is nothing much and that soon you will be recovered and although you are now deprived of the pleasure of walking in the garden, you can always sit there and so have the same advantage of the fresh air. Mama said that we will be going for a little ride on the lake in a boat. I hope my dear Henrietta that you will go also, as it will be a very relaxing diversion for you, thus one will not have to get tired walking; the weather is nice and favourable today. I will not write any more till that little pleasure trip; we will talk about it more tomorrow. I wish you a good day, good health and much pleasure. It is in the hope of seeing you enjoy this pleasure today that I congratulate myself at being among those who helped with this plan. I am your sister who loves you always / EB

1. Conjectural dating based on handwriting.
2. Ink blot.
3. See letter 37, note 2.

---

60. EBB TO MARY MOULTON-BARRETT

[Hope End]
[ca. 1818]¹

Ma Maman bien-aimée

Helas Je n'ai pas des bas propres– en effet Je suis bien malheureuse mais Madame Fortune le veux et elle veux aussi d'etre obeit– en verité ce Madame Fortune c'est un femme dont la pudeur et la coquett[e]rie est estimable. Je suis beaucoup enrhumée J'en conviens et peutetre il me fait de bien de rester ici mais malgré tout cela c'est un chose bien effroyable de rester seule—mais n'en parlez plus Je suis bien mecontente. J'avouerai tachons de nous contenter. À present Je veux mettre au papier ce que J'espere vous demander la ba[s]. N'est t'il point d'autre livre que Je puis lire[?] J'ai lu tous que Je crois les plus beaux pour l'amour de moi ma chere Maman ayez pitié de moi!– envoyez Henriette Je vous prie avec votre reponse– J'espere que vous vous portiez mieux car J'ai envie de vous voir tout-a-fait *en-bon-point*–

    Helas Je ne peux vous baiser autrement mais assurez vous Je vous aime toujours de toute ma petite cœur–

Votre fille heureuse
Elizabeth–

Address, on integral page: Mʳˢ Barrett / Hope End–
Publication: None traced.
Manuscript: British Library.

Translation: My beloved Mama / Alas I do not have any clean hose. In fact I am very unhappy but Madame Fortune wants it so and she wants also to be obeyed. Truly Madame Fortune is a lady whose modesty and coquetry are estimable. I have a bad cold, I admit, and perhaps it will do me good to stay here even though in spite of all it is a frightening thing to stay home alone—but say no more about it, I am very discontented. I will acknowledge that we should try to be happy. Now I must put down on paper what I hope to ask you there. Is there no other book I could read? I have read all that I think the best, for the love of me, my dear Mama, have pity on me!—send Henrietta I beg you with your answer. I hope that you are feeling better, because I would like to see you in complete good health. / Alas I cannot salute you any other way, but rest assured that I always love you with all my little heart. / Your happy daughter / Elizabeth–

    1. Conjectural dating based on handwriting.

61. ELIZABETH MOULTON TO EBB

[?London]
[ca. January 1818]¹

I trust this will find you my dearest Elizabeth and the rest of the dear Circle, in the enjoyment of perfect health—long may such blessing be yours my dear Child, and may each New Year bring an increase of happiness to all my beloved pets at Hope End, to all of whom, Individually, you will offer my good wishes & best affections—— I have great pleasure in telling you our dearest Babes is quite well, & in *fine spirits*, indeed my Beloved Ba, she promises to be very clever, no present seems so welcome to her as a Book, two hours every Mor^{ng} she is closeted with Minny at her lessons—she send[s] her very best Love to all—— Your poor *Granny* has been confin'd to the House for the last three Weeks—I have only just risen from my Bed & finding the Box on the wing,[2] I cou^d not resist the temptation of enclosing a few lines to you; the Box is directed to Storm knowing it will please him to distribute to each a small parcel—the Cake is yours, with a frock &c— six pocket Handkerchiefs, dont mind their being *coloured* ones, they do very well for the Country- Harry has the same with my best Love— Mamas Account of Darling Storm is quite enchanting, tell him Gr Ma is very very happy to hear he is such a good Boy—— Doct^r Nuttall[3] was here last Even^g & begs to be rememberd to all of you; I assure you he has been extremly kind in his attention to me—— I hope you have a clearer Atmosphere than we have, there is now so thick a fog that we can scarcly see—— If Gr^d Mama is with you present our best Love & every good Wish for her happiness, the same to dear Bum Charlotte & Jane—— Trep joins me in best affections

Your Sincerely attach^d
Granny EM—

Remember us Kindly to Mr Mac Swiney
Kiss dear Papa & Mama for us——

Address, on integral page: Miss Barrett.
Publication: None traced.
Manuscript: Pierpont Morgan Library.

1. Dating based on internal references. After spending the summer of 1817 at Ramsgate, the family and Mr. McSwiney returned to Hope End. Arabella was left behind with Minny and they made occasional visits to Mrs. Moulton in London.
2. Messages, parcels—even produce—according to the custom of the time, would be sealed in a narrow deal box and transported from one household to another by public coach.
3. George Ricketts Nuttall, M.D., born in Jamaica, was admitted a Licentiate of the College of Physicians in 1817, and was for some years at the Westminster Dispensary. He died in 1831, at the age of 43. His family was known to the Moulton-Barretts through the Jamaican connection, and Mary Trepsack, writing to Elizabeth Barrett Williams on 2 October 1810 (SD144), said: "Mrs. Nuttal's son is now here, he is going to Jamaica. ... I hear he is to be patronized by many—he is a good looking young man—& every respect his fathers exact counterpart."

62. EBB TO ARABELLA GRAHAM-CLARKE (AUNT)

[?Hope End]
[ca. January 1818][1]

My sweetest old Maiden aunt

I take up a bad pen with the intent of fulfilling my promise th'o according to custom to skim over it with that idleness which is so peculier to *me*, th'o perhaps "rude am I in speech"[2] yet I can justify myself by repeating I do not love you less. If I might with the leave of Fancy transport myself, thro' her abodes to the no less delightful ones of Fenham I could easily suppose you all in the library, *you*, painting some tremendous caricature, or cracking some of the favorite jokes, as

"My life and soul your nose is broke,
And all your teeth are down your throat"

(I quote from *memory*); Jane composing that which makes "you sick" at least *me*. Charlotte with a grave face & a pair of spectacles painting or at that *much admired* loom. Grandmama reading the newspaper to Grandpapa, who I will suppose is sitting in the great arm chair lending an attentive ear——

I will say nothing of James, for I fancy by his long silence he still is hugging his golden chains, in defiance of the Muse, Apollo, and all the other deities!—

You will here my dearest *Bum* suffer me to break the coarse black worsted thread of this paper,—And tho' in defiance of Fashion, I shall neither say this letter is a "*wretched*," or a "*shabby scrawl*" I do not think the less. I will however allow that to be judged by you, who will always be loved & remembered by your attached *niece*

Ba ——

Henrietta is very much offended with Lotte for not remembering her promise; she has grown quite fat, and rosy and is at present only troubled with a cold —

EBB

[Continued by EBB's mother, immediately after the word "cold"] which is *nearly* well. I never saw a child so improved, since my mother left us—

Address, on integral sheet: To / The dear Bum / of Fenham.
Publication: None traced.
Manuscript: Lady Elisabeth Cooper.

1. Dated by internal references. Bummy and EBB's grandmother, Mrs. Graham-Clarke, were no longer at Hope End, where they had spent the recent holiday season. There is a reference to the presence of "Grandpapa," who died later in 1818.
2. *Othello,* I, 3, 81. In this and subsequent Shakespearean quotations, the line numbers correspond to those used in *The Riverside Shakespeare* (Boston, 1974).

---

63. EBB TO MARY MOULTON-BARRETT

[Hope End]
[February 1818][1]

My very dear Mama
    I beg you to look over this and to burn it if you find fault with it as I have only writen it for your inspection pray do not mention any thing about it[2] You will oblige me if you tell me exactly what you think of it it is not near finished– I hope you will tell me exactly the truth about it as it is a very lerringl humble attempt—which I am afraid I have failed in if I have pray do not be angry with me as it is writen with true humility dearest Mama DO[3] send your thoughts in a note to me by John[4] to the schoolroom I await it anxiously do not disapoint
                                        your affec.te child
                                        Ba

Publication: None traced.
Manuscript: Berg Collection.

1. Mary Moulton-Barrett dated this letter "Feb.y 1818."
2. What accompanied the letter is not known.
3. Underscored five times.
4. John Lane, one of the Hope End servants. He was employed principally in the house (letter 228 mentions his serving at table), but EBB refers to his acting as coachman also (*Diary,* p. 187).

---

64. EBB TO MARY MOULTON-BARRETT

[Hope End]
Feb.y 14.th 1818[1]

Dear Sweet Mama Take this Dream for my sake and *if* you DO love [me] let me go to Ledbury to day —
                                        EBB Do Do Do

    Send an answer quick / in a hurry yours —

Address, on integral page: Mrs Barrett / Hope End / I hope in a *good humour.*
Publication: None traced.
Manuscript: Berg Collection.

1. EBB's note comes at the end of a fanciful essay ("The little waves," *Reconstruction*, D1376), which Mary Moulton-Barrett dated "Feb.y 13.th 1818." EBB's own 14 February date appears on the address panel.

---

65. EBB TO MARY MOULTON-BARRETT

[Hope End]
March 1st 1818.

Sweet Mama you must excuse the faults in this[1] for I have read a good deal & have written 41 lines of poetry to day besides this

Publication: None traced.
Manuscript: Berg Collection.

1. This note comes at the end of an unpublished essay entitled "A fragment– Imitation of Sterne" (*Reconstruction*, D1295).

---

66. EBB TO HENRIETTA MOULTON-BARRETT

[Hope End]

To our dearest Pet Henrietta
On her birthday so welcome to us
March 4th 1818[1]–

Euterpe[2] from Apollo's breast,
Snatch the bright lyre,
My Spirit fire,
And lull thy cares to rest

Sweet Spirit let thy warbling lute
Its accents raise
And Addles praise
While Philomel and Heaven are mute

In thy happiest gayest measure
Softly sad
Sweetly glad
Let the strain be joy, be pleasure

Oh Goddess sing the quarel dread
Betwixt the nine
Who dared to shine
To reign supreme in Addle's head

First wrapt in state great Clio came
And in her hand
A burning brand
To fire the glorious pile of Fame

With scorn beheld the haughty Fair
She mocked her state
Nor deigned to wait
And left the Goddess to despair

Next Thalia came and at her side
The sheperds crook
The sheperd flock
The first her strenght [*sic*] the last her pride

Nor then replies—with calm disdain
She blasts her hope
Who dares to cope
Within her swelling heart to reign

Urania[3] next with downcast mien
With lovely face
With youthful grace
Her patient suffering form is seen

"Away" the maid replies with scorn
Nor thou shall dare
To blight with care
The breast that never felt thy mourn

She spoke—Erato tried her power
Melpomene
Calliope[4]
Were all rejected in that hour

Then forth appeared the graceful three
With dimpled smiles
The fair beguiles
["]With all the soul of Harmony"

Oh Henrietta sister loved so well
Euterpes self can scarce its limits tell
Accept ah child beloved my lowly lay
So humbly wreathed upon thy birth today

And be my sister blest in every spot
In every station and in every lot
Long may she live with sweet contentment here
For ever cherished and for ever dear

Publication: None traced.
Manuscript: Berg Collection.

  1. Her ninth birthday.
  2. The Muse of music.
  3. Clio, Thalia and Urania were, respectively, the Muses of history, comedy and astrology.
  4. Erato, Melpomene and Calliope were the Muses of erotic poetry, tragedy, and epic poetry.

---

67. EBB TO MARY MOULTON-BARRETT

[Hope End]

To my dearest dear Mama
On her birthday May 1st 1818[1]

So supremely distinguished in the anals [*sic*] of our little lives and oh may Phebus celebrate this dear day with us

---

Sweet soul of sacred Poetry
From Helicons sequestered fanes
From blest Triconias [*sic* for Tritonia's] loveliest plain
To wake the lyre I call not thee

Untaught by art my lowly lay
Forth from my breast Affection springs
And sweeps the lyre's rebounding strings
To greet a Parents natal day

Then hail dear harbinger of May
Protector of our early youth
Guide of our steps to sacred truth
And hail this fondly pleasing day,

Mary Moulton-Barrett

Edward Moulton-Barrett

Where sorrow sends the palm to mirth
Where grief is joy where woe is bliss
Where every pleasure yields to this
E'en thus to celebrate a Parents birth

If filial love could e'er have ta'en
From Heaven one blessing on thy state
The pleasure from the arms of fate
Thy children have not lived in vain—

nor has Eliz[th] B Barrett

Address, on integral page: M[rs] Barrett / Hope End–
Publication: None traced.
Manuscript: Berg Collection.

1. Her 37th birthday.

---

68. EBB TO EDWARD MOULTON-BARRETT (FATHER)

Hope End

To my dearest Papa
On his birth day
May 28th 1818.[1]

Euterpe! On Parnassus rocks
Who loves to pass the hours
And twine thy glossy raven locks
With Helicons pure flowers.

Where gently bending oer thy shell
Thou pliest the tuneful note,
To Heaven the flowing numbers swell
In mid air, trembling float.

I call thee not to tell of fame
Or pride, or pomp, or monarchs bliss
That lyre deserves a sacred name
Which winds a lay, so dear as this.

A Parent's birth to celebrate
Euterpe strings the lyre
With face of joy and heart elate
She smites the echoing wire.

Oh Parent loved so justly, hail!
To us so dear, so justly dear
And hail the day, where sorrows fail,
Their shadowy forms to rear.

When joys on joys, & smiles on smiles
Disclose each longed for wish
When time each joyful hour beguiles
Progressive—bliss on bliss!

Low lies his head, who on this much loved day,
First came to being,—low the Statesman lies
Inert in death—who shook just freedom's sway
Made Britain tremble for her liberties.

Now sleeps in peace—there let him sleep
Within deaths narrow precincts let him lie,
Let man forget, who made blest freedoms weep
His name a Pitt—his victim liberty!

Oh may his earliest days, for ever live!
His age!– Ah let that sleep, & never wake!
His shame forget, the dead forgive
Forgive his vices for his virtues sake.[2]

Yet more have seen the light this day
Yet more to earth their dust consigned
A heart than thine, the Muse can say
Ne'er breathed more gently good & kind

Farewell! no blessing need I pray
From Heaven upon a Parents head
What joys are wished, 'tis vain to say
And most is felt, where least is said.

Publication: None traced.
Source: Copy in Mary Moulton-Barrett's hand in "Poems by EBB," Berg Collection.

  1. His 33rd birthday.
  2. Footnote by EBB's mother indicates that this passage refers to William Pitt, who shared her husband's birthday, having been born on 28 May 1759.

69. EBB TO EDWARD MOULTON-BARRETT (BROTHER)

To my dearest dear Bro, alias Edward, on his
Birth day– June 26th 1818.[1]– Hope End

To sing no mighty deeds, I call the Muse
To sweep those chords once more,—I bid them swell
In fainter notes to tell a Sisters love
A Brothers birth– Oh day so dear, how oft
The lyre has welcomed thy returning joys–
When love unites her garland to the flowers
Of liberal Natures hand, & joy completes!
And Oh my Brother, may the hand of Heav'n
Preserve in happiness thy growing years!
May truth & Virtue guide thy steps to fame,
May Heav'n in peace & joy prolong thy days!
Years from thy life remorseless time has stolen
With ten fold interest, years may he repay!

Publication: None traced.
Source: Copy in Mary Moulton-Barrett's hand in "Poems by EBB," Berg Collection.

1. His 11th birthday.

70. EBB TO GEORGE GOODIN MOULTON-BARRETT

To my sweetest Pudding
On his birthday
July 14th 1818.[1] Hope End–

Celestial Muse who on the Olympian mount
Tunes thy soft lays deign once again to lend
Thy sacred spirit now, to grace this day
So dear to us and oh! so blessed by Heaven
Then hail sweet George sweet smiling infant hail
Smiling in innocence unknown to thee
All the harsh sorrows of proud Fortunes gifts
If then her gifts be woes—oh what her favors?
Unknown to thee sweet Babe unknown to thee
The joys alike and sorrows of the world
Unknown to thee of Virtue or of Vice
The names—blest child of innocence & truth
Such ever mayst thou be & when thou rise
For rise thou must to mans degen'rate state

Free from all vice that threats his weary path
Untainted gain Truths highest pinacle
There undisturbed by all that harms the mind
With peace there mayst thou rest & "smile at grief"[2]

My Sweetest Puddings affec^{te} Sister
Elizth B Barrett.

Address, on integral page: Master G G Barrett / Hope End–
Publication: None traced.
Manuscript: Berg Collection.

  1. His second birthday was on 15 July 1818.
  2. Cf. *Twelfth Night*, II, 4, 115.

71. EBB TO MISS FANCE[1]

[Hope End]
[?9] [August 1818][2]

My dear Miss Fance will excuse the absence of Mama this evening being only a fortnight confined of a fine boy but tho illness prevented her enjoying your society at Malvern happy would s⟨he⟩ have been to have s⟨een⟩ you here had not the late unhappy event of the death of Grandpapa prevented it This was indeed a heavy blow on our feelings as none was so deservedly beloved as he whom we lament but we trust in Him who is always merciful that he has met with his reward. Pardon ⟨this⟩ digression dear Miss Fance for it is a subject that comes spontaneously from the heart–

Believe me yours sincerely
EBB

Publication: None traced.
Source: EBB's draft copy, Berg Collection.

  1. Probably the daughter of Major Fance, a neighbour of the Moulton-Barretts.
  2. Dated by the reference to the birth a fortnight since of Henry Moulton-Barrett, who was born 27 July 1818, and to the death on 7 August 1818 of EBB's maternal grandfather.

72. EBB TO MRS. FANCE[1]

Hope End
August 10th 1818.

I sincerely trust that my dear Mrs Fance will dismiss any anxiety she may experience on the health of our very dear Mama as indeed it surpasses our most affectionate and most ardent hopes.

She begs her best love and commissions me to tell you how happy she would feel if assured that you had the same endeared prospect of returning health. The Baby is astonishingly well and is a fine little fellow and as you may well imagine is chief favorite in the *Nursery*– The country is lovely at this season every thing smiles under the benignant rays of a summer sun. Our family circle unite in the most affectionate loves to you and the dear little children and believe me dear Mrs Fance

Always to remain yours very sincerely
E B Barrett.

Publication: None traced.
Manuscript: EBB's draft copy, University of California (Clark Library).

1. Presumably the wife of Major Fance.

---

73. EBB TO MARY MOULTON-BARRETT

Hope End
Sep! 1818

Tres Tres chere Maman. Je relis sur votre bonte qui est toujours la meme pour rasembler du courage de preparer mon petition—le faveur le plus grand qui peut etre demandé[.] Allons courage. Chere Mama laissez Esther[1] aller avec nous à Cheltenham[.] Je veux la donner un surpris. Elle n'a jamais eté dans une carosse de sa vie– Elle n'a jamais ete à un ville hormis Ledbury– Elle est de tres bonne fille et elle fait tout ce qu'elle pourait pour nous[;] il faut lui donner une recompense. Oh Je crois qu'elle sera si surpris si hors d'elle quand Je la dit qu'elle aille à Cheltenham avec nous. Qu'elle bonheur pour elle! Elle nous sera tres utile aussi C'est impossible que Betsy[2] prenait garde de six– Esther dit l'autre jour Comme vous etes heureuse d'aller à tous ces beaux choses! Alors Je la dis que Je vous demanderai si vous la permetterez d'aller mais elle dit que cela etait impossible elle croyait– Ah chere Maman faites elle cette plaisir il y a de place en la carosse et tout chose qui convient– Maman consentez ce ne sera pour elle de bonheur inexprimable—pour moi ce sera Je crois presque plus de delice de lui dire ce nouvelle— Maman ouvrez votre cœur Je vous prie–si vous consenterez Je vous promis que Je vous ecris un lettre Francais tout fois par semaine– Je vous donne ce petit fragment en dehors comme vous m'avez dites que vous avez perdu l'autre ecrit en six minutes et que vous voulez avoir un autre ec[r]is Je crois et beaucoup superieure à l'autre– Maman ne me refusez pas ce faveur[.] Je n'en ai pas demander longtemps– chere chere Maman si vous m'aimez ne me refusez pas–ecrivez moi un petit reponse tout de suite car Je suis tout impatience[.] Oh qu'elle sera favorable! Allons il faut quitter mon plume mais il me semble toujours que Je n'ai pas prier assez—encore un fois– Ne me niez pas mon priere. Oh faites heureuse

Votre toujours affeteuse enfant.[3]
Ba.

[Written across page 2] Read this first
[Written across page 3] This next
[Written on page 6] This third

Publication: None traced.
Manuscript: British Library.

Translation: Very Very dear Mama / I rely on your goodness which is always the same to gather courage to make up my petition—the biggest favour that can be asked. Come, courage! Dear Mama, allow Esther[1] to go with us to Cheltenham. I want to give her a surprise. She has never been in a coach in her life. She has never been to any town except Ledbury. She is a very good girl and she does all that she can for me; we should reward her. Oh, I believe she will be so surprised, so beside herself, when I say that she goes to Cheltenham with us. What happiness for her! She will be very helpful to us besides, it is impossible for Betsy[2] to take care of six. Esther said the other day How fortunate you are going to all these nice places! Then I told her that I would ask you if you would allow her to go, but she said that that would be impossible, she believed. Ah, dear Mama, give her this pleasure, for there is room in the carriage and everything convenient. Mama, give your consent, it will not only be indescribable joy for her, but for me, I believe there would be scarcely any greater delight than to give her the news. Mama, open your heart I beg you—if you will agree, I promise you I will write you a French letter every week. I give you this little piece separately as you told me that you had lost the other, written in six minutes, and that you wanted to have another one, I think, and much superior to the other. Mama, do not deny me this favour. I have not asked you for anything for a long time—dear dear Mama, if you love me do not refuse me—write me a little reply right away because I am all impatience. Oh that it may be favourable! Well I must put down my pen, but it still seems to me that I did not entreat enough—once more, do not deny my prayer. Oh make happy / Your always affectionate child / Ba.

1. Apparently a nursery maid at Hope End.
2. Beyond her assistance in the nursery, nothing else is known about this servant. It is possible she was the Betsy Willis mentioned by Mary Moulton-Barrett at the end of letter 132.
3. See letter 37, note 2.

74. EBB TO MARY MOULTON-BARRETT

[Hope End]
[September 1818][1]

When I read it over after having written it[2] I found many words renewed—also I thought that "charm" was better than "reach" in the last line of the second verse but I believed it better to leave it as it is; as I thought you would not like me to alter it before you had seen it– for MY sake dearest Mamma let poor Esther go.[3]

Publication: None traced.
Manuscript: Berg Collection.

1. Mary Moulton-Barrett dated the original manuscript and her own copy "August 1818," then corrected the latter to "Sept 1818." See *Reconstruction*, D306–7.
2. Refers to an unpublished poem of 12 lines, "A fragment occasioned by immagining the music of the spheres," which EBB had just written in four minutes. Note reproduced here appears on back of same sheet.
3. In "Poems by EBB," Mary Moulton-Barrett added the words "with us to Cheltenham!——".

---

75. HENRIETTA MOULTON-BARRETT TO EBB

[Cheltenham]
[September 1818][1]

⟨★★★⟩ really and truly

your affec[te] Henrietta

Address, on integral page: Miss Barrett / Hope End.
Publication: None traced.
Manuscript: Berg Collection.

1. Along right margin of address panel, Mary Moulton-Barrett wrote "Cheltenham / Sep! 1818."

---

76. EBB TO EDWARD MOULTON-BARRETT (BROTHER)

[Cheltenham]
[September 1818][1]

My dearest Bro,

Your funny letter received this instant gave us no small pleasure as it both afforded us the inexpressible delight of hearing you were *safe and sound* & told us that you had niether forgotten *us* or your promise!

Our own LUXURIES these three days have not far exceeded yours as a deluge of rain has abjured both the pleasures of shopping and of physicing ourselves! I should suppose that you were an agreable interuption to Mr Mc Swineys meditations. They indeed must have been solitary! How delighted Rosa must have been to see you! and how pleasant a companion Mrs Kings![2] The Coachman waits and Papa hurries (for he has returned) & I have only time to tell you that we will have the pleasure *on Monday* of beholding you and Hope End once more!

Mc Swineys Novel![3] It ⟨is⟩ really intolerably provoking. And the garters! shameful! I hope you found Moses well and all the out of doors pensioners biped and quadruped! You beg pardon for having asked me to write twice. I shall *not* pardon an offence *not committed* as you have certainly only asked me once! And is not that sufficient for your insatiable soul? The beds MUST be well aired by Monday– Good bye dearest Bro.

Ever your affec^{te} Sister.
Ba.

Our united remembrances to M^r McSwinney in spite of the novel The wafer IS excused![4]

Address, on integral page: Master Barrett. / Hope End.
Publication: None traced.
Manuscript: Pierpont Morgan Library.

1. It is known that most of the family were in Cheltenham at about this time in 1818.
2. Probably Mrs. Kings, innkeeper of the Unicorn, Southend, Ledbury.
3. No record of a novel has been found. Several works of verse by him are preserved (see *Reconstruction*, L168–71).
4. Cf. letter 202, note 2.

---

77. EBB TO SAMUEL MOULTON-BARRETT (UNCLE)

[?Hope End]
November 1818

Offered for sale by Sotheran, Catalogue 737 (1913), item 258. 3 pp., 4to. EBB covers a wide range of literary topics: "I have read 'Douglas on the Modern Greeks.'[1] I think it a most amusing book . . . I have not yet finished "Bigland on the Character and Circumstances of Nations.'[2] An admirable work indeed . . . I do not admire 'Mme. de Sevigné's letters,'[3] though the French is excellent—the idioms beautiful—yet the sentiment is not novel, and the rhapsody of the style is so affected, so disgusting, so entirely FRENCH, that every time I open the book it is rather as a task than a pleasure– the last Canto of 'Childe Harold' (certainly much superior to the others) has delighted me more than I can express. The description of the waterfall is the most exquisite piece of poetry that I ever read, 'The Hell of waters where they howl and hiss and boil in endless torture'[4]—tis really fine, really POETRY. All the energy, all the sublimity of modern verse is centered in these lines— they are models which would not dishonour any man to imitate.''

1. *An Essay on Certain Points of Resemblance between the Ancient and Modern Greeks* (1813), by Frederic Sylvester North Douglas (1791–1819).
2. *An Historical Display of the Effects of Physical and Moral Courses on the Character and Circumstances of Nations* (1816), by John Bigland (1750–1832).
3. Marquise de Sévigné (1626–96). The letters for which she is famous were published posthumously, the first collection (31 letters) in 1725, much enlarged in later editions.
4. Byron's *Childe Harold's Pilgrimage, Canto the Fourth* (1818), stanza 59.

---

78. EBB TO CHARLES JOHN MOULTON-BARRETT

To our beloved Storm
On his birthday
December 28th 1818[1]
Hope End.

If theres a Muse that sweeps the lyre
Sacred to jollity and play
Now be it hers our thoughts to inspire
Be it hers to reign to day

If theres a Muse that can declare
The feelings of the breast
And all affections influence there
And how supremely blest!

Be it hers to tune the joyful lay
Our petty griefs forgot
Be it hers to ride our hearts today
And bless our Stormys lot!

Nor thou Charles John despise my strain
This day four years have shed
Their simple joys deprived of pain
Upon thy darling head

Oh child beloved Papas dear Boy
Whose days thus happy flow

Play's soft delights thy souls employ
Unknown to grief or woe–

And if by chance some petty sorrow
Should wake the pensive tear
Thou weeps today then smiles tomorrow
And griefs thy joys endear

Four years thy little life has past
With swift and silent tread
Unruffled by afflictions blast
They've faded o'er thy head–

Rejoice ye nymphs and tune your song
To celebrate this day
And wind the festive dance along
With gladsome footsteps gay

Let play the livelong hours employ
That Happiness may cheer
With bosoms light & heartfelt joy
The Winter of the year.

Oft may the present circle meet
To hail our darlings birth
And this loved day may happy greet
With kindred joy and mirth.

My sweet Charles Johns
affectionate sister
E B Barrett.

Publication: None traced.
Manuscript: Berg Collection.

1. His fourth birthday.

---

79. ELIZABETH MOULTON TO EBB

[?London]
[1819][1]

My very dear Ba
    Your preface my dear Elizabeth was so formidable that I expected
it w^d end in nothing less than a call on me to pay the national DEPT
[*sic*], or the seven *millions* which it is said will be *required* to build the
Prince a new palace;[2] however like many other formidable alarms, it

ended in trifle– I wish that of the Nation cou^d be so easily settled– with pleasure I comply with your request my dear Child, & I hope on all *occasions* you will never hesitate making known your WANTS[3] to *Granny*, who will ever be READY to meet your wishes as far as her abilities will allow, indeed my dear Ba you cannot know half the Love I bear you, not only as my Child, but for the many good & amiable qualities you possess– May you in riper years fulfil the early promise given & you cannot fail being the comfort & happiness of all connected with you– Mr Welsh[4] is so seldom to be met with, that I did not send to him, at the same time wishing you to be Independant I purchased the Musick & it becomes your own– I wish we cou^d witness your performance; we sh^d feel so affectionately Interested, as to lose all remembrance of the absence of Miss O Neil–

Trep^s best Love & will at all times pay postage with the greatest pleasure indeed her regard for all of you is not to be expressed, one, & all, share her warmest affections– Say all kind things to Mama for us & thanks for her few lines– Trep will write her soon–

I was delighted with my Stormys Letter, Kiss & tell him Granny thinks he writes very well indeed for a little Boy– We have not heard from Babes[5] these ten days, but we have no doubt of her being very well, as Minny promisd always to let us know whenever she was indispos'd.

Remember us affectionately to your Dearest Papa & all our D^r pets——

$\qquad\qquad\qquad$ D^r Ba
$\qquad\qquad\qquad$ Your Devotedly Attach^d Granny
$\qquad\qquad\qquad$ EM—

Comp^{ts} to M^r Mc Swinney

Address, on integral page: Miss Barrett——
Docket, probably in Elizabeth Moulton's hand, immediately above address: Drawing of several musical notes.
Publication: None traced.
Manuscript: Pierpont Morgan Library.

1. Dated by reference to a letter from Storm and reference to the Prince Regent. Moulton-Barrett children usually started writing letters at about age four, and the earliest known dated one from Storm was written in July 1819 (SD314). The Prince Regent became King George IV on 29 January 1820, upon the death of his father, George III.
2. Upon the death of Queen Charlotte, the Prince Regent's mother, on 17 November 1818, Buckingham House fell into his hands. He threw himself into its reconstruction, with Nash as architect.
3. Underscored three times.
4. Of the firm of Welsh and Hawes, Music Sellers to His Majesty and the Royal Family, 246 Regent Street.
5. Arabella.

80. EBB TO MARY MOULTON-BARRETT

[Hope End]
[ca. 1819][1]

My dearest Mama

Tho the sorrow of separation was amply compensated by the delightful hope of a return yet we still felt very unhappy when you went away My sorrow was doubly strenghtened [*sic*] by dearest Papas kind present in making me feel what two sweet good people we had losst [*sic*] I will not attempt to deny I felt TRUELY MISERABLE when you departed which not even the remembrance of my elevated rank could eleviate[;] for a few hours I could fancy that I was "unheard alone" and I could consider you "for ever ever ever lost"[.][2] Mr McSwiney you may imagine added not a little to my anxiety & tho I must confess I did not in the least consider which was most to be prefered "To be or not to be"[3] yet I might be considered by a friend to roin[4] and to be in REAL despair– And now my dearest Mama I believe I shall pronounce this subject to be banished I hope for very long I dare not [say] for ever[.] Tho you are so very far away from us you dear creatures I can easily penetrate my way into your hearts & can guess that your greatest wish is to hear how we are & how we have been since your departure I believe your hopes will not prove vain– In the first place Boy[5] is as well as can be imagined if a piece of Apple Dumpling had not interfered you must allow very rudely indeed[;] secondly tho storms SPIRRITS a[re] very much AFFECTED in being seperated so cruelly from Robinson Crusoe yet he is in perfect health[;] thirdly *old mischief*[6] might be truely thought to be envied by Neptune but the jealous God has at lenght [*sic*] gratified his rage by bestowing on his victim the *curse* of such an appetite mortal before never possesed which at the same time has exposed him to the laughter & ridicule of our little hilly world[;] fourthly Addles has partaken his curse t⟨o⟩ such a degree *that* it is often necessary to [ration] her food[;] you will conclude the God of the sea did not act without provocation– [fifthly] His imperial Majesty is in perfect health– Sixtly I would have enjoyed with him that blessing if Eolus[7] had not very rudely declared against me and his powers beat me about so cruelly I have not yet recovered [from] it– Mr McSwiney believes Greece to surpass Rome in every respect but in conquests he says that tho she is trodden under foot by the Turks yet even in the countenance of the inhabitan[t]s she bears the marks of her former greatness of soul virtue & grandeur he says she is conquered but still 'virtue' is not banished what can be more favorable to my DARLING

EBB with Edward and Henrietta Moulton-Barrett

George, Arabella, Samuel and Charles John Moulton-Barrett

project.[8] Sweet Mama I wis⟨h I⟩ was kissing you– I am with love ⟨to⟩
Papa sweet little John & all

Yours

EB

Kiss Papa a thousand kisses for me M[rs] John Clarke & John &
dont forget sweet little John[9] pray forgive me for not writting [*sic*] to
you on Tuesday I was wrong enough to forget it sweet Mamas dear
child Elizabeth

Write very soon indeed

Friday– Between twelve & one– Dear dear dear Mama how very
sweet you are.

Address, on integral page: M[rs] Barrett / Kinersly Castle / Near Hereford.
Docket, in unidentified hand: M[rs] Barrett / Letters [illegible word] at Ledbury.
Publication: None traced.
Manuscript: British Library.

1. Dated by the references to Henry Moulton-Barrett.
2. Pope's *Ode for Musick. On St. Cecilia's Day* (1713).
3. *Hamlet*, III, 1, 55.
4. "To growl" (obs., *OED*).
5. Henry, the last-born child.
6. "Old mischief" and the later reference to "His imperial Majesty" are assumed to refer
respectively to George and Bro, the only children not otherwise named in EBB's report.
7. Æolus, the god of the winds.
8. Her poem, *The Battle of Marathon*.
9. EBB's aunt, Mary Graham-Clarke (*née* Parkinson), her husband, and their first-born,
John Altham Graham-Clarke.

---

81. EBB TO SAMUEL MOULTON-BARRETT (BROTHER)

To
Our dear Sam
On his birthday Jany 13th 1819[1]
Hope End.

Again oh Goddess sweep the lyre
A sisters thoughts declare
Light up my soul, my bosom fire
    Oh hear my prayer!

And if the tenour of my lay
Might times least course beguile

Or cheer one pleasure of to-day
        Or gain a smile

For this I ply my humble strain
For this my heart aspires
For this I strike those chords again
        And sweep those wires

I sigh not for the wreaths of fame
Nor for such joys I soar
To please is all my only aim
        I ask no more

And those for whom benignant Heav'n
Its choisest gifts combines
To whom are days the happiest given
        Accept my lines!

And as old Time returning brings
Thy birth, to us so dear,
By us so loved, upon his wings
        And turns the year

May he ever find us thus elate
To meet with social mirth
Unhurt amidst the storms of fate
        To hail that birth

Farewell may Heaven its blessings shed
With sweet returning joy
Dear Sam upon thy youthful head
        Without alloy.

                Your affectionate Sister
                E B Barrett

Address, on integral page: S M Barrett Esqr Junior. / Hope End / n^r Ledbury /
Herefordshire.
Publication: None traced.
Manuscript: Berg Collection.

    1. His seventh birthday.

82. EBB TO HENRIETTA MOULTON-BARRETT

[Hope End]
March 4.th 1819

To the Rig.^{t} Revd D.^{r1} Harry Parry Barrett.
With Compliments and Wishes
for her prosperity.

_____

Awake my Muse; and strike the lyre,
My soul uplift, my breast inspire.
    Awake again
    The joyful strain
    Let grief be mute
    Upon this festive day,
    And on the lute,
    Thy warbling fingers stray.

For Time again upon his wings
Another festive birth day[2] brings;
Another day of sports and joy,
Our thoughts, our hearts employ.
    Another day
    Of mirth and play!–
    Let joy wing the hours,
    Away sorrow and sadness,
    Let Time glide in the flowers,
    Of pleasure and gladness!

A Sisters birth day comes again
To raise our joys, & wake the strain,
A birth day must be welcome here,
A Sisters! doubly justly dear!
    Then Harry hail!
    The Muse would fail,
    If she should shew, but to disclose
    The feelings of my soul
    Where all affection glows,
    Nor meets control!

Then Harry do not thou despise my strain
That "list" with Hamlet, I may cry in vain,[3]
Justice I ask not, then the critics blows
Will bid my modest Muse, sink where she rose.
    Then Doctor hear!
    Thy suppliants prayer

In mercy then thy brow incline
Like Jove in fable big,
Like Jove! No—thou art more divine
Then shake thy bushy wig!

Dost thou not yet, in sovereign pity nod,
And canst thou yield in mercy to the God!
Then I must try a compliments address,
And by the bye, I would not do much less.
    Oh mercy sweet
    I do entreat.

And may the fates thy breast endue
With blessings but to angels given,
To angels? then ah what are you?
At least, the loveliest angel out of Heaven!
Ah Doctor!– but I see you smile,
C'est often—you my cares beguile,
Then Oh, avert the critics stroke,
For I should die, beneath the shock.
    No more I'll say,
    At least today,

Nor more my gabbling Muse shall tell,
Now have I done—with Oh and Ah!
And I must——Must I say farewell?
Then– pray forget not loving Ba!

Publication: None traced.
Source: Copy in Mary Moulton-Barrett's hand in "Poems by EBB," Berg Collection.

1. The form of address appropriate to a bishop. EBB's mother explained in a footnote:
"For this dignified appellation, she is indebted to her hair–"
2. Her tenth birthday.
3. *Hamlet*, I, 5, 22.

---

83. CHARLES JOHN MOULTON-BARRETT TO EBB

[?Hope End]
[?6 March 1819][1]

[In child's scrawl] Storm's kisses to his dear Ba.

Address, on integral page: to Ba.
Docket, in hand of EBB's father: Poet-Laureat / Hope-End.
Publication: None traced.
Manuscript: Berg Collection.

1. Conjectural dating based on handwriting. This may have been Storm's first attempt at a birthday greeting to EBB.

84. EDWARD MOULTON-BARRETT (BROTHER) TO EBB

[Hope End]
[6 March 1819][1]

To Miss Ba on entering her teens.

Now be my strain a sisters birth to greet,
While tears & sighs lay humbly at thy feet,
Let not fierce anger, rage, or fear, depress
Nor the long day by passions be oppressed;
But may this day by nought but joy be blest
And nought but joy the happy hours invest
Till tired with fun and quite o'ercome by play
Papa says go to bed must I away?

Edward Barrett

Address, on integral page: To / Miss Ba Barrett / Hope End / Herefordshire——
Publication: None traced.
Manuscript: Berg Collection.

1. Mary Moulton-Barrett dated this poem "March 6th 1819" when copying it in "Poems by EBB," Berg Collection. EBB would have reached her teens on this date.

85. EBB TO EBB

[Hope End]
[6 March 1819][1]

My dearest Ba,
    I love you so,
I could not let the postman go
Without a letter from me too
Not that I've got so much to say
For I am passing dull to day
But just my dearest Ba to prove
How much you share my partial love
Then oh may blessings best of all
That Fate has given—Upon you fall!

Then you must be my instrument
To give a handsome compliment
To Mistress Hen & Master Bro
To Master Storm & Sam also
To George & lovely Arabel
Thats all—then dearest Ba farewell!

Address, on integral page: For / Miss Ba Barrett / Hope End—
Publication: None traced.
Manuscript: Berg Collection.

1. In "Poems by EBB," Berg Collection, Mary Moulton-Barrett dated her copy of this poem "March 6th 1819." She also gave it the title "To Myself."

---

86. HENRIETTA MOULTON-BARRETT TO EBB

[Hope End]
[6 March 1819][1]

My dearest Ba

I hope we may all succeed in pleasing you on your birthday; we shall all try to do so, as we have tried to make you happy on all your birthdays but I cannot expect that my little letter can give you as much pleasure, as your beautiful verses gave me and wish I could write verses for your sake, but I love you as dearly and wish you as happy as if I could tell you so in verse and hope you will have a great deal of fun with

my dearest sisters affec[te]
Doctor Harry

Address, on integral page: To / The dearest Ba / On her birthday.
Publication: None traced.
Manuscript: Berg Collection.

1. EBB's birthday was 6 March. The year 1819 is assumed because on Henrietta's birthday in that year, just two days earlier, EBB had addressed her as "Rig[t] Rev[d] D[r] Harry Parry Barrett" (letter 82).

87. SAMUEL MOULTON-BARRETT (BROTHER) TO EBB

[Hope End]
[6 March 1819]¹

My dear Ba
    I wish you many happy birth days and hope that we shall play and laugh till we to go sleep to night
                                                    your affec^{te} Sam

Address, on integral page: the dear Poet!
Publication: None traced.
Manuscript: Berg Collection.

    1. Dated by the handwriting, which matches a birthday greeting written to Henrietta two days previously (SD307).

---

88. EBB TO SAMUEL MOULTON-BARRETT (UNCLE)

To my dearest Sam¹
On his birthday.
Hope End March 31st 1819.

Again, Euterpe, and again
Rouse the accustomed strain
Wake every Muse whose fairy shadow strays
Near purest Helicons benignant waters
And bid them each confine their several lays
And dream no more of battles & of slaughters!
And those on sunny glades midst flowers reclining
For mortal pangs in heavenly pity weeping
With myrtle wreaths their floating locks confining
Those pensive musing, and these softly sleeping!
Thou! with thy magic numbers
Awake them from their slumbers!
Euterpe now their souls inspire!
And strike the deep toned lyre!
With one accord they rise they spring
They snatch each warbling lute
E'en echo lingers while they sing
And Heaven and Natures mute!
Then hail dear Sam we strive once more
For thee our strains to raise
May Heaven have gifts & joys in store
To gild thy coming days!

And may each wish thy heart declares
That might to Man be given
Be granted to our supliant prayers
(What e'er it be) by Heaven!
May every joy that mortals own
Prolong thy destined years
And may thy life be still unknown
To sorrow & to tears!

Y.^r affec.^{te} Child
E B Barrett

Address, on integral page: S M Barrett Esqr / Hope End— /or London!
Publication: HUP, I, 143—144 (from unknown source, as to her brother Sam).
Manuscript: Pierpont Morgan Library.

1. The date written by EBB in the heading indicates that the poem was for her uncle
Sam, not her brother as stated in *HUP*. The uncle was born on 31 March 1787.

---

89. EBB TO MARY MOULTON-BARRETT

Hope End
May 1.st 1819

Ode to my dearest Mama
On her birthday[1]

Hail fragrant Summer, hail delightful Spring,
Amidst the year, with generous plenty smiling,
And all the ravages of Winter sting,
With sweet profusion, and with hope beguiling;
Hail lovely month! Within thy generous train,
And dancing sportively to fairy measure,
And crowning each and all thy plenteous reign,
Are gentle Mirth, and Hope, & young eyed Pleasure;
And Gayety with dimpled brow;
And Flora's[2] self, unbidden now,
Her mingled beauties showers;
Her hand combines each different hue,
Each petalled herb, that sips the dew,
And sows the turf with flowers.—
I call thee not, Oh Muse to fire,
My breast & strike the chorded lyre;
My soul, my heart desire to prove,
Th' inspiring lay of filial love,—

Let every pleasure now combine,
And every kindred mirth,
To gild this day with joy divine
And hail a Mothers birth.
May every bliss that Heaven bestows,
Await thy coming days,
And happiness unmixed with woes
Renew—as life decays!–

Publication: None traced.
Source: Copy in Mary Moulton-Barrett's hand in "Poems by EBB," Berg Collection.

1. Her 38th birthday.
2. The Roman goddess of flowers.

---

90. EBB TO EDWARD MOULTON-BARRETT (FATHER)

Ode
On dearest Papas birthday.[1]
Friday May 28.th 1819. Hope End

Welcome sweet returning gladness
Welcome foe to grief and sadness,
Joy within thy sparkling eye
Yes I hear—I see thee nigh,
I hear thy footstep swift and light–
Opening to my eager sight
Thy gait thy face thy smile I see!
And all is mirth and all is—thee.
Goddess, I confess thy power
Gild *thou*[2] each moment, every hour,
But most[3] of all, oh Gladness, sway
The limit of this blissful day,
This day that gave a Parent birth—
Then bless the day that blest the earth.
For all in him has Heaven combined
The feeling heart, the noble mind
The spirit freed from dusts controul
And all thats godlike in the soul!
A Fathers just and worthy praise
Not Glory—but his children raise.
His praises earth and fame may ring
All may confirm—but *we* will sing!

Then Goddess as each coming year
This day within its course may bear,
Ever attend—each hour beguile,
And chear *our* bosoms by *thy* smile!—
                    E B Barrett, May 28th 1819
                    Hope End

Address, on integral page: E B Barrett Esqr / Hope End / Herefordshire.
Publication: None traced.
Manuscript: Pierpont Morgan Library.

1. His 34th birthday.
2. Originally written "Thou gild"; then reversed with superior numbers.
3. Written above the line over "first" which has not been deleted.

---

91. EBB TO SAMUEL MOULTON-BARRETT (UNCLE)

                                                                        Worthing
                                                                June 19.th 1819

My dearest Sam,

     I shall always be grateful to those who will trouble themselves to
admonish me or to warn me of my faults and I am sensible that I
deserve a great deal of your censure and many of your remarks! But I
cannot plead guilty to what you believe concerning my wishing to "pry
into individual characters" or to "expose the blemishes" of those
friends to whom I owe so much! The lines to which you allude[1] were
the production of an idle hour and were never meant for any other eye
than my own and it was entirely by an *accident* that it was ever known
that "Vissions" [*sic*] were in existance—for I was and am sensible of
the impropriety of my judgeing of characters which are so far superior
to mine—and confident in my own *integrity* though not in my
perfections I never *wished* and I trust in God I never *shall* to "draw the
veil['] from the frailties of those beloved relations whose kindnesses I
never *never* can repay— Having thus warmly and believe me sincerely
exprest myself, I own that I have acted both wrongly & inconsiderately
in having allowed myself to sketch even the virtues of my friends: and
forgive me if I assure you that if I did wrong I did it unintentionally &
that in Mr Mac Swineys; Malice did not in the slightest degree influence
either my *heart* or my *pen.*[2] And now my dearest Sam to prove to you
my *real sincere* repentance and the value I attach to your opinion I
promise you that I will *never* indulge myself *again* in triffling with the
frailties of others and that as long as I live upon that point (as far as I

am able) you shall *never* have a moments uneasiness– I confess and I have ever allowed that I borrowed *the idea* of that stanza in the hymn from an anectate [*sic*] in a book (whose name now I forget) where a soldier prays before a battle in these words "Lord if I forget *thee* on the day of battle, do not *thou* forget *me!*"[3] A Thousand thanks for the bracelet! can I ever be grateful enough for all your kindness?

Publication: None traced.
Source: EBB's draft copy, Pierpont Morgan Library.

1. Apparently an unpublished poem titled "Visions" (copy in Mary Moulton-Barrett's hand at Berg), dated 17 January 1819, using fictitious names in discussing the characteristics of several people, including her mother and father (see *Reconstruction*, D1097).
2. Malice or not, EBB's delineation of McSwiney is far from complimentary, including such comments as "With love of titles writ upon his face"; "does not, *quite detest* a glass of wine"; "Ambitious—nor of fame, as yet quite sick"; "For Paddy's heart it cannot be denied / Joins Irish prejudice, to Irish pride."
3. The prayer offered before the battle of Edgehill (1642) by Major-Gen. Sir Jacob Astley (1579–1652), recounted by Sir Philip Warwick in his *Memoires of the reigne of King Charles I* (1701).

---

92. EBB TO MARY MOULTON-BARRETT

[Hope End]
[August 1819][1]

My dearest Mama
    To set your heart at ease at once from all anxiety I must leave all the flowery sentiments of oratory and relieve you with the welcome tidings that little Henry is a great deal better he slept last night without either coughing or waking—so much as he [h]as done since the unfortunate colds began. Bro Henrietta Sam Storm and George are equally improved in health and in that appendage to health—Spirits– As for myself the *violent cough* that I had when you were last here has not left me and I fear will accompagny [*sic*] me to the end of my life– My constitution and my appetite is as *bad* as ever! But do not be uneasy for you know that *natural ill health* generally continues to *death* so it is nothing *outrée*.[2] And have you really the assurance to suppose that in this short period of separation buried as we are amidst hills rocks and woods that we have any news or even scandal to regale your ears! Alas if you have I fear you will be terribly disapointed– M! Mac Swiney is rather better I wish he was well: indeed his illness has not *the best effects*—THOSE of *preserving* his natural good humour. Love to dearest Papa I dare say he is now wishing to be in his own dear home in spite of all the Hereford gaieties and *our* noise. If I was not writing to *you* I

should *be* half tired for this pen is stiff and lazy & it requires great muscular exertion to drive it on– Pity me & forgive the shortness of this letter–

Ever your affec.te child—
Elizabeth B Barrett

I hope to have a good deal of my Preface done by the time you return.[3]
Thank you for your kind permission about the gooseberries

Address, on integral page: M.rs Barrett / Hotel / Hereford.
Publication: None traced.
Manuscript: British Library.

1. EBB's mother and father were in Hereford, pursuing political interests. An oath "taken by those that are admitted Freemen or Guild-Merchants of the City of Hereford" was sworn by Edward Moulton-Barrett on 23 August 1819 (SD 320).
2. "Excessive."
3. Presumably that of *The Battle of Marathon*, published in the following year. The manuscript (Texas) is dated: "Hope End, 1819." See *Reconstruction*, D69–70.

93. ARABELLA MOULTON-BARRETT TO EBB

[Worthing]
[ca. August 1819][1]

My dear Ba many thanks for your kind Letter tell dear Storm I should like to go home in a donkey cart very much, do you rememb'r simple susan and whim and contradiction[2] I have just read them I often take a dip in the sea and drink a little sometimes my best love to dear Papa and Mama and all my Brothers and sisters your affect sister

Arabella Barrett.

Publication: None traced.
Manuscript: Myrtle Moulton-Barrett and Ronald A. Moulton-Barrett.

1. It is known from family letters that Arabella was sent to Worthing for her health in May 1819, and remained there until March 1820. Letter 91 shows that EBB was also at Worthing in June 1819, and no. 92 that she was back at Hope End in August. Arabella's references suggest that this letter was written after EBB's visit in June.
2. "Simple Susan" was one of the stories included in the 3rd edn. of *The Parent's Assistant* (1800) by Maria Edgeworth (1767–1849). *Whim and Contradiction: A Tale* was published anonymously in 1815.

The

Battle of Marathon

A Poem

Behold
What care employs me now, my ... they
To the sweet Muses, teachers of my youth!
Athenians.
—Ancient of days, august Athens! where
Where are thy Men of might, thy grand in ...
Gone glimmering through the dream of things
First in the Race that led to Glory's goal, that were
They won, & past away—

Byron—

E. B. Barrett—

Hope End: View from the Lower Pond

94. MARY MOULTON-BARRETT TO EBB

Foxley.[1]

Wednesday. [*Postmark:* 25 August 1819]

My beloved Eliz[th]
I fear you will be sorry to hear that you will not see us till Sunday Morning; We are obliged to stay till after Saturday, and you will I trust my darling Children be all well & happy; if otherwise pray send off to me instantly and we will be with you: I feel very impatient to hear from you, and trust I shall do so today– you are never out of my thoughts, & dear Papa thinks not less of you in spite of the Election– Col: Mathews opposes M[r] Scudamore, & it is going on very actively, & must be a very severe contest[2]—this is the reason we delay returning, in great measure. I had a delightful walk in the beautiful valley before breakfast this morning, by myself, & wished I had my dearest children with me– I write in such haste and in so much talking, that you must forgive it my beloved Eliz[th] Write to me directly, and kiss all my darlings for me.

Ever, my sweet Childs
Affec[t] Mother
MB–

Order our letters to be forwarded here, until Saturday—& remember us kindly to M[r] M[c] S– do not let this scratch be seen.

Tell me exactly how the coughs are, & do *not* stay out late—or sit on the grass——

Address, on integral page: Miss Barrett / Hope End / Ledbury.
Publication: None traced.
Manuscript: British Library.

1. Foxley, seat of Uvedale Price, 7½ miles N.W. of Hereford. This is the earliest letter of 20 that EBB wrapped in a cover sheet which she labelled "Letters of my for ever beloved & kindest Mama." The last of the series is letter 321 and carries a notation by EBB "The very last I ever received from *her.* . . ."
2. A parliamentary election had been necessitated in Hereford by the death of a sitting member, Col. Symonds. Despite Mary Moulton-Barrett's forecast of "a very severe contest," *The Times* reported on 24 September 1819 the election of "R. P. Scudamore, Esq. . . . without opposition." Col. John Matthews, of Belmont, had been M.P. for Hereford 1803–06.

95. EBB, Edward, Henrietta, Samuel & Charles John Moulton-Barrett to Mary Moulton-Barrett

[Hope End]
[September 1819][1]

Madam,

We have the honor to announce to you the representation of a new tragedy this evening "Laodice" or "The dying Queen" never before represented— We beg the honor of your attendance & if you would distribute the tickets we would feel obliged.

We are Madam,
Your humble servants
E, E^d, H, S, & C. Barrett.[2]

The honor of an answer is required—

Address, on integral page: Mrs Barrett—
Publication: None traced.
Manuscript: Berg Collection.

1. A ticket of admission (MS at ABL, with fragments of the play itself) indicates that EBB's play "The Tragedy of Laodice" was presented by the Barrett children on a Saturday evening in September 1819.
2. Entire letter, including signatures, appears to be in hand of EBB. Initials at end represent Elizabeth, Edward, Henrietta, Samuel, and Charles Moulton-Barrett.

---

96. Arabella Moulton-Barrett & Mary Robinson to EBB

[In Arabella Moulton-Barrett's hand]   [Worthing]
[ca. November 1819][1]

My dear Ba I am very sory I am not going to Hope End to see you all But dont forget your own child

Arabella Barrett

[Continued in Mary Robinson's hand] My dear Ba Excuse Babys Short Letter She did not know till just now Papa was going and has not time to write more

Address, on integral page, in hand of Arabella Moulton-Barrett: Miss Barrett.
Publication: None traced.
Manuscript: Berg Collection.

1. This letter may follow one to Arabella from her mother of 7 November 1819 (SD323), in which Mary Moulton-Barrett says "My heart longs to see you, but Papa thinks we ought not to move you just yet."

97. MARY MOULTON-BARRETT & EMMA HESELTINE[1] TO EBB

[In Mary Moulton-Barrett's hand]   [Kinnersley Castle]
                                    Finished Friday Morng. Nov[r] 26. [1819][2]

My beloved Elizabeth,
    We arrived here at past six o'clock on Sunday, and found all the
dear party, dressed & *very hungry*, tho' not too much so to be
overjoyed to see us, & you may believe how many *hugs* were
interchanged– They are all looking blooming, excepting poor dear
Lotte, who has been kept for the two last days in bed by a severe cold
which has sadly damped the pleasure of our party– John is very much
grown, & Leonard Edmund, is a *beautiful* child, and very intelligent[3]–
We all went to church to see him Christened, where he learned to say
Amen after the Clerk– the Clergyman & his Wife dined here, the party
were all smartly attired in white excepting Grandmama– We had a
concert in the evening, which concluded with a game at forfeits–
Yesterday morn[g] M[r] Price & L[y] Caroline came to take Miss P. home,
who was very sorry to leave our merry party[4]– Emma was much
pleased with your note, & entirely understands your explanation—
before I came she had learnt the 1st scene– I hope certainly to hear
from you tomorrow, my sweetest Puss—to say the truth I am *sadly*
disappointed not to have heard already—it is sometimes not quite a
sufficient consolation to believe "*no news* good news." I am sorry to
say we cannot contrive to get to our beloved children till Tuesday—I
hope certainly to bring Fanny[5] & Emma, if it be possible for them to
meet us in Hereford– Poor Charlottes cold is still so bad as to confine
her to her bed otherwise she would have written to thank darling
Henrietta for her note– A thousand kisses

[Continued by Emma Heseltine]

Dear Baz, I take this opportunity M[rs] Barrett so kindly offers me, to
write you a few lines about our grand theatricals indeed dearest Baz it
will be quite delightful. I think your additions to the Merchant of
Venice will be a great improvement tho I do not exactly understand yet
whether I am to learn what you told me in your first Letter as well as
what you last wrote to me about, but it does not much signify as I am
afraid I shall not be able to learn *all* my part till I go to Hope End
as M[rs] Clarke[6] cannot give me the Book, as she does not exactly know
where it is, Miss Richards however lent me it for a short time and as I
took the opportunity to write out Fannys part there will therefore be no
impediment to her, and she will learn it all before she sees you again; I
have tho learnt quite perfectly all the first scene and I shall not be five
minuits learning the rest when ever I can get the Book so dearest Baz

you not be in the least disstress yourself about my part as I shall be sure to know it by some means or other quite soon enough. I long to be with you again and have *all* the squabling delights of the Green Room to go through, I here [*sic*] you are making great preparations. I have no room to say anything more as this page is my limited quantity. I must however find room to thank you for your *three* kind Letters–

Dearest Baz's affectionate Cousin–

E Heseltine

[Continued by Mary Moulton-Barrett] Kiss from every one here to you *all–* We work & talk, & talk & work, which with Music occupies our time very industriously

God bless all my treasures–

Ever my own Eliz[ths]

Most Affec! Mother.

I suppose we shall have G.Mama &? with us in about ten days——
We go to Whitfield (M! Clives) tomorrow[7]

Address, on integral page: Miss Barrett / Hope End / Ledbury.
Publication: None traced.
Manuscript: British Library.

1. Emma Heseltine was the daughter of Mary Moulton-Barrett's first cousin, James Altham Heseltine.
2. 1819 dating based on content and the fact that 26 November fell on Friday in that year.
3. John and Leonard were children of John Altham and Mary Graham-Clarke.
4. Uvedale Price (1747–1829), his wife Lady Caroline Price (*née* Carpenter, 1754–1826), and their only daughter, Caroline (1783?–1853).
5. Frances ("Fanny") Heseltine, Emma's younger sister.
6. Their hostess, Mrs. John Graham-Clarke.
7. Edward Bolton Clive, for many years M.P. for Hereford. He did not stand for the general election of 1820 and Edward Moulton-Barrett was asked to offer himself as a candidate. He refused and endorsed Mr. Scudamore for re-election. Whitfield is 7 miles S.W. of Hereford.

98. EBB TO ARABELLA GRAHAM-CLARKE (AUNT)

[Hope End]
[ca. December 1819]¹

A Welcome
for sweetest
Bum
To Hope End

———————

1

My Muse twice Welcome to this happy day
Welcome to her for whom I strike the lyre
Who raises in my breast celestial fire
Oh Muse benignant listen to her sway

2

Tis thou oh Virgin Fancy pure and bright
Tis thou I woo thou balmy nurse of love
Through flowerets wild and thorny paths I rove
To catch a glance of sweet affections light

3

And may these groves this prospects wide extent
Smile welcome to thee Mistress of my heart
For from my breast affections greetings start
And oh how joyfully on thee their [*sic*] bent

———————

Elizabeth Barrett

Address, on integral page: A Welcome / To dear dearest Mʳˢ Bum / To / Hope End.
Publication: None traced.
Manuscript: Lady Elisabeth Cooper.

1. EBB's aunt is known to have visited Hope End during the Christmas season of 1819.

99. EBB TO SAMUEL MOULTON-BARRETT (BROTHER)

To my beloved Sam on his birthday with appologies for haste
In consequence of my Muse being on such rapid wing that
she could not stop to make any corrections.

Hope End January 13th 1820.[1]

The ambient Morn with rosy fingers streaks
The dusky Heav'ns– the sun in rising splendour
Flames fiery red amidst the grey horizon–
Hail glorious orb of everlasting light!
Thou seem'st to me more purely beautiful
Than when I gazed upon thee yestermorn
In unobscured, eternal, bright effulgence
For now thou gladst a cherished Brothers birth
A Sisters prayer! Oh *thou* inspire my song
Bright image of thy bright Creator! Raise
My thoughts to Heav'n, and cheer my anxious breast!
And thou my Sam! my Brother! tis for thee
I twine this hasty garland on thy birth
A Sisters love alas! can do no more!
Then oh may Sense and goodness guide thy path,
And pour joy's endless sunshine o'er thy head!

Yours affecte Sister
Elizabeth.

Address, on integral page: To / Master S Barrett.
Publication: None traced.
Manuscript: Berg Collection.

1. His eighth birthday.

100. EBB TO HENRIETTA MOULTON-BARRETT

Ode to my beloved Henrietta
on her birthday. March the fourth 1820[1]
Baker Street 62.

Time was when Phebus self was young
And music trembled from his tongue!
And every Muse in youthful pride
Tuned the sweet lyre on blest Parnassus side–

When glorious Fame on mighty pinion bending
Near Helicons eternal waters,
Swift from the Heaven of light descending
Addrest Apollos daughters–
"Go hence oh progeny of Heav'n" he cries
(While lightening flashes from his radiant eyes)
"Go hence to Thracias wild and ample side
Where far famed Hebrus² rolls his golden tide–
Ye, near that sacred flood Apollo waits
To leash the awful mandate of the fates!
This day most blest mysterious signs declare
Peace on the earth, and sunshine in the air–
This day with happiness the Gods will bless
And Hells worst influence *shall* not make it less!
Though Mis'ry strain each nerve and ev'ry wile
Yet on the 4th of March the Heav'ns benignant smile!
Fly hence already Morning yields to day
Apollo wills, it fits ye to obey!["]
He said and breaking from their eager sight
Poised his strong wings and soared to realms of light!
The heavenly Sisters to his words assent
And thro the liquid air their flight celestial bent!
Where Thracian Hebrus flows on golden sand
The god of poesy they found
While waiting his austere command
Circling his throne and all around—
Those renowned or famed in story,
Warriors high in lists of glory
The mighty God surround––
The graces at his feet
Their wonted garland twining
With low submission meet
Above the flood reclining!
"Children of earth and of those azure skies"
With accents sweet the power eternal cries—
"This day the pitying fates with joy bestow
(To ease your cares) an antidote for woe
For on this day the awful power decree
A happy boon shall future ages see
Where native goodness and unblemished truth
With all the sweetness all the glow of youth

Attractive beauty grace without a fetter
Will smile unsullied in a Henrietta!["]
He said and paused——the heav'nly muses raise
The swelling strain to Henriettas praise;
Their notes the lofty vaults of Heav'n rebound
And earth rejoices in the welcome sound!

———————

Then ah if thus the Powers of Hea'vn
Rejoiced with kindred mirth
What joy shall to *my* heart be giv'n,
Upon a sisters birth?

Why should I strive with empty sounds to bless
Thy birth my sister *ever* EVER dear?
Oh what can all the pomp of words express?
Heav'n *reads* my heart & *knows* it is sincere!
And if my Henrietta thou'd beguile,
And cheer my labours on this happy day
My wearied fingers and poetic toil———
Ah *love* me *still*, and smile upon my lay!

My beloved Henriettas
Affec.te Sister
Ba.

Address, on integral page: Miss H Barrett / Baker Street / 62.
Publication: None traced.
Manuscript: Berg Collection.

  1. Her 11th birthday.
  2. The most important river in Thrace, associated with the worship of Dionysus.

———————

101. EDWARD MOULTON-BARRETT (BROTHER) TO EBB

[London]
[6 March 1820][1]

To dearest Ba
on her birthday[2]

———————

No haughty strain of verse employs me now,
No fall of despots and no bo[a]st of Kings,
To sweet affection do I pay my vow,
And sweet affection speaks of milder things;

For tis a sisters birthday that I greet,
A sisters virtues & a sisters song
Which rolling energeticaly sweet
Swell on the ear & to the feelings throng

But could a crown of ivy deck her brow
Yet would she rather hear affections voice
Than, from the capitol the trump of fame should blow,
This sounds her praise that bids her heart rejoice.

Address, on integral page: To / Our dear Sapho. / 62 Baker Street.
Publication: None traced.
Manuscript: Berg Collection.

1. Date and writer's identity based on copy in Mary Moulton-Barrett's hand in "Poems by EBB," Berg Collection.
2. Her 14th birthday.

102. HENRIETTA MOULTON-BARRETT TO EBB

[London]
March 6th 1820

My dearest Ba
    Would you deign to read this little letter as a pledge of my affection to you; I should be glad if your genius would allow me a little of your pœtic taste, but as the muse turns her back upon poor me, and as I believe you know I try to do it as well as I can, perhaps you may excuse very dull prose and let me offer my humble wishes as well as I am able, that you may be the happiest of the happy! I hope on your next birthday I shall have more time, and more skill, to tell you how dear you are to Henrietta.

Address, on integral page: To my dearest Ba / Smiling at Grandmama's / good dinner.
Publication: None traced.
Manuscript: Berg Collection.

103. SAMUEL MOULTON-BARRETT (BROTHER) TO EBB

Baker Street
March 6th 1820

My dear Ba
    I wish I could tell you how much I love you, but I think you can

guess it and will believe the old toast that I wish you many merry
returns of this happy day and that I am, tho' very sleepy,

your affec^{te}

Sam

Address, on integral page: The dear Poetess
Publication: None traced.
Manuscript: Berg Collection.

---

104. EBB TO MARY MOULTON-BARRETT

Hope End

May 1st 1820.

Ode to my dearest Mama
on her happy birth day.[1]

Hail lovely month! the incense breathing shower
Of oderous roses, thy fair form array
Veiled in a blushing canopy of flowers
While midst thy locks delightful breezes play!
Hail Queen of Flora's tribe! thrice hail celestial May!
The hours of wint'ry gloom at length are past.
And genial warmth succeeds, and brighter skies;
Far from our smiling land, the wint'ry blast
To some less happy shore reluctant flies
Awed by the laughing bliss of May's re[s]plendant eyes!
And thou for whom I raise th' untutored song
To bless a Mother on her natal day.
To thee my verse, to *thee* my thanks belong!
Oh partial smile, and cheer my humble lay
Loved, cherished as thou art, the fairest flower of May!
For thou hast watched my infant helplessness
I owe thee *all* for thou hast all bestowed!
Thou taught my lisping accents first to bless
That azure Heav'n, man's last secure abode
And turned my infant thoughts to a redeeming God!
No! I can ne'er my gratitude express!
And never can I all thy care repay!
And yet accept the offering that *would* bless
Thy future hours—accept my simple lay!
Then who so blest as Ba upon this joyous day?

Your most affec^{te} Child

EBB.

Publication: None traced.
Source: Copy in Mary Moulton-Barrett's hand in "Poems by EBB," Berg Collection.

1. Her 39th birthday.

---

105. EBB TO EDWARD MOULTON-BARRETT (FATHER)

To my dearest
Papa
on
his welcome birthday[1]
May 28.th 1820—Hope End.

The young Morn breathes her first soft sigh
So low so plaintive and so sweet
And breathing from the thin grey sky
The light airs kiss her fairy feet.
The smiles, engagingly serene
The burst of joy but half supprest
Danced in that throbbing breast
In vivid flashes seen–
Oh why's her airy footstep lighter
Her smile more cloudless and serene
Why is that eye of radiance brighter
Today, than it *has* been?——
Yes!! tis his welcome birth who blest
Her eyes, with this delightful scene
Who bade her sight enraptured rest
On rocks—and hills of verdant green–
For half her beauties does she owe
To him for whom those pillars rise
Who bade perlucid waters flow
And waving foliage seek the skies!
His birth, no brazen trumps proclaim,
No sounds which gladness' self annoy
No meanless clang, no noisy fame,
But heartfelt mirth, and smiling joy
Murmur to the listening gale
And laughing echo tells the welcome tale!!
And thou my Father ever ever dear
So fondly loved and cherished as thou art!
Accept my lines unstudied, but sincere,
The simple offering of a grateful heart!

Majestic verse the deeply learn'd may pay
The noble offspring of an ample mind—
Affections fondest tide impels *my* lay,
Natures own strain unskilled, & unrefined!
This pledge of love, of gratitude receive
(But how can words that gratitude express?)
Accept my verse!! the ALL I have to give—
But when the pen is still the heart shall bless!!

Your most affec.^te child

Ba

Address, on integral page: E M Barret Esqr / Hope End.
Publication: SBHC, 9 (Fall, 1981), 26–27 (in part).
Manuscript: Armstrong Browning Library.

1. His 35th birthday.

---

106. EBB TO EDWARD MOULTON-BARRETT (FATHER)

Die natali patris
Carissimi.
May 28.th 1821 [*sic*, for 1820].[1]

Vos sacræ castæque Divæ
Supplice prosequor votas!
Audite! accipe precem!!
Tu pater carusne horâ
Candidâ esse ne tuum
Lætite ardorque vitæ
Filia delect invocat
Tibi dulcissime rerum!!!

Elizabeth

Publication: None traced.
Source: Copy in Mary Moulton-Barrett's hand in "Poems by EBB," Berg Collection.

Translation: Because of irregularities in syntax, this text poses problems. The following translates the spirit, if not the exact letter, of EBB's verse: "On the birthday of my dearest father. / May 28th 1821. / As a suppliant I offer prayers to you, / holy and pure goddess! / Listen! receive this prayer!! / You, surely my dear father, at this special time / That is truly yours, be happy / The light of your life, your delighted daughter, / Asks for you the sweetest of things!!!"

1. Although clearly dated 1821, EBB's mother has copied this verse in "Poems by EBB" immediately following the preceding letter and before two odes by Bro to his father dated 1820—one in Latin, one in English (SD343).

107. SAMUEL MOULTON-BARRETT (UNCLE) TO EBB

[London]
[ca. July 1820]¹

My dearest Ba,

As Tripsack is writing to you, & seems bent on giving you an extract from all the daily papers with a few dips into futurity, I think I may well be spared. I will therefore reserve myself for another opportunity, assuring you only at the present thinking far from wishing you to abandon your political principles (Is this to a female Baby?) I wish to confirm you in them— But do use some delicacy both towards the individual of whom you are writing, & towards to whom you are addressing yourself— With this little piece of advice which may save hereafter both your understanding, your taste, & your feeling being impeached, I shall take my leave of you referring you to Tripsack for a full account of our yesterdays proceedings which have convinced me more than ever that the House of Commons is the most blackguard hole a man can be found in.

Ever most affectionately Yours
SMB

Publication: None traced.
Manuscript: Pierpont Morgan Library.

1. Dated from the reference to "our yesterday's proceedings" in the House of Commons; Samuel Moulton-Barrett had been elected as member for Richmond, Yorkshire, in the general election of 1820. It seems likely that his disenchantment stemmed from the acrimonious debates in both houses of Parliament on the Bill against Queen Caroline, proposed on 5 July (see letter 109, note 1). He was recorded in *The Annual Register for 1820* as having voted on 26 June against the motion to appoint a secret committee to investigate the charges against the Queen.

---

108. EBB TO ARABELLA MOULTON-BARRETT

Ode to my beloved Arabel
On her birthday
Hope End July 4ᵗʰ 1820¹

Sweet month again with joy returning
And breathing from the pure blue sky!!
Thy warmth congenial, incense burning
Smiles these wat'ry mists away
Which oer the silent azure fly
And veil the loveliness of day!

Hail sweetest month! be it thine to bless
Our clime—with gentle sway presiding
O'er the soft and beautiful scene,
Earths glories—and that blue serene
In the Heav'n of radiance gliding
So silent, still, and motionless!!
Delightful Month! the loveliest, fairest,
Most grateful of the circling year—
Within thy course HER birth thou bearest
HER birth to us so fondly dear!
Oh oft upon this thrice blest day
The smile has mingled with the tears
Which joys self could not laugh away—
For SHE to whom belong
The birthdays jest the birthday song
SHE was not here!!²
But now no more the pensive sigh
Disturbs the joyful hour
And the live long day beams happily
Where never now afflictions lower–
The shadowy form of mournful sadness
Fades neath the fairy touch of gladness
And young eyed Peace like the soft breath of even
Smiles sweetly from the mild blue Heav'n

Accept my verse my dearest Arabel
The little all that verse can thus express
Accept the lay from her who loves thee well
Accept the off'ring that would strive to bless!
My Babes, my sister gentlest, dearest
Accept my lowly lay
For thou inspirest me and cheerest!
I ask not glory or a name
I sigh not for the wreaths of fame
But—one sweet smile of thine!!

                    Your ever affectionately attached
                              Ba–

Publication: None traced.
Manuscript: Pierpont Morgan Library.

1. Her seventh birthday.
2. A reference to Arabella's absence from Hope End on previous birthdays.

109. EDWARD MOULTON-BARRETT (BROTHER) TO EBB

[London]
July 7.th 1820

My ever dearest Ba

I am afraid you will think me inconscionably stupid when I tell you that I can give you no information with regard to the interesting yet detestable SECRET COMMITTEE[1] except what you must have already heard, and the only breath of news that I can collect to regale poor dying Ba; is that *her* counsel desired the day before yesterday to be heard in her defence but the House refused to hear them at the same time promising that yesterday they *should* be heard and yesterday M[r] Brough[a]m and M[r] Denman made speeches[.] I have not yet seen the paper for to day and therefore cannot tell you any thing about them. I doubt their effects very much in the House but I think they will certainly make a great impression amongst the people as they will tend to proove more forcibly her innocence and their guilt in charging an innocent person with such crimes as they have accused her of! They have already dropped the charges of forgery and murder; do you not think that they who attempt to accuse any person, much more their Queen upon English ground of what they knew them not to be guilty ought to suffer the same punishment as he whom they accused would have suffered had he been guilty and prooved so. Nothing more is to be done at present in the House of Commons and the bill must pass through the House of Lords before any thing *can* be done. In my energetically enthusiastic opinion she stands but a poor chance of escaping from the shot of these experienced menslayers such as Castlereigh and Canning innocent as she is they will find some means of finding her guilty if she is really guilty she deserves but I would rather have the guilty escape unpunished than that such proceedings as these should pass unnoticed in England no if they *do* give the unjust sentence guilty! let her throw herself upon the mercy of her countrymen at large, though english justice may have flown from the hearts heads and hands of such men as Castlereigh and Sydmouth it still lingers in the breasts of the people Oh yes! *"The laurel though faded still is there."* M[r] M[c] Swiney was here yesterday and was so kind as to set me lessons both in Latin and Greek and promised to be here to day to hear me. In your next letter pray tell me what are your reasons for not thinking the pamplet [*sic*] written by him. Granny sends you her best love and gives you ten thousand thanks for your letter. Give our best love and kisses to every body round

Believe me my dearest Ba
Your affec[t] Brother
E M Barrett.

Publication: None traced.
Manuscript: Edward R. Moulton-Barrett.

1. This and following references are to the *cause célèbre* of 1820, the trial of Queen Caroline. Caroline Amelia Elizabeth (1768–1821), second daughter of Charles William Ferdinand, Duke of Brunswick, had married George, Prince of Wales on 8 April 1795, but had lived apart from him, on the Continent, since 1814. Upon the death of George III and the accession of her husband, she returned to England on 6 June 1820. Two days later, a secret committee of the House of Lords was appointed to investigate charges against her of adultery. Following the report of the committee, the Prime Minister, the Earl of Liverpool, proposed on 5 July "A Bill to deprive her Majesty, Caroline Amelia Elizabeth, of the title, prerogatives, rights, privileges, and pretensions of Queen-Consort of this realm, and to dissolve the marriage between his Majesty and the said Queen." The effort against the Queen stirred high feelings, both in and out of Parliament, but came to no clear-cut conclusion. She was, however, excluded from the coronation of her husband, George IV, on 19 July 1821. She died on 7 August of that year. The Queen was popular with the public, who for the most part thought her innocent of the charges.

The Queen appointed Henry Peter Brougham (1778–1868) her attorney-general, and Thomas Denman (1779–1854) her solicitor-general. Other references are to Viscount Castlereagh (1769–1822), George Canning (1770–1827) and Viscount Sidmouth (1757–1844).

EBB wrote an unfinished poetic drama ("Oh! why so sad") on Caroline's 1814 departure from England (see *Reconstruction*, D743). It can be found in *HUP*, I, 150–161.

---

110. EBB TO GEORGE GOODIN MOULTON-BARRETT

To my sweet George
On his birthday
Hope End July 15.th 1820. [1]

Where Helicons soft streamlets glide
Oer the gently blooming shore
Rolling its pure sparkling tide
Its sweet rasplendant [*sic*] silv'ry fountain
Softly murmuringly oer
The flowery turf of that blest mountain!
And near, where those pure waters gush
The margin of that heavenly river
The sweetly budding flow'rets blush
Breathing incense thus, for ever.!!
She stood aloft, the Goddess Queen
With downcast eye and pensive mien;
The muse who loves the tender sigh
The tear which trembles in the eye
In all the sympathy of woe!
Twas hers to swell the mournful heart
Dispair grief sorrow to impart
And bid the pure drop flow—
Within her lovely hand she bore

The soul inspiring lyre!
But ah! in HER cold grasp no more
Those strings had power to fire!
The lay no longer now beguiled
But ofttimes oer the silver wire
The wind abruptly broke,
But in that thrilling chord awoke
A strain so desolately wild,
That all appalled the Sisters stand
And none dare snatch it from her hand!

2

For as Calliope lay sleeping
Rest upon the soft turf seeking,
Urania from her sacred breast
Snatched the celestial lyre—
No spirit in that hour of rest
The injured Maid could fire
Nor did she ope her heavy eyes
Till that pale Muse had ta'en the glorious prize!

3

And thus she stood and boldly dared
(Tho weak, unarmed, and unprepared)
That bright celestial sacred throng
With steady look of stern command
To tune upon those strings a song
Or snatch it from her hand!
In haste, abashed, they backward drew
Till instant from the trembling throng
An airy form now trips along
And oer the green turf flew!!
Life sparkled in that radiant eye
Pale melancholys foe
And as that bright glance flashes by
Oh who would think of woe?
And oer her shoulders fair the ambiant tresses flow!

4

She siezed she grasped the sacred lyre
And swept the echoing strings
Those notes the joyous sisters fire
And all Parnassus sings!

"I come from those delightful glades
Where ne'er I meet alloy
I come from Hope End's fragrant shades
Upon a blest employ
Sisters I come from thence, my name is Joy!
I come not sisters to oppress!
For ah! tis Georgy's birth to day
I come to celebrate and bless
Then all your might display
And wake the song!
Call happiness and blue eyed pleasure
And hope and gladness without measure
A festive throng!
Bless my George and oer his head
Delight and heavenly blessings shed
Awake the song!"
The strain was hushed yet echo lingers
And air enchanted floats—

Around her fairy fingers
To catch those last pure dying notes!
My George farewell the lay's no more
Accept, I once must beg, my humble strain,
Thy Sisters lowly verse is past, is oer—
And yet a Sister's love a Sisters's prayers remain!!

Your affectionate Ba.

Address, on integral page: Master G G Barrett.
Docket, in unidentified hand: July 1820.
Publication: None traced.
Manuscript: Huntington Library.

1. His fourth birthday.

111. EBB TO HENRY MOULTON-BARRETT

Ode
On my sweet Henry's
birthday
Hope End August. 1820. [1]

Goddess of the gentle eye
Meekest nymph, Humility

Hope End: View from the Lower Pond

Hope End: View from the Deer Park

To thee belong
The modest burden of my song—!
In vain Euterpe's fingers
Would strike the echoing lyre,—
The purest best note lingers
Mutely on the trembling wire
The powerless tones would die away
Like Eve's resigned & faintest ray
Or like the bubble on the River
Which dances now—then bursts for ever!
Without thine aid
Divinest Maid!!!.
For at the magic of thy sway
The lowly unassuming lay
Triffling, may please affections ear
And Taste perhaps may list, & not disdainful hear!
And thou dear Boy let one sweet smile
Upon thy Sisters efforts beam
And tho unconsciously beguile
The labours of her humble theme
And let not PATS, or TURNCOATS deem
Those labours unrepaid;
If from those laughing lashes play
One sweet rewarding ray
Of glad applause . . or kindred pleasure
Or joy unceasing, without measure,
To glad her lowly lay!!

                        Your ever affectionate
                        Ba.

Publication: None traced.
Manuscript: Armstrong Browning Library.

1. His second birthday fell on 27 July 1820.

---

112. EBB TO EDWARD MOULTON-BARRETT (BROTHER)

[Hope End]
[August 1820][1]

My own beloved Bro,
    I must compliment you on the excellence of your birthday

effusion– It possesses a depth of feeling and an elegance of diction which none of your former productions have betrayed in so eminent a degree– The last four lines are so very good that I might almost imagine the didactic spirit of Pope guided your pen– The great fault "for all have faults"[2] is the too frequent repetition of the word "D⟨A⟩Y"[3] for which you might easily substitute "year" or "hour"–

Yours my dearest Friend
with the fondest affection
EBB—

Address, on integral page: Master Barrett—
Publication: None traced.
Manuscript: Berg Collection.

1. This letter probably refers to a twelve-line birthday ode (MS copy in "Poems by EBB"; SD350) written by Bro to his brother Henry and dated August 1820. He used the word "day" three times. The last four lines read as follows: "Sweet Henry! may this day be spent / In joy and Mirth, and Merry play / In happiness and in Content / Which last *must* make a happy day!"
2. Cf. Goldsmith's *The Goodnatur'd Man* (1768), act II, sc. 1.
3. Ink blot.

---

113. EDWARD MOULTON-BARRETT (BROTHER) TO EBB

an accident[1]   [London]
Septimo die Octobris [1820][2]

Mea carissima Ba

Duas a te accepi litteras ex quibus una mandata mei delectissimi patris continent, quæ me exire a scholâ prohibent etiam ad ludos spectandos nisi cum urbem venerit et domum alicujus nunquam adire cum mea proava in urbe non sit. Me valde piget quód tuam epistolam citius non accepi ut aliquod periculum incurrerem potius quam meo patri displiceam. *Dominus* M.ᶜSwiney, cujus in me amicitiæ semper memor ero cùm scholam venisset me videre perspexit me tussi et frigore laborare et dixit se venturum saturno die scire quomodo valebam et cúm me pejus vidisset putabat esse melius venire domum Dominæ Williams[3] ut medicum consultarem qui dixit me non posse redire sine magno periculo utpote qui haberem aliquantum febris et magnum dolorem pectoris séd redeam cras. Vale

Mea delictissima soror.

My dearest Ba
    I received your kind letters this morning from M^r M^c who called
here as usual to hear me my lessons (for that he has done ever since I
have been at home so that I have not lost any thing of the schools
lessons) I thank you a thousand times for them, particularly as they are
Post Paid. When M^r M^c called on wedbesday week last at the Charter
House to see me I had a cold with a pain in my chest of which both he
and I thought but slightly and therefore did not take particula⟨r⟩ notice
of it however on his calling on saturday after he thought it so bad that
he determined upon taking me somewhere to get advice and not
knowing where else to take me and having no place of his own to
receive me as he would wish we went to Mrs W.^{3} where Mr Green^4 saw
me and declared to M^r M^c who asked him particularly that if he had
not brought me home an inflammation of the lungs ⟨★★★⟩

Publication: None traced.
Manuscript: Edward R. Moulton-Barrett.

Translation: Seventh day of October. My dearest Ba, I received two letters from you, one
of which contained the orders of my most esteemed father, which prohibited me from
leaving school, even to watch games, except when he came to the city, and from ever
going to someone's home when my grandmother was not in town. I am really disgusted
that I did not receive your letter sooner as I might have met with some danger of displeasing
my father in some manner. Master McSwiney, whose friendship toward me I shall always
remember, saw when he came to the school to visit me that I laboured with a cough and
cold and said that he would return on Saturday to see how I was doing, and when he saw
I was worse, he thought it would be better if I went to the house of Mistress Williams^3 to
consult a doctor, who said I could not return without great danger seeing that I had some
fever and severe chest pain, but I may return tomorrow. Goodbye my most delightful sister.

    1. Explaining an ink blot at the top of the page.
    2. Bro began attending Charterhouse in 1820. He was elsewhere (with EBB) at this
particular time of the year in 1821; had he written the letter in a still later year he would
have mentioned his brother Sam, who entered the school in 1822.
    3. Mrs. Elizabeth Barrett Williams (*née* Waite), who lived near Mrs. Moulton in London.
Mrs. Williams (1754–1834) had had a long relationship "without benefit of clergy" with
Mrs. Moulton's brother, Samuel Barrett (1765–94), and had borne him four sons. Bro was
taken to her house instead of his grandmother's, because Elizabeth Moulton was out of town.
    4. Possibly Dr. Jonathan Green (1788?–1864), of Gt. Marlborough Street, who qualified
in 1810.

114. EBB TO CHARLES JOHN MOULTON-BARRETT

To my ⟨belo⟩ved Storm.
On his birthday—
Hope End December 1820.[1]

Wake Muses wake! and oer the echoing strings
Of the melodious pipe or soft tuned lute
Your gay, light fingers fly on fancys wing
Nor bid the voice of joy be mute!!—
A Smile, young eyed Hope on the sweet lyre flings
Like pleasures rainbow on youths soft skies.
Mirth from her couch of roses springs
And Heaven seems to smile in the light of her eyes!—

Awake from sleep's long trance
Nymphs of the flood and Spirits unseen
Fauns of the wild woods glance
Joy, upon the beautiful scene
And sylvan Satyrs dance!——

And thou my Storm accept my humble lay
Tis all, my child, a sister can bestow
Then let one sweet smile from those bright eyes play
Nor knit thy brows and proudly answer "no"!
I will not bless thee it were vain to bless—
Tho justly dear & cherished, love, thou art
For how can words the souls own thoughts express
And what can speak the language of the heart?

                         Your own affec.te Ba–

Address and date, on integral page: Dec.r 28.th 1820. / To Ba's own Storm who is so dear
to all of us and who merits our affection by his industry and his cleverness!—— /
Long live the Queen!
Publication: Marks, pp. 323–324 (in part).
Manuscript: Wellesley College.

1. His sixth birthday fell on 28 December 1820.

115. EBB TO THOMAS CAMPBELL[1]

[?Hope End]
[ca. 1821]

M.r Editor, There has appeared in a former series of your magazine an
article under the very comprehensive title of "Talking and Talkers"[2]

the author of which seems a strong advocate for that vulgar mode of communication the tongue!!– Now though for the last forty years I have been universally remarked as a silent man whose thoughts were reflected back into his own bosom, and decidedly hostile to chatterers blabbers and the whole multitude of Talkers, yet when I beheld that (oh the depravity of humanity) that six pages of a public magazine were employed in striving to immortalize that contemptible race and to vitiate the public taste like Esop with divers dishes composed entirely of tongues, I consider it high time to immerge from solitude, wake like a giant from his slumbers!——

My friends are astonished at my resolution to appear in your pages so inconsistent with my usual habits of silence & peaceful obscurity but some sacrifice is necessary for the wellfare of society and even I will not shrink from the painful duty!! Better oh better that one man should not hold his peace than that the whole race of men women & children should stun sense & scare reflection by their rantings. For what else can be the language of the tongue! which springs spontanously [*sic*] from the lips like mushrooms from the dunghill niether nurtured by the glorious sun of intellect or by the soft showers of reflection! After the usual course of sylogisms and logical reasoning this is my determination . . namely not only to appear in the horizon of literature but also to enter into society proclaiming the doctrines of Pythagoras and fully prepared to cope with the talkative and aver him into silence!——

The mind M! Editor is a mystery which foils the eye of genius & the ingenuity of the philosopher! Such depth, such reason and yet such perspicacity! A thousand links A thousand emotions which seem like the colours of the Iris[3] all combined yet all separate———all melting into one another yet all distinct! Imagination like the phantasmagoria flings hues, so exquisite so flowing upon this mystery of God while reflection an unflattering mirror arranges and receives the lovely picture! For without reflection fancy is but a day star which shoots in vain its ineffectual fire—she is but a beautiful woman loaded with jewels but devoid of that grace & that simplicity which embellish perfection!——

There are ideas inexpressible unutterable indescribable which rush across the memory—bright emanations from the soul like the mysterious comet!! There are thoughts which silence more eloquently expresses than All the pomp of words!! Thoughts which the mind alone can comprehend—too lofty—too exalted for the powers of hyperbole—too sublime for rhetoric to reach!——!

Oh for the glorious understanding of Plato & Longinus Oh for the pure & magnificent mind of Homer! If their works excite even in these ages admiration, enthusiasm rapture what must have been their secret thoughts their aerial visions—their splendid glimpses into immortality??

Ossian ex[c]*laims* "There is in my bosom a power which ye cannot hear."[4]

And yet M[r.] Editor probably you may agree with me when I remark that perhaps Homer had done better if he had transferred the following beautiful description of Menelaus to Ulysses instead of making the disciple of Minerva a votary to guarrulity!

Παῦρα μεν, ἀλλὰ μαλα λιγεως, επει ου πολυμυθος

Ουδ αφαμαρτοεπης, η και γενει υστερος ηεν. book 3[d]. 137.[5]

"Words pay no debts"[6] says Shakespeare with great truth!

There is certainly no greater tormentor than a great talker!!—Oh the horrors of being awakened from a philosophic reverie by a pun! or in the midst of mental composition being startled by the laugh of folly or the quotation of the Pedant! Unfortunately for me M[r.] Editor my whole family are curst with this detestable propensity to the use of the tongue!! You may imagine the agonies I endure!! But no! you cannot! They are above the conception of most lofty imagination! To be always in the same situation with poor Horace when he exclaims in the bitterness of his heart "Fugit improbus ac me Sub cultro linquit!".[7]

These are indeed some few of those miseries which language fails to describe and which can only be adequately felt by the mind of the unhappy sufferer!——

Silence it must be allowed is the strongest proof of true wisdom for what says Sallust!

["]Satis eloquentiæ sapientiæ parum"[8] is the remark of the great & learned historian! That a reflective mind is seldom a communicative one is an observation which few can confute for what is reflection but depth of thought and how can depth of thoughts exist—when the tongue is ever in motion and when the ears are open to the eternal & monstrous rattle of the great talker—! In fact reflection and chattering are sworn foes. Mankind cannot unite them for *Reason* the Parent of the former has a decided antipathy to the latter! I M[r.] Editor have passed most of my days in silence refraining both from the gloomy & forbidding conversation of the pedant and the frivolous chit chat of the Drawing room!! The offspring of my meditations and mental commune is this: that untill Mankind adopt the doctrines of Pythagoras . . until they abjure all the different sects of talkers they will never reach the glorious goal of heavenly perfection!! It is to reveal this sublime truth that I tear aside the veil which till now has separated me from society! it is for this gentle readers that I intrude myself in your attention!!!— sequestring from me all

That time acquaintance custom & condition
Made tame & most familiar to my nature

& here to do you service am become
As new into the world!–[9]

I know not if amidst the everlasting din of tattlers my admonitions will be heard or whether they will die away like the prophetic words of Cassandra unmarked & unremembered. If this former glorious event should take place then shall my name be extolled by my cotemporarys And immortalized in "ages yet unborn"[10] if on the contrary my voice be disregarded I shall again retire into the privacy of my own closet . . forsake the pen forever . . lay my spectacles on the dusty shelf and seat myself for life in my old arm chair, philosophically to ruminate and silently contemplate the bright visions of that future world, where niether talking or talkers will assail our ears but where all will be reflection, silence & wisdom—!

I am Sir
Your constant reader
Silentius . .

"Hunc neque dira venena nec hosticus auferret ensis
Nec laterum dolor aut tussis nec tarda podagra
Garrulus hunc quando consumet cumque. Loquaces
Si sapiat, vitet"[11]

HOR—

Publication: None traced.
Source: EBB's draft copy, Berg Collection.

1. The reference to "Talking and Talkers" identifies the recipient as the editor of *The New Monthly Magazine.* Reference to "a former series" dates this letter after the commencement of the 2nd series, under the editorship of Thomas Campbell (1790–1858), in 1821. Although Campbell continued as editor for some years, the style of handwriting in this letter points to the earliest year of his tenure.
2. An article "On Talking and Talkers" was printed in the first series of *The New Monthly Magazine* in October 1820 (no. 81, vol. 14, pp. 395–400).
3. Rainbow.
4. A paraphrase of lines 147–148 of Ossian's poem "Oinammorhul":
   "Within this breast is a silent voice
   (It reaches not the ear of strangers)"
5. "[One of] few [words], but clear, since he was not a man of lengthy or rambling speech" (*Iliad*, III, 214–215).
6. *Troilus and Cressida*, III, 2, 55.
7. Horace, *Satires*, I, ix, 73–74: "The rascal runs away and leaves me under the knife."
8. *The War With Catiline*, V, 5: "he possessed a certain eloquence, but little discretion."
9. *Troilus and Cressida*, III, 3, 9.
10. Pope, *The First Epistle of the Second Book of Horace, Imitated* (1737), line 228.
11. Horace, *Satires*, I, ix, 31–34. The verse (including the final phrase "simul atque adolverit ætas," omitted by EBB) is translated as:
    "No wicked drug shall prove his end,
    No foeman's sword shall death him send,

[ca. 1821]

No cough or pleurisy or gout—
A chatterbox shall talk him out:
And if he's wise, as he grows old,
He'll steer quite clear of talkers bold."

---

116. EBB TO SAMUEL MOULTON-BARRETT (UNCLE)

[?Hope End]
[ca. 1821][1]

"Bella horrida bella"[2]
VIR
"And Aaron said 'let not the anger of my lord wax hot' "[3]—
Exodus

"Woe to thee rash & unrelenting chief
In vain thou heapest ashes on thy head"[4]

for the day of vengeance is arrived, the hour of retribution draweth
nigh and as Shakespeare says

"Give passion words—the rage that does not speak
Whispers the o'er fraught heart & bids it break"[5]

Tho I have had ample room & time for reflection I hardly know
whether it will be more prudent to vent my anger in empty words or
wait till I see you in order that vengeance may take the shape of a box
on the ear or a shower bath! Shakespeare exclaims—

"I am not yet so low
But I may reach your eyes"[6]—

However on second thoughts & second thoughts have PROVED BEST
ON MANY OCCASIONS (vide the attack on you) I have at length made up
my mind to thunder in your ears cannons charged only with the
gunpowder of oratory which may give you the headache for a
twelvemonth tho it may not prove the instrument of your death! My
dear member of Parliament you are all this time I dare say hanging like
Mahomets coffin between Earth & Heaven with astonishment &
anxiety[7]— Aristotle comes very near your case in the following passage
παντα[8] &c!——

And you really have had the desperate assurance & affrontery not
only to insult Derrydown[9] by talking to him about petticoats but
moreover to abuse me for not sending the Hereford Paper!——

Monster of iniquity! if I believed you to be half as bad as I dare
say you are I should have sent you a paper which is a Tory

publication—servile as the dust we tread on—& patronized by my Lord Somers!

Well! I forgive you—I forgive you! only write instantly and thus I take leave of you in the words of Shakespeare– "Come shake hands! I'm sorry I beat thee but mind another time keep a civil tongue in thine head!——[""][10]

Your dutiful niece
Ba—

Publication: None traced.

Source: EBB's draft copy, Folger Shakespeare Library.

1. Conjectural dating based on handwriting and style of expression, and the fact that the letter was written some time after Samuel Moulton-Barrett's election to Parliament in March 1820.

2. "War dreadful war" (Vergil's *Æneid*, VI, 86).

3. Exodus, 32:22.

4. A slight misquotation from Byron's *The Bride of Abydos* (1813), II, 651–652.

5. *Macbeth*, IV, 3, 209–210, also slightly misquoted.

6. *A Midsummer Night's Dream*, III, 2, 297–298, misquoted.

7. Cf. *Hudibras*, III, ii, 602, by Samuel Butler (1612–80).

8. "All; everything." The passage EBB had in mind cannot be identified from this one word.

9. Not identified.

10. *The Tempest*, III, 2, 111–113, misquoted.

117. EBB TO UNIDENTIFIED CORRESPONDENT

[?Hope End]
[ca. 1821][1]

What honors that
"But tedious waste of time, to sit and hear
So many hollow compliments, and lies,
Outlandish Flatteries?"[2]
MILTON

"Davus) Non hercle intelligo! Simo) Non? hem! Davus) Non!
Davus sum, non Œdipus"—[3]
TER[ENCE]

Mr Editor,

I am one of those unfortunate beings who are too conscientious to be happy, and who have sacrificed the world at the eternal altar of Truth. I have pursued the unprofitable meteors of ideal pleasure, admired the glittering kaleidescope of Fashion and gazed with anxious expectation on the bodiless visions of enjoyment, but Mr Editor I have turned with listless impatience from the animated scene, for in my search after happiness, sincerity has faded from my sight. It had never been my intention to lay the tale of my misfortunes before the public eye, but yesterday morning, finding at my booksellers a number of your most valuable publication, I have endeavoured to awaken myself from the constitutional indifference, which has lately siezed my intellectual powers, that the world may learn how disgusting to the votary of truth, is the prevailing taste for insincerity, and compliment.

> "Con arte ed inganno
> Si vive mezzo l'anno
> Con inganne et [*sic*] con arte
> Si vive l'altra parte"[4]

I do not however desire to stigmatize complimenters in general, it is the hyperbolical compliment that I would accuse, that universal rage for complimenting which renders it impossible for an old fashioned, plain spoken man like myself to pass thro' society without fixing on my unhappy shoulders the opprobrium of being a boor, or what perhaps is as bad . . a philosopher!— Nothing is composed of such delicate Materials as a compliment and it may not improperly be compared to the rainbow whose lovely tints cease to be exquisite when deprived of the reflecting rays of Candours bright and ineffable luminacy!—At least the *shadow* of truth should be conspicuous, for without it Praise ceases to please and must unavoidably disgust. When Pliny composed his magnificent "Panegericus Theodosio Augusto dictus" he displayed the whole depth of his Philosophical knowledge in that inimitable declaration,—"Neminem magis laudare Imperatorem decet, quam quem minus necesse est".[5] Preceded by such a sentiment the fine Panegeric that follows could not appear extravagant, and could not produce disgust even in the mind of the elegant Theodosius; for praise only sinks into adulation when it is not spontaneous. Shakespeare might have intended a satire on extravagant compliment in the well known dialogue between Viola and Olivia in the "Twelfth Night"—

> Olivia) "Come to what is important, I forgive you the praise.
> Viola) Alas! I took great pains to study it, and tis poetical!
> Olivia) It is the more like to be feigned, I pray you keep it in—"[6]

Bacon says "There be so many false points of praise, that a Man may justly hold it in suspect—"[7] The remark is philosophical, but perhaps the Philosopher himself was not invulnerable to the irresistable might of vanity! as Pope once said "It is vanity which makes the rake at twenty, the worldly man at forty, and the retired man at sixty".[8] I always admired the sincerity of Sir Godfrey Kneller, when he frankly acknowledged his fallibility, and human weakness. "I cant do so well"

exclaimed he to the immortal Poet, who was in silence gazing on the
beautiful delineations of the Artist's pencil, "I cant do so well as I
should do unless you flatter me a little; pray flatter me M.ʳ Pope, you
know I love to be flattered"——⁹

Swift was not perhaps a man of exquisite refinement, or peculiar
delicacy, but when a member of the present adulatory school assured
him, that he loved him better than his nearest relatives and best friends,
silence alone expressed the Deans disgust who afterwards exclaimed
"The man's a fool"—! And yet when Rollin assailed Swift with a letter
of elegant compliment, he was not displeased for while his vanity was
flattered by it, his good sense was unoutraged!¹⁰

The philosopher would judge of causes from effects, and perhaps
if we analyse the present rage for compliment we shall discover that the
evil originates from the increasing vanity of humanity. "Omnia
vanitas"¹¹ indeed! As a Philanthropist, M.ʳ Editor, I should desire to
believe that that Christian precept, "Do as you would be done by."
occasions the multiplicity of Adulators, but I acknowledge also with
due deference that the exalted hyperboles, and complimentary episodes
ushered in upon the fashionable stage, are even far above my limited
powers of comprehension. I am naturally diffident, and most willingly
do I believe that the present race of mortals are far above me both in
capacity of intellect, and elasticity of imagination, for certainly my
mental powers will expand no further and my fancy is incapable of
soaring higher. But the words of Cicero hang in consoling sweetness on
my ear "Non est enim parum cognosse, sed etiam in parum cognito
turpe atque diu perseverasse stulti est".¹² I do not desire M.ʳ Editor to
persevere in my ignorance, and if it be in your power to initiate me in
these mysteries of the complimentary orgies my obligation will be
eternal. But alas! how can you reconcile this constant, and habitual
practice of deception with the beautiful simplicity which dignifies
Truths untutored tongue? How can the glittering web of complimentary
ingenuity bear unbroken the holy, and pure drops of sinceritys
translucent dew? I can behold dipravity without scorn, audacity
without resentment, folly without contempt, but I cannot gaze on
deceptions refined tissue of elegant untruths, uninfluenced by feelings
of inexpressible indignation, and unutterable disgust!! I have laid
before you M.ʳ Editor the sentiments of one, unfortunately addicted to
the weak propensity of being vulgarly candid, though I sincerely
confess that I consider my own case hopeless. For while the world is
vain it will not want Flatterers, and while Deception yet cowers over the
earth she will not want an altar. I can no longer even hope to behold
Insincerity unmasked: Friendship and Antipathy have changed liveries,

Malevolence stalks abroad under the bright semblance of a smile and
Hate grins applause with affable serenity. And yet why should I
despair? Truth does not turn from me for ever; even now she
sometimes gleams in momentary splendour, a sunbeam on a stormy
sea. For instance as somebody says,

"Who hangs himself or beats his brains
The devil's in him, if HE[13] feigns"[14]–

EBB.

Publication: None traced.
Source: EBB's fair copy, Folger Shakespeare Library. A draft copy is also at the Folger
Library, and two incomplete copies exist, one at Bibliotheca Bodmeriana and the other
with Philip Kelley. All three of these copies vary in differing degrees from the text
reproduced here.

1. The cover sheet accompanying Philip Kelley's draft copy bears EBB's notation:
"Essays, poems and Translations . . . written in the years 1820 and 1821."
2. *Paradise Regained* (1671), IV, 122–125.
3. *Andria* (166 B.C.), act I, sc. 2: Davos) "By Hercules, I don't follow you." Simo)
"You don't? Well!" Davos) "I don't. I'm Davos, Not Œdipus."
4. Giovan Maria Cecchi (1518–87), *L'Esaltazione della Croce* (1585), act IV, sc. 9:
"By art and swindling here / Men live for half the year; / By swindling and by art / They
live the other part."
5. EBB is confused; Pliny's *Panegyricus* was addressed to the Emperor Trajan, not to
Theodosius. The passage she quotes appears in the *Panegyricus Theodosio Augusto dictus*
of Latinus Pacatus Drepanius, written in A.D. 391 (*MPL*, 13, 480). It translates as: "It is
fitting to praise no emperor more than the one to whom less praise is necessary."
6. *Twelfth Night*, I, 5, 192–194.
7. "Of Praise" (1597) in *The Essays of Francis Bacon.*
8. Samuel Weller Singer's edition of Joseph Spence's *Anecdotes, Observations, and
Characters, of Books and Men. Collected from the Conversation of Mr. Pope* (1820, Sec.
V, 203).
9. *Op. cit.*, Sec. IV, 180. Kneller (1646–1723) settled permanently in England in 1678,
after being commissioned to make a portrait of Charles II; he subsequently became the
principal court painter, and ten reigning sovereigns sat for him. After his death, Pope wrote
the epitaph for his monument in Westminster Abbey.
10. *Op. cit.*, Sec VII, 256.
11. "All is vanity."
12. "For it is no small thing to have understood, but to have continued in that little
knowledge shamelessly and long is the mark of a fool" (*De Inventione*, II, cap. 3).
13. Underscored three times.
14. Samuel Butler's *Hudibras*, Part II (1663), I, 497–498, slightly misquoted.

118. EBB TO CHARLES JOHN MOULTON-BARRETT

[Hope End]
[ca. March 1821]¹

My dearest Sir,
    Neglect you? not for worlds! but at the same time let me tell you that I accuse you of shameful dereliction (tell Puppy to explain that long word) from your political principles! "How is that pray Ba"? you will exclaim with your ugly little nose cocked up and your eyes on fire with indignation! Why M! Storm I will tell you how that comes to pass! Because Sir you have not obeyed my positive commands. For this half hour have I been employed in examining the list of prisoners in the newspapers and have been reading with a penetrating eye the names of those condemned to the gallows! Of course I expected to see "Master Charles John Barrett aged 6 years" at the head of them! But no! you were not even mentioned in the papers as being taken up for a slight riot—for a triffling row—or even for breaking my Lord Castlereaghs kitchen window!— Pray Sir what is the use of singing Wallace till you are hoarse²—what is the use of professing radical principles if you do not act up to them? A sudden thought has struck me!! I really believe that you are afraid of being hanged! If you ARE, let me tell you Sir that you are unworthy of the cause! Nothing is more pleasant than that little tickling sensation about the throat caused by the friction of a rope! And then such a delightful view from the top of Newgate!³ I hope this consideration will have some weight with you if you are not influenced by any nobler sentiment and I trust that I shall ere long read this paragraph in the newspapers!
    "This morning Master Storm Barrett a young man of prepossessing appearance was launched into eternity! He was remarkable by the *air degageè*⁴ with which he stepped his head into the noose"–

Adieu my dear Fellow
Your affec.ᵗᵉ Ba——

Address, on integral page: Master Storm Barrett–
Publication: None traced.
Manuscript: Pierpont Morgan Library.

1. Storm reached age six on 28 December 1820. He apparently was in London at the time of this letter, and letter 125 shows that he was there in March 1821.
2. From the context of the letter, it is assumed that the reference here is to Thomas Wallace (1768–1844), Member of Parliament 1790–1827, an advocate of various reforms.

3. The infamous prison of the City of London, finally abandoned in 1880 and demolished in 1902.
4. "Off-hand manner."

---

119. EBB TO EDWARD MOULTON-BARRETT (FATHER)

[Hope End]
[ca. March 1821][1]

My ever ever dearest Puppy,

Sams letter to Mama recieved yesterday was certainly the bearer of a severe disappointment to me as it contained the tidings of your being yet UNCERTAIN whether to allow me the long anticipated happiness of beholding my beloved Bro, Granny, Trip yourself and sweet Storm or to withhold the delightful boon!– When I showed you Sams letters in which he declared an intention of bringing down his own carriage in order to return with *me*, you did not object, and I fondly believed that a kind consent was implied by your silence! I am undeceived, and am I actuated by presumption when I thus come forward to throw myself on your mercy? I believe I am not, for whilst I supplicate a smile I will submit to a disappointing frown without a murmur, tho not perhaps without a pang! So thoroughly am I convinced of my ever dearest Papa's affection for me, and so perfectly am I aware of the superiority of his judgement that I would not complain tho the awful fiat were to pass his lips, and yet while my fate is not decided I may HOPE, and I may sollicit a merciful sentence!

You may perhaps exclaim with Apollo "Magna petis BA" but you cannot add "Non est mortale quod optas"[2]– Consider my dearest Puppy that by ONE smile accompanied by that politest of all little words—"Yes", you may make me more happy, more grateful than all the pomp of Ciceronian eloquence can express! Oh! do not, pray do not, refuse! at least do not be angry with me for pressing on you a boon which has been so long, so joyfully anticipated!

Your grand objection is on account of my singing!! I promise you most faithfully and on my HONOR, that if you allow those features to relax into a becoming smile I will practise carefully every day in London my "do re fa" which if I do Mrs Orme[3] ⟨. . .⟩[4] thinks will even IMPROVE my voice? I also promise most faithfully that on my return home I will turn all my energies towards understanding, & excelling in, both vocal and PRACTICAL Music!

When I *promise* my dearest Puppy I do not consider myself SLIGHTLY BOUND but under a sacred obligation to fulfil it!

Thus have I offered every thing in my power in order to obtain that fascinating solitary word "YES"! I have bid as high as my purse will admit! Oh let the kind, the affectionate Auctioneer exclaim "Going . . going . . gone."!

My heart whispers that you will not refuse, that you will not turn from me in anger! My dearest, dearest Puppy grant my request! ONE week in London! Let me not be acused of presumption in thus entreating so urgently for a petition to which perhaps you annex no importance! But to me my beloved Puppy it seems worthy to ma⟨ke⟩ "*worlds* CONTEND"– Imagine yourself my age once more, how your heart would beat with joy at the prospect of an excursion to the metropolis! Have I tormented you? If I have, oh! forgive me, and let the kind verdict be "Guilty but to be recomended to mercy"——

Your always affectionate
and fondly attached Child
Ba–

Publication: HUP, I, xlv–xlvii.
Manuscript: Berg Collection.

1. Conjectural dating based on EBB's disappointment at not going to London during Charles John's visit.
2. Cf. Ovid, *Metamorphoses*, II, 54–56: "thou askest too much, Phæthon" and "not for mortals is that thou askest."
3. Governess to the children at Hope End. Her forte seems to have been music.
4. Two illegible words, covered by ink blots.

120. EDWARD MOULTON-BARRETT (BROTHER) TO
EBB & HENRIETTA MOULTON-BARRETT

[London]
[March 1821]¹

To—
Ba and Henrietta
on
their birthday——

I've heard, or seen it writ, I know not where,
In Homer, Virgil, Ovid, or Lempriere.²
Some give these worthy gentlemen the lie,
And say they dont believe't, no more do I;
But whether meant in earnest or in fun
It answers still my purpose, and all's one.
And thus the story runs, one day was found
By prying boy, on tree top or the ground
Hid in a well strawed barn, on thick grown rushes
Perhaps in blackbird's nest, perhaps in thrushes
A *largish* egg, (I hope the term is granted
One cannot always find the word that's wanted
I'd bring authorities of our first shining
Poetic lights, who never stick at coining,)
But to resume the thread of my discourse,
This egg was going to aid the second course,
The ready cook applied the spoon so well,
*That two large babies tumbled from the shell
But Cook enraged (such things were common) waddled
Away in rage and swore the egg was ADDLED
One was called Castor t'other Pollux, this
Is an example which I would not miss;
And therefore do include in this one sheet
The wish I lay at Ba's and Addle's feet.

EMB—

*This accident however saved, no doubt,
Alderman Somebody a fit of gout,
Eggs are inflammatory I've heard tell
Does Asculapius³ say so?—no Bell–

Address, on integral page: For / Ba and Co / Hope End / Ledbury.
Publication: None traced.
Manuscript: R.J.L. Altham.

1. Conjectural dating based on handwriting and these facts: there exists a different birthday ode from Bro to Henrietta for 1820, and Henrietta and EBB were not together at the time of their 1822 birthdays.
2. John Lemprière (1765–1824), compiler of *Bibliotheca Classica* (1788).
3. Æsculapius, son of Apollo, was the Greek god of medicine and healing.

---

121. EBB TO HENRIETTA MOULTON-BARRETT

[Hope End]

Ode
To my dearest Addles
On her birthday
March 4th 1821–[1]

The Minstels harp was quickly strung
And o'er those wires my ready fingers
In melancholy sadness hung!—!
The first sweet pensive note yet lingers
Within the silent snare of air!
My eye was raised to Heavens pure vale
Expectant, lest some Spirit there
Might breathe a sweet inspiring tale.!
It came at last! that heavenly lay
Upon my soul melodious state;—
So wild, so beauteous, it might seem
The memory of a Poets dream!
Bright as the dewy tears of day
The glorious numbers roll!!–

"Why Minstrel is thy harp so mute?–
Nay! strike once more a bolder strain!
Let not Urania's pensive lute
(Tho' deemed the fairest of the Nine)
Oerwhelm with sighing tones again
The splendid harmony of thine!
Crown the red bowl! and let the swelling note
Winged on the pinions of triumphant mirth
Upon the brilliant Heavens superior float
Proclaiming Hope End's joy and Addles' birth".

And thou my Addles, while th' awakened strings
Break into rapture, fired by smiling Bliss!

Thou, while Affections Muse untutored sings
The welcome of a day so dear as this,
Accept my verse! accept the humble line,
The prayer for *thee*, which moves thy Sisters breast!
May health, content, joy happiness be thine,
And may Heav'n smile while young Hope speaks the rest

Your always affec^te
Ba —

Address, on integral page: Miss H Barrett——
Publication: None traced.
Manuscript: Pierpont Morgan Library.

1. Her twelfth birthday.

---

122. ARABELLA MOULTON-BARRETT TO EBB

[Hope End]
[6 March 1821][1]

My ever dearest Ba
Once more is your birthday come I hope that you will have many
more What shall I do to oblige you on your birthday Last year I was
not here to rejoice your little party but now I am here to wish you many
happy returns of your birthday

your very affectionate
Arabell

Address, on integral page: To / dearest Ba / On her birthday.
Publication: None traced.
Manuscript: Myrtle Moulton-Barrett and Ronald A. Moulton-Barrett.

1. Conjectural dating based on handwriting and the fact that Arabella had been in
Worthing at the time of EBB's 1820 birthday.

---

123. GEORGE GOODIN MOULTON-BARRETT TO EBB

[Hope End]
[6 March 1821][1]

My dear Ba
I hope ou will let dear George kiss ou as he loves you too much
and he is for the good Queen happy turns ou birth day my dear Ba I am

very glad ou is for the Queen and ou say down king for he is very
naughty

Ou very dear
af[fectiona]te George

Address, on integral page: To s[w]eet dear Ba / with Georgy's / love.
Publication: None traced.
Manuscript: Berg Collection.

1. Conjectural dating based on the reference to the Queen. In the previous March,
Queen Caroline had not yet returned to England, to precipitate charges against her, and
she was no longer living in March, 1822.

---

124. HENRIETTA MOULTON-BARRETT TO EBB

[Hope End]
[6 March 1821][1]

My ever very dear Poêtess

This is your learned birthday. I am afraid you will not deign to
read this letter, but Oh what am I saying? when I think who you are
and what qualities you possess, I am afraid I am going mad; pray don't
take it as a compliment; I am sure you won't, as you know I love you
too much to think of such a thing; and I flatter myself that you love me
better than [to] think it is conceit. My love for you will never never
cease but this you know. I must use an old phrase, which is, with all my
heart and soul I wish you many returns of this ever happy day, which I
hope will last till the end of my happy day's. Good bye my dearest
Poêtess and always

Believe me your dear Addles.

This is to dearest sweetest Ba,
Who is as bright as any spar.
And is so very *very* dear to us,
That really we cannot help making a fuss.
So if dear Mama will us once excuse
We will take care to no one abuse.
But now my dearest Ba I must away,
For it will soon be the middle of the day.

Address, on integral page: To dearest Ba / On her ever happy birthday.
Publication: None traced.
Manuscript: Berg Collection.

1. In a series of birthday odes from Henrietta to EBB, none is dated 1821 or 1823. The quality of the handwriting places this letter in the earlier year.

---

125. EDWARD MOULTON-BARRETT (BROTHER) & DANIEL MCSWINEY TO EBB

[In Edward Moulton-Barrett's hand] [London]
March. 18.th 1821.

My ever dearest Ba

I am extremely sorry to have thus offended your *mightiness* to such a degree in not answering your enquiries about Silentius but I cannot ascertain at present from M[r] M[c]Swiney, much information concerning them, however he says that they desire to shorten it before they insert any of it. I hope you will in your next letter tell me whether you would concent to cutting short of poor Silentius which cost you so much trouble and concerning which you expended so many Elegant and complimentary phrases toward your humble Servant.[1] Wonders upon wonder well they will never cease M[r] M[c]Swiney and Miss Edwards again reconciled to each other he who but a fortnight ago had returned all her letters and picture this last week walked so many miles on purpose to see her. M[r] M[c] I and Papa have been so much engaged this evening with a latin verse (which after all turns out to be impossible to be done) that here I am after dinner before I can get on with your letter and therefore you must excuse the length of this letter however, *if possible* on Wedensday I will endeavour to make up for it by writing to you again. Last wedensday M[r] M[c]Swiney called upon me to tell the bad news to me (though perhaps you may acuse me of selfishness) of Papa's and Stormy's departure for dear Hope End and I leave you to guess my surprise and delight when, on calling for me on Saturday he told me that he was not gone. I am delighted to hear how well you are coming on with S[t] Paul and I think if you put your whole powers to it (which (however[2] you do, to whatever you undertake) you are sure of success. I completely approve of the plan of the mail[3] but I think when it is once altered it would be better to let it remain[.] M[r] M[c]Swiney begs me to leave him a little space as he wishes to write you a few lines, therefore for the present beleive me my dearest Ba

ever yours affectionately.
E M Barrett. –

[Continued by Mr. McSwiney]

My Dear Ba /

I was not a little astonished on reading your answer to Miss

Trepsack's letter to find that instead of *eulogizing* my recent *Heroism* you should assimulate it to the most ordinary rencontre among *ordinary men.* Know then, Miss Sauce-box that nothing has happened of late years so deserving of *Public approbation* or that has approached more nearly to the feats of your beloved Antients if you will except the Scene of Action. Drury lane, I confess is not the most rythmical term, but as you look to things not names, you will I trust reconsider the subject & ⟨give⟩ *my name* its proper locality in the Temple of Fame.

Your's eve⟨r affectionate⟩ly

Much underrated *Hero* —

Addressed and franked by EBB's uncle on integral page: London. March nineteen. 1821 / Miss Barrett / Hope End / Ledbury / S M Barrett.
Publication: None traced.
Manuscript: Edward R. Moulton-Barrett.

1. Apparently Bro is referring to one or more essays that EBB had submitted for publication using "Silentius" as her *nom de plume.* See letter 115.
2. Writer used two opening parentheses.
3. This is taken to refer to an agreement that while Bro was away from home he would write to EBB each Saturday, and she to him in mid-week. As later letters show, he was a more faithful correspondent than she was.

---

126. EBB TO SAMUEL MOULTON-BARRETT (UNCLE)

[Hope End]

Ode to my ever dearest Sam
on his birthday
March 31st 1821[1]

It is not that my heart is sad
Tho' to my eyes these tears will gush
For Poesy's sweet soul is glad
And wildly pure her numbers rush!
It is not that youth steps less lightly
On unculled flowers in garlands wreathing
It is not that Joy smiles less brightly
On young Hopes cradle—gently breathing
On the slumb'ring form of Care
That still sleeps gently, sweetly there!!
Grief wakes not yet, & smiling Bliss
With laughing taunts assails her foe!
It is not—no! it is not this
That bids these tears unbidden flow!

Tis gratitude that swells my breast
And bursts in rapture o'er those wires,
Swims in the tear drop unreprest
And triumphs when the strain expires!!
And thus beloved, and justly dear
The strain untrue *thou* wilt not deem
But think the lonely heart sincere
That trifles on so dear a theme!
For Ah! when sweet affection sings,
Natures untutored, prattling child,
Her numbers flow untaught & wild!
And here, a radiant smile she flings
Refulgent on the glittering wire—
And there perchance, she knows not why
Her musical sweetness trembles in a sigh!!
And tho' amidst the Senates lofty walls
Amidst the thunders of a worlds applause
When Tyranny, another Cæsar falls
And Patriots triumph in their Country's Cause!
Tho' round thy head, th' immortal laurel twine
Which graced a Russells or a Sydneys tomb
(In spite of "Couriers" and the right divine)
With incorruptible, eternal bloom
Tho Fame's loud trump oerwhelm my sighing lyre
And drown those numbers that would strive to bless
Tho' ABSENCE bid the ling'ring notes expire
Yet—dearest Patriot wilt thou love me less??

Your own affec^te child
Ba.

Publication: None traced.
Source: Copy in Mary Moulton-Barrett's hand in "Poems by EBB," Berg Collection.

1. His 34th.

---

127. EBB TO MARY MOULTON-BARRETT

Ode
To my dearest Mama on her birthday
Hope End May 1st 1821[1]

The Minstrel of the sacred lyre
Retired beneath the sombre shade—

Those softly sighing tones expire,
The Minstrel's breathing harp had made!
Gently among her hallowed strings
Untaught the roaming zephyrs sigh.–
The musical gale harmonious sings
In sweet toned melody . . . to die!!–
For sickness oer the Minstrels brow
Had cast a light and transient shade–!
But ah! what untaught Spirit now
Breathes within the sacred glade?–
So gently, and so sweetly flying––
Then floating on the desart air—
As Music when the Swan is dying
Swells in her throat, and lingers there!
"Awake"! it said or seemed to say—
"Minstrel awake,! thy pains[2] forego!
Oh hail the harbinger of May,
And bid the splendid cadence flow"–
Yes! Not in vain the Spirit spoke,
My Mother, truly, fondly loved!
For on the lyre wild Music broke,
And all this hearts affection proved!!!–

And wilt thou then these simple lines approve?
Oh! if thou *wilt*, my labours are beguiled!
Then sweetly smile with kind parental love
And gently bless the efforts of thy child!!.
I seek not laurels! oh! I seek not fame!
Unenvied let the trophic glories blaze!
Affection lingers on a *Mothers* Name,
And only supplicates a *Mothers* praise!!–

My dearest Mama's
Own affectionate Ba—

Publication: None traced.
Manuscript: Armstrong Browning Library.

1. Her 40th.
2. This word is written above "cares." The latter, not crossed out, is underscored four times.

128. EBB TO ALFRED MOULTON-BARRETT

Ode
To my dearest Alfred
On his birthday. Hope End May
20th 1821.[1]

Air was all quiet—and the lute
Upon the silent breezes slept–
Those flowing notes were still, and mute,
And one might deem that Echo wept
Their silence—for she seemed to sigh,
Untaught by minstrels silver tone,
Beneath that deep—etherial sky
And sweetly breathe her Matins lone,
With wildest music that was all her own!
But ah! a graceful Muse advances,
And in her arms a Cherub bears—
Whose laughing eye, joy . . sweetness, glances
Whose smile was sunshine—and whose tears
(Pleasures own rainbow) seemed to flow
In mocking at the frown of woe!
Instant the silent lyre awoke,
To hail its Muse, and favor'd child
Upon those things, pure numbers broke
In Music beautiful, and wild!!
My Alfred! May I call thee so?
My tributory toils beguile–
One glance from those soft eyes bestow—
And fondly gaze, and sweetly smile!
And tho' thy Ba would strive to bless,
Tis not poetic claims to prove—
For while she greets thy kind caress
She only seeks her Alfred's love!–

                                        E B Barrett —

Publication: None traced.
Manuscript: Berg Collection.

  1. His first birthday.

129. EBB TO EDWARD MOULTON-BARRETT (FATHER)

Ode
To my beloved Papa
On his birthday Hope End
May 28.th 1821¹

Sweet Poesy! divine untutored maid!
Oh! gently from chaotic slumbers wake—
Thine influence o'er thy humble vot'ry shed,
And into purest music, proudly break!

Tis thine to elevate, and fire the breast,
And bid exalted numbers wildly roll—
Inspire the noble thought—and unreprest—
Awake the energetic strenght [sic] of soul!–

Oh! for the voice mysterious, which has charmed
My lonely hours!! and on my silence breathed—!
This heart, with bright poetic fervor warmed,
And my young brows, with fancied laurels wreathed!!

Oh for that voice so sweetly pure, that stole
(Like the low murmuring of the distant wind)
Upon those chords, that thrill within the soul!
Ecstatic rapture!—music of the mind!!–

Parent beloved! within this lowly lay,
No studied tropes, or hacknied types appear–
And yet, Sincerity, Affection say!
Is Puppy to his child, less truly dear?

Ah no! not all that flatt'ry might impart
Could sweet Affection's HUMBLEST accent prove,
Could speak the simple language of the heart
Or breathe th' enduring strains of filial love!!–

Your own fondly and
Gratefully affectionate
Ba —

Publication: None traced.
Manuscript: Pierpont Morgan Library.

1. His 36th.

130. GEORGE RICKETTS NUTTALL TO EBB

[London]
[*Postmark:* 31 May 1821]

I take it kind, my dear Elizabeth, in you, to deliver so clear a
description of the symptoms which necessarily obtruded themselves on
your own observation; but before I can advance any opinion further,
than that, already in the possession of your Father; there are other
symptoms of which I wish to be apprized, of the existance or
modification of which you could not be aware unless your attention
had been attracted to them, & there are a few more besides which are
obvious to none but the practised eye, & touch. Under the last class the
pulse is to be ranged, & also the action of the Heart, as to number of
strokes during the minute, their regularity, or otherwise; their force,
compared with that of others; at the present time, as well as during a
paroxysm: Under the former class, are to be included sensations arising
from pressure on a part &c. Having offer^d these general remarks allow
me to request, that you will answer the following questions as early as
you shall have gained the necessary information. What is the state of
your pulse, and Hearts action, during the *advancement* of a paroxysm?
What, when you do not suffer? If you apply moderate pressure to your
sides below the short ribs, pit of stomach, & bowels, what sensations
arise? does pain ensue? or does a positive sense of uneasiness? when
actually, or passively suffering. Are your bowels distended more than
before your complaint began, & has your appetite vascillated; food
oppressed, bowels torpid, or irregular in their action? At the time you
suffer so much commotion, & distress, when rising do you suffer much
distension from wind, & does it escape when the, "tendons &
lineaments—break"–? How long after breakfast is it before the agony
begins, & what do you take for breakfast? Does any one part of the
bowels seem more tumid, at one time, or constantly, than another, &
harder, as if distended with air? or even something more solid?

The severe pains you experience about the chest, & right side,
proceeding towards the back, are in all likelihood owing to irregular, or
spasmodic action, then occurring in the Heart; arising sympathetically
from some disorder advancing in the alimentary canal, generating
flatus, which pressing *in* the midrif, or internal boundary of the chest,
& consequently impeding the Hearts free action renders it for a time
irritable. Your active turn of mind, & *inactive state* of body, together
with your age &c incline you, as well as other young bodies under
similar circumstances, to dyspeptic complaints. It not unfrequently
happens, that the Bowels become loaded, with vitiated matter, which
does not sometimes become obvious, notwithstanding the best means

have been adopted to remove it, for 10 days a fortnight or three weeks, nay more. The sure criterion that all is not right there, is the appearance of clay-coloured, or greenish, or blackish, or frothy, or mucous, or yeasty motions, fœtid in character, but sometimes these conditions do not occur till the disease is about to be removed.

You have too much good sense, my dear Elizabeth, not to be candid with me, on a point, of so much moment to yourself, & those who love, & value you. In matters of this kind, false delicacy might, & have, often, led to the most ruinous consequences; therefore scrupulously attend to all I have suggested to you, for observation. Get the following prescription made up directly, & take the two pills the same night, & ⟨obs⟩erve ⟨what t⟩hey shall cause to be dislo⟨dged⟩ from the ⟨bow⟩els next morning. Give my best love to Father, Mother, Brothers, & *sympathetic Sisters.*

Yours truly
G R Nuttall

Rx   Estracti Jalapie   gr: ⟨. . .⟩
          Estracti Aloes —   gr:ii
          Hydrargyr: Sub-mur: gr:ii
Bene contunde, & divide in pilulas duas.
nocte sumundas hora somni[1]–

G R N

Address, on integral page: Miss Elizabeth Barrett / Hope end / Ledbury Herefordshire.
Docket, near address, in unidentified hand: Illness– / 1821.
Publication: B-GB, pp. 346–348.
Manuscript: Pierpont Morgan Library.

1. The prescribed ingredients were extract of jalap root and extract of aloes, both purgatives, and hydrargyri submurias (submuriate of mercury) to promote operation of the purgatives. The final instructions translate as "Pound well, and divide into two pills. To be taken at night at bedtime."

---

131. EBB TO MARY MOULTON-BARRETT

[Gloucester]
[ca. June 1821][1]

My ever, ever dearest Mama,

I am perhaps too tenacious of the good opinion of my Friends and yet believe me were I not so thoroughly assured of yours and my beloved Puppy's affection as I am your letter might perhaps have proved a dam head to the impetuous torrent of my vanity. When my dearest Mama I promised to exert myself I spoke sincerely and the promise I made I intended to keep. If it were possible believe me that any mental exertion could shake off bodily torture it should be effected without reluctance as without hesitation. I HAVE exerted all my energy all my locomotive intellects all the muscular power of MIND and I HAVE found that though in some degree bodily anguish may be repressed from APPEARING yet it has failed to be overcome. Today D.ʳ Baron² comes to examine my back accurately and with particular care in order either to remove or satisfy his own DOUBTS. I trust in God it may prove not to be the spine, the restraint attending such a disease would indeed be irksome! He told me yesterday that did that disease absolutely appear he thinks I might as well be at home as elsewhere but on the contrary should it not he would recommend my absence from Hope End. Either case however he observed would not incapacitate me from travelling tho' it might influence the "absolute necessity". I do not wish to return home my dearest Mama till I am well and perhaps the wish may be natural considering that illness casts a shade of apathetic gloom over scenes which in health and enjoyment were once so dear.

I am as happy here as possible and my dearest Sam's kindness perfectly exemplary!! Dear Granny & Trip too! how can I forget their affection?³ D.ʳ Baron advises great quiet and a recumbant posture. I was out in my chair the day before yesterday but was certainly the worse for it. Yesterday the bath was tried but no sooner had the hot water touched my back than I was in agony. I could not remain in, an instant. I will not my dearest Mama assure you that I am much better but though my pains continue I feel the privation of health so much less and have such uniform good spirits (which enable me to support the regular paroxysms without sinking) that I *feel* you MUST⁴ rejoice!!!

My own dear Mama's

affec.ᵗᵉ child Ba–

Address, on integral page, in hand of Edward Moulton-Barrett (father): For Mary.
Publication: None traced.
Manuscript: Berg Collection and British Library.

1. Written shortly after EBB went to Gloucester for treatment of an illness. For a professional description of her symptoms, see SD389.
2. John Baron, M.D. (1786–1851), of Gloucester, the friend and biographer of Edward Jenner.
3. Elizabeth Moulton, Miss Trepsack and uncle Sam were with EBB in Gloucester during most of her illness.
4. Underscored three times.

132. MARY MOULTON-BARRETT TO EBB

[Hope End]
[ca. June 1821][1]

My dearest Eliz[th]

That you may not be disappointed of your daily despatch, I must *blot* this unhappy half sheet– would it were to have a better fate than to be the bearer of the ignoble productions of a pen under the soporific dominion of a wet day, & sick room!– the good tidings from thence however will be a sure passport to your favor for all my dullness, as I can so comfortably confirm the good report I made an hour or two ago of our beloved Addles to Papa– She is going on very well, with Minny *patting* her, which she seems to consider an absolute essential, to a sick bed; there never was such a little *cozy* coaxing invalid; She is very uneasy lest you should think her unkind not to write, but I venture to *answer* for you! Indeed my beloved girl, I was grieved to hear you have been at last obliged to submit to Cupping, of which you had such a dread, but a dread no longer I trust, if it has been of the use to you which I pray it may– Never did any thing try my patience more, than the perversity of this post, taking as long a time to bring a letter from G[loucester]. as from London! Yes, this poor little stock of patience of mine is *still more* tried by being this long time without seeing you tho' so near, but necessity speaks in the imperative mood & the mind *somehow*, finds obedience– If I have only the blessing to see my Eliz[th] better, it will be *tenfold* compensation for every anxious minute.– Great joy has been diffused over every countenance by the news that the poney is sent for to bring dear Bro to pay us a *visit*, for such it must be, while his dearer Ba is at G. & a short one too I suppose—there has been great alacrity at lessons to have less to do tomorrow, & Stormy has been fagging to complete his verbs, before the joyful arrival of the paragon of learning. You must not expect to hear for a day or two from Hen[tta] as she is so covered with measles from top to toe that it will be impossible for her to put her hands out of bed– her cough is a great deal better, & she is going on very well—but yesterday she had many troubles which *your* pleasant little visit of measles did not exhibit– Minny, amongst her other perfections, turns out to be an excellent *French Cook* as Hen[tta] pronounces, after eating the other day, some potatoes à Maitre d'Hotel which she insisted on her preparing for her– Not so well does she like the barley water, & other *measles diet*, which she terribly scorns, & sometimes *scolds* us, before she will condescend to touch it– I cannot say my beloved Ba how grievously I am disappointed not to have a line today, as I conclude Papa is not coming by the moneys being sent for only today. Love to all Woodyatt[2] is on the wing, & I can only wish my beloved Eliz[th] good night!—

Tuesday

How much I should thank Frost if she would enquire of your hostess at Dowlings[3] or elsewhere, whether there is a chance of getting places for two young girls, who rather than not go out, would for the first year, be contented almost without wages; In some of the tradesmens families in your gay city, such places might be heard of— they are both strong & willing enough to work, & can also work neatly at their needle—they are Betsey Willis,[4] & one of the Browns; that poor widow[5] has *five* daughters at home, & is unable to maintain them.

Address, on integral page: S. M Barrett Esq[r] MP– / Spa Hotel / Gloucester.
Publication: None traced.
Manuscript: British Library.

1. Reference to Henrietta's having caught measles from EBB places this letter early during the latter's removal to Gloucester.
2. William Woodyatt lived at Home-End, Ledbury, and in this instance was obviously being used as a courier.
3. Mr. Dowling was the proprietor of a hotel in Gloucester. In a letter of 24 August 1821 to Henrietta (SD400), Mary Moulton-Barrett speaks of a visit to Gloucester by the King, when "the Mayor & Aldermen, the Dean & Prebendaries all arrayed in their robes, were assembled at Dowlings, all the richest fare that time allowed spread out, the inhabitants crowding the Streets & bells ringing. When lo & behold his Majesty had the cruelty to drive as fast as his horses would carry him thro' the Town, without taking notice of any body in it. The Aldermen tried to comfort themselves for the affront by Eating up the Royal Collation, & the disappointed crowd by Abuse. Dear Bro was of the latter Class."
4. Thought to be the Betsy who earlier worked in the Hope End nursery (see letter 73).
5. Mrs. Brown was the tenant of Cummins Farm, about a mile east of Hope End.

---

133. MARY MOULTON-BARRETT TO EBB

[Hope End]
[ca. June 1821][1]

I well know how pleased my Eliz[th] will be to receive the enclosed acct, of all the wandering thoughts of her dear Hen[tta] which were I believe for one day & night very bewildering to her aching head, but now, thank God, it is perfectly restored to its *usual clearness & precision*; All fever is gone, & in spite of the roseate tint being rather too promiscuously strewn, her dear little contented face has recovered much of its beauty, & she looks clean & happy in her snug nightcap, & lilly white night gown. Bro visits her very often & makes her laugh very merrily, and when she has no visitors, she amuses herself with a book or reading the newspaper, which she says "she has GOT a great fancy for just now," so I conclude with *your* measles she received also, the infection of politics– To⟨morrow I dare⟩ say, she may be up

⟨. . .⟩²

first hours of his arrival last night, & they are all gone out together to try how far this propitious wind will favor its flight, & reward their ingenuity. Mrs Watson & Miss Skinner³ have just called & are to take this on with them to Ledbury, so that I am in great haste Miss S. looks dreadfully ill tho' she ⟨★ ★ ★⟩

Address, on integral page: ⟨S M Barr⟩ett Esqr MP. / ⟨Spa⟩ Hotel / Gloucester.
Publication: None traced.
Manuscript: British Library.

1. Dated by Henrietta's progress in recovering from the measles mentioned in preceding letter.
2. Lower half of page torn off.
3. Probably Mrs. G. Watson, who lived at Bronsil, near Eastnor Castle; a Miss Elizabeth Skinner, milliner, lived at Southend, Ledbury.

---

134. EBB TO HENRIETTA MOULTON-BARRETT

[Gloucester]
[ca. July 1821]¹

How can I thank my own Addles for her sweet and pretty letter? A most difficult and comprehensive question addressed to the brain but answered by the heart!! I am as happy as possible and have delightful fun though Dr BARREN (see your letter) has confined me to my bed and my sofa. He seems to have a penchant for the *pillow* in any case as he has desired me not to get up on any account till VERY LATE. I have no doubt but that I shall ere long be perfectly restored to health indeed it is physically impossible to be long an invalid at Gloucester– You know my ever loved Addles that sickness is not an inspiring theme and I protest I have nothing to say of any thing else– Let me hear from you soon–

My Henriettas
own affectionate Ba–
May I be allowed to condole on the subject of the dove

Publication: None traced.
Manuscript: R.J.L. Altham.

1. Dated by reference to Henrietta's dove having died. Uncle Sam promised Henrietta on 7 July 1821 (SD391) to "replace Dovey by a little Canary."

135. MARY MOULTON-BARRETT TO EBB

[Hope End]
[ca. September 1821]¹

That Thursday may not be a blank day, I must scribble for the post, tho'
I much suspect that an earlier report of the present hour, may reach my
beloved Ba, by Papa tomorrow. Sams two last notes have been very
cheering, and I trust you continue to go on, *"Very well indeed,"* which
is the blessing I most anxiously pray for. Heavy clouds have hung upon
the Malvern Hills all today, & tho I went out after breakfast to see two
of the old straggling apple trees cut down, which hung over the carriage
road near the house, I found neither Papa's wit, nor the approving laugh
of the delighted & busy audience sufficient to prevent even MY *shrinking*
from the cold chill air– these rains however have agreed marvellously
with vegetation– the shrubs about the ice house, will soon form a *forest*
in *their* way, where I trust my beloved Ba, will often wander with *Homer*
or *Virgil*, as all sufficient compensation for more animated scenes. A
poets lasting preference for dirty streets & hackney coaches, would be
an unheard-of inconsistency, tho' to love "the busy haunts of men"² for
variety's sake now & then, is both natural & wise– I wish you could hear
how brilliantly a duett from the "Creation"³ sounds, as performed by M.ʳˢ
O[rme]. & Henrietta. I really hope she is improving, but tho' fond of
music, I do not think she has much more fancy for the mechanical labor
of practice, than her elder sister. M.ʳˢ O. hears that M.ʳˢ Moneys⁴ indifferent
state of health, prevents their going abroad till the spring, and that they
are all gone to her Fathers at Ramsgate. it will be a sad disappointment
to them thus to be deprived of one of the winters they had dedicated to
the culture of the *fine arts*, which are not likely to flourish much, in our
good English seaport.– I have not yet heard from Fenham, of the bridal
festivities– perhaps you have– I trust they are to be followed by that
happiness to Jane, which her own affecᵗᵉ heart & amiable temper, are
well calculated to bestow, tho' I hope she has no visionary hopes of
finding it upon yours & M.ʳˢ Wolstonecrafts system;⁵ if so, it may *at best*
be anticipated that she will *oftener* find herself wrong than *right*: however
it may do very well for an *old maids singleness* of *will* &c[.] I would not
put you out of conceit with it, as long as it is y.ʳ intention to belong to
the sisterhood. I assure you it is by mere stratagem I have scribbled thus
far my darling Eliz.ᵗʰ therefore pray do not complain of words & sense
unintelligible, for here sits Alfred⁶ the little on my knee, doing all he
can to get the pen into his own hands, & the paper on the floor—but he
is *too sweet* to be sent away, & *you* must suffer, my poor Ba, for your
Brothers *winning* ways– I think you would forgive him, could you see
how pretty he looks in Grannys blue frock– Stormy George & Henry,

יוֹנַת אֵלֶם רְחֹקִים :

This portrait of E.B.B was taken by 1821
her Mother, — during the great illness, —
and is given to me by Arabel.
See also the faint outline on R B.
the otherside, which is even more like.

EBB Aged 15

EBB Aged 15

are running round the table comforting themselves as well as they can for their confinement to the house, with not much consideration for the ears of fellow prisoners– All are united in loves to you & your dear little circle–

God bless my beloved Ba!

Publication: None traced.
Manuscript: British Library.

1. Dated by reference to the forthcoming wedding of Jane Graham-Clarke to Robert Hedley. According to a letter from Mary Moulton-Barrett (SD411) this was to take place on 18 October.
2. *Tale of the Secret Tribunal* (1819), pt. 1, line 203, by Felicia Dorothea Hemans (1793–1835).
3. Haydn's oratorio *The Creation* was first performed in England in 1808. One of Henrietta's descendants has Mary Moulton-Barrett's copies of some of his works (see *Reconstruction*, A1158).
4. Mary Thomasina (*née* Ffrench), wife of the Rev. Kyrle Ernle Money, Vicar of Much Marcle.
5. Mary Wollstonecraft (1759–97), best known for her *Vindication of the Rights of Woman* (1792), an argument for the equality of women. EBB wrote "Fragment of an 'Essay on Woman'" (*Reconstruction*, D308) at about the time of this letter.
6. Alfred Price Moulton-Barrett, born 20 May 1820.

---

136. EBB TO HENRIETTA MOULTON-BARRETT

[In the hand of Edward Moulton-Barrett (brother)]   [Gloucester]

September 12.th 1821.

My dearest Addles

I shall make the same use of my friend Bro's slippery fingers as the monkey did of the cats paw,[1] in order to assure you of the sincere delight I experience from the perusal of your facinating letters, and that though Doctor Barons medical wand, may menace me with awful fierceness, yet can it not break one of those secret links of fond affection which must ever bind me to my dear Henrietta, I send you in return for your unmatched and exquisite feathers, the enclosed which may remind you of one whose greatness of spirit and loftiness of soul, towrs over death and speaks a lesson from the grave. Thank dear Mrs Orme for her kind letters, and give her my best love. I am sorry that Arabel finds so great a difficulty in collecting her ideas and that the epistolary Cibyl will not allow her, to greet me with a line, assure her however of my undiminished affection, and distribute kisses from me to the lovely and beloved circle, let not dear Minny be forgotten, though she still considers my complaint "aerlike-dispersible[.]" Thank her from me for the offer of a thousand pounds, if at the end of six months her wish be realized and I be again on my legs I shall indeed have reason to be thankful. I am going on as well as possible. Adieu my dearest Henrietta and ever beleive that no one can more fondly love you than your affectionate—

Ba

written myself[2]

You are [to] take your choice Sam[3] advises you to choose the black one as it is mor⟨e⟩ like the Queen.—— Sam says if the old cock still continues to peck you had better take it out of the cage.——

Addressed and franked by EBB's uncle on integral page: Gloucester September Twelve / 1821 / Miss H. Barrett / Hope End / Ledbury / S M Barrett.
Publication: None traced.
Manuscript: R.J.L. Altham.

1. In La Fontaine's fable, "Le Singe et le Chat" (1671).
2. The signature and "written myself" are in EBB's hand and were circled by her.
3. EBB's uncle, who also franked the letter.

---

137. EBB TO HENRIETTA MOULTON-BARRETT

[In hand of Edward Moulton-Barrett (brother)]   [Gloucester]
October. 5.th 1821.

There now! we have turned them all out of the room and I have cocked my learned companion Master Bro by the side of my classical couch hurling a look of contempt at Doctor Baron and of defiance at little Tommy Cooke[1] while I prepare to chat for half an hour with my own Addles. First of all let me reiterate my grateful thanks for that unceasing affection which ever prompts my beloved Henrietta to give me such pleasure, by sacrificing at my altar the sweetest flowerets of her epistolary garden—and now I suppose I am expected to give the bulletin of my health. Indeed my dear Addles upon that subject Hope speaks eloquently and casts so soft a gleam of happy sunshine over future scenes blest with the delightful visions of returning health, that your kind heart must be gratified, my sufferings are much diminished in consequence of the seatons [*sic* for setons], which have certainly relieved me wonderfully, by striking into the very center of the disease as Mr Carden expresses it.[2] Indeed my dearest Hen I now admire the little man quite as warmly as you do, and I am sure I have reason to exclaim blessed is the hour when Mr Carden entered Spa Hotel. I wish you to take my memorandum book out of my little room and if you turn over the leaves, you will come to an article entitled "Bro's character and mine compared" tear the whole article out and keep it,[3] for as I do not wish it to be read I commit it entirely to your care; If you would then my dearest Addles send me the book, by the first conveyance you really oblige me much. Little Tommy Cooke is quite divine and excels at my toilet with as much grace as ever. God bless all the beloved inhabitants of Hope End. And may Henrietta sometimes think—

[continued in EBB's hand]   of her own most tenderly attached
                                                    Ba–
                                        A thousand loves!
                                Isnt that well written considering
                                        a spine complaint!

[Continued in hand of Edward Moulton-Barrett] I wish you would see if Mrs Hartfords children[4] are all well stocked with flannel peticoats, stockings shifts &^{c} &^{c} and send me a full account of them. Treppy sends her very best love to Arabel and returns many thanks for her present and letter and will write to her soon.

Address, in hand of Edward Moulton-Barrett, on integral page: Miss H. Barrett / Hope End / Ledbury.——
Publication: None traced.
Manuscript: R.J.L. Altham.

1. Several families of Cooks/Cookes lived near Hope End. Tommy probably was the son of Thomas Cook, one of the Hope End tenant-farmers. He appears to have been in Gloucester during the whole of EBB's illness.
2. On 8 May Mr. I. Carden wrote from Worcester to Edward Moulton-Barrett, advocating a change of air for EBB (see SD379). A seton is a piece of thread or tape drawn through a fold of skin to facilitate the discharge of matter.
3. Henrietta did as directed. The essay "My Character and Bro's Compared" was cut from the notebook. The essay (*Reconstruction*, D1324) is published in Appendix III, part 3. The notebook has not been identified.
4. Mrs. Hartford (or Harford) and her children (three of whom are named in later letters) seem to have been under EBB's especial care, receiving gifts of charity.

---

138. EBB TO HENRIETTA MOULTON-BARRETT

[Gloucester]
[ca. November 1821][1]

My own ever dear Addles will not expect any very brilliant corruscations of the imagination or very glowing ebullitions of wit from my pen when she considers that the Muse who deigns to visit me in my present disconsolate state must either take the uninspiring form of Dr Baron or that of his illustrious coadjutor little Tommy Cook. Now whether the Nine have some insuperable—some unaccountable objection to the faculty, or whether Apollo is jealous of little Tommys medical skill remains to be determined, but certain it is that I never felt more of the dross of Mortality—never more thoroughly unintellectual than I do at this instant! I would thank my beloved Henrietta for her kind and MOST ENTERTAINING letters– I would thank her for the interest of the Composition and her attentive affection could I find words to express my surprise at the MERIT of the former or eloquence to describe my gratitude for the latter! As it is, Silence perhaps may speak stronger to the heart than the most sublimated rhetoric! "Words pay no debts" says Shakespeare[2]– "Thanks have no intuitive value" responds a young lady on her back! I am unwilling to enter on the subject of my illness—it is an endless theme– Suffice it to declare that there is DECIDEDLY a SURE tho slow improvement in my health!!–

Give my most affectionate love to all those so very, very dear to me, whether I shall behold them all this Winter & have the happiness of gazing on my dear ever dear Addles is under our beloved Puppys consideration! This you however of course have heard!

God for ever bless you all!—
Your fondly affectionate Ba–

My best love to Mrs Orme! Tell her how sincerely I trust her headaches continue better–

In the distribution of loves let not my dear Minny be forgotten— she NEVER CAN[3] be by ME!!–

Thank my dearest Mama for the entertainment her affec^{te} letters afford me—

Address, on integral page: Miss H Barrett. / Hope End.
Publication: None traced.
Manuscript: R.J.L. Altham.

1. Dated by reference to forthcoming winter, and to Mrs. Orme's headaches, which are also mentioned in a letter from Mary Moulton-Barrett to Henrietta dated 14 October 1821 (SD411).
2. *Troilus and Cressida*, III, 2, 55.
3. Underscored three times.

---

139. MARY MOULTON-BARRETT TO EBB

[Hope End]
[28 November 1821][1]

I had begun to despair of dearest Papa's arrival last night, the windows were all shut, & the school room & nursery were at tea, when his anxiously expected voice was heard! Never was he more welcome, for he brought me the good tidings of my dearest child, being free from all the pains which have teased her during the last week, & which I was sadly disappointed to find could not be MORE SATISFACTORILY accounted for. Poor Puppy was half frozen, for the air was *bitterly* cold, however we sat down directly to our soup & chicken & half an hours basking in the arm chair before a blazing fire, enabled him to get thro' the even^g very comfortably roasting chesnuts till the rioters all went to bed, and then in a more sober chat with Hen^tta & I, of which our loved Ba was the heroine!– How I long to see certain observations on Bacon of which I hear so much!² I had a note last night from Sam from Cheltenham³ to desire I would write to Mrs Bussier for some of her enchanting little airs in *Spanish Portuguese Italian & Venetian.*⁴ As I know not where M^rs B— is I have written to her Mother making the *modest* request that she will send me them forthwith, as Sam is in the *utmost* haste for them– how far poor Mrs D. may be *linguist* enough, to write them out, in less than a *months* [time,] *spelling* & putting together, I know not—however she has her *pastoral* daughter to assist her, & I hope they will gratify Sam's impatience as quickly as they can— I have had a closely written vol. from Jane, from Turin dated Nov 10th which I want to answer or I would send it you. it breathes of happiness & of the delights of her interesting journey. They were enchanted with the situation of Lyons, with the walk on the Quai of the Rhone, which joins the Saone a little below that ancient & dirty Town– the scenery from thence to the foot of Mont Cenis, delighted her. At the little Inn there, they supped on excellent trout & roasted *thrushes*, whose sweet notes I should have grieved to see thus *stilled!* They had six horses to ascend the mountain, three abreast, & after winding at right angles over a road without a pebble, they reached the top in 3 hours– there was just a sufficiency of snow to complete the grand & imposing effect of the scenery which seems to have deprived the *untravelled* Jane, of all power to express her feelings! She however apostrophizes the great Napoleon who by this work enables his fellow beings to climb to the clouds with as much ease, as they bowl along the flat roads of our less aspiring part of creation–⁵ Neither did banditti or avalanche threaten their safety. They reached Turin without a single misadventure & with glorious weather– From thence, they were going to Genoa for some days, which I much envy her, for I have a longing desire to see that beauteous bay, & to spend some little time at Florence on their way to Rome— She and her sposo were writing over a good wood fire like *Darby & Joan*, & she talks of having some new books to cover the first of her *domestic cares.* She desires me to tell her dearest Ba, how much distance appears to encrease her anxiety to hear of her— by some mischance she has rec^d only one letter from England since she left it– A thousand loves & kisses she sends you, some of which you are to distribute to dear Granny Tripsack & Sam. Poor Hen^{tta} has not time to scribble to you today, & we could not do so as usual last night, out of *compliment* to our *guest–*

And so you discovered the true *Il Hoskins*, which Hen^{tta} had believed a perfectly impenetrable secret![6] May God bless my beloved Ba, & may she love her Mother only *half* as well as she is loved.

Wednesday 1 o'Clock– all gone to dinner!– Pray ask Dr B. his opinion of Dr R. & let me know it—*do not forget!!*

Address, on integral page: S M Barrett Esqr MP– / Spa Hotel / Gloucester.
Publication: None traced.
Manuscript: British Library.

1. Mary Moulton-Barrett used, as her final page, the cover sheet from another letter, franked and dated "Cheltenham November twenty five / 1821 / Mrs Barrett / Hope End / Ledbury / S M Barrett." She also writes "Wednesday," and 28 November was the first Wednesday after the receipt of this letter, which she says came "last night."
2. It is possible that these "observations on Bacon" relate to an early draft of *An Essay on Mind*, as the first extant draft is on paper watermarked 1813, 1820 and 1821 (MS at Texas). Note (h) to Bk. II (p. 102 in the first edition) criticizes Bacon's dedicatory remarks to King James I, a subject EBB dealt with at some length in letter 309.
3. Samuel Moulton-Barrett, not Mrs. Barrett Williams' son Samuel Barrett, who lived at Cheltenham. This is established by reference to note 1.
4. We have not identified anybody of this name, and the British Library's Music Catalogue does not list any published scores under this name. In view of the Moulton-Barretts' habitual carelessness in spelling names, taken together with the later reference to "her *pastoral* daughter," it is possible that the composer of these "enchanting little airs" was the wife of the Rev. Peter Edward Boissier, mentioned in letter 229.
5. Napoleon ordered the construction of a road over the Mt. Cenis pass (6,893′); it was built between 1803 and 1810.
6. Although obscure, this remark is believed to refer in some way to Hungerford Hoskyns, the 17-year-old son of Sir Hungerford Hoskyns (1776–1862), of Harwood, Herefordshire.

---

140. MARY MOULTON-BARRETT TO EBB

[Hope End]
[ca. December 1821][1]

Here is frost enough my dearest Ba to make the water look like a mirror, tho' partly frozen over, and to dry & prepare the ground I trust for seed– Mrs Waller is much better, & our gouty *Senechal* can stand upon a foot & a half I hear.[2] "Murad the Unlucky,"[3] (or rather the *improvident*) amused us all greatly last night! it is greatly superior in moral to the Arabian tales, & little inferior in incident, tho' it wants the splendor of their scenic decoration– Bro copied your half finished drawing of ⟨. . .⟩s Cottage extremely well. I really think there ⟨is⟩ talent enough for the graphic art amongst all the jun.[r] branches of this house to turn it into no unworthy academy, if we had nothing else to do.– I rejoice to find that Bro has not forgotten his French either in accent or grammar– I cannot say so much for geography. We looked over some Maps yesterday with a very wandering & unsteady gaze, & tho' I could not help feeling mortified, that knowledge to *my* mind so needful, & to his own once so familiar should be so impaired, I still believe it is very readily regained, & willingly admit the Classics for the present to be all in all, satisfied that there *are* seeds sown of every-day knowledge which in due time will not fail to yield their fruit– I am surprized to find that Sams Latin exercise consists merely of *Copying* from the grammar the four principal parts of the verbs, which any one may do who can write, but the plan of the school rests upon this *extreme* attention to the most simple rudiments, & I have no doubt that the strength of the superstructure will prove its efficacy. I cannot however give up the progress Stormy is making in the most advanced stage of exercises on the united noun adjective & verb, which he writes very correctly. Poor Arabel is in sad distress about her Canary, who sits moping with his head under his wing, & looks rough & miserable– it is not from want of food, but probably it feels the change from the constantly warm atmosphere of the school room, & there are some thoughts of making them ⟨o⟩ver to the snug comforts of the Housekeep⟨er's⟩ room for the present. I feel very anxious about hearing from Sam; the time for M[rs] O[rme]'s return is rapidly advancing. Tonight I trust will bring me good tidings of my beloved Ba. In the midst of a political tirade from Bro at tea time last night, Henry placed himself with his back to the fire, & with the Colossus stride, & his hands behind him, called out with all his might, "*Imm for Teen*"![4] Kisses to my best loved Ba from all & *to all!*

Indeed if M⟨. . .⟩[5] do not make the proposal to ⟨separ⟩ate herself, *now*, I have many doub⟨ts w⟩hether we shall be justified in ⟨giving⟩ her this very summary dis⟨missa⟩l!——

Address, on integral page: S.M. Barrett Esq.[r] MP. / Spa Hotel / Gloucester.
Publication: None traced.
Manuscript: British Library.

1. Dated by references to winter conditions and the illness of Arabella's canary (which had died by 3 January 1822).
2. Mrs. Waller is perhaps in the Moulton-Barrett employ, and the "gouty Senechal" could be a manservant named Phillips.
3. One of Maria Edgeworth's *Popular Tales* (1804).
4. "I'm for Queen," a reference to the late Queen Caroline. Henry was three years old at this time.
5. Seal tear.

141. CHARLES JOHN MOULTON-BARRETT TO EBB

[Hope End]

[Written below pencil sketch of a house] Storms love to his dear Ba, dec.[r] 8th 1821

Publication: None traced.
Manuscript: Edward R. Moulton-Barrett.

---

142. EDWARD MOULTON-BARRETT (BROTHER) TO EBB

[Hope End]
December 23rd, 1821.

My ever dearest Ba

We were this morning agreable [*sic*] surprised by Sam's getting up quite recovered[.] All his fever and headache has forsaken him and the tooth-ache and Giddiness in his head which troubled him very much have left him. he is now practising his hymns for Christmas morning, to awake Pap⟨a⟩ with. A book has just pitched on my mouth thrown by Sam so that I am happy to say he can use both his tongue and hands, I can almost say it is with me as with Dares "mixtosq⟨ue⟩ in sanguine dentes."[1] Papa has gone to Ledbury Church and I am affraid he will have a most wretched rid⟨e⟩ for it has rained almost ever since he went away. Good bye my dearest Ba and as I write in the dark excuse all blunde⟨rs⟩

ever believe me
your devotedly attached——
Bro

Best love——

Address, on integral page: S M Barrett Esqr / M P / Spa Hotel / Gloucester.
Publication: None traced.
Manuscript: Edward R. Moulton-Barrett.

1. "And teeth with blood commingled" (*Æneid*, V, 470–471). Dares was a famous pugilist and friend of Æneas.

---

143. EDWARD MOULTON-BARRETT (BROTHER) TO EBB

[Hope End]
December 26.th 182[1]¹

My ever dearest Ba
I can not say we spent a very Merry Christmas day for there were too few of us Georgy and Heny went to bed soon and then there were very few of us however I dressed up as an old woman and frightened ⟨poor⟩ Heny out of his wits I dressed Henny in his nightgown and nightcap and whitened his face all over. Sam was dressed up too in Papa's clothes short knee breeches and a tremendous paunch stuck out with a pillow and an Opera Hat on, he certainly was a most capital figure he looked very much like what I could imagine an old French Doctor. We made an attempt at Grand Muffty but as there were so few of us we soon gave it up as a bad job. Papa And I are going this evening to ride to Mrs Griffiths² this evening to dine and I fear we shall be wet through before we get half way as it has been snowing all the morning and is now snowing and seems likely to snow the whole evening. I must wish you good bye as the post is going.
Ever believe me
your devotedly attached
Bro——

Address, on integral page: S. M. Barrett Esqr M P. / Spa Hotel / Gloucester.
Publication: None traced.
Manuscript: Edward R. Moulton-Barrett.

1. Bro wrote off edge of page. Year determined by reference to the following letter.
2. Charlotte Griffith (1762?–1837), widow of Thomas Griffith. Her residence was Barton Court, the estate adjoining Hope End.

144. EDWARD MOULTON-BARRETT (BROTHER) TO EBB

[Hope End]
December 27.th 1821.

My ever dearest Ba
I sit down to give you a short account of last nights gaieties, (but it must be but a short one as I am very busily engaged in preparing the birthday ode for Stormy¹ which is tomorrow.) When we started from her⟨e⟩ I rode my poney and Papa his horse it sno⟨wed⟩ a little and I was well wrapt up with a pair of Papa's gaters on as over-alls[.] we sat a

little in the drawing room When dinner was anounced and after dinner Master Payton[2] brought out an elegant collection of mine⟨rals⟩ and shells, tea soon after arrived with plenty of cake which I know will be very interesting to you to hear[.] after tea Mr. Watts,[3] Papa, Mr. Payton and Mrs. Griffiths played a game at whist and Miss Glasco[4] and I played a[t] chess, supper then came in so that upon the whole I think I did very well. we did not get home till one o'clock in consequence of a hard frost the rodes [*sic*] were so slippery that Papa slid nearly the whole way however I suppose in consequence of my poney's being ruff [*sic*] shod I did not slip once. Good bye my dearest Ba I must go and invoke my Muse

Ever believe me
your devotedly attache[d]
Bro —

Address, on integral page: S M Barrett Esqr. M P. / Spa Hotel / Gloucester.
Publication: None traced.
Manuscript: Edward R. Moulton-Barrett.

1. SD413.
2. Reynolds Peyton (1815–61), eldest son of Nicholson and Eliza (*née* Griffith) Peyton.
3. Probably the Rev. James Watts, Vicar of Ledbury since 1810.
4. A member of the Barton Court household, probably in the office of companion to Mrs. Peyton or Mrs. Griffith, or as governess for the Peyton children.

145. Edward Moulton-Barrett (brother) to EBB

[Hope End]
December 31st [1821][1]

My ever dearest Ba

Papa will by this time have arrived at Gloucester unless he has taken a ride down the Severn with the flood,[2] and I dare say you are too busily engaged talking to him, to attend much to any thing else, however I shall trouble you but a short time to day as the post is now going. Mr. Bayford yesterday evening gave us another sermon.[3] I certainly think it was much better than the morning as he was much more collected and *I*[4] think upon the whole it was much better, for though the matter was capital in the morning he delivered it in a confused an[d] hesitating manner. Today being the first fine day we have had for so long we enjoyed it extremely and Henrietta rode down to Mrs. Hartfords your childs house and gave her, your clothes with which she was delighted. I must wish you good bye my dearest Ba, for today;

Ever believe me
your devotedly attached——
Bro —

Publication: None traced
Manuscript: Edward R. Moulton-Barrett.

1. Dated by reference to their father's going to Gloucester. Letter 147 reads as if he had done so.
2. The river Severn was notorious for its tidal bore, which was capable of reversing the flow as far upstream as Tewkesbury, often causing considerable damage and flooding.
3. John Bayford and his family, who lived in London, were on friendly terms with Elizabeth Moulton and Miss Trepsack. His wife Frances (*née* Heseltine) was Mary Moulton-Barrett's first cousin.
4. Underscored twice.

---

146. EBB TO ARABELLA GRAHAM-CLARKE (AUNT)

[Gloucester]
[ca. 1822][1]

My dearest Bum must have a few little lines from me today to assure her that her many kind letters have made my heart a debtor to her which will not require much DUNNING– I have often entertained hopes that you and dear Grandmama might be inclined to enliven my confinement but alas! how often have I been disappointed! I fear many months must yet pass ere I change my position and tho' I endeavour to be as patient as I can yet dearest Bum the prospect is melancholy. Oh! how I *do* wish you were here but it would be too much I fear to ask!

I expect my dearest Sam every day as he has promised to spend a few weeks with us to breakfast in my room "as is his custom"–

Dear, dear Bum forgive this stupid scrawl for the *Graces* of Composition with all other *Graces* desert me just now–

Ever your own attached
Ba–

Love to dearest Grandmama–
Pray write by return of post–

Address, on integral page: Miss Graham Clarke. / < . . . >
Publication: None traced.
Manuscript: Pierpont Morgan Library.

1. Apparently written early in 1822 while EBB was recuperating at Gloucester.

147. MARY MOULTON-BARRETT TO EBB

Hope End.
Jany 1st *1822*

A Happy new year to my beloved child, was the first thought that presented itself to my waking intellect this morng. May it please God to make it a year of convalescence to her, and of blessing to those whose happiness rest so much on her health!– To dearest Papa Granny & Trep, say all that is most affec^{te} on the commencement of this new term of life, which I trust will abound in the blessings of mutual affection to us all, & in thankfulness & content!– We were all collected round the breakfast table this morning, & another fine day, enables them to get out, tho' much rain during the night, prohibits yesterdays excursions over the hills, & limits them to the walks– Sam is exercising Moses, & they want only our dearest Ba to complete the happy groupe, but *there* is a *blank*, that hangs heavily about our hearts! & our only comfort is to hope that before next new years day, it will be joyously filled!– Bum sends you the enclosed, to compound which, a gracious Providence, (rather than philosophy) has supplied you with every material. the recipe is not indeed new to you for you have swallowd these pills during all your illness, even with more regularity than M^r F's[1]— Bum sends you dozens of kisses & prays that long before next Xmas, you will be restored to all the pranks & pleasures of Hope End. Poor Butler is well in health, but his low spirits resulting from his late loss, casts a gloom over their Xmas fire side– Carlow is still quiet, but it is a most uncertain quiet.[2] They rather expect Richd B. at Fenham this day; They have not still determined whether to go this month to Ireland, but wait first I suppose to see Richd B.— On Xmas day—little Arabella[3] had a *tea party* & the magic lantern & the poor people dined at Fenham as usual– Poor Clements has had an alarming attack but is better– Rowcastle[4] was very ill Jane said in consequence of their sea voyage & had lost an eye from the bites of the musquitoes, whose bites had covered Jane also with a thousand bumps– She was pleased to meet Mrs Cockle (late governess to Miss Pearson) at Florence, & who for the sake of information, she meant to take with her in their wanderings over that interesting city, of which, they had then seen nothing– Lotte is just finishing her picture from Sam's Paestina ruins,[5] which Bell says is quite beautiful. Lotte is very well, & rides every day. Papa may remember old Mrs Clavering– her death was hastened by her maids letting her *drop* as they were putting her into bed & breaking her thigh– She has left all her property to Mrs Werg.– Miss Russel arrived only the day before her melancholy death. Mr Witham gave up his room to her,

& M.[r] Blackburn's[6] escape was great sleeping in the next room– L.[y] Arabella Vane marries M.[r] Russell's son, to L.[d] Darlingtons great satisfaction.[7] One of the antiquated Miss lRouthsl who must have reckoned 65 good years at least, gives her wrinkled hand to some stranger she has met on a late visit– Catalani[8] is to have concerts this week in N[ew]-Castle & on the 10.th Aubone Surtees,[9] new Mayor, gives a fancy ball at the Mansion House, to which all the *Country* are going– The poor Heseltines are in a wretched state again– Fanny is gone to her Aunt Rives, & her Father is concealed in Paris over head & ears in debt.– Phillips is laid up with gout, & M.[rs] W[aller]. not much better– I trust dearest Papa has got rid of his pains & sleeps better– Affec.[te] love to him & to all. This is but a dismal new years day, separated from those most dear to our hearts! but no separation can make the fond affection less warm of that of your own

Mother.——

Address, on integral page: S. M. Barrett Esq.[r]—. / Gloucester. / *MP.*
Publication: None traced.
Manuscript: British Library.

1. Possibly Fothergill's Tonic Female Pills. These were advertised extensively, and recommended for "general Debility of Constitution . . . they tend to strengthen the Organs of the Stomach, correct bad Digestion, remove Nervous Giddiness, Head-ache, &c, &c."
2. There had been widespread eruptions of violence in Ireland for the previous three months, protesting tithes, taxes, and absentee landlords. Tipperary and Limerick, west of Carlow, were two of the principal centres. A report in *The Times* (6 November 1821, p. 3) spoke of the populace being "all armed, and very daring . . . murders are committed in open day, and in the sight of hundreds . . . The object of these wretches is . . . by a conspiracy of the lower against the higher classes of society, to drive the latter out of the country, and to remain lords of the soil themselves."
Sir Thomas and Lady Butler were waiting for his brother Richard to arrive with the latest news before deciding the date of their return to their home in Carlow.
3. Arabella Sarah Butler, eldest daughter of Sir Thomas and Lady Butler.
4. Thought to be Jane Hedley's dog, taken with her on her recent honeymoon to Italy.
5. Pæstum (Posidonia) in Lucania (*fl.* 540 B.C.) was sacked and partly destroyed by Saracens in 871 and later by the Normans. As Samuel Moulton-Barrett was no artist, one supposes that he acquired a painting of the ruins while travelling in Italy, which Charlotte Graham-Clarke, a talented amateur artist like all her sisters, was copying.
6. *The Newcastle Courant* of 22 December 1821 announced the death on the 19th, aged 82, of "Mrs. Clavering, widow of George Clavering, Esq. of Greencroft, in the county of Durham." The only reference we have found to Mrs. Werg is in extracts from a diary kept by Elizabeth Cook (*née* Surtees), which mentions "Captain and Mrs. Werge" dining with Arabella and John Graham-Clarke, Mrs. Cook's aunt and uncle and EBB's maternal grandparents (manuscript with Mary V. Altham). The other persons mentioned—Miss Russel, Messrs. Witham and Blackburn—are presumably north-country acquaintants, but have not been identified.
7. Lady Arabella Vane (1801–64) was the daughter of William Henry Vane, 3rd Earl of Darlington (1766–1842). The projected marriage did not take place; she did not marry until 1831, and then not to Mr. Russell. Hope End had been purchased from a member of her family, Lady Tempest.

8. Angelica Catalani (1780–1849), Italian opera singer. Her first appearance in London was in 1806. In 1814 she participated in the Grand Musical Festival in Newcastle, of which John Graham-Clarke was one of the patrons. At this time, EBB heard her, and wrote "On Hearing Catalani Sing" (September 1814), subsequently published in *HUP*, I, 59–60. The first of the concerts mentioned here was to have been given on 3 January, but *The Newcastle Courant* of 5 January reported its postponement due to Catalani's having caught cold. The concerts were given on 5 and 7 January. It is likely that Mary Moulton-Barrett, and possibly EBB, called on her during their visit to Paris in 1815, as Mary Moulton-Barrett had mentioned that intention in a letter to her mother dated 25 October 1815 (SD236).

9. A prominent Newcastle-upon-Tyne banker, who had married Mary Altham, eldest sister of EBB's maternal grandmother. Henrietta Moulton-Barrett later married their grandson, Williams Surtees Cook.

---

148. EDWARD MOULTON-BARRETT (BROTHER) TO EBB

[Hope End]
January 2ᵈ 1822.

My ever dearest Ba

We went out today in a large party with bows and arrows to shoot however we were unfortunate enough not to make our dinner in our rambles over the hills Henrietta went with us, and I can tell is becoming a famous marksman. This morning it was a very frosty morning though not quite hard enough to slide but tomorrow morning I anticipated a good slide and of course a few good falls, however I was disapointed by an untimely thaw which blasted all my hopes and spoiled all my sliding. My dearest Ba I must wish you good bye as the letter must go.

Ever believe me
your devotedly attached
Bro—

Address, on integral page: S. M. Barrett Esqᵣ M. P. / Spa Hotel / Gloucester.
Publication: None traced.
Manuscript: Edward R. Moulton-Barrett.

---

149. MARY MOULTON-BARRETT TO EBB

[Hope End]
Janʸ 2ᵈ 1822

Minny arrived last night in so much better cue than from the *last visit* she paid my beloved Ba that it did me infinite good to see her smiling face when she came down to make her report arrayed in Henᵗᵗˢ smart blue cap, the new years gift! How did my head follow every line of dearest Papa's kind letter, thanks to him for his great kindness in writing to me thus fully. The turkey went down with bon apetit, yesterday, & our president insisted on various toasts—of which in some shape or other you formed the essence & those around you, & the *three* times *three* with Henrys voice not least audible, gives me the head ache to remember– We did all we could to be gay last night, but new years night wanted its inspiriting coadjutors, you & Papa, & seemed to me more gloomy than the *every-day* evenings, which suggest their regular occupations– When those we best love are not near, the heart is most at ease when nothing occurs to excite its sympathies, or note of time to call up recollections!– We breakfasted this morning on Minny's New Years offering of Gloucester Cakes, & then Bro wrote his Virgil, Sam & Stormy their Latin, & Hen^tta & I, had I hope a profitable research into all our thorough bass lessons learnt at Logiers,[1] & ended with the duetts, which she really plays very nicely– At twelve o'clock, she was transformed into Diana with her bow slung across her shoulders, & went out with Bro, Sam, & Stormy, on some fanciful chase over the hills, which look more like Summer now than they have done since August— The rest of our business is to be finished when this short day begins to close—& we shall draw & read in the eveng^s tho' how to assimilate our reading to the various comprehensions of our audience is not easy– Parks travels[2] I proposed this morn^g but was overruled by an unanimous preference of one of *dear* Miss E's. Moral tales,[3] as being within the reach of all! I do not enter into the detail of the Harford visit yesterday, as I conclude it to be Bro's & Hen^tta profit. My confirmation however may be acceptable of the cleanly healthy state of the family, (tho' crimson cheeks will turn blue), the royal Carolines thriving state, & likeness to Ellen, M^rs H's abundant loves to you, & her bounty to us in showers of nuts & walnuts. She drank y^r health in a glass of ale, with all her heart & soul!– They were all dressed in *your* gifts; the slip fits Ellen nicely– So the Browns & Cotterel[4] still preserve their locks! Perhaps to be clipped after the Christmas Wasseling, before the school meets on Monday.

God bless my beloved Ba, &
all around her!——

I have heard or read somewhere that "Celestina," & "Julia Mandeville"[5] are superior to the common run of novels——

Address, on integral page: S. M. Barrett Esqr MP. / Spa Hotel / Gloucester. Mary Moulton-Barrett used a cover sheet from another letter as stationery. It was addressed to her at Hope End by an unidentified correspondent.
Publication: None traced.
Manuscript: British Library.

1. John Bernard Logier (1780–1846) had invented a machine called the chiroplast, designed to facilitate the correct positioning of the hands on the pianoforte, and devised the system of music teaching known by his name.

2. Mungo Park (1771–1801), surgeon, traveller, author, and a friend of Sir Walter Scott, was famous for his *Travels in the Interior of Africa* (1799), an account of an exploration along the River Niger.

3. *Moral Tales for Young People*, published in five volumes in 1801, by Maria Edgeworth (1767–1849).

4. Mrs. Brown, a widow, had five daughters at home (see letter 132). "Cotterel" is taken to refer to one of the children of Sir John Cotterell, who lived at Garnons, Herefordshire.

5. *Celestina*, by Charlotte Smith, and *The History of Lady Julia Mandeville*, by Frances Moore.

---

150. SAMUEL MOULTON-BARRETT (BROTHER) TO EBB

[Hope End]
Jan 3.^{d} 1822.

My dearest Ba,
Who shines like a star,
And as bright as a piece of spa[r].
But no more compliments must I pay,
Or else I will waste all my head away
But Arabel's bird is dead,
For want of being bled.
O poor, unfortunate bird,
It died without saying a word.
Arabel's pocket hankerchief is quite wet,
And she is in a little bit of a pet.
And her tears do fall
Exactly like a ball.
So therefore I wish you good bye,
My ever dear little fly.
Your ever affectionate Sam,
Who likes nothing better than a *dram*.
(not physic!)

Address, on integral page: For the lady in the crib, / With a pain in the rib, / And without a wig.
Publication: None traced.
Manuscript: Edward R. Moulton-Barrett.

---

151. EDWARD MOULTON-BARRETT (BROTHER) TO EBB

[London]
February 5.th 1822

My ever dearest Ba
You must excuse my not writing to you yesterday as in the first place at the only time I possibly could have the least time to write there was not a drop of ink in the room and in the second place nearly all my time was occupied in preparing for an examination which the Doctor[1] threatens us, and in which he says he is going to work us most properly and most thoroughly. according to my agreement I wrote a note to Mr Bayford and went to Doctor Nuttals where soon after my arrival the Doctor ipse[2] arrived and after talking a little he went out of the room and soon appeared with little master George the son in heir who is really a very fine little fellow, the first question he asked was who I thought he was like I said I really could not judge as he was so young the Doctor then exclaimed "is not he like me, has he not got my aquiline nose, like an eagles beak, hey!! and his mouth is it not his mother's hey! hey!!['] in the evening we went to Mrs Simson's[3] to drink. she is better, but I think looks very ill. she asked very kindly after Papa. On Sunday we took a long walk to Brompton through the Park & after tea we started for the Charter House so that upon the whole we spent a very happy Saturday and Sunday, with, goose one day and roast beef another for dinner. I must be gone good bye
ever believe me
truly attached & ever affec.^t
Bro

Many many thanks for your letter though I complied with your request in one point I could not comply with it in another. Thank Mama for her kind letter and Henrietta for her promise of one. ——

Publication: None traced.
Manuscript: Edward R. Moulton-Barrett.

1. John Russell, D.D. (1786–1863), educated at Charterhouse and Christ Church, Oxford, returned to his old school as Assistant Master in 1806. He was appointed Headmaster in 1811 and held that post until 1832. He was described as "a man of exceptional vigour and capacity, a born reformer, and possessed of imagination and of original ideas" (*Charterhouse in London*, by Gerald S. Davies, 1921, p. 264). Under Russell's guidance, the school became very popular.
2. "Himself."
3. A friend of Elizabeth Moulton, referred to in letter 165 as "old mother Simpson."

152. EBB TO HENRIETTA MOULTON-BARRETT

My beloved Sister, ⟨my own dea⟩rest Henrietta
On her birthday.
Hope End. March 6.th 1822.[1]

Oh! once again, my trembling hand shall wake
The breathing sweetness of the magic lay—
Bid the o'erhanging shadows gently break,
And, radiant, brighten to a gladder day!
What though the fleeting hand of Suff'ring may
Still snatch a smile from Joy, and prompt a sigh—
Yet Hope be it thine, in mimic guise, t'array
The rugged form of stern Reality,
And calm, with laughing brow, the terrors of her eye!

What tho' perhaps, my Sister, it MAY be,
This hand shall falter o'er the untuned wire,
And the loved chords of sweetest minstrelsy
Shall breathe faint notes of intersepted fire!
What tho' the music of the sighing lyre
Be mute, or dead. Yet, Addles, faithfully,
Affection lingers while those strains expire,—
Gleams oer the broken string, and, "fancy free,"[2]
Smiles softly the fond smile of tenderness on thee!

⟨. . .⟩rian attached
Ba

Publication: None traced.
Manuscript: University of Durham.

1. EBB dated this letter two days after Henrietta's actual 13th birthday, 4 March. Henrietta, in turn, dated her birthday verse two days after EBB's, 6 March. EBB was in Gloucester when this birthday greeting was sent; the heading refers to Henrietta's own location, Hope End. EBB's fair copy of this birthday ode, at ABL (*Reconstruction*, D553), bears a sub-title: "Written on the prospect of recovering from a dangerous illness."
2. *A Midsummer Night's Dream*, II, 1, 164.

---

153. ARABELLA MOULTON-BARRETT TO EBB

[Hope End]
[ca. 6 March 1822][1]

My dearest M^{rs} poet
        I hope that the Doctor may please you on your birthday as I have phisic for you to take, and I hope that you will take some of it now, as

you are a young woman, you must take a larger quantity. well Mrs Poet I think I will soon cure you.

> "When thou art feeble old and gray,
> My healthy arms shall be thy stay;
> And I will sooth thy pains away.["]

Your ever dutiful
Doctor Thomson.

Address, on integral page: for M^{rs} poet.
Publication: None traced.
Manuscript: Berg Collection.

1. Identity of Arabella as writer conjectured from handwriting. Conjectural dating based on handwriting and references to EBB's illness.

---

154. HENRIETTA MOULTON-BARRETT TO EBB

[Hope End]
Wednesday [6 March 1822]¹

My ever dearest Ba

Well I must say I am rather pleased that you are of my opinion and I am *more* pleased that two people and more than two should agree that Bro's to my opinion exquisite and sublime birthday ode is so much superior to any of his *other works* it shews that he has attained the God of learning and what is more facinating and more godly he has by his warm heart his forgiving temper and his cultivated and polished manners if it is not too conceated a word for me to use perfectly won the hear[t] to my view of the heavenly muse of vertue some faults must *sometimes* always intrude in our path to heaven and certainly few he has[.] People who do not study his character cannot know him he is not fond of shewing off that you know he is not vain——

All your children were here yesterday but their cake was not made I am sorry to say but for all that they had a capital feast with mince pies and bread and Jam and when they were going away and we were at dinner we gave the children a glass of ale and a tumbler to Mrs Harford the little children namely Elen and Annette were rather terrified at the appearance of the glasses but they soon got over that so upon the whole they fared very well——

We had famous toasts after dinner in three times three the first that you might this time next year may be here enjoying both health and happiness the second for your nurses third for the hospital inhabitants of this mansion and fourth for Sir Frances Berdebt² all these were succeeded with great raps on the table so upon the whole you may think it made a little uproar[.] The dinner bell my dearest Ba I must withdraw to serve my stomach

Your afft
Addles

Address, on integral page: dearest Ba.
Publication: None traced.
Manuscript: Edward R. Moulton-Barrett.

1. Apparently written on EBB's birthday while she was ill and away from home. 6 March fell on a Wednesday in 1822.
2. Sir Francis Burdett (1770–1844), politician, was a very vocal critic of the abuse of power by government, an advocate of parliamentary reform, and a champion of the rights of the commonalty.

---

155. MARY MOULTON-BARRETT TO EBB

[Hope End]

To my own beloved Elizabeth.
March 6th 1822

Fondly I would invoke Parnassus heights
To bless me with one strain of love to thee,
Unheard my prayer– chill silence sadly blights
Th' ambitious hope so vainly formed by me!

But tho' the magic of thy own loved Muse
Be to my lay, for ever thus denied
Tho' she the concord of her lyre refuse
Won by *thy* hand, it is much more my pride!

On thee, my dearly loved, the tuneful nine
All emulous have smiled, in reasons dawn,
And sought in thy sad sufferings to entwine
The cheering laurel, with thy couch of thorn!

But tho' thus cradled in th' "enchanting shell"
Lulled by th' Æolian lyre thy infant rest,
Strong tho' the charm of genius' magic spell,
'Tis not for this thy Mother loves thee best!

More dear to her the unrepining smile
Which radiant in thy suffering brow does shine,
The patience that could months of pain beguile
The Christians peace! sure pledge of love divine!

For this her heart in thankfulness is raised
To Him who gives the sorrow & its balm
Well, for affliction, may His name be praised
While Resignation brings thee, Heaven-sent calm!

Thus richly blessed! child of my fondest love
What would thy Mother's prayer add to thy store?
But that returning health, may gladly prove
"Mercy that does so much, can still do more."

And while thy Parents bless thy natal day
Hushed be each sigh, & dried be every tear,
While Hope shall cheering shed her brightest ray
On Health & peace thy lot! for many a year!

If a darkened room[1] did not conceal my *blushes*, I should not find courage to send these uncouth lines to my dearest Ba! but critic as she is, the hasty & faulty effort shall go, for it comes from the heart & disowns all connection with the head!– Vanity makes only one clause, & that is, that no one sees it but *your* own dear self—on this, I must be peremptory—

Homer himself could not tell you how earnestly I wish you *many* happy years, nor how dear you are to your fondly attached

Mother.

Excuse a *trembling* hand!–

Address, on integral page: To / My dearest Ba.
Publication: None traced.
Manuscript: British Library.

1. Septimus had been born less than a month before. Apparently Mary Moulton-Barrett was still recuperating.

---

156. HENRIETTA MOULTON-BARRETT[1] TO EBB

[Hope End]

To my dearest Ba
On her happy birthday
March 8th 1822[2]

Hear the birds how they warble their praises to God
But who can behold him but those that are good
Then goodness what art thou? and what is thy name?
That thou wilt never lend thy beauteous fame

Except to those who doth combine truth patience and good
　humour
And whose heart is as warm as the last day in summer
But goodness I pray thee behold and is it not so?
You are a relation to E B Barrett you know
A near one and dear one I really and truly do think
For your qualities in her are as fresh as a Pink
Then Oh my dearest Ba are not you happy
Do not you know that this is not false flattery
Then may you once more be restored to sweet health
For that would I know be to you the greatest of wealth

Address, on integral page: For / dearest Ba.
Publication: None traced.
Manuscript: Edward R. Moulton-Barrett.

　1. Correspondent identified by handwriting.
　2. See letter 152, note 1.

---

157. EBB TO HENRIETTA MOULTON-BARRETT

[Gloucester]
[ca. May 1822][1]

My time is limited & I cannot therefore write more than a line. A
thousand thanks for your information my beloved Addles it has given
me real delight & in return you shall hear all I have to tell since I last
wrote. Papa settled every thing with M! Brydges[2] as he came through
Ledbury & it is agreed that when the day is fixed for my removal Papa
is to write to M! B who wishes to come to Gloucester to be with me in
case of accident during the journey– Tommy Cook also is to attend me
so that I cannot want medical assistance.

　This Papa told me the first day he came but has been quite silent
since– I could not help letting it out to Mama in my last letter, give her
a hint not to mention it when she writes– If you hear any thing pray my
dearest Addles let me know as I am quite in the dark——

Y! own attached
Ba!

Publication: None traced.
Manuscript: R.J.L. Altham.

　1. It is thought that EBB returned to Hope End, after her long stay in Gloucester,
around May 1822.
　2. W. H. Brydges, described as a "Medical Gentleman" and surgeon, High-Street,
Ledbury (*Hints of Ledbury*, 1831).

158. EDWARD MOULTON-BARRETT (BROTHER) TO EBB

[London]
June 17.th 1822.

My dearest Miss Basy

Upon my word and honor your impudence I think encreases every day in proportion with the movement of your toes at least I hope so for it must make a most rapid progress I suppose by the time it reaches the knee you will be setting up in opposition to Dr Bailley[1] and all the first Physicians in London, you will then write criticism upon Locke &^c &^c Swear Sir Isaac Newtons[2] discovies [*sic*] are all a humbug, & that you are the only wise person in the world, upon my honor the very idea of your giving your opinion in opposition to Mr Greens,[3] now as it happens a blister would be useful if the swelling in my knee did not go down for the swelling is occasioned by too full a supply of (I^4 do not know the medical term though perhaps a lady with so much "MEDICAL EXPERIENCE" as you are master of, may) what is *comonly* denominated joint oil though I suffer no pain the swelling is still there, though not so large, for farther particulars enquire of Mr Green who attends me. Sam left us last night for Charter House, I am to remain here a few days longer– My knee is much smaller though not yet at its proper demensions. Mrs Orme was here this Morning & says she recieved a letter from Henrietta in which she says Henny expects an answer she wants to know what to for she has recieved no letter from him. Now I tell you what Miss Basy I have no idea of writing every other day to you as I hitherto have done without having some return. I have now written you four letters and I have had from you ONE, Dab it but your [*sic*] a cool hand by Jove!! Papa desires me to say that he shall comply with your request by writing to you very soon. I must wish you good bye now my dearest Ba but you shall here [*sic*] from me soon

ever believe me
your affectionately attached—
Bro— .

Address, on integral page: Miss Barrett.[5]
Publication: None traced.
Manuscript: Edward R. Moulton-Barrett.

1. Matthew Baillie (1761–1823), morbid anatomist, was Physician Extraordinary to George III.
2. The philosophers John Locke (1632–1704) and Sir Isaac Newton (1642–1727).
3. Possibly Jonathan Green (1788?–1864). See letter 113, note 4.
4. Underscored twice.
5. Written over the address is a 16-line draft poem signed with initials "HT" [Henry Trant?] (SD437). The first line reads "While here forlorn & lost I tread."

159. EDWARD MOULTON-BARRETT (BROTHER) &
MARY TREPSACK TO EBB

[In hand of Edward Moulton-Barrett]   [London]
                                                        June 18.th 1822.—

No! No!! Miss Basy you certainly cannot tell a slight lie when you are
hard pressed, your letter prooved this to me most fully, and YOU as well
as your FANCY must have no very small share of IMAGINATION[1] to
invent such down right thumpers! Eh! Basy Do you take. Eh!? Well I
must say that was rather good, certainly upon the whole considering the
extreme labor it put you to and that you worked hard a whole half hour
at it I could not do less than drop a compliment, poor Girl! she really
deserved a little encouragement if it was only for her industry. If
modesty is my failing (as you kindly took upon yourself to say for me,)
it never was yours & never will be. Fancy is certainly a wonderful
GANIUS [*sic* for genius] to fly away from you to seek refuge on his
perch I'l be bound you bellowed so loud in the poor things ear and he
being in his cage was OBLIGED[1] to where he COULD GET,[1] I'l be bound I
would make your toes rattle (in spite of excommomunication [*sic*]) if I
were to run in and tell you the house was on fire and the beams were
falling in. Dab it how you would jig Eh! But I say Basy I cant bolt a
stale PILL[1] it sticks in my throat, no it wont do, and to bring it forward
too with your usual impudence as your own, you say "upon MY SOLE"[1]
now as it happens it was MY pun and Mr Mc Swiney's HOLY SOLE[2]
Come I see it is necessary to refresh your memory now and then when
[you] so conveniently FORGET.[1] Well my INIMITABLE[1] sister I must wish
you good bye, but you may depend upon hearing from me soon. You
will be a sharp young lady to get learned notes and introductory
treatises from me.

                    Believe me your affectionately attached
                    Bro—

I[3] am as anxious to hear that YOUR FACE is free from the tyranny of
your fingers as YOU are to hear that *I*[3] am free from the tyranny of the
doctor!–

    [Continued in Mary Trepsack's hand] Bulletin of the Inimitable
Youth's health– The distressing Symtoms are (we are happy to say)
progressively vanishing If we cou[l]d induce the patient to exercise his
Tongue a little more It w^d be more pleasing to his friends– We are
afraid the air of London agrees not with that Member—but mayhap the
shock he received on coming away so suddenly is the sole cause of his
present Melancholy– The only fault we can find in him is the want of
speech– as you are considered to have some knowledge of diseases, &

remedies, perhaps you can point out some cure for this Young Man's complaint, If so, you will oblige the Medical board now sitting on this disease of Silence, by giving them the earliest information– We are truly happy to hear of the improvement in the Spine, God send you every blessing my dearest Girl——

Addressed and franked by EBB's uncle on integral page: London June eighteen 1822 / Miss Barrett / Hope End / Ledbury / S M Barrett.
Publication: None traced.
Manuscript: Edward R. Moulton-Barrett.

1. Underscored three times.
2. Underscored six times.
3. Underscored twice.

---

160. EDWARD MOULTON-BARRETT (BROTHER) TO EBB

[London]
June 20.th 1822.

My ever dearest Ba

On tuesday evening just as we were sitting down to tea we heard a rap at the door[.] Trepy run to the top of the stairs to tell Tomkins to say not at home however he is fortunately so deaf that he could not hear her, and presently anounced M.[r] Cockral or some such high sounding name we all expected some grand acquaintance of Sam's one was putting [on] her petticoats Granny pulled off her apron and put herself in her most elegant position, in short we all put on our most INSINIVATING [*sic*] appearances when who should walk in but little Tommy Cooky, he had a dish of tea with us and said the reason he had come to town was that during his illness a gentleman had given him a carriage & he had come to see about it, he is on his way to M.[r] Hunter at Brighton and above all what do you think he has never seen the sea yet, he says [he] is in a most debilitated state from his late illness and a dip will brace and strengthen his nerves. Yesterday who should walk in but M.[r] M.[c]Swiney I dont know when I have seen him looking so well he is realy very much improved he says the second day he was at the school he knocked a boy down in his own words gave him his full length on the ground, he has bought a net for one pound and fishes every day with it, in giving a description of the country he says there is very little wood but remarkably fine HEDGES I with my usual wit answered can you turn a coach and six on them sir, rather sharp eh! By the by I HAVE had a blister on Miss Basy in spite of you and your medical experience, yes and it drew too famously what do you say to that eh, ⟨as⟩ it was put on on tuesday night we cannot yet tell if it has had the effect of reducing the swelling now because I have a blister on do not set your imagination to work and swear you saw me with my legs swelled and in blisters (you understand me), for Mr Green says I am coming on as well as possible but that the blister will hasten my recovery: Good bye my dearest Bazy ever believe me

your affectionately attached
Bro

Trepy's love and she meant to have written to Mama today, but has not time.

Address, on integral page: S M Barrett Esqr MP. / Hope End / Ledbury / Herefordshire. "Ba" is written below the seal.
Publication: None traced.
Manuscript: Edward R. Moulton-Barrett.

---

161. EDWARD MOULTON-BARRETT (BROTHER) TO EBB

[London]
June 22^d 1822—.

Upon my honor Miss Basy I hardly know how to express my indignation at the *atrocious, barefaced, unpresedented, impudent,* abominable &^c lies that you are guilty of telling, dont think because yesterday the more urgent calls of hunger prevented me from paying you, that you will escape my clutches today, no, no, it is rather too good a joke to let you have your confounded whackers to pass with impunity. The charge is this that you, E.B.B. have been guilty of telling most *unfounded* falsehoods (alias confounded) concerning the Latin reading of Master E. M. Barrett, you said that the aforesaid youth declared he could read Latin better than any persons or person in the united states of Great Briton [*sic*] and Ireland, which declaration is as false as it is unfounded, he the said E.M.B____tt swears to the contrary and in consequence of this abominable falsehood in the presence of a M^r M^c S____y &c &c he was yesterday compelled to read aloud from the sixth book of the Æneid, and tormented most desperately. Sam has come and I am going for the first time walk, tomorrow I am to go with Sam to school. I must wish you good bye.

Ever believe me
your affectionately attached
Bro.

Address, on integral page: S. M. Barrett Esq.ʳ MP. / Hope End / Ledbury / Herefordshire. "Ba" is written below the seal.
Publication: None traced.
Manuscript: Edward R. Moulton-Barrett.

---

162. EDWARD MOULTON-BARRETT (BROTHER) TO EBB

[London]
June 24ᵗʰ 1822[1]

My ever dearest Ba

I believe the fates have decreed that I should not give you your deserts for your impudence however I can assure you that I shall not forget you at some other time yesterday just when I was in the middle of my bang up in came master Sam, and I was obliged to finish my letter in a great hurry before I had given you HALF[2] your due. I should advise my friend as a well wisher of yours to send me no more of your impudence or else you shall repent it by Jove too late, no fates or any thing else shall save you. Sam yesterday came home in triumph, looking half a head taller for he has got up another form, he asked Watky[3] he heard him the Greek alphabet & then put him up. Mʳ Mᶜ Swiney dined with us yesterday and was shown your Greek epitaph, in the first place he says Anacreontic measure is not proper for an epitaph, it ought to be Hexameters & Pentameters, in the second place you must send down the translation of it, as he cannot make out your meaning. He also saw your lines which were sent to Colburns[4] and thinks them quite beautiful but it is not adapted to the public, as it is not so interesting to them not knowing the circumstances which attended it. I enclose Colburns note which he sent with the verses now dont be in a passion my friend Basy because all authors must meet with disappointment you know, I should advise you next time to send, a subject more interesting to the public. I could not go last night to school with Sam because Papa had forgotten to send a note to Watky to apprise him of my coming and therefore my bed could not ⟨be⟩ ready however Sam took one last night and I go this evening. Good bye my dearest Ba you must not expect to hear from me so often.

Ever believe me
your ever affectionately attached–
Bro.

Granny desires me to say that though she has neglected to write to you there is nobody in this world she loves better. —

Address, on integral page: S. M. Barrett Esq! M.P. / Hope End / Ledbury / Herefordshire. "Ba" is written below the seal.
Publication: None traced.
Manuscript: Edward R. Moulton-Barrett.

1. Altered from June 23ᵈ
2. Underscored three times.
3. The Rev. Robert Watkinson (1775–1869), Second Master at Charterhouse, later Rector of St. Laurence, Newland, Essex.
4. Henry Colburn (d. 1855), publisher. He was instrumental in starting (1814) *The New Monthly Magazine.*

---

163. EDWARD MOULTON-BARRETT (BROTHER) TO EBB

[London]
June 30!ʰ 1822.

My ever dearest Ba

You must excuse the scratch I sent you yesterday but Granny came in a glass coach to fetch us and went afterwards to visit so many people, and so many of them were at home, that we did not get here till the last bell was ringing. I must confess that it was not worth a penny of itself, but as you have not heard from me for a week I flattered Myself that you would like to hear, that I have not lost anything by my long absence and that I have not suffered any thing from any return of my rheumatism the whole week. We have had a most precious row this week, the cake man used to put down the boys name and some of them had bills for cakes and fruit to the amount of pounds. Russell found this out and made every boy pay what he could and bring the rest with him after the holidays, the table at which Russell sat to recieve the money was completely strewed with gold and silver I dare say there were about thirty pounds in gold besides an immense collection of five shilling pieces, half crowns, shillings, & sixpences. Mʳ Mͨ Swiney was here yesterday and saw your translation he says the Greek is wrong but will be easily altered and I am to try today with his assistance to alter it, he offered to take Papa to a Catholic chapel today to hear some very emminent man but his time which he fixed has elapsed and he has not made his appearance. I am glad to see Miss Basy that your impudence is at length silenced, however I wish you would favor me a with [*sic*] line now and then, whilst you are *resting your toes*, however I suppose you find the charges against your impudence qui⟨te⟩ unanswerable. Mʳ Mͨ Swiney brought yesterday, the New Monthly Magazine and there are two songs of Campbells own,¹ which are realy the greatest stuff you ever read, and, (though I do not wish to raise your vanity higher than it is) are no more to be compared to yours, than (I wont make you too vain) you are to be called a modest young lady. I must wish you good bye as we are just going to church and I have no more room in my paper. Good bye my dearest Ba

ever believe me
your affectionately attached
Bro.

Address, on integral page: S. M. Barrett Esq[r] M.P. / Hope End / Ledbury / Herefordshire.
Publication: None traced.
Manuscript: Edward R. Moulton-Barrett.

   1. On pp. 572 and 576 of Vol. IV (1822).

---

164. EDWARD MOULTON-BARRETT (BROTHER) TO EBB

[London]
July 13.th 1822.

My ever dearest Ba

Do not imagine that I meant to imply that your "authorieal disappointments, are trifles"[1] far from it, on the contrary "tristia"[2] signifies things that are worthy of being greived for, I only mean, I HOPE you will in the course of time & by experience be able to bear these sorrowful things with fortitude, next I send *you* a classical quotation I shall translate it word [by word] underneath and then you cannot misinterpret it Miss Basy however I will try you once more & I do not think you can well misinterpret it, "tu es stultus."[3] I can tell you another thing too Miss which you have completely mistaken in me and which I am sure you ought to know "Tempore et usu"[4] i.e. that you can never surprise me, by any IMPUDENCE either in words or deeds of yours so had better keep quiet on that subject. Now I have given you your due, I must thank you most sincerely for your letter, and condole with you on this abominable fresh attack in the head, which prevents you so provokingly, from pursuing your classical studies, with as much ardour as you wish. I hope you will not exert yourself TOO much even though you discontinue your delight [in] the "ars Poetica" for a short time, you will find the advantage of your privation. I must wish you good bye but you shall hear from me again tomorrow. Good bye my dearest Ba pray comply with my request.

Ever believe me
your ever affectionately attached.
Bro. —

Address, on integral page: Miss Barrett—
Publication: None traced.
Manuscript: Edward R. Moulton-Barrett.

1. Possibly a reference to a discouraging letter EBB had received from Henry Colburn (see letter 162).
2. "Sorrowful."
3. "You are a fool."
4. "By time and practice."

---

165. EDWARD MOULTON-BARRETT (BROTHER) & MARY TREPSACK TO EBB

[In the hand of Edward Moulton-Barrett]   [London]
                                                    July. 28th 1822

Though it threatens us rain, yet dear Granny is gone
To see "old mother Simpson" & "Good M[rs] Dun,"[1]
Where your verses my Basy will make a commotion
Like Burdet or Hume[2] on some Popular motion
The end of each sentence, & oft in the middle
With the sense incomplete & doubtful as riddle,
Dear Granny will sing till her cough interferes,
And respite is given to her auditors ears.
"What a wonderful child, what a pity it is
That her brother should have such a Mandarin phiz!
What a wonderful child, of all knowledge no lack
What a contrast the brains to her leachy[3] old back,
Her strains are well worthy the very best of the Nine,
And her head how deserving a far better spine—
But look at her extracts—Tis not to abuse you
Though in Latin it is "tempore et usu"[4]
Greek, Latin, & Hebrew, serve her for quotation,
And in Justice, she brings them out in rotation,
To Italian & French she will only descend,
In writing to Minny, or some Hereford friend,
Or to Bummy her aunt, or some mean burgage holder
Some reformer, Huntite,[5] or "Worthy Freeholder"–
At all languages used she turns up her nose
And declares against Pittites[6] all placemen & Prose.
Dear wonderful child I would fain she wore bree⟨ches⟩
That her back was reformed, and abandon'd the leaches⟨."⟩
In chorus all cry, "We would fain she wore breeches
That her back was reformed & abandon'd the leaches"

Thus in church at our prayers, for "fruits in due season"[7]
And many more things in and out of all reason
When the Parson is done and complete is his word
We cry out "we beseech thee to hear us good Lord."[8]
It were useless to tell you the talk of Patch work
Or their female idea on the famine at Cork
Dear Granny's returned & complains of my prose
My "BLUE *little* PINS eyes" and scarce visible nose
She adds too with her love (so well as she knows you[)]
Her wonder you can't find a good rhyme for Brozy.
Your wit M^{rs} Ba as I've always declared
To your impudence certainly can't be compared
With respect to your wit, I must say without pause
I've heard many worse things in a far JUSTER cause.
In one line you call me a piece of perfection
⟨In the⟩ next on my head piece you make a re⟨flection⟩
A ⟨word⟩ to YOURSELF may be justly applied
Which you cooly gave me when you lied.

[Continued in Mary Trepsack's hand]   [29 July 1822]

The Boys returnd to school last Eve in perfect health, looking forward
with the highest pleasure to Wednesday, your Ladyship must not be too
impatient– The small Esq[uir]e is desirous of paying a visit to Soho
Bazaar & as St. Swithin may weep on Thursday & not on friday, we
keep them those two days, Saturday they will proceed on their Journey,
that is If your father does not counter order– God bless you dear Girl—
         [Illegible scrawl]

Address, in Edward Moulton-Barrett's hand, on integral page: S. M. Barrett Esqr M.P. /
Hope End / near Ledbury / Herefordshire.
Publication: None traced.
Manuscript: Edward R. Moulton-Barrett.

1. Mrs. Dunn is mentioned several times in secondary material in a social context, mainly in letters from EBB's brother Sam. In one to Henrietta (SD715) he mentions attending a ball at Mrs. Dunn's, and in one from Henrietta (SD835) Sam is stated to be a "great favorite" of Mrs. Dunn.

2. Francis Burdett (1770–1844) and Joseph Hume (1777–1855), contemporary politicians. According to *DNB*, the latter spoke "longer and oftener and probably worse than any other private member" of the Commons.

3. A reference to the use of leeches during EBB's illness.

4. "By time and practice."

5. An adherent of Henry Hunt (1773–1835), a radical politician and advocate of universal suffrage, who had been imprisoned for two years for his part in the Peterloo massacre of 1819.

6. Followers of William Pitt the Younger (1759–1806), statesman and one-time Prime Minister.

7. Cf. Matthew, 21:41.

8. Cf. Acts, 26:3.

166. EDWARD MOULTON-BARRETT (BROTHER) TO EBB

[London]
August 1st 1822.

My ever dearest Ba,

Directly I arrived here yesterday evening I scribled a line though the last bell was then ringing, in hopes that I should be in time but the postman was off out of reach before Neddy,[1] as Sam calls him [*sic*, for his] rat, could overtake him. The reason I was in such a hurry that you should hear from me was I knew how anxious you would be to hear how we past the examination, and above all I knew how delighted you would be to hear that I was yesterday promoted to the higher form namely the fifth, Doctor Russell called over all the boys names who for their ill conduct were to have double holiday tasks, and in the midst he called out my name I was in a most horrible frightened for thought he was going to set me a good long holiday task instead of which he told me I might go to the higher form. As Treppy Sam & I are going to the Bazaar I must wish you good bye till I see your elegant face on Saturday evening. We are waiting anxiously for Papa's answer. Excuse my hurry for, it seems very much like rain before we start.

Ever believe me
your affectionately attached.
Bro ——

Publication: None traced.
Manuscript: Edward R. Moulton-Barrett.

1. The reference to Neddy is unclear. Although a diminutive of Edward, it is unlikely that Bro means himself; it is possible that he refers to a fag of that name, whom he sent to catch the postman.

167. THOMAS CAMPBELL TO EBB

30 Foley Place Portland Chapel — [London]
Aug: 28 1822.

Madam

I should have answer'd your letter sooner but I have been unwell & very much occupied— It certainly would be very unhandsome on my part to refuse a dedication from a lady and from one who offers me so flattering an expression of her literary estimation[1]—but as you ask also my opinion of the composition I will give you my opinion frankly for the very reason that your addressing me with confidence inspires me with a real kind wish that my advice may contribute to your happiness

EBB Aged 17

& not to the contrary.– I would advise you to pause at least & to consult some other literary person with whom you can have more immediate discussion about the merits of the piece than with my self before you publish it—at least with your name– The voice of public criticism is hard & the poem is open to many objections– It bespeaks an amiable heart & an elegant mind—but it is the work of an inexperienced imagination & though the versification & expression are such as should make me very loth to exhort you to give up poetical composition Yet I should decieve you if I anticipated the story & main effect of the poem being likely to be popularly admired– I have marked one or two passages to which I particularly object – I object in general to its lyric intermixtures– They are the most difficult of all gems to set in a Narrative poem & should always be of the first water.——

I should be heartily sorry if this unsparing criticism were to damp your poetical hopes & ambition– It is with no such intention that I comply with your request to give my judgement of this work– And rationally taken my opinion if it were of more weight than it is ought not to depress you– I am accustomed to applications of the kind & nine times out of ten decline them from a fear of discouraging an inexperienced author who may not have sense to distinguish my motive for sincerity– Something in your letter gives me an idea that you are not of this injudicious order of literary consulters– I determined therefore to answer your note– And though it might look more like gallantry & good nature to encourage you to speedy publication yet in reality if I should mislead you by false hopes I should be acting a very unmanly & cruel part.– Give me leave at the same time to assure you that unless the perusal of your composition had given me a personal interest in you I should not risque that appearance of arrogance and severity which advice of this complexion is so apt to bear however kindly it may be meant— I trust you will believe you have a

sincere & respectful well wisher
in
Tho.ˢ Campbell

Address, on integral page: Miss Eliz^th B. Barrett / Hope End / Ledbury——
Publication: None traced.
Manuscript: National Library of Scotland.

1. A manuscript title-page including a dedication is at the Armstrong Browning Library. It reads "Leila, / A Tale: / with other Poems. / . . . / To / Thomas Campbell Esqr. / as a humble tribute / of respect for his genius, / and gratitude for his kindness, / the following pages are inscribed, by / his obliged Servant / The Author." It is followed by a preface commencing "In opening the little volume, which so humbly solicits his clemency, the Critic must not expect . . ." The work was first printed in 1913. (See *Reconstruction*, D459–460.)

168. EDWARD MOULTON-BARRETT (BROTHER) TO EBB

[London]
[*Postmark:* 12 October 1822]

My ever dearest Ba

I must write you a fewe lines to tell you that on Monday, tuesday, & Wednesday were examination days we did not go into hall to be examined till tuesday we then went and the D^{rs} set us a thesis to write verses upon the subject was "sol sciens"[1] and there all sat round a long table and we had to make twelve verses Hexameters and Pentameters when we had all finished we gave up our verses and we found one poor unfortunate boy who had only done one verse and that was all wrong, he had to walk to Dr Russell with his single verse in his hand all scratched out however he is to have one more chance next three weeks, another boy (whom Russell has booked as a regular downright "idle, shuffling blockhead") described the sun as adorned instead of adored by the Ancients and his verses were upon the whole so bad that Russell read them loud out not one of them would scan, on Wednesday we went in again and were examined in our Homer parsing and construing, our Ovid repetition &^{c} and Greek vocabulary all of which I got off famously and am now pretty high in my form 3^d or 4th I dont know if I tolled you of a boy who said the Westminsters boys licked him, however his story was this he said he went to Westminster on Sunday to see it and that some of the big boys caught him & licked him so terribly that two men were obliged to come to his assistance. On hearing this Russell imediately wrote to the head Master at Westminster who after inquiry found it was all a lie and wrote to Russell that effect Russell enquired of the boy and after some time he confessed it was not true, and upon confession was sentenced to recieve sixteen stripes, accordingly yesterday morning he was brought to the block & recieved his punishment with four rods,[2] ten shillings Watky was executioner and every now and then through the key hole, between the boys groans we could distinguish Watky's voice desiring him to "take away his hand" or telling the Monitor to "hold him tight["] &^{c} &^{c}– And between every stroke Watky waited about half a minute so that he had it most sweetly the blood flowed most copiously. Granny sends her love to Papa and begs ⟨him⟩ let Mathews exterminate the rats (as she ⟨knows⟩ he can) for fear they should bite any body's nose off for such things have been known you may think I am joking but upon my honor this was Granny's message and she was quite grave when she desired me to say so. I must wish you good bye my dearest Ba but you shall hear from me in the week again.

Ever believe me

your affectionately attached——

Bro——

Treppy desires Mama will in her next letter acknowledge the reception of her 2 pair of shoes and Cocoa nut & raisins (which were for you) by Treahern[3]——

Address, on integral page: Miss Barrett / Hope End / Ledbury / Herefordshire.
Publication: None traced.
Manuscript: Edward R. Moulton-Barrett.

1. "Knowing the sun."
2. "The Block, shaped something like an executioner's block, with one step to kneel upon, and another over which to bend the head . . . Six cuts were generally given, and always *in camera*" (*Charterhouse Old and New*, by E. P. Eardley Wilmot and E. C. Streatfield, 1895).
3. Probably John Treherne, a tenant on the Hope End estate, or his son William, who was employed in the Hope End stables.

---

169. EDWARD MOULTON-BARRETT (BROTHER) TO EBB

[London]
[*Postmark:* 2 November 1822]

My ever dearest Ba

I am very sorry that you should be uneasy about your "ars Poetica" but you may set your maternal fears at rest for I have his word for not showing it to any one but himself I believe he is neither writing for his own amusement nor is he writing it as a lesson but is only translating it from the book and so there you need not be uneasy so my dear Miss Bazy you need not fret yourself into the Lumbago, nor keep your "*well leg*" in bed a bit the more for it nor need it prevent the other from following it a bit the more tardily. I am really both surprised & delighted at the comparative swiftness of your recovery to what it was a few months ago I must say that I anticipate happier holidays this Christmas that [*sic*] I have had for the last year by your total recovery at least so far so as to be able to join in all our cozy little fireside round games, or chats and birthday processions or gambols, I hope again to see you transformed from the delicate invalid living upon pills and draughts to the healthy & livley Mrs Pickle.[1] With respect to your new poem[2] you talk about *blushing* to own that you have not yet finished your second canto, in the first place this is the very first time I ever heard you COULD blush atall [*sic*] in the second place even supposing you were endowed with this newly acquired genius I think in this case it would indeed be misapplied, for instead of blushing I think may well boast of your rapid progress, particularly as you seem to have bestowed so much pains upon it to suit the taste of your "friend Tom."³ I have no news at all from Charter House this week except that I got off my examination capitally, Sam was not examined.

Ever believe me
your affectionately attached ——
Bro——.

Who do you think has just made his appearance, no less a person than Mr Mc Swiney he says he has come to attend the Radical dinner on Tuesday he is looking as well as ever I remember him.

Address, on integral page: Miss Barrett / H⟨ope⟩ End / Ledbury / Herefordshire.
Publication: None traced.
Manuscript: Edward R. Moulton-Barrett.

1. In *The Adventures of Peregrine Pickle* (1768), by Tobias G. Smollet (1721–71).
2. Possibly an early draft of *An Essay on Mind.*
3. Presumably Tommy Cook.

---

170. EDWARD MOULTON-BARRETT (BROTHER)
& EDWARD MOULTON-BARRETT (FATHER) TO EBB

[In the hand of Edward Moulton-Barrett (brother)]   [London]
[ca. November 1822]¹

My ever dearest Ba
    I sit down without a word to tell you out of the comon order of things but I know, (though by the bye my friend you played me rather a shabby trick this week) if I did not send you something in the shape of a letter you would swear at me, shake your raven locks, (I beg your pardon I forgot you had none)² kick about your WELL LEG, in short I should never hear the last of it[.] I have I think as good an excuse as possible for not letting you have a line today but I disdain to make use of such mean artifice and write to you today for the sole purpose of giving you a bit of a remembrance and to teach you how to treat with such slite [*sic*] a person of my distinguished character it is now some time since I have mentioned your *unparalleled impudence* and I have forborne from so doing in hopes that a little salutary advice and a few occasional *bang ups* had had the desired effect and that you were RATHER less insolent, and as your *toes* began to *approach* the ground *you* were begginning to *approach* to something having the semblance of

humility, but alas! how vain were all my hopes! all my expectations! how ungrounded are all hopes of humiliation in a young lady raised four feet from the ground on a spine crib! for instead as I fondly hoped that you were improving I find you are not only as bad as ever, but that you are breaking out in fresh places, and becoming more incorrigible than ever, that instead of your impudence *falling* with your TOES, I begin to fear it will *raise* with your HEAD. As I have nothing more to bring against you I shall wait for a fairer opportunity of giving you your full measure and dare say by next Saturday if you are not greatly improved I shall feel myself justified in giving you a second edition. For the present I shall wish you good bye.

Ever believe me

your affectionately attached.

Bro——

Love to Bumy and the rest your dear party. —

[Continued in the hand of Edward Moulton-Barrett (father) at top of page 1] Sam is coming to Town for Mail Summond by Boddington[3] on particular Business—

Address, in hand of Bro, on integral page: Miss Barrett / Hope End / Ledbury / Herefordshire.
Publication: None traced.
Manuscript: Edward R. Moulton-Barrett.

1. Conjectural dating based on references to EBB's illness and to her "well leg," which was mentioned in previous letter.
2. At this time, EBB's hair had been shorn—a contemporary sketch by her mother shows her wearing a skull-cap. (See *Reconstruction*, F7.)
3. Of Boddington Philips Sharpe & Co., London merchants. Edward Moulton-Barrett wrote to his father, Charles Moulton, on 13 February 1807 (SD70), "I am compelled to apply to some Merchant to assist me in my difficulties, I therefore entered into an agreement with the house of Boddington and Sharpe to allow me a specific sum for my own private expences and other sums that they name to advance for the payment of these debts I have contracted." The Moulton-Barrett family used the firm as a clearing house for their Jamaican interests well into the latter part of the nineteenth century.

171. THOMAS CAMPBELL TO EBB

10 Upper Seymour Street West—London
Dec[r] 1. 1822.

My dear young Lady

I addressd you in the sincerity of my heart when I applauded the symptoms of promising talent in the Ms which you first sent to me—[1] It was very natural for your youth & ingenuousness to throw yourself again on my confidence—& I should be most sorry if this

communication in the least annoyed your feelings– There is no
necessity that it should do so– I like you nothing the worse for a
mistake originating in simplicity– But, it *is* a mistake to suppose that
with an incessant succession of papers which I must read as a matter of
business I can possibly admit of renewd applications for criticisms on
the worths of young authors however promising they may be– I have
neither eye-sight nor leisure for it– I return you therefore the Ms[2]—&
remain

Your very sincere well-wisher
T. Campbell——

Address, on integral page: Miss E. B. Barnett [*sic*] —
Publication: None traced.
Manuscript: National Library of Scotland.

  1. See letter 167.
  2. Possibly of EBB's poem "The Enchantress," the fair copy of which is on paper
watermarked 1822 (*Reconstruction*, D232).

172. EBB TO CHARLES JOHN MOULTON-BARRETT

Addressed to my beloved Storm
on his birthday
Hope End. December 28.th 1822.[1]

The chords, the Minstrels fingers strike,
Now proudly soar, now softly sigh,
Yet are the echoing strings alike,
Though oftimes their wild melody
May swelling rise, or sinking die!
There let me wreath my votive lay
With gift more prized, and verse more gay–
For if Affection wake the lute,
My Brother will not wish it mute!
And while a day so glad as this
Gives Music to my harps soft tone,
I'll ask no loftier praise than his,
No smile more radiant than his own!
Young Hope in gay perspective shews
Long dreamt of Healths seraphic form,
Led by the Mercy that arose
Like Iris from the bursting storm;
And I am blest, yet seek I where
Affection lingers—! then the while

I give thee all I CAN . . . a prayer . .
Oh! grant me ALL *I ask* . . . a smile!–
                              Dearest Storm's
                              own Ba.

Publication: None traced.
Manuscript: Pierpont Morgan Library.

1. His 8th.

---

173. EDWARD MOULTON-BARRETT (BROTHER) TO EBB

[London]
Feb.ʸ 9ᵗʰ 1823——

My ever dearest Ba

I believe I forgot to tell you that we were examined on tuesday and on Wednesday in our Ovid & Homer by Russell and came off extremely well, Russell has made a new regulation, that there are to be only eighteen in each form mine and the one above, so he turned down the four worst to make up the number, so I am afraid it will be rather more difficult to get up into the higher form, on tuesday we had an English theme to make, the subject was Justice, and I got first in it, the following day we had, thesis verses on the North Pole in Latin, and I was again first. Can you fancy Sam spouting English poetry he actually learns eight lines every day and was spouting in bed this morning "Ye IMPS of SOLOMON." instead of "Ye nymphs of Solyma."[1] Watky has quite recovered from his gout or rheumatism or whatever he chooses to call [it] but his temper seems to fall off with every attack I always thought him RATHER passionate, but now he does nothing all day in school but fly over the benches, knock the boys down &ᶜ, &ᶜ, to be sure he is very good-natured when he is not in a passion but he puts one in mind of a man who was going to part with his servant why says he "John what are you going to leave me for" "Sir says "John[2] you are too passionate" "too [*sic*] be sure" says he "I am sometimes put in a passion but I am soon out of it and then I am always very indulgent" "Yes Sir" says John "but you are no sooner out of one than your [*sic*] in another." I must finish my letter my dearest Ba ⟨as⟩ tea is nearly ready

ever believe me your affectionate
Brozy——

Addressed and franked by EBB's uncle on integral page: London Feby. twelve 1823 / Miss Barrett / Hope End / Ledbury / S M Barrett.

Publication: None traced.
Manuscript: Edward R. Moulton-Barrett.

1. The opening words of Pope's pastoral poem "Messiah" (1712).
2. Quotation marks occur as shown.

---

174. EDWARD MOULTON-BARRETT (BROTHER) TO EBB

[London]
[*Postmark:* 22 February 1823]

My dearest Bazy.

For the third time I have come home by myself without poor Sam, he stopped on account of having been reported irregular, I staid a long time begging Russell & Penny[1] but all to no purpose. Oh Bazy, Bazy, I have been writhing in agony ever since thursday with that very unromantic complaint vulgarly called the stomach ache which I attribute to having eaten some sliced, hard, dried, beastly bits of beef with a sprinkling of cabbage passing at Charter House under the fashionable nomination of Bubble and Squeak, well I eat a little of this, but I had hardly swallowed half a dozen mouth fulls before I thought I had at least taken a pint of julep if not poison. Oh what pain I was in all day, in the evening Watky sent me over to Spry's the doctors[2] who gave me a calomille pill that night, a black dose, alias black soup in the morning, a saline draught last night and another this morning which I am happy to say has set me quite right again, and I am now quite ready [to] tuck down all the good things 67 Baker Street can afford.

We had a half holiday on Thursday in honor of a boy of the name of Saunders[3] who was at Charter House some time ago obtaining a very respectable degree at Cambridge. We have had two rows this week three of the very biggest boys have been flogged for throwing a stone which went through a window which [hit] a poor man on the forehead and hurt him severely, another boy threw a stone and hit one of the little boys in the eye and they are not sure but what he will loose [*sic*] his eye. Granny desires me to remind you for the second time to enquire of Matthews the price of his box.[4] My dearest Bazy I must finish my letter as dinner is just ready & I have to wash my hands,

believe me
your affectionately attached
Brozy.

Sam[5] left town on thursday evening for Gloucester being unwell with a severe cold in his head.

Address, on integral page: Miss Barrett / Hope End / Ledbury / Herefordshire.
Publication: None traced.
Manuscript: Edward R. Moulton-Barrett.

1. Edmund Henry Penny, M.A. (1797–1879), Assistant Master at Charterhouse. Thackeray, who was a pupil during Bro's time there, and who immortalized the school as Grey Friars in his novels, was a boarder in Penny's house. Penny later became Rector of Gt. Stambridge, Essex.
2. Dr. J. Hume Spry, of Charterhouse Square.
3. Augustus Page Saunders, M.A., D.D. (1801–78). He was a pupil at Charterhouse 1817–19 and followed Dr. Russell as Headmaster in 1832, holding the post until 1853, when he was appointed Dean of Peterborough.
4. A cabinet maker by the name of Mathews had premises on New Street, Ledbury.
5. Uncle Sam.

------

175. EBB TO HENRIETTA MOULTON-BARRETT

[Hope End]
[4 March ?1823][1]

"I dont know what to write."
LAUREATES MEDITATIONS.

Nothing being certain but death, taxes, & birthday letters, certainties are not always pleasant things. In this note of mine, I have to do with nothing but the last. i.e. birthday letters . . & I heartily hope it may be the *last I have to do with*. It is miserable to be obliged to put your thoughts *into papers*, before you put your thoughts *on* paper,—to make your imagination *frisser*,—& your good taste *frissoner*[2] at leisure. I cant bear writing birthday letters.

Today there is an extra difficulty. We are taught by compositional rules to adapt our style to our subject—and I am apprehensive that, on this occasion, mine will be found deficient in the difficult requisites—simplicity, elegance, & grace.

Many happy returns of the day to my dearest, dearest Henrietta! I like her much better than I like her birthday; &, out of compliment to her, make my birthday note resemble the venus de medicis, in being . . . . *very short*!!

Her always attached Ba.

Address, on integral page: Miss Henrietta Barrett.
Publication: None traced.
Manuscript: R.J.L. Altham.

1. This letter was probably written in 1823, a year for which there is no dated birthday message from EBB to Henrietta.
2. EBB misspelled the French words "friser," meaning "to curl," and "frissonner," meaning "to shiver."

176. EDWARD MOULTON-BARRETT (BROTHER) &
MRS. ORME TO EBB

[In the hand of Edward Moulton-Barrett]   [London]
[*Postmark:* 8 March 1823]

Well Miss Bazy what is the matter with you now or what new flights of fancy, or humour have you taken into your head that you would not deign to write me a line today, is it that because you have got down stairs you think yourself too fine a lady to condescend to notice [a] Charter House boy if this is your reason let me inform you that a Carthusian scholar is as good any day in the week as a young lady just recovering the use of her spine, pray what is the matter with you. I had almost a mind to pay you off in your own coin, and not write to you today but I am too much enraged to let you off so easily, and to let my anger evaporate in cool contempt. [Continued in the hand of Mrs. Orme[1]] My dearest Ba Bro seems lost in thought endeavouring to collect his ideas but alas! There is a chatty lady here who entirely prevents him. My cold is better and I am looking forward with anxiety to a despatch from you My best love attend you all. C Orme. [Continued in the hand of Edward Moulton-Barrett] In short to sum up your coolness is past bounds, & your impudence is proverbial. We are now doing Cicero in the evening instead of doing Homer both[2] morning and evening. We were examined on Thursday by Russell for the purpose of turning down the six worst as the form was two [*sic*] full, I am happy to say that I was not one of the unfortunate fellows who got turned down. We had had such a heavy fall of snow yesterday that we had more snow balling, but the Watkyites I am sorry to say got the worst of it, I got rolled twice and my retreat was cut off, from getting into my own house again and I was obliged to take refuge in Churton's[3] with three other boys here we collected the Churtonites and Pence[4] and after several unsuccessful sallies we at last cut our way through the enemy. Good bye my dearest Bazy and believe me

your affectionate–
Brozy.——

Love to all, and thank Henrietta for her letter, I think your letter to her beautiful.

Address, on integral page: Miss Barrett / Hope End / Ledbury / Herefordshire.
Publication: None traced.
Manuscript: Edward R. Moulton-Barrett.

1. Bro apparently intended to continue beyond the word "contempt," but was interrupted. Mrs. Orme began her note on the same line which he had left unfinished. When Bro resumed writing, he added a period after "contempt," crossed out a word ("you"), then continued his attack on EBB.

Charles John, Samuel and
George Goodin Moulton-Barrett

Septimus and Octavius Moulton-Barrett

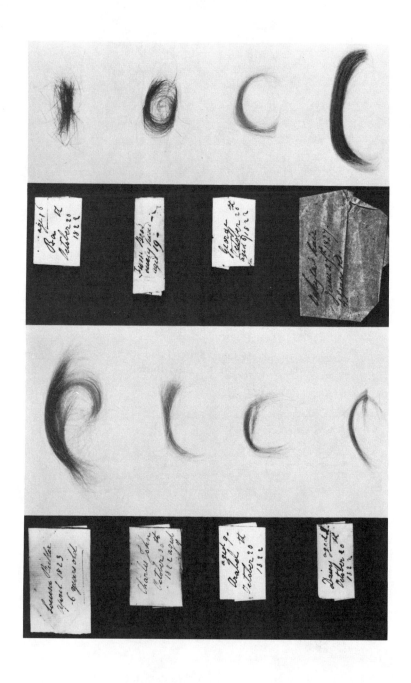

2. He originally wrote "both Homer," then transposed the words by numbering them 2 and 1 respectively.
3. Edward Churton, M.A. (1800–74), was admitted to Charterhouse as a scholar in 1810, going on to Christ Church, Oxford, where he took his B.A. in 1821. After obtaining his degree, he returned to his old school, and until 1830 was Assistant Master. He later became Archdeacon of Cleveland. The reference here is to his house in Wilderness Row, holding 56 boys, one of three new houses opened in 1821 to relieve overcrowding. Prior to that, 148 boys were crammed into Watkinson's house, and 144 in Chapman's.
4. This is thought to be Charterhouse jargon for the boys of Penny's house.

---

177. EDWARD MOULTON-BARRETT (BROTHER) & MARY TREPSACK TO EBB

[In the hand of Edward Moulton-Barrett]   [London]
                                                    April 5.th 1823.

Some young ladies have a great deal too much impudence, and some young gentlemen a great deal too complaisant in putting up with their impudence, I must certainly place you at the very head of this class of young ladies, the idea of your impudence in writing such a letter as this Miss Bazy. In your letter which I got on Thursday you allowed that you entirely forgot yesterday was thursday, & consequently (which (as you say) is uncommon occurrence) forgot me altogether, these are your own words, now in your letter today, you begin with your airs and graces again and talk about young ladies, and young gentleman Carthusian scholars, and the Haymarket (by the bye you ought to learn the Geography of London before you talk about it) and then you say that the fault was that of the Guard and not of your memory, now how to account for this contradiction, all I can say is that it is what Russell would call a downright shuffle. We are going to have the school room made double the size it is now as it is now too much crowded, there was a regular consultation of masters and Architects with maps and plans of buildings in the flogging room. There has been another boy flogged most severly this week a fourteen cutter for stealing a sovereign, he screamed and bellowed most dreadfully and now fellows have all cut him, and now the poor wretch goes moping about by himself and nobody speaks to him.[1] One of the poor old Pensioners[2] was found with his throat cut in bed and pen knife in his hand, he had got drunk the day before and was going to be expelled so he thought he would put an end ⟨. . .⟩[3] by ending his life, many of th⟨e . . .⟩ I had no such curiosity. I ⟨. . .⟩ surprised at any thing ⟨. . .⟩ or any thing else I shall ⟨. . .⟩ marks either your fancy ⟨. . .⟩ or your impudence. Well ⟨. . .⟩

my rage as much as I can I shall finish with; my dearest Bazy believe me
your affectionately attached
Brozy. ——

[Continued in Mary Trepsack's hand] What say you to Mrs Orm[e]
going to live with Mrs Murray in Bryanston Sq$^{re\,4}$ 150 p^r year & a regular
Establishment of Servants at her command she is to go to Italy with them,
she fixed her own salary—

Address, on integral page: ⟨Miss Barre⟩tt / H⟨o⟩pe End / Ledbury / Herefordshire.
Publication: None traced.
Manuscript: Edward R. Moulton-Barrett.

    1. "It was considered poor-spirited to squeal over a flogging" (*Charterhouse Old and New*, by E. P. Eardley Wilmot and E. C. Streatfield, 1895).
    2. Charterhouse was constituted in 1610, by Letters Patent of King James I, to afford a home for eighty male pensioners ("gentlemen by descent and in poverty, soldiers that have borne arms by sea or land, merchants decayed by piracy or shipwreck, or servants in household to the King or Queen's Majesty"), and to educate forty scholars.
    3. Large tear in seal area.
    4. A William Murray and his wife lived at 40 Bryanston Square, according to an 1823 Directory.

---

178. EDWARD MOULTON-BARRETT (BROTHER) TO EBB

[London]
April 19.th 1823.

My ever dearest Bazy,

    I am sorry to say that the boy who I told you of in one of my former letters as having fallen down and had leg cut open, died on Wednesday morning of a lock jaw,[1] but it turns out instead of having *fallen* down, one of the big boys had PUSHED him down and occasioned his death by cutting the pan of the knee completely open, the poor fellow is now however perfectly miserable, he hardly ever speaks, eats very little, and will sit with his eyes fixed upon the ground for a few minutes and will then burst into tears. Chapman[2] in whose house the boy was in has also been crying almost ever since, and did not come into school till yesterday evening, in short the whole school has been very melancholy ever since it happened. How do you think we came home today, by no less a conveyance than the Paddington coach[.] Brookes,[3] another boy who came with him Sam and myself formed a very cozy little party. Here is Mr Mc Swiney determined not to be laughed at again for his parson like appearance for he is looking quite smart in a new smock coat lined throughout with silk & white waistcoat, he has been swearing against the house of Commons, and cursing all the ministers one by one, he says, Canning is as great a rascal as ever lived, and those who spoke for the Catholicks are the only honest men in the house.[4] M[r] Robinson[5] has sent twice to know where Papa is now, he wrote to him and has not recieved an answer he wishes to know if he is at Bath or not if there what direction will find him. M[r] M[c] enquired at Drury lane at [*sic*, for and] finds that your share[6] is in Papa's name and to make the ticket pay, he must fill it up. Granny will send it up by the first opportunity. Good bye my dearest Bazy believe me

your affectionately attached
Brozy. —

Granny knows nothing of the book which you say she sent you, and you must be indebted to some other friend for it.

Address, on integral page: Miss Barrett / Hope End / Ledbury / Herefordshire.
Publication: None traced.
Manuscript: Edward R. Moulton-Barrett.

1. The Charterhouse Registers identify this boy as the Hon. John Howard, 3rd son of Thomas, 16th Earl of Suffolk. He entered Charterhouse in May 1822 and died on 14 April 1823, ten days after his 12th birthday, as a result of an accident during a game some weeks earlier.
2. The Rev. William Herbert Chapman (1782–1861) was admitted to Charterhouse as a scholar in 1794, and returned as Assistant Master in 1812 after taking his degree at Pembroke College, Cambridge.
3. George Brooks (1809–54), son of a Jamaican landowner, who was at Charterhouse from September 1822 until May 1823.
4. One of the current issues in Parliament and the country was "the Catholic question." By law, Catholics were still unable to vote for Parliamentary candidates or to stand for election themselves, and repeal of the penal statues still affecting Catholics was being hotly debated. EBB's poem "Visions" (see letter 91) shows that McSwiney was himself a Catholic.
5. A letter from James Scarlett to Edward Moulton-Barrett of 19 September 1808 (SD114) speaks of a Mr. Robinson, of Richmond, Yorkshire, "a very respectable & steady man of business," undertaking negotiations on behalf of Samuel Moulton-Barrett. This reference is probably to the same man.
6. EBB wrote to R.H. Horne [ca. 1841] (*Checklist*, 41:1) that she had "something to do with the proprietorship of Drury Lane, by virtue of five shares given to me when I was a child."

---

179. EDWARD MOULTON-BARRETT (BROTHER) & MARY TREPSACK TO EBB

[In the hand of Edward Moulton-Barrett]   [London]
April 27[.th] [*sic* for 26[.th]] 1823.[1]

My ever dearest Bazy

I feel myself under the highest obligations to you for your kind intentions in sending me your Greek Epigrams to translate, but really I have got so much to do for myself particularly as the examination is drawing near, that I fear I shall not have time to do what you require, I have now got ten verses to do to show up on monday morning however if I have a few minutes spare time I will try what I can do before Sunday evening, I admire your English translation very much indeed and only hope I may succeed half as well in my latin. Poor Sammy is much better today. I admire the shape of the gardens very much for this reason because I think the fantastic shapes of the beds, are a very exact resemblance of the twistings and windings of your brain and fancy. We have had nothing new going on at Charter House this week, which would interest you nothing but Cricket matches, and battles, there was one poor fellow who came into the play ground yesterday and some of the very big boys siezed him and bumped against a tree, pulled his hair nocked him down and I really think treated him most shamefully, for nothing atall [sic] but because he came into the green. The gold medal is decided to a boy of the name of Walford,[2] and they say that the verses are quite beautiful, the subject is King Lear. Every thing now indicates that the Holidays are fast approaching for places are taking in all the coaches to all parts of the kingdom from Scotland down to the land's end, the trunks are packing &c &c and we are certainly to break up on the seventh which is next Wednesday week. Russell works us most properly now in Grammar, and Ovid which we are to be examined in on the examination day. Good bye my dearest Bazy, if I can I will certainly do the verses to be sent in my sunday's letter.

Believe me your ever affectionate
Brozy ——

[Continued in Mary Trepsack's hand] Bro has kept his Letter so long in hand as scarcely to leave me time to say that Mr Green is just gone from here— he thinks our dear Sam better— his head is quite relieved & his Tongue which was very foul is nearly quite clear— his fever has been slight the last two days It has changed from a regular period of coming on, to different hours & much slighter— numbers have it, & it is so very tedious that it lasts three weeks or more—but I trust our dear Boy will get well much sooner— there is great improvement in him, & I hope to give you a much better account on Monday when I shall not fail to write— he sends his Love with Grannys & Treppys— Bro is looking uncommonly well, & hard at the task you have given him, you will receive it with my next dispatch.

[Continued at top of page 1 by Edward Moulton-Barrett] Now Bazy what do you think of me I have been inspired and have done your verses.

Ad lapidem vitâ vertebar numine divûm,
Remutare jubet Sculptor, me, marmore, vitæ.[3]

Address, on integral page: Miss Barrett / Hope End / Ledbury / Herefordshire.
Publication: None traced.
Manuscript: Edward R. Moulton-Barrett.

1. Postmarked 26 April 1823.
2. John Desborough Walford (1805–76). His prize verses, 145 lines in Latin hexameters, were published in *Charterhouse Prize Exercises, from 1814 to 1832* (London, 1833), pp. 105–109. He was a pupil at Charterhouse from January 1817 to May 1823.
3. "By the will of the gods, in life I am turned to stone; the Sculptor orders me to change back from marble into life."

---

180. EDWARD MOULTON-BARRETT (BROTHER) & MARY TREPSACK TO EBB

[In the hand of Edward Moulton-Barrett]   [London]
                                                          April 27.th 1823.

My ever dearest Bazy

As I knew you were not the most patient of human beings, I sat down yesterday evening, and in the little time which was allowed whilst Treppy was writing a few lines in my letter, I managed to finish the task which you had given me, however I was in so great a hurry that I forgot the second verse ought to be a pentameter instead of an Hexameter, I therefore set to again today and with my usual condescension and patience altered it into a short verse–

    "Me vitam, rursum Sculptor habere jubet,"[1]

I also find upon second consideration that the "Ad lapidem" in the former line ought to [be] "In lapidem".[2] Now Miss Bazy what do [you] think of that when you write to your friends, as Papa says, I dare say you will exlaim [*sic*] with him, he is breaking out in fresh places, never Bazy talk to me of idleness again, for I have sweated today as we ilegantly [*sic*] term it most properly both in body and mind, for Mr McSwiney, Brooks, Griffith,[3] and myself went into Kensington garden, where we all set on him with sticks and we all got so hot with running after him and he after us, that we were very nearly walking into the Serpentine up to our middles by way of cooling ourselves[.] Sam was put into a warm bath today and feels much the better for it. M.^{r} M^c has seen your two lines and thinks them capital, he also [saw] mine but I can assure you he did not assist me in the least as I had finished them before he came nor did he make any alteration. My dearest Bazy I must finish my letter as it [is] past eight and I expect to be called for directly to set out for Charter House, only one more w⟨hole⟩ week Bazy!!
                    Ever believe me
                        your affectionately attached
                            Brozy —

[Continued in Mary Trepsack's hand]

Monday 5 oclock —— [28 April 1823]

Tiney Sam's best Love & thanks for your Letter– he is much better, yesterday & today he was put into a warm Shower Bath which delighted him beyond every thing—he hopes to have it every day[.] It was a fortunate thing for his little Lordship that he was kept at home, taking his Complaint in hand at once has perhaps saved him a serious fit of Illness– he is greatly distressd at not being at School, the opportunity is lost he says for getting into another form this quarter you must love him my dear Ba, he is a little angel—so good, so amiable every way– he has been amusing me this mor^g with a variety of little anicdotes about his School, Hope End &c– talks much of going home & what he is to day– he is now engagd with a Bread pudding & sends his love to all

Address, on integral page: Miss Barrett / Hope End / Ledbury / Herefordshire.
Publication: None traced.
Manuscript: Edward R. Moulton-Barrett.

  1. "Once more, the Sculptor commands me to life."
  2. Ad lapidem: to stone; In lapidem: into stone.
  3. Charles Griffith (1805–86) was admitted to Charterhouse in 1817 and so was a senior at this time.

————————————

181. EBB TO THOMAS CAMPBELL

[?Hope End]
[ca. May 1823]^1

Mr Editor,^{2}

Though we have been patronized by no one more liberally, than by yourself, yet it may require some little apology to your readers to occupy these pages with the history of those, whose family may be the only one of which they may not wish to know the history. When I furthermore declare myself the humble chronicler of the much abused, and misrepresented race of the Thoughts, I imagine I hear a young Lady exclaim with a yawn which might be termed ominous "Bless me the Thoughts of Devonshire—I'll bet my life!" while a better informed, and more matronly damsel, stealing a trembling glance at her no longer flattering mirror, may cry "Was any thing so unlucky? I've been avoiding these people all my life, and now to stumble on them here!! Can any thing be more unfortunate!"

The Commencement of my descriptive narrative must give a slight outline of the history of some old family relatives, whom it will be necessary to introduce to the reader, before he can understand a sentence of my biographical sketch. I allude to the ancient and respectable house of the Words, lineal descendants from the Alphabet and near connections of the Sylables. These little gentlemen are of very inflammable tempers, being ever quarrelling among themselves; so much so indeed that the "War of Words" is proverbially mentioned as the most unending, while Gray speaking of their fiery temperament says "Words that burn".[3] Indeed the Poets seem rather to have a spite against this hapless race, and [among] many other attacks we may mention Lord Byrons contemptuous expression "Away with Words",[4] and Shakespeare's more serious libel on their reputation when he asserts "Words pay no debts."[5] ⟨Nevertheless the Words are at present a family of much consequence; having made themselves of great weight in the Cabinet. Many a Chancellor of the Exchequer has, by their aid, paid the national debt ––– as much as he meant to pay it; and M.[r] Canning has lately sent them into Spain instead of arms, and ammunition.⟩[6]

In former times the Words were the most intimate friends of the Thoughts, and, to do them justice, were extremely kind in introducing them into the best society. I cannot either help acknowledging that when several of the Thoughts were falling fast into poverty, the Words in the most benevolent manner lent them every assistance, and equipped them in court suits. In return however for this charity they exacted so much from the Thoughts that the latter, who are of noble blood, could not help feeling indignant, remembering that the Words were a younger branch of the family, and, tho' replete with pride, quite divested of natural talent. At this the Words took offence, and libelled the Thoughts in so public a manner that the latter were obliged to cut their acquaintance, and now it is considered the height of ill breeding to invite the relatives to the same party in the fashionable circles. The quarrel has even gone so far that there is a flitting report of the dispute being about to be placed in the hands of the Gentlemen of the bar, in which case M.[r] Editor you will allow with me that "Words versus Thoughts" will have a most *nil ultra*[7] echo both in politics and Ethics.

The first individual in the Thought family, of which I intend making mention, is M.[r] Philosophical Thought, a Gentleman of eccentric habits and singular disposition. He was acquainted with Plato, Socrates, Cicero, and Bacon, and was so intimate with Sir Isaac Newton, that the *on dit*[8] assures us that he held him down, in a malicious frolic, opposite a burning fire till that distinguished man's proper person, subdued by the torturing flames, was instantaneously converted into the *centre* of GRAVITY[9] This however may be a calumny for I always considered M.[r] Philosophical Thought a very excellent

Person, tho' rather too sensible of his own importance, and too fond of studying his own pedigree. As a proof of his original disposition, I will cursorily mention, that a silly report being spread of his children, the young *Ideas*, having had the free use of their eyesight before they came into the world, he took the trouble of dictating a long chapter to his secretary (Mᵣ Locke) in order to prove that his infants could not discern objects till after they were born.

Mᵣˢ Poetical Thought, first Cousin of the Gentleman above mentioned, is a venerable old Lady who boasts of having wet nursed Homer, and led Shakespeare about, in leading strings. She however is still a great dresser, and flirts away most valiantly with the Words, who continue her humble servants, though at variance with the rest of the family– Her three Sons are all of great celebrity in the literary world and are talked of with raptures by the Critics– I can't help thinking that Sublimity Thought, her eldest born, lifted Lord Byron to a word or two in "Childe Harold"– as to Brilliant Thought he is too ready with a quotation from "Lallah Rookh"¹⁰ to escape my suspicion; and Refined Thought confessed to me the other day in confidence that he snatched the pen out of Campbell's hand and wrote "The Pleasures of Hope" himself.

Unlike other writers, Mᵣ Editor, I keep my own portrait to the last, but as I am unwilling to pass quite unnoticed, I shall just assure you that I am a good natured hanger on of the family, and generally better recieved that [*sic*] the rest of my connections. I am of so condescending a disposition that I have often helped a damsel to distribute her patches becomingly, besides having presided over the Cabinet of a Lady's dress in order to enable her to confirm her *government* by good policy and adorn it with new CONQUESTS. I am also skilled in the more dignified employments of drawing accurate likenesses in the fire on a winter evening, and building castles in the air on a summers night, for which I am known by the illustrious title of Architect Thought.

Having thus Mᵣ Editor graciously allowed you to take a coup d'œil¹¹ of our family concerns, I must entreat you to honor us with your protection, and defend us from the many attacks on our fame which hourly assail us. For even proverbs are aimed in tremendous phalanxes against us, such as "A thought strikes me," "a penny for your thoughts," and other sayings equally unjust, and injurious. If however you will allow us to assemble under the shield of your distinguished character we may once again be at peace, and, with the hope that you will not be quite deaf to our entreaties, allow me to assure you, in behalf of all our illustrious house, that as we have ever been, so we shall always be,

Yours to command.

Postscriptum

I had just laid my pen in its resting place, when I heard a shrill voice at my elbow, and turning beheld Concise Thought, an eccentric Cousin of ours, so close in his economy that we may term him the Ricardo[12] of our household. His dwarfish form was contracted into half its natural dimensions by the help of tight stays, and his own extraordinary efforts; for as it is the aim of the generality of Mankind to be believed great, so is it the ambition of our Cousin to be thought little . . Now as Concise Thought holds the Words in utter detestation, I expected the most flattering praises from his tongue! when imagine my astonishment to hear him begin as follows. "No doubt my dear Sir (said my Cousin with a twirl of his left hand which in itself was an epigram) no doubt you imagine you have done much service to our family, by the above article, and much injury to our enemies, that horrible aristocracy who would have stretched us on a Procrustian bed[13] to their own inordinate dimensions. How!! have you not the wit to observe that in every line you have courted the assistance of those very words whose authority you deprecate, and that to have said *less* would have answered your purpose *more*."?

I know not whether my Cousin is right, M! Editor, but shall hasten to conclude, lest your readers should think he IS.

Publication: Athenæum, 23 July 1836, pp. 522–523 (after revisions).
Source: EBB's fair copy, University of Texas. Two of EBB's drafts are extant, one at Wellesley College and one at the Armstrong Browning Library. A further fair copy exists, enclosed in a letter to H.S. Boyd (no. 423).

1. Conjectural dating based on the reference to George Canning, who became Foreign Secretary in September 1822. In April 1823 he strongly protested against a French invasion of Spain, following the Congress of Verona, but took no military action.
2. On a separate cover sheet, EBB wrote "For the new Monthly Magazine." Campbell was its editor at this time, but EBB's reference in the body of the letter to his poem *The Pleasures of Hope* suggests that she was not aware of the identity of the editor to whom she was writing.
Above the salutation, EBB wrote her title, "A Thought on Thoughts." The magazine did not publish this essay. A revised version was printed in *The Athenæum* in 1836.
3. Thomas Gray (1716–71), *The Progress of Poesy* (1754), III, 3.
4. *Childe Harold's Pilgrimage, Canto the Fourth* (1818), line 972.
5. *Troilus and Cressida*, III, 2, 55.
6. The bracketed passage was actually written farther down in the manuscript, after the words "Thoughts that the latter . . ."; EBB indicated its revised location with asterisks.
7. Literally "nothing beyond." It is difficult to see what EBB intended to convey; perhaps "meaningless echo."
8. "Gossip; rumour."
9. Underscored three times.
10. *Lalla Rookh* (1817), by Thomas Moore (1779–1852).
11. "Glance at."
12. A reference to the English economist David Ricardo (1772–1823).
13. In Greek legend the robber Procrustes placed all his victims on an iron bed; those too tall were cut to size, those too short were stretched to fit.

182. EBB TO MARY MOULTON-BARRETT

To my dearest Mama.
On her birthday
Hope End May 1ˢᵗ 1823.[1]

"Benedetto sia'l giorno, e'l mese e il anno"[2]—
Petrarque's 46ᵗʰ Sonnet

Within the merry month of May,
When eyes are bright and hopes are gay—
The rustic train the pale embowers,
In vernal wreaths of laughing flowers–
(A votive off'ring to the Sun
Which he may smile to look upon)
Dancing around to those sweet lays
That light hearts breathe on sunny days.

So while thy children round thee climb,
And fondly lisp the birthday rhyme,
With them I'll twine my offering here,
To deck the *May pole* of the year–
For like yon orb of bright degree
Thou nursed the flowers, thou'lt smile to see!

Your always affectionate
Ba.

Address on integral page: Mʳˢ Barrett / Tea Urn / near Slopbasin / Breakfasttable / China.
Publication: None traced.
Manuscript: Pierpont Morgan Library.

1. Her 42nd.
2. "Blest be the day, and the month and the year" (Sonnet 47, not 46).

---

183. EDWARD MOULTON-BARRETT (BROTHER) TO EBB

[London]
May 14ᵗʰ 1823.

My ever dearest Bazy.

Though coolness is a very desirable thing at this season of the year and on such a roasting day as this yet there is a particular sort of coolness which only tends to put you into a fever, and it is this description which you have practised towards me in not writing to me this week[.] There you go again, last quarter you missed several letters and I was fool enough to write to you on Saturday but I shall completely alter my plan, and next time I come home and do not find a letter from you, I will be as cool as you and let you foam away as much as you please. When I went to Charter House I was surrounded on all sides and deafened with exclaimations such as "I thought you had left" and some went so far as to address me as my ghost for [there] had been a report spread that I was dead, I find the school not so much altered as I expected they have only enlarged the windows which certainly is a great improvement, but I believe they have reserved the more extensive alterations for the long holidays, I am now reading sentences from Xenophon—which I find pretty easy. Watky enquired after Papa very particularly, I can assure you he is a great favorite with him. M.ʳ M.ᶜ Swiney came for us today to the Charter House and hearing that John was in Town we took the Hummum's[1] where he lodges in our way but he was not at home however he has promised to be hear [*sic*] either today or tommorrow to see us, Good bye my dearest Bazy ever believe me

your affectionately attached
Brozy

    You may depend upon hearing from me next Saturday, provided you are not too lazy to write to me——

Address, on integral page: Miss Barrett / Hope End / Ledbury / Herefordshire.
Publication: None traced.
Manuscript: Edward R. Moulton-Barrett.

    1. A contemporary Directory lists two lodging houses of this name, Old Hummums and New Hummums, both in Covent Garden.

---

184. EBB TO ALFRED MOULTON-BARRETT

To dear Alfred,
On his birthday
Hope End. May 20.ᵗʰ 1823[1]

Saith Locke (I think his system answers)
"Dreams are the scraps of waking fancies,
Touching love, physic, or the weather,
But rather oddly put together." [2]
If this be so, or not, I ween
Some day, or other may be seen–
At present I'll content my pen,
With sketching briefly how, and when,

I saw a vision, rather gay,
And quite appropriate to the day.
For as I slumbered yesternight
(My slumbers were not very light,
With my poor cranium cut in two
Between a birthday ode, and LOO)
Reclining neath rose twisted bowers,
And weaving garlands for the Hours,
I saw young Hope, to Poets dear,
(Sweet offspring of a smile, and tear,
Caught by the Sylphs in airy ewer)
So luminous and yet so pure!
A veil concealed each feature's Grace,
For Man shall never see her face,
Till (when yon Heav'n, around him breaking,
Shall greet him in th' eternal waking)
He, midst the choir of angel song,
Shall find the Hope he loved so long!

The laughing Hours were round her playing,
And, decked with wreaths, seemed gone a maying,
When in a musical voice, & clear,
She called those followers of the year,
Winding her various words together,
Like Sun, and rain, in April weather—!
"Ye—(winged Sons of Time) tomorrow
Shall pay no tax to Care, or Sorrow—
For know, tomorrow's Sun shall gild
The birthday of a Cherished Child,
Whom, if your memories be not lazy,
You'll think of by the name of DAISY!
Then fetch with speed the seraph Joy,
My offspring, but a truant boy,
Who, like a little selfish elf,
Thinks only how to please himself,
And, mindless of poor Mortals pain,
Just flies FROM Heav'n & back again.
Catch him in haste, my much loved Hours,
And place him in a Cage of flowers,
At Hope End—where his eye of blue,
Thro laughing wreaths, may just peep thro',
Making what is lovely brighter—
Light hearts gayer—gay hearts lighter!!"

She ceased—no more with verse I'll cope—
For what can I^3 say after HOPE?

Dearest Daisys
Affectionate Ba—

Publication: None traced.
Manuscript: Pierpont Morgan Library.

1. His 3rd.
2. A paraphrase of one of the propositions contained in *An Essay Concerning Human Understanding* (1690), bk. II, ch. 1, sec. 17.
3. Underscored twice.

---

185. EBB TO EDWARD MOULTON-BARRETT (FATHER)

To my ever dearest Papa
On his birthday May 28.th 1823 [1]
Hope End.

Oh! sacred be the pure, and gentle song,
That may the hearts of list'ning friends beguile,
Flowing in modulated verse along!
Whose first Ambition is to please awhile,
A Parents birth, its theme—its hope, a fathers smile!

Then let Affection bring, in fairy urn,
Kind words, and looks, to youthful mem'ry dear,
And little tales, that never can return—!
Fondly, I'll sketch the loved memorials here,
T' excite the tender smile, & wake the grateful tear.

My Father! fondest! kindest! dearest! best!
Who taught my infant fingers first to bear
Th' Aonian lute—oh! mayst thou be most blest!
From a benignant smile can Heav'n forbear?
Thy worth exacts the wish—thy children breathe the prayer—!

Your own affectionate child
Ba.

Publication: None traced.
Manuscript: Pierpont Morgan Library.

1. His 38th.

---

186. EDWARD MOULTON-BARRETT (BROTHER) TO EBB

[London]
June 22.^d 1823.

My ever dearest Bazy

In compliance with your desire I sit down, (though in no great humour for writing,) to fulfill your commands, with respect to the verses. An Hexameter verse consists of ten feet, the four first feet may be either dactyls or spondees the fifth *must* be a dactyl the last *must* be a spondee, there must be three cæsuras in every Hexameter verse for instance. "Jura dablat¹ popullis posilto modol consul arlatro.² Another, three cæsuras Tytyre tu patlulæ reculbansl sub tegmine fagi[.]³ H is considered as no letter and therefore another vowel is cut off before it,⁴ like two vowels coming together, as "frigida hyems"⁵ scans "frigid' hyems," M is also cut off as "Sepulchrum horrificum"⁶ i e sepulchr' horrificum, if a vowel precedes two consonants it is long and you may not have a word of more than three syllables at the end of a line. I know not whether you will be able either to understand or even make out this uncorrected scrawl but really when I wrote the former part as far as "sepulchr' horrificum," I was so disconcerted by those rheumatic pains in my head that I hardly knew or cared what I wrote accordingly I staid here last night and feel certainly better today though all pain is not quite removed, I expect to go back to Charter House again tommorrow as I shall most likely [be] pretty well recovered by that time. Beautiful Sam⁷ is in town, arrived last monday, he looks dreadfully ill and talks of going down into Herefordshire for the purpose of consulting Mr Blizard.⁸ We are expecting every day to hear some good news about your coming to London.

Ever believe me my dearest Ba
your truly attached
Brozy.

Addressed and franked by EBB's uncle on integral page: London June twenty three /
1823 / Miss Barrett / Hope End / Ledbury / S M Barrett.
Publication: None traced.
Manuscript: Edward R. Moulton-Barrett.

1. Directly above this word, Bro wrote "cæsura" to illustrate what he had said previously.
2. "The consul put aside the plough just to give laws to the people" (Ovid, *Fasti*, I, 207). In this and the following Latin quotation, the vertical marks are Bro's own, not editorial additions.
3. "You, Tytyrus, recline in the shade of the wide-spreading beech" (Vergil, *Eclogues*, I, 1).
4. Bro originally wrote "is cut off before it another vowel." Then he placed numerals above the words to rearrange them in the order shown here.
5. "Chilly winter."
6. "Dreadful tomb."

7. i.e., their cousin Samuel Barrett.
8. Thomas Blizard lived at Donnington Hall, near Ledbury. "No medical man ever gave more time and attention to the Sick & infirm even when paid for their Services" (Biddulph Diary, 22 July 1832, MS at Hereford City Library).

---

187. EBB TO HENRIETTA MOULTON-BARRETT

Hope End
March 4th 1824

I sent a message to the Muse,
Last night, to leave Castalian dews,
And speed here, if twere in her power,
This morning at the breakfast hour—
But, above all, to keep in time,
As Reason would not wait for rhyme!
When lo (I never heard a better)
'Stead of the Goddess, comes a letter—
A curious *MS*, to be writ
By hand divine—and this is it!!

"You will not think I treat you ill,
When, tho' my presence I refuse,
I use a whole Mæonian quill¹
To write a billet in excuse.

Nor call my absense unpolite,
Nor want of condescension deem,
For all that stays my Hope End flight,
I speak sincerely, is your *theme!*

To say the truth, on Beauty's eyes,
When gentle Poets softly think,
I oft Parnassus' glowing dyes,
Have mingled with my vot'ry's ink!

And some instead of charms of face,
Good humour's charms have lov'd t' impart,
And then my smile hath gilt each grace,
Each dear enchantment of the heart!

But modesty with beauty joined,
And temper's sweetness, in *one* letter?!
Oh no! I *cant* sing all combined,
I wont attempt your Henrietta!!

Yet let not *this*, my note, astound her,
Nor be *thou* wroth at my excuse!
With all the laughing Graces round her
She surely will not miss

The Muse—[''']

Many many happy returns of the day to my dearest Henrietta,[2] and if
she be inclined with Pope to "trust the Muse"[3] for the sincerity of her
apology, may she also forgive her uninspired votary for attempting so
weighty a subject without divine aid, remembering amongst other
classical quotations that I am not the only one who has been in at *the*
SCRATCH without being one of the FANCY!

Ever my dearest Addles most affec^te

Ba—

Address, on integral page: To / Miss H Barrett.
Publication: HUP, II, 38–39.
Manuscript: University of Texas.

1. An allusion to Homer, sometimes called the Mæonian poet.
2. Her 15th birthday.
3. *Rape of the Lock* (1714), V, 123.

188. CHARLES JOHN MOULTON-BARRETT TO EBB

To dearest Ba:
Hope End, March 6th, 1824.

1

Dear Ba! this is your birthday
So let us all be merry when we play
Come dear Ba! this is your birth,
And long may you live in joy and in mirth!

2

And pray now always love me,
And depend upon it, I'll pay thee;
Now dear ma'm. I must go away
To think of *you*, this happy day!

Your affec^te brother
Charles John Barrett

Address, on integral page: To dearest Ba.
Publication: None traced.
Manuscript: Berg Collection.

189. GEORGE GOODIN MOULTON-BARRETT TO EBB

[Hope End]
March 6.th 1824

My dearest Ba
    How old you are today! I hope you will be as happy as you are old, & as good. & so strong that you may jump over the moon! for you are very dear to your affecte

George G. Barrett

Address, on integral page: To the old lady.
Publication: None traced.
Manuscript: Berg Collection.

---

190. HENRIETTA MOULTON-BARRETT TO EBB

[Hope End]

To dearest Ba
on her birthday
March 6th 1824

No aid Apollo I need ask of thee.
Nor thou Minerva, thou e'er scorneth me,
Thy presence e'en today thou wilt not give
Although I write to one you so much love;
Yes she is loved by you, and that I know
On her, thy bounty thou doest e'er bestow;
But is she loved by none but you
Oh no, she's loved by *many many* too
And why? is it because to her thy aid is given
No, not that alone, for she is loved by Heaven,
Yes, she is good, I love her well,
How much I do, I feel, to you I need not tell—

May I be allowed to wish dearest Ba *most perfect* health and happiness for *many* years and may I flatter myself that I am her dearest

Henrietta—

Address, on integral page: To / Miss Barrett.
Publication: None traced.
Manuscript: Berg Collection.

191. EDWARD MOULTON-BARRETT (BROTHER) TO EBB

[London]
April 4.th 1824.

My dearest Bazy.

I can assure you I felt the full force of your rage, and must allow that I was stupid about the business, however, although tis most true that I owe you many a grudge yet unpaid which would have fully justified me even supposing it intentional, yet I disclaim having entertained any desire of showing my "MALICE" (as you please to denominate it) in half so mean and underhand a manner, and I at the same time feel suitable indignation at the insinuations which you have thrown out to that effect, now that I have gratified my desire to be candid, and at the same time my wish to justify my "DISPOSITION" from your unjust, unfounded, and "MALICIOUS" hints, I will no longer seek to gratify my revenge but in your own words *"blot your sins from the tablets of my memory"* "to which you so poetically allude," you see Bazy I can make your own words turn upon yourself, as the scythes attached to the wheels of Roman chariots in a route [*sic*] used to do as much execution among their own army as they were intended to do against the enemy, and I think one or two of your expressions would apply more aptly and with greater justice to yourself, however Bazy a truce for the present untill we meet, which by the bye will be now in the course of about four weeks and a half. Your last letter by way of seasoning has so much good news with it that it fully compensates for———but I am entering on forbidden ground; in short I am quite delighted to hear ⟨of G⟩randmama's visit to Cheltenham, ⟨wh⟩ich I am in hopes will induce her to stay some time at Hope End; I am also very glad to hear of the Trants[1] being at Malvern, remember me to them, James in particular. Good bye friend Bazy, I shall expect to hear from you during the week.

Believe me your affectionate
Brozy.

I know not if you can read this scrawl, but my hands are so cut and quartered with chops[2] that [I] can hardly bend a finger.

Address, on integral page: Miss Barrett / Hope End / Ledbury / Herefordshire.
Publication: None traced.
Manuscript: Mary V. Altham.

1. Mary Trant (*née* Barrett), the widow of James Trant, was a first cousin of EBB's paternal grandmother. She had three sons: Henry, Dominick and James.
2. i.e., strokes of the cane, as punishment at Charterhouse.

192. EBB TO EDWARD MOULTON-BARRETT (FATHER)

[Hope End]

To my dearest Papa.
On his birthday. May 28th 1824.[1]

Amidst the days of pleasant mirth,
That throw their halo round our earth—
Amidst the tender thoughts, that rise,
And call bright tears to happy eyes—
Amidst the silken words that move
And syllable the names we love—
There glides no day of peaceful bliss
More soothing to the heart than this–
No thoughts of fondness ere appear
More kind than those I write of here–
No name can ere on tablet shine,
My Father! more beloved than thine!

Tis sweet, adown the shady past,
A ling'ring look of love to cast;
Back the enchanted world to call,
That beamed upon us first of all—
And walk, with Mem'ry, fondly o'er
The paths where Hope has been before!
Sweet! to recieve the floating sound
That breathes, in tenderness, around—
Repeating to the list'ning ear,
The names that made our Childhood dear!
For Joy, like Echo, gently kind,
Hath left her dulcet voice behind—
To tell, amidst the magic air,
How oft she smiled, and lingered there!

Oh! let the deep Aonian shell[2]
Breathe sweetest numbers, clear, and well!
While the light Hours, in fair array,
Lead on the buxom holiday–
For, neath thy gentleness of praise,
My Father! rose my early lays!
And, when the lyre was scarce awake,
I loved its strings for thy lov'd sake.

Woo'd the kind Muses—but the while
Thought only how to win thy smile—
My proudest fame—my dearest pride—
More dear than all the world beside!

And now, perchance, I seek the tone
For magic, that is more its own—
But still my Father's looks remain
The best Mecænas[3] of my strain!——
My brightest joy, upon his brow,
To read the smile that meets me now—
And hear him, in his kindness, say
The words, perhaps he'll speak today!——

"Many, many happy returns of my dearest Papa's birthday" is the
first wish of his most attached.

Ba—

Publication: An Essay on Mind, 1826, pp. 109–111, greatly altered from original.
Manuscript: Berg Collection.

1. His 39th.
2. Aonia was the home of the Muses, otherwise known as the Aonides.
3. Intended as "Mæcenas," after Gaius Cilnius Mæcenas (d. 8 B.C.), a Roman patron
of letters.

193. EDWARD MOULTON-BARRETT (BROTHER) TO EBB

[London]
[*Postmark:* 21 June 1824]

My dearest Bazy
   It is now nearly three weeks since I saw you, and during all that
time I have not recieved a single line either from you or any one else at
Hope End, which if you do not make up for next [week] I shall take full
vengeance upon you next Saturday, but I am sure you will not fail in
your correspondence for another, whole, which however if you should
by any mishap forget you know what to expect. I am happy to inform
you that with the assisstance of a good dish of black soup, more
elegantly styled a black dose, I feel no effects from my unfortunate
wound except a black eye which however will soon clear off.[1] We have
had a great row here this week, Russell has lately been extremely severe
with those boys whom he has caught fagging and they being as

EBB Aged About 19

Edward Moulton-Barrett

determined to mantain there [*sic*] privileges wrote a note to Russell signed by most of the biggest boys in the school to, declare there intention, of still adhering to this custom,[2] and if he refused them, his permission to fag, they threatened to resign their several offices such as Monitors, Sub Mon[i]tors, &ᶜ &ᶜ this as you may well suppose put the Doctor in a violent passion, and he obliged many of them to sign a paper of his drawing up, the purport of which I cannot atall [*sic*] learn, however—after giving them a long speech, or *pill*, I believe the row has ended pretty amicably on both sides. Mʳ Churton one of our Masters who has been lately made a Revᵈ, gave us his first sermon today in Charter House chapel he certainly has a most monotonous tone of deliver[y], and I could discover no recommendation, of which the sermon could boast greater than that it lasted *only* one quarter of an hour, however the ⟨. . .⟩[3] and he wa⟨. . .⟩ as he obtai⟨. . .⟩ -tainly ⟨. . .⟩ Bazy a⟨. . .⟩ attached ⟨. . .⟩

If you dont write next week—— but I wont put myself in a passion, with so insignificant, little,—— but as I said before, I *wont* put myself in a passion

Address, on integral page: Miss Barrett / Hope End / Ledbu⟨ry⟩ / Herefor⟨dshire⟩.
Publication: None traced.
Manuscript: Edward R. Moulton-Barrett.

1. A passage in letter 197 indicates that his "wound" was caused by a cricket ball hitting him in the face.
2. Dr. Russell opposed both the system of fagging and the imposition of corporal punishment, and attempted to abolish both, substituting fines for the latter. The boys "thought flogging was very gentlemanly . . . but fines most ungentlemanly . . . and burst forth one day in School in a general cry of 'no fines.' Dr. Russell was induced to reconsider his intention" (*Charterhouse Past and Present*, by William Haig Brown, 1879). As this letter indicates, his efforts to abolish the traditional fagging were also opposed.
3. Bottom corner of page, with signature, torn off.

---

194. EDWARD MOULTON-BARRETT (BROTHER) TO EBB

[London]
[3 July 1824][1]

My dearest Bazy

I recieved your letter which contain the news of Sam's death, and I cannot say I am sorry for it as indeed in his state it must have [been] a most happy release, the only thing to be regretted is his unhappy ignorance of the state he was in till the last. I think you wished last holidays to have a specimen of the subjects which are given to the second form for english verses, I accordingly send you the thesis for next Saturday, which is the only one for this quarter;—Ex: $^{ch}4$–11 verse. "Who maketh the dumb or deaf." you will see that it is not quite in your style, however I have an idea that if you were at Charter and in the second that you would beat a good many of them in the english verses, if not in any thing else! Russell has given us a few good strict examinations in Homer, and the repetition of the Ovid, from all of which I am happy to say I came off extremely well, Sam has also been examined by him several times since we came back. They still talk of McAdamizing the green,[2] and they are certainly going [to make] a most material alteration in the chapel, and greatly enlarge it[3] however I have since heard that the story of our not being allowed to go out any more on Saturdays after this quarter is a complete lie, for which I assure you I am not atall [*sic*] sorry. I have this week recieved a most [pleasing] letter from Hastings in which Treppy says she likes the place much better as the summer advances, and that Granny is much better than she was a short time ago, but all this I suppose you have heard yourself and as STALE NEWS is not much adapted to interest, and as I have nothing else to communicate to you but what is stale, I shall wish you a very good morning, for it is past six o'clock and nearly time to go into school.

Believe me my dearest Bazy—
your ever affectionate
Bro

    You deserve by the bye to be ROASTED for your shameful neglect of correspondence however you shall be excused, if you write me a good long letter of reconciliation this week.

Address, on integral page: Miss Barrett / Hope End / Ledbury / Herefordshire.
Publication: None traced.
Manuscript: Edward R. Moulton-Barrett.

    1. Day and month determined by postmark; the year by reference to the death of Samuel Barrett, son of Mrs. Elizabeth Barrett Williams and a first cousin of EBB's father, on 13 June 1824.
    2. The Green was about 330 feet square, and Dr. Russell had reported to the Governors as early as 1819 that it was "uneven, full of holes, and quite unfit for the playing of games." In 1821 he was given permission to level and improve it. (*Charterhouse in London*, by Gerald S. Davies, 1921, pp. 268–270.)
    John Loudon McAdam (1756–1836) devised a system for hard-surfacing roads; his name became a synonym for the process.
    3. This was not done, however, until 1826, when "a recess (it cannot be called an aisle) was added to the north side" (*Chronicles of Charter-House*, by William J. D. Roper, 1847, p. 144).

195. MARY MOULTON-BARRETT TO EBB

Kiosk– [Hope End]
July 5.th Monday. [1824]¹

In calling to my minds eye the circle of ladies single & double in *N° 8.*,² Etiquette that grand mover of all my courtly manners, directs my pen to Miss Barrett, to whom my thanks are due for a most acceptable letter, or I should be puzzled to which of the attractive phalanx to pay my devoirs– *All* I suspect, are looking a little *shy* at my weeks silence, but if they knew how much I have thought of them I think I should be honored with a few gracious smiles!– My *rustic* sensibilities were much excited by being so affectionately thought of dearest Ba, in your gaieties, Inhanced as they are by all the kindness of which you boast, & which my imagination so readily apprehends, in union with your own devoted preference to the social charms of a Town, they might chanced to have turned that *curly head* of yours, & for a time driven Hope End & its homely appurtenances out of it; Your dear letter therefore made me hold up my head, & feel very proud, & Papa & I agree you really are a kind good girl– I can scarcely envy my own dear children any blessing or enjoyment, as has been fully proved by this test—for no happiness to *me*, can ever be so enviable, as that they enjoy at this moment—and scarcely secondary to it, is the delightful feeling, that they are with my beloved Mother & Sisters! Here are two letters for you, dearest Ba from *two beaux* . . one on Saturday, & of so interesting a character that I should have sent it off by express I believe, had not all my interference being checked by Papa's saying he intended himself to write to you– I hope you have heard from him, but as the days may have been too temptingly dry, I had best tell you that the letter was from Sam, offering thro' you the olive branch to Papa, & proposing to come here with Mary as soon as he can leave Town³– I opened the letter, thinking it was from Bro, & having read it, I felt it to be expedient to give it to Papa to read for which it was evidently intended– Nothing can be more like the writer than its kindness, expressing Marys desire to know Papa, & his own that the past should be buried in oblivion– Not much is said, as it is only a note, but it is kindness itself– Papas only observation was that he should write to you– My hopes I own are great, but they *may* be erroneous! Either way, I am sure it will be a struggle with dearest Papa, that I anxiously wish was over—should it end to our wishes it will indeed be joy! Sam & Mary have been at Hastings, where they are more & more pleased with her— The other letter is from Bro, with a scold for your not writing; he has had some strict examinations in Homer & Ovid from Dr Russel in which he makes a flattering report of his success, & of Sam's in a no less strict examination— It is not true that they are not to go out on Saturdays— this I think is the pith of the letter— In the Globe & Traveller of 30ᵗʰ June appears Lines on the death of Lᵈ Byron, which we beg to recommend as worthy your notice. As Papa took up the paper in the Dining Room a glance satisfied me whence they came, but I said nothing till he came into the Drawing Room, when taking the paper, with a becoming carelessness of air, I asked him what he thought of those lines, he said, "They are very beautiful indeed the only I have seen at all worthy the subject." ["]I cannot help thinking,["] replied I, ["]that we know something of the Author." ["]They cannot be Ba's" said he, taking the paper from me to read them again, ["]tho' certainly when I first read them, they reminded me greatly of her style—have you any idea they are hers?["] "I have a *conviction* of it," said the conceited Mother, pouring out the tea with an air that threatened to overflow the tea tray—& thereupon followed eulogiums that must not appear here!—suffice it to say, my beloved child, that Papa is quite delighted with these feeling & beautiful lines, & thinks them superior perhaps to any you ever wrote— Sam gives hopes that he shall be equally successful with the others— I write in the dear Kiosk, while George & Stormy are cleaning the walks, A. *scuffling* up Henᵗᵗᵃˢ walk to the Cottage & Henry helping Emma[4] to spread out the Nursery tea on the grass— a busy but very quiet school day we have had—the Boys attend to your directions— The only *events* since your departure are visits from your friends *Mistresses* Drummond, Webb, & Watts, & the Wigrams[5]— *My* visits have been to Mʳˢ Barker & old Jonathan,[6] where we had a delightful walk in last nights sun shine—let *your* gaieties hide their diminished heads. A. availed herself of dearest Henᵗᵗᵃ kind permission & gave us a gay cottage breakfast[7] on her birth day, under Minnys directing taste—it rained the rest of the day— Delighted are we in the hope of seeing dearest Jane on Wednesday—tell her so with a kiss—& Tell dearest Lotte that she must not *move* without my dearest Mother & Bum under her arm—she must bring her *whole heart* with her, or *mine, will only half* welcome her— I cannot let her be seperated from them while she remains in England[8]— Bummys appetite is to be sure rather *alarming*, but dearest Grandmama will not I think, *considerably thin* the flock of sheep, & dearest Bum, perhaps may *eke* out her dinner with Lottes share—indeed they *must come!*— The bell rings, Papa is come in, & away I run— Kisses innumerable to my loved Children, Mother, Sisters, & Nei[c]es— (who ever was so rich as I am) kindest loves too to your Uncles[9]— Seppy[10] is sneezing with a little cold—he often talks of you, & is as sentimentally melancholy during your absence as the strawberries will permit– Papa will eat no salad now, & it [is] a remarkable fact, that we miss you & Addles greatly– Papa says he is sure you are crowding Grandmama unconscionably– Pray when are you coming back?—— Marg^te has been for a day at Mrs Blizard & wrote a note of regret that she could not come here, or find time to write to Bell before she came away– She has taken 95 Glouc[este]^r Place for the present & gone–

Ever my dearest childrens
Most affec^te Mother—

You must bring all with you— tell Bum to write to me— all my gardeners & *scufflers* send you H. &^c &^c a thousand kisses– the roses are begin⟨ning⟩ to be ⟨beau⟩tiful No hay cut yet, the weather has been so wet.

A vile pen!

Address, on integral page: Miss Barrett / Cambray Street / Cheltenham.[11]
Publication: None traced.
Manuscript: British Library.

1. Dated by the reference to EBB's "Stanzas on the Death of Lord Byron," which appeared in the London *Globe and Traveller* on 30 June 1824.
2. EBB and Henrietta were in Cheltenham with their maternal grandmother, at No. 8 Cambray Street.
3. Samuel Moulton-Barrett had married at Gloucester, 20 March 1823, Mary Clementina, daughter of the late Rev. Henry Cay-Adams, of Painswick. What caused a break in the brothers' relationship has not been determined; possibly it related in some way to this marriage.
4. Thought to be Emma Mathews, daughter of the man mentioned in letters 53, 168 and 228.
5. Members of the local social circle. The Drummonds lived at Underdown, the Richard Webbs at Donnington Court, the James Watts at the Ledbury Vicarage. The Wigrams are unidentified.
6. Mrs. Barker lived in a cottage by the south gate of Hope End, and acted as gatekeeper. In a juvenile poem (*Reconstruction*, D418) EBB described her thus: "And Madam Barker with the sallow cheek / The lanky shape and the long slim neck / Sweet Madam Barker!" Jonathan has not been identified.
7. There was a summer cottage in the grounds of Hope End. A sketch of it by Henrietta is reproduced in *Diary*, facing p. 112, and there are numerous references suggesting that it was acknowledged to be her particular domain.
8. Mary Moulton-Barrett's sisters, Jane Hedley and Charlotte Butler, were staying in Cheltenham—the latter on a visit from her home in Ireland; she had married her brother-in-law, Richard Pierce Butler, in 1822. He was Vicar of Trim, 25 miles N.W. of Dublin.
9. John and James Graham-Clarke, Sir Thomas Butler and Richard Pierce Butler. A copy of Burns's *Works* (1821), with a notation by EBB: "Elizabeth B. Barrett, kindly given to her by the Rev. Richard Butler, Cheltenham, July, 1824" formed lot 533 of *Browning Collections* (see *Reconstruction*, A539).
10. Septimus, EBB's seventh brother.
11. Near the address appear notations: "opened"; "opened twice."

196. MARY MOULTON-BARRETT TO EBB &
HENRIETTA MOULTON-BARRETT

[Hope End]
[ca. July 1824]¹

A thousand congratulations to my loved Ba on this ["]joyous reconciliation"—a source of such comfort & delight for many a year I trust!— Your dear letters were both gratification & amusement to me– Most happy I am sure you are, I hope you will persuade dearest Grandmama to try Malvern Waters– My sweet Addles, thank you for your dear note! the affec^te attention of my dearest absentees is welcome to our hearts. Papa read Ba's letter with the greatest delight–
May God bless you both!――

Address, on integral page: Eliz^h & Hen^tta.
Publication: None traced.
Manuscript: Scripps College.

1. Preceding letter indicates that EBB's uncle Sam was seeking her help toward a rapprochement with her father. Presumably that is the "joyous reconciliation" mentioned here.

197. EDWARD MOULTON-BARRETT (BROTHER) TO EBB

[London]
July 29.th 1824.

My dearest Bazy
You no doubt were, or pretended to be disappointed at not hearing from me last Saturday; Knowing my power over you, and conscious of my great superiority as a punctual correspondent, and of the great debt of letters which you owe me, and which I am sorry to say in spite of all I can say or do you still suffer to accumulate; I tell you *plump* without any attempt at exculpation, or any supplications of pardon, which are rather due from *you to me,* I forgot you; after this declaration you cannot I think impeach my candour, and that I may preserve it from the slightest imputation of underhand proceedings, I will furthermore declare that I consider your mode of life amidst the gaity and dissipations of Cheltenham, as injurious to yourself, as it is disagreable, and inconvenient, to your friends and correspondents, it teaches you to forget your AFFECTIONATE BROTHER, who continues punctually every week to waste his time, pens, ink, and paper in the unprofitable service of writing to an ungrateful sister. Bazy, Bazy, as each week passes over my head without my receiving a line from you, it excites in me fresh

wonder, at your heinous ingratitude, and your incorrigible impudence. Well, now that I have exhausted all the rhetoric of my indignation, I suppose I must enter into more amicable terms with you, as I wish to obtain your sympathy on a most EYE BREAKING subject, only think Bazy, again this week has that most detestable engine of cruelty the cricket ball hit me on the very same unfortunate eye, and a second time both nearly obscured my "visionary ray" and turned that unhappy member black, blue, green yellow, in short every colour, upon the face of the earth, except the natural one, now is not this too affecting, it brings tears into my eyes when I think of it, into the one for its *own* misfortunes, into the other those of sympathy (which by the bye I shall espere[1] from you) for the wretched fate of its brother. Granny desires me to thank you for your kind letter, (more than *I* can do), and is delighted to hear yo⟨u ar⟩e all so well (more than my EYE is[)]. I wr⟨ote to⟩ Papa on Monday to apprize him of the near approach of the holidays, which ⟨com⟩mence on Thursday next, but have not yet received an answer from him. Good bye my dearest Bazy and believe me

your affect.
Brozy.

Sam is so much better that Dr Nuttall has this morning driven him out in his gig. Treppy desires me to say that she wrote to you last.

Addressed and franked by EBB's uncle on integral page: London July thirty one. 1824. / Miss Barrett / 8 Cambray S^t / Cheltenham / S M Barrett.
Publication: None traced.
Manuscript: Edward R. Moulton-Barrett.

1. "Hope for."

---

198. EDWARD MOULTON-BARRETT (BROTHER) TO EBB

[London]
[August 1824][1]

My dearest Bazy

You realy are quite incorrigible, after all my effusions or rage, indignation &.^c &.^c you take it coolly and answer me only by your impudent silence, which provokes me more than the most violent passion you could assume. I suppose you will plead as your excuse, the round of uninterrupted business you were pursuing at Cheltenham, no, no Miss Bazy that's "all my eye,"[2] if you did not postively wish to seek some excuse tolerably digestable, for indulging your idleness in not answering my letters, by even a line in return. you could have found plenty of time to scribble me a few lines, however it is of no use, to waste both my time and patience, upon so inattentive, & careless a ear, however all I've got to say is, that if the distance between you and me, was converted from miles into inches I would soon make that said member of yours a little *more susceptible* to my *more urgent* remonstrances. Yesterday on going into the hall after school, what was my astonishment at seeing M.ʳ M.ᶜ Swiney standing there as large as life, and as great a dandy as ever, he certainly was not looking quite so interesting, as the day he went in the celebrated lilac coat to pay his repects to the late lord Castlereigh,³ no, *"we shall never see its like again,"*⁴ but a frock coat of latest and most fashionable cut, brown duck trowsers, a MIGHTY NATE [*sic*] pair of sharp pointed boots, a stock six inches in length, and as inflexible as iron, with a very HILIGANT [*sic*] GOLD PIN by way of a polisher, he answered to the letter, the description which was given of him a short time ago, that of a "DASHING HIBERNIAN", but joking aside he is looking as well as ever I saw him, and I assure you I was very glad to see him; he says he likes Brighton very much and is as comfortably settled as possible. When we arrived here we found another old acquaintance, no other than M.ʳˢ Orme who looks all the smarter for a little Frenchification, curls half a yard long &.ᶜ &.ᶜ and is also very well; she is now looking out for another place as governess. Good bye my dearest Bazy, I hope you wont forget, me this next week, for I shall have my revenge if you dont.

Believe me
your ever affectionate
Brozzy

Love to all.

Publication: None traced.
Manuscript: Edward R. Moulton-Barrett.

1. Bro addressed the preceding letter, dated 29 July 1824, to EBB at Cheltenham. This one reads as if her visit there had just recently ended.
2. Goldsmith's *The Goodnatur'd Man* (1768), act III, sc. 1.
3. Lord Castlereagh (1769–1822), British statesman and Foreign Secretary (1812–22).
4. Cf. *Hamlet*, I, 2, 188.

199. EDWARD MOULTON-BARRETT (BROTHER) TO EBB

[London]
[*Postmark:* 20 September 1824]

My dearest Bazy
    I am to inform you that we arrived in town at five o'clock in spite of one or two of the little inconveniences which generally attend travelling, when we arrived in Cheltenham we got our tea and went to bed at nine o'clock by way of seasoning ourselves for the journey but I am sure I had twenty times rather have travelled all night than have slept in the bed they put us into, however to cut short a *long story* we had more bedfellows than were by any means pleasant, and we hardly either of us had a wink of sleep all night, for my own part I never closed my eyes, and I am sure Sam was not much better; but though this beyond doubt was bad enough, my new acquaintances formed such an attachment to me that I unknowingly carried a few away with me in the coach and I assure you I was most heartily tired of their company before we reached London; we went in new coach named the Berkeley hunt, which took us at a famous pace all the way, and as we arrived in London by five o'clock, I went to see Sam[1] on my way to Charter House, and staying with him some time we started once more and arrived here in excellent time. They seem to me to have made a very poor job indeed of the play ground, it is covered all over with gravel, but still retains the wet as much as ever,[2] and I dont think if left in this state it will ever be fit to play upon, McAdam I think has certainly completely failed here. My dearest Bazy I must now wish you good bye for dinner is just coming on the table.

Ever beleive me
your truly affect.
Brozy

    Pray write directly.
    Sam joins with me in love to all, and particularly *happiness in all things to our sweet Ba*

Address, on integral page: S. M. Barrett Esq[r] MP. / Hope End / Ledbury / Herefordshire.
Publication: None traced.
Manuscript: Edward R. Moulton-Barrett.

1. i.e., uncle Sam.
2. See letter 194, note 2.

200. EDWARD MOULTON-BARRETT (BROTHER) TO EBB

[London]
[*Postmark:* 30 September 1824]

My dearest Bazy.

You will no doubt be extremely sorry to hear of melancholy death of young McCinnon who was drowned during these holidays whilst bathing at Boulogne,[1] I heared it from a boy who was there all the time, it is the eldest son who was here, and I understand his father and Mother are almost broken hearted, in the morning he had asked his mother for a franc that he might take a machine, but she told him she had not one about her, and told him to bathe off the sands which he accordingly did, and his body was not found till two days after, when he was taken up in the most dreadful state. I have had a good deal of conversation with this boy and I assure you it was very interesting talk over our old haunts and acquaintances.[2] I enquired very particularly after a most intimate friend of ours who resides near the bottom of the Grand Rue on the right hand side, and with whom he was also upon very friendly terms, the said person is going on as usual with this exception that the mince pies were not quite in such requisition as when *we were there.* I am sorry to be obliged so soon to complain of your idleness in not writing to me, you are really too bad, and I tell you plainly that unless you answer my letters as regularly as I write them, I shall write to somebody else, ⟨who will be more punctual, there are plenty of correspondents to be found in the family besides yourself. As Sam tells me he has written to you, he will of course have told you all the Charter House news which is but scanty, and in consequence of his writing I have detained my letter untill today in hopes that something might happen worth communicating to you but as nothing of the sort has happened I shall now close my letter.

Believe me my dearest Bazy
your ever affectionate,
Brozy—

If you make this out⟩[3] I think you must be a juggler but you must excuse it as could get no darker ink till just this moment.

Address, *on integral page:* ⟨S M Barrett⟩ Esqr MP. / ⟨Hop⟩e End / Ledbury / ⟨Her⟩efordshire. "Ba" written adjacent to the seal.
Publication: None traced.
Manuscript: Edward R. Moulton-Barrett.

1. The Charterhouse Registers record the death by drowning on 20 July 1824 of William Henry Mackinnon. He was 18, and had been a day boy at Charterhouse from January 1820 to February 1824.

2. EBB and her family spent seven months in Boulogne in late 1823/early 1824.
3. Bracketed passage, from "who" to "out," is very faint, affected by the ink problem mentioned in the postscript.

---

201. EDWARD MOULTON-BARRETT (BROTHER) TO EBB

[London]
Oct.^{br} 6.th 1824.

Better late than never Bazy, I can assure your letter came none too soon, for I was in a most terrible rage with you, for your shameful idleness, and unless you had taken the prudent measure of writing as quickly as you did, you might have waited long enough before I should have condescended to have written you a line, however in consideration of your very many and humble appologies but more particularly because though I am disarmed of all excuse for *giving it you* on my own account, I am delegated from another quarter *not to spare you*, this from no less a person than Miss Trepsack who is almost as much out of patience with you as I was, she says they have not received a letter from you for an immense time and moreover she is extremely angry with you for not sending your poem[1] down to her. I read your account of the imaginary fire under the floor with great pleasure, and was much amused by it, except in one part where you allude to your slow retreat from the scene of action, this awoke in me feelings of a different nature, and I felt truly concerned when I see so clear a proof of the great weakness which must yet exist in your legs, and when I remembered with what astonishing velocity they carried you down stairs on the memorable day when the school room chimney was on fire, I could not have a more convincing proof that your legs are still in a very debilitated state; as for your boastings upon the subject they only made the feelings of compassion with which I regard your still deplorable state still more acute, as, I have been informed it is the nature of the disease, this however I will allow MAY be as much the nature of the BEAST as the DISEASE to boast of strength of MIND when strength of BODY *was at fault*, & pray dont mention this subject again as all your expostulations will only go to STRENGTHEN my ideas of your WEAKNESS. Yesterday I received a letter from Treppy she says it is uncertain whether they stay the winter at Hastings or not; there was she says a report of the Typhus fever having broken out there which frightened away many of the visitors, and no doubt amongst the rest they felt no small degree of the general fear, this report however, I somehow GUESS must be untrue, as like you they seem shy of *running*. Good bye for the present my dearest Bazy as I must now write to Hastings.

Believe me your affect
Brozy.

I am happy to hear *Mama's legs* are pretty strong.
Sam joins with me in love to all.

Address, on integral page: S. M. Barrett, Esq.ʳ M.P. / Hope End– / Ledbury / Herefordshire. "Ba" written adjacent to the seal.
Publication: None traced.
Manuscript: Edward R. Moulton-Barrett.

　1. Perhaps EBB's most recently-published poem, "Stanzas on the Death of Lord Byron."

---

202. EDWARD MOULTON-BARRETT (BROTHER) TO EBB

[London]
October 10.ᵗʰ 1824.

Well Bazy if these are your delights of London, I can only say as [I] do upon many other subjects, that I pity your taste, a wet Sunday in London has been considered by many, as the summum[1] of earthly misery. Now as to such disatisfied wretches I would just put them in the same situation with the small addition of being at Charter House, and then see if [they] would not wish themselves, any where even dripping in the middle of the street, in preference, to being shut up here on such a day as this, the play ground is completely flooded, the Library in the house is shut up, and if it had'nt been for you I know not what I should do, so here for once in a way you are of some use. You will no doubt admire my great condescension, unbounded kindness and implicit obedience to your earnest requests when you hear that I have changed my seal which gave you so much offence and have now got a plain one of which I hope you will approve,[2] if not I am affraid you must remain displeased as I am sure your opinion will not make me change again, I hope you will [feel] all due gratitude, and will consider yourself highly flattered for my so condescendingly submitting to your taste this once, from which my own very frequently so essentially differs. I have today been writing to Hastings, and hope you either have or will soon, direct your pen in the same direction. I assure you they are by no means pleased at your silence, and they will no doubt think it extremely unkind of you, if they dont hear from you soon, this do for both them and myself so sit down directly and make us each a good long apology for your idleness. As I wrote to you so short a time ago I have little more to tell you, except that from an exactly different cause on your part I shall expect shortly a different result, and that I shall soon receive a good long letter from you, as I am sure you must have plenty to tell me after so long a silence.

Ever beleive me
your affectionate
Brozy——

Sam's love.

Address, on integral page: S. M. Barrett. Esq.ʳ MP. / Hope End / Ledbury / Herefordshire. "Ba" is written adjacent to the seal.
Publication: None traced.
Manuscript: Edward R. Moulton-Barrett.

1. "Highest."
2. As all Bro's letters of this period that we have examined were sealed with wafers, his comment must be taken to refer to them, rather than to a signet for use with wax. Letters prior to this one were sealed with a ridged wafer that was apparently hard to undo without tearing the paper; use of this kind of wafer was discontinued with this and subsequent letters.

---

203. EDWARD MOULTON-BARRETT (BROTHER) TO EBB

[London]
[*Postmark:* 30 October 1824]

My dearest Bazy

You were no doubt greatly enraged at not recieving a letter from me last week, but to tell you the truth I was not atall [*sic*] well on Sunday, from a bad cold, which gave me a slight touch of the rheumatism, particularly in the back of my head, however I am happy to say a black dose has set me up again, and I am now quite well, I should have written during the week but Sam told me [he] had written so I thought I might as well put if off till today; in his turn Sam has now got a stiff neck and a bad cold, in short colds and coughs are so prevalent that every body is now complaining of them. I hope next week to have a chance of getting made a præpositus,[1] as we are to write verses without dictionary or graders, besides which we are to be strictly examined by Russell when the best will be elected. We have been examined four or five times this last week by Russell, and have come off well each time, he examined us once or twice for the purpose of explaining the plans of the school to a man who is going to establish a school at Corfu,[2] and of whom Russell has the nomination. I am quite delighted to hear you are getting on so well with your poem[3] and if I were you I certainly should not relinquish certain little hopes and ideas which you will remember you expressed to me.

I have not heard from Hastings since I wrote last, I hope you have not forgotten to write to them if you have you may depend upon it you never hear the end of it, for they were by no means pleased at your silence when I mentioned it last. I hope Bazy you will excuse this very short letter as I have got no less than four and twenty verses which must be done before tommorrow morning but I cannot close my letter without thanking both you and Henrietta for your very kind letters, I assure you they were most acceptable. Good bye ever believe me my dearest Bazy

your ever affect
Brozy

Address, on integral page: S. M. Barrett. Esq.ʳ MP. / Hope End / Ledbury / Herefordshire.
Publication: None traced.
Manuscript: Edward R. Moulton-Barrett.

1. Præpositus: one set in command. In 1821, there were only five masters at Charterhouse for 431 boys. To help compensate for the lack of teaching staff, a "picked boy of each form" (præpositus) was set "to teach the rest of his form, and keep order as best he could" (*Charterhouse in London*, by Gerald S. Davies, 1921, p. 265).
2. Probably the Ionian Academy, founded by Lord Guilford (1766–1827), who was its first chancellor in 1824.
3. Probably a draft of *An Essay on Mind*.

---

204. EDWARD MOULTON-BARRETT (BROTHER) TO EBB

[London]
Novᵇʳ 10.ᵗʰ 1824.

My dearest Bazy.

You will no doubt be greatly enraged, and most strongly indignant, that I, I who am always complaining of your idleness, should myself be so heinous an infringer of our epistolary laws. I can assure you it was quite unpremeditated on my part, as a very bad sprain in my thumb totally disabled me from further service with the pen for some time, it is indeed now very stiff, but I could not let another day pass without returning you my most grateful thanks for, your very regular and amusing correspondence. Your poem you say is coming on most rapidly I am delighted to hear it, but those hundred lines; they seem to me something like the hundred heads of the monster Hydra, except that your hundred lines remain the same though every letter from you speaks of the number of lines which you have written, whilst the Hydra by loosing [*sic*] a head gained two, it seems to me certainly a very extraordinary hundred lines, when I came away you had A HUNDRED LINES[1] to complete the poem, and though you have most certainly, got on most surprisingly, you are still in the same place, with a HUNDRED LINES before you.

According to your desire I questioned Sam about these nine shillings, which he wanted to pay the hair cutter, and I find, that it is not only for hair cutting, which would be quite impossible, but also for brushes which he has had of him. I have got a very nice addition to your library, not however to be monopolized by you as you must allow many of my books have been, but only to be stuck up in the shelves by way of ornament; so don't flatter yourself I am going to make you a present of it, as it was given to me by one of my greatest *cronies* who left it me as a legacy, it is Potter's Antiquities[2] very handsomely bound in half Russia in two volumes. We have not yet as I expected been examined, but I expect it very soon when you shall know the result. Good bye for the present my dearest Bazy– you shall hear from me again on Sunday.

Ever believe me your affec[t]

Brozy——

Address, on integral page: S. M. Barrett Esqr M.P. / Hope End / Ledbury / Herefordshire.
Publication: None traced.
Manuscript: Edward R. Moulton-Barrett.

1. Underscored three times. The poem in question was probably *An Essay on Mind.*
2. John Potter (1674?–1747), Archbishop of Canterbury, published his *Archæologiæ Græca: or Antiquities of Greece* in 1697–98. The two-volume, 1820 edition, with EBB's inscription, sold as lot 1016 in *Browning Collections* (see *Reconstruction*, A1888).

---

205. EBB TO MESSRS. KNIBB & LANGBRIDGE[1]

Hope End.
Thursday. [ca. December 1824][2]

Miss Barrett thanks Messrs Knibb & Co for their punctual attendance to her wishes, and would be much obliged if they would recieve back "Warburtons letters", and "Pizarro", about which she has changed her intentions. She would be glad to purchase Reid at 4[s] 'Suetonius' at 3[s] and Rogers in boards—also M[r] Campbells new Poem "Theodric." If made up in a parcel they shall be called for. The Money for all except 'Pleasures of Memory' & 'Theodric,' is enclosed.[3]

210 [ca. December 1824]

Address, on integral page: Messrs Knibb & Langbridge.
Publication: None traced.
Manuscript: Huntington Library.

1. Worcester booksellers.
2. Dating of this letter is based on the fact that EBB, in drafting her original order list, used the address page of the previous letter from her brother Edward, which is dated 10 November 1824. The list and accompanying price calculations are as follows:

Reids Enquiry into the human Mind– (calf gilt.	£ 0.6^S
D Stewarts "Philosophical Essays"—	7–6^d
Bowles St Michael's Mount—	1–6.
Warburton's Letters to Bishop Hurd.	8^S
Bossuet's Oraisons funebres."	2–6^d
Suetonius	2–6.
Voltaire's Siècles de Louis 14 et de Louis 15. 5 tom.	15^S
Sophoclis Tragœdiæ Gr. et Lat. ed. T Johnson 2 tom	12^S

3. Of the books mentioned here, only one can be identified as having been sold in *Browning Collections*, namely *Theodric; a Domestic Tale, and Other Poems*, by Thomas Campbell (London, 1824). EBB added the inscription: "E. B. Barrett, given to her by her dearest Papa." (*Reconstruction*, A565.) Of the items listed in note 2, two were sold in *Browning Collections*. They were *Philosophical Essays*, by Dugald Stewart (Edinburgh, 1816), (*Reconstruction*, A2211); and Sophocles' *Tragœdiæ Septem*, 2 vols., ed. T. Johnson (Etonæ, 1799), (*Reconstruction*, A2175).
   EBB wrote a 25-page essay on another of Stewart's works, *Elements of the Philosophy of the Human Mind* (see *Reconstruction*, D1286).

---

206. EBB TO CHARLES JOHN MOULTON-BARRETT

Written on dearest Stormy's
birthday. Hope End Decr 28.th 1824[1]

My Fancy's steps have often strayed
To some fair vale, the hills have made—
Where sparkling waters travel o'er,
And hold a mirror to the shore;
Winding, with murmuring, in, & out,
To find the flowers which grow about.
And there perhaps, in childhood bold,
Some little elf, three summers old,
Adown the vales may chance to run,
To hunt his shadow in the Sun—!
But when the waters meet his eyes—
He starts, and stops, with glad surprise,
And shouts, with merry voice, to view
The banks of green—the skies of blue—
Th' inverted flocks, that bleating go—
Lilies—and trees with apple blow—
Seeming so beautiful below.

He peeps above—he glances round
And then looks down—and thinks he's found
Reposing in the stream to woo one,
A world even lovelier than the true one.

Thus, with visions gay, & light,
Hath Fancy loved my page to dight,
Yet *Thought* has thro the vista seen
Something less frivolous, I ween!
Then while my chatting pen runs on,
I'll tell you what she mused upon.

Memory's the streamlet of the scene,
Which sweeps the hills of life between—
And, when our walking hour is past,
Upon its shore we rest at last;
And love to view the waters fair,
And see lost joys depictured there.

My Brother when thy feet are led
To press those banks, we all must tread—
Let Virtue's smile, and Learning's praise,
Adorn the waters, to thy gaze,
And o'er their lucid course be lent
The sunshine of a life well spent.
Then if a thought should glad thy breast
Of those who loved thee *first*, and *best*—
MY name perchance may haunt the spot
Not quite unprized—nor all forgot!

Publication: An Essay on Mind, pp. 120–122 (as "Memory"), slightly altered.
Manuscript: University of Texas.

1. His tenth.

---

207. ALFRED MOULTON-BARRETT TO EBB

[?Hope End]
[ca. 1825][1]

Dearest Ba Though you don't love me
I love you you now may see
As I can walk in with my letter
I think you ought to love me better

Your dear Baby

Address, on integral page: Dearest Ba / look kind at me / And something attracting / you will see.
Publication: None traced.
Manuscript: Berg Collection.

1. Conjectural dating and identity of writer based on handwriting.

208. EBB TO HENRIETTA MOULTON-BARRETT

[Hope End]

"Fortune-telling"

To my dearest Henrietta
On her birthday. March 4th 1825.[1]

Whose Fancy would turn Trappist, and go slave
At digging her own grave? Who would not cope
At hide & seek with Hope? Albeit the time
In youth's sweet concord chime, and Happiness
Shew her sunshiney face– Albeit the hour
Be pleasant with the power of merry hearts,
Playing their laughing parts—and musical
Voices which freshen all, making life gay!
Yes! Fancy steals away, when Thoughts asleep,
Trying to over-peep the shoulder of Time,
And read the Sybil rhyme of future years.

While thus my Spirit dreams,—looking upon
Thy face, oh dearest one! I fondly guess
That thy words of tenderness, and actions mild,
And goodness undefil'd, and gentle eyes
Tell us thy destinys . . . *to be BELOV'D!*

Your always attached Ba.

Address, on integral page: Miss Henrietta Barrett.
Publication: None traced.
Manuscript: R.J.L. Altham.

1. Her 16th.

209. EDWARD MOULTON-BARRETT (BROTHER) TO EBB

[London]
[*Postmark:* 5 March 1825]

My dearest Bazy

I am I must confess a little disappointed at not receiving your accustomed Saturday's epistle this week but in consequence of the very melancholy strain you wrote in last week, and knowing you are so very busily engaged about the corrections of your poem[1] I conclude you realy cannot find time to scribble to me. I hope you are getting on more to your taste with your poem than your accounts last week expressed, for two reasons, first because I think it must be most truly diasppointing to you after all your exertions and industry, to fail in your most favorite scheme, of being————— (you may guess the rest,) and secondly from a much more selfish motive, namely that you may not write so illhumoured and savage a letter as you sent me last week. I beg your pardon Bazy but realy your temper *generally* so sweet and calm, (upon again reading this sentence, the insertion of that little word "*generally*" seems very necessary.) was at the time you wrote to me last; most unaccountably ruffled. By the bye this prooves to me that you had a hand in a little trick that was played Sam, for that in consequence of being yourself very much out of humour you are determined to annoy every body else as much as possible, this is even more like you than making bad practical jokes which SAM accuses you of, and I am now QUITE sure that it was you who had the kindness to send Sam a shilling instead of his sovereign. He desires me to thank you for your kindness, and in consideration of the trouble you have taken he sends you back the shilling with the utmost contempt, he says moreover he is convinced it [is] yours from the badness of the joke, and he adds that he does not know which is the worst your wit or your poetry, and that neither one nor the other is worth what you have had the impudence to send him. With this affec.t adieu I shall now leave you to your meditations, but pray let me hear from you soon, believe me

your ever affec.t
Brozy.——

Publication: None traced.
Manuscript: Edward R. Moulton-Barrett.

1. *An Essay on Mind.*

210. ALFRED MOULTON-BARRETT TO EBB

[Hope End]
[6 March] [?1825][1]

To dearest Ba
On her birthday

_____

1

Let this day pass away
In mirth festivity and joy
And you must come and with us play
And always love your darling boy.

2

We'll deck your chair so very fine
With flowers both green and white
I hope we'll have some cake and wine
And then we will be happy quite

3

My dearest Ba that's all we want
To make us enjoy this happy day
I hope no one you will taunt
Now no more I have to say

ou's dear Dais[y][2]

Address, on integral page: To the Queen / of the day —
Publication: None traced.
Manuscript: Berg Collection.

1. Dated 1825 in a contemporary hand, but the quality of Alfred's handwriting raises the possibility of a later year.
2. Signature was obviously intended as "Daisy," the nickname of Alfred Moulton-Barrett, but it ran off the edge of the page.

_____

211. ARABELLA MOULTON-BARRETT TO EBB

[Hope End]
March 6th 1825

As my dearest Ba this is your birthday I must try to find out something to say to greet you on it my store is very empty so I must call in Apollo to aid me, so great is my affection towards you, that it is very difficult to find words to express it. And indeed my dearest Ba my fervent prayer shall always be for your health and happiness may Heaven grant it and may you have many happy returns of your birthday as my sincere wish. I must now quit the presence of Apollo and attend the summons of Comus.[1]

Always remember
Your ever affect[e]
Child *Arabell*

Address, on integral page: To dearest Ba, whom I hope won't love me the less / By saying, she is the image of good queen Bess.
Publication: None traced.
Manuscript: Myrtle Moulton-Barrett and Ronald A. Moulton-Barrett.

1. The god of pleasure or revelry.

---

212. CHARLES JOHN MOULTON-BARRETT TO EBB

[Hope End]

To dearest Ba
On her birthday
March 6th 1825[1]

Come Comus come and give us mirth
For this is the day of your birth
And I hope that you will live long
And always do what's right and never wrong.
By any chance ma chère sœur[2]
For if you remember Je vous aime de tout mon cœur[3]
Now dear Ba this is your day
So let us pass it merrily away
But now I must wish you good bye
Without a heave or without a sigh.

Your affectionate
Storm vel[4] CJB—

Address, on integral page: To / Dearest Ba.
Publication: None traced.
Manuscript: Berg Collection.

1. Year was originally written "1824," but was changed to "1825" in Mary Moulton-Barrett's hand. She also wrote "March 6th 1824." below the address, but changed the year to "1825."
2. "My dear sister."
3. "I love you with all my heart."
4. "Or else."

213. GEORGE GOODIN MOULTON-BARRETT TO EBB

hope End
March 6.th 1825.

My dearest Ba
I wish that you may be good and happy for a long life, and that I shall continually improve in the language you are so fond of, and teach us so cleverly, tho' I do not like it, quite so well, as I love you.

facere non possum sine te, ad senectusm¹ pervenias me docēre, soror carissima, et sis felicia!

G.G. Barrett

Address, on integral page: ad doctissimam Bam.²
Publication: None traced.
Manuscript: Berg Collection.

1. Originally written "senectum," then altered to "senectus" without crossing out the "m." The sentence translates as: "I am unable to do anything without you, may you reach old age to teach me, dearest sister, and may you be happy!"
2. "To most learned Ba."

214. HENRIETTA MOULTON-BARRETT TO EBB

Hope End
March 6th 1825

As my beloved Ba knows that *like* herself I am not a great advocate *at any time* for birthday addresses, she can hardly imagine I should venture to attempt one, on such *a natal* day as this; for indeed I very much doubt a pen *however skilled* could succeed in the expression of those feelings with which my heart now beats; could she think then that *I* whose pen is so unskilled would dare to tax myself with so tremendous a task? No, it would indeed be as presuming as unfeasible. But I will not demand a pardon for my inexp[i]ability I will leave it to her to imagine my feelings.

Yet this my much loved Ba I cannot omit to wish you every happiness this world can afford, that all your wishes both *now & ever* may be fulfilled & that you may ever believe me

Your devotedly attached
& most affectionate
Henrietta

Address on integral page: Miss Barrett.
Publication: None traced.
Manuscript: Berg Collection.

215. HENRY MOULTON-BARRETT TO EBB

[Hope End]
March 6.th 1825

My sweet Ba

How merry you are, & how clever to write such a magnificent Poem. I am so glad you were born for indeed your are very dear to

Your affec^{te}

Henry

Address, on integral page: Miss Basy
Publication: None traced.
Manuscript: Berg Collection.

---

216. EDWARD MOULTON-BARRETT (BROTHER) TO EBB

[London]
March 14.th 1825.—

My dearest Bazy

You are so very ticklish when your wit, (which I really believe you like, and ADMIRE equally with your poetry,) is called into question that you make no scruple of venting your rage against any unfortunate wretch that you may most conveniently light upon, you fly into a violent passion with me, who was only the innocent instrument in offering you this imaginary insult,[1] now I had nothing more to do with it than merely being the means by which it was conveyed to you, you abuse me for my want of discernment, now Miss Bazy I flatter myself I may in this respect turn the tables upon you, could you possibly be so stupid as not to see that what I said to you was meant for Sam, to divert his suspicions from this part of the world, now I think you have exposed yourself most completely and almost deserve every thing that was said about you.

We went yesterday to Warrens Hotel and saw Jane,[2] she has been very unwell all this week with the fashionable complaint, viz a bad cold however is now recovered and went out for the first time during the week to dine on Friday, she talks of staying some time in town. Sam[3] has gone to day with a gentleman in a gig to West Molsey about fifteen miles from town to look at a house which he proposes taking for the summer, and riding up to town three or four times a week, this I think is almost a[s] bad a plan as staying in town, as I should think the exertion of riding so far and not being used to it will be almost as predjudicial to his health as the smoky atmosphere of London. Russell

has given it out that we are to be examined next week, I am, as you may suppose a little nervous. Good bye my dearest Bazy
> ever believe me your
> affec! Brozy.

Addressed and franked by EBB's uncle on integral page: <Ma>rch fourteen 1825 / Miss Barrett / Hope End / Ledbury / <S M Barre>tt.
Publication: None traced.
Manuscript: Edward R. Moulton-Barrett.

1. The suggestion in letter 209 that EBB was responsible for sending Sam a shilling instead of a sovereign.
2. Jane Hedley, their maternal aunt.
3. i.e., uncle Sam.

---

217. EDWARD MOULTON-BARRETT (BROTHER) TO EBB

[London]
[*Postmark:* 26 March 1825]

My dearest Bazy

You were no doubt greatly offended at not hearing from me last week, and have I confess paid me in my own coin, by not writing to me this, however I hope somewhat to appease your anger, by assuring you that the omission was quite unpremeditated on my part, for I had actually taken a frank with me on Sunday night with the intention of writing to you on Monday morning when quite unexpectedly we were ordered in to write verses, by which means I was prevented from using my frank. We have been examined twice this week, by Russell and I expect a third will take place next, for the election of præpositi. Tell Arabel how much obliged I was for her most edifying, entertaining, and witty letter, tell her I acknowledge the justice of her complaint in not thanking her for the former one, it was certainly a most unpardonable piece of neglect, but having repented of my inattention I hope I shall soon receive a letter of forgiveness from her. I send you a very beautiful *silver remember* medal of Lord Byron, which I hope you will value and preserve as it deserves, it struck my fancy last Saturday in Oxford St. from its extreme elegance, and beauty of execution, and a still stronger recommendation was, that I was at a loss to discover which it most resembled Ld Byron, or myself.

You must excuse a long letter today as Jane has been kind enough to invite us to dine with her this evening and go to see Mathews,[1] I am sure you will envy us.

> Good bye my dearest Bazy
> ever believe me your truly affec!
> Brozy

I shall expect a doubly long letter next week to compensate for your idleness this.

Love to all.

Addressed and franked by EBB's uncle on integral page: London March twenty six 1825 / Miss Barrett / Hope End / Ledbury / S M Barrett.
Publication: None traced.
Manuscript: Edward R. Moulton-Barrett.

1. Charles Mathews (1776–1835), actor. The production was "Mr. Mathews's Memorandum-Book," at the Lyceum Theatre. Jane was aunt Jane Hedley.

---

218. EBB TO EDWARD MOULTON-BARRETT (FATHER)

[London]
[28 May] 1825

To my beloved Papa.
On his birthday. 1825.[1]

If every thought of love could find a sound
To speak its life—if Tenderness might steal
A touch from Orphean harps, pulsing around—
Yea! if the heart were MUSIC,[2] to reveal
In most melodious tones, what hearts, in fondness, feel—

Then might Affection, like the Bulbul,[3] be,
When every gadding bird is hush'd on spray,
Keeping to Heaven her holy minstrelsy—
Oh! then nor Chiron's art,[4] nor Loxian sway[5]
Would match these simple rhymes . . eclipse my artless lay.

But if, as Poets write, Feeling be *dumb*,
And can alone by *gesture* show her meed;
If, to fond thoughts, Expression seldom come,—
No wonder tho' my song be rough indeed—
Nor shall my Father's ear a sweeter cadence need.!

He'll think my broken measures sound more soft
Than all the pomp, sublimer themes inspire!
For tender words are never heard too oft,
Tho breathed as thickly from the murmuring lyre,
As wild Ogygian tales[6] at Gossip's evening fire.

Albeit the sound be harsh, the image dim,
Grateful Affection writes her language here—
And *her* true language makes it all to *him!*

Let me aread thee right, oh! fondly dear!
For what no tongue can speak, a Parent's heart may hear.

Yours always attached Ba

Publication: HUP, II, 48–49.
Manuscript: University of Texas.

1. His 40th.
2. Underscored three times.
3. A member of the thrush family, sometimes called the nightingale of the East.
4. Chiron was the centaur who taught music, hunting and medicine to Achilles and other heroes.
5. Loxias (Interpreter) was a title bestowed on Apollo, in recognition of his prophetic knowledge of the will of Zeus.
6. Odysseus was shipwrecked on the island of Ogygia, the abode of Calypso, under whose spell he remained for seven years.

219. EDWARD MOULTON-BARRETT (BROTHER) TO EBB

[London]
[*Postmark:* 15 June 1825]

My dearest Bazy

You were no doubt surprised at not hearing from me for so long a time, but as I met my very great friend M! Webb at the Bull and Mouth and he promised to convey the news of our safe arrival,[1] I thought there was no occasion to hurry myself particularly, in setting your anxious fears at rest for our safety, which I am sure must have been very strongly awakened. When we left you and arrived at Chances Pitch[2] we waited for more than a quarter of an hour for the Mail but when it arrived we were lucky enough to find two places vacant, and arrived in Worcester about half an hour before the London coach started, nothing of any importance happened to us all the way except that we both slept extremely well, and drank a very comfortable tea at Oxford, instead of arriving at the Bull and Mouth as we expected at seven we did not get in till past nine, when after a good breakfast we tumbled into a coach and got here a little before eleven. We met with a very civil reception from Russell who was not the least angry at our not returning in time.

We have had a letter from Treppy who talks of returning to Hastings very soon, but talks of coming to see us before they go. I must wish you good bye for the present, but shall spare a little more time to you next Saturday

Beleive me
your ever affectionate
Brozy ——

Remember me very kindly to Emily and Angela³ and tell them I disspatched their letter immediately on our arrival, and I hope it has been safely received.——

Address, on integral page: Miss Barrett / Hope End / Ledbury / Herefordshire——
Publication: None traced.
Manuscript: Edward R. Moulton-Barrett.

1. A reference to meeting a neighbour, Richard Webb, and sending a message by him to Hope End.
2. A place on the turnpike road, about two miles from Hope End, where the public coach could be boarded en route from Ledbury to Worcester.
3. Emily and Angela Bayford, daughters of John and Frances Bayford, were visiting their cousins at Hope End.

---

220. EDWARD MOULTON-BARRETT (FATHER) TO EBB

Hope End,
August 16. 1825.

My dearest Ba

My only object in writing is to say that if you and dear Granny and Trippy like to keep the Boys another Week you may¹– Before the expiration of that time I shall know something certain of Mama's intentions as Charlotte's confinement has taken place, and who with her little girl were doing well when she wrote–² I met your friend Carden in the streets of Worcester yesterday he says, you may bathe with profit in the sea provided it be not too early nor you too cold when you take your plunge. If Knight delays giving you an answer soon I would beg Sam to remove your Poem into some other hand–³ We know from the length of it that it could not require a sixth portion of the time he has had it, to form a judgement as to its publication, where he runs neither hazard of Character or Expenditure by so doing– You will be sorry to hear that the youngest Brother of Col: Money, who was in the East India Company's China Trade, cut his Throat about a week ago, and was buried last Saturday.–⁴ He was for a long time in a very dejected state– I requested Bro to write me word, all the information he could acquire of the state of the Hop yards in his way to Hastings; but not a line from him have I received– Tell Henrietta "to season her admiration"⁵ that a Preacher should be a Physician for the Dʳ she heard in favor of the Home Missionary Society was a L.L.D not a MD. I believe he is a learned Man and above all possesses a Wisdom that will not descend to the grave but must mount up aloft after life– I hope she gave largely, as I am connected with the Society,—that is to say, if she could find no better motive; but from an observation of hers to me, I have no right to suspect this— Dearest Sette told me at Din⟨ner⟩ to-day that he had behaved purtty well, not very well, that he had said his pictures, what t⟨hat⟩ is I dont know, his counts, his multication [*sic*], his speling, his reading and his catsimn![6] he certainly is the dearest thing in the natural and sensible World, he sleeps with me every night and often has occasion to tell me Oh ou skeese[7] me! Tell those who may feel an interest in it that this Week I hope to finish nearly my harvest, all very good and well won. I dont presume to retouch this on face— God bless you all my dear Loves and make you, what I never cease to pray for, good, healthy and spiritual—

Yͬ dearly attached EMB ——

I write almost in the dark on the eve of going to bed—and but ten o'clock— I get up at six—and therefore feel disposed for Bed early. I am rejoiced to find our beloved Sam has quite recovered but am concerned to hear his Mary is complaining. He is however where he can get the best advice and the result we must leave to a merciful *Providence*

Address, on integral page: Dear Ba ——
Docket, at left side of address page near seal, in EBB's hand: My beloved Papa.
Publication: None traced.
Manuscript: British Library.

1. Bro and Sam were with EBB and Henrietta at Hastings.
2. EBB's mother had gone to Ireland in July. While there her sister Charlotte gave birth to her first child, Charlotte Mary ("Arlette") Butler.
3. EBB had submitted the manuscript of *An Essay on Mind* to Charles Knight (1791– 1873), author and publisher.
4. Col. James Money-Kyrle (later Major-General Sir James, 1775–1843), was a neighbour of the Moulton-Barretts, living at Hom House, Much Marcle. His brother, John Money (b. 1786) had died unmarried on 6 August.
5. *Hamlet*, I, 2, 192.
6. Catechism.
7. Squeeze.

---

221. EBB TO JAMES GRAHAM-CLARKE

1 Kentish Buildings. [Hastings]
[*Postmark:* 12 November 1825]

My dearest James,

Hearing that you have been so very unwell, & finding that, from the purposed journey of all your dear companions, writing to THEM would be vain, I cant help sending you one line to enquire how you are. If it is fatiguing to you to answer this enquiry, you will make us uncomfortable by doing so, but otherwise you must not refuse to give us one bulletin (however short) of your health. In the health of one whose kindness to us has been so great, how could we feel otherwise than interested? Believe dearest James, that we are not ungrateful!

Henrietta and I have been four months from home, & our visit seems inclined even now to lengthen itself. Hope End letters make no very pathetic lamentations over our absence, & Hope End seems to do well enough without us. For ourselves we are as happy here as we well can be, eschewing every human discontent to good purpose. We find Hastings an exceedingly pleasant place, and our loved Granny more than kind—while letters from home, bringing us tidings of the health & well doing of all there, set our hearts quite at ease.

There has been a pleasant degree of romance in our situation during the last week,—inasmuch as this time last year the inhabitants of the house we inhabit were put to flight by a holy alliance between the sea before our windows & the adjacent river on our right. A like route seemed to be in reserve for us, when on waking this morning we found the meadows behind us completely flooded, & the sea advancing in three leagued boots. High tide has past however without attempting our security, a little to my disappointment— We are in search of a more sheltered habitation, but one much less attractive.

I hear constantly from the Bayford's who speak of you with eloquent gratitude. And indeed dearest James the extreme kindness with which you lent yourself to our convenience must be long remembered by all of us. We spent some happy days, and had to thank you for so spending them.

Have you met with Southey's new Poem "The Tale of Paraguay[")]? The extracts I have seen delight me maugre the reviewing commentary which speaks I think much too harshly and partially. If I do not mistake, the style appears to be a remarkably good imitation of "Gertrude," given with a high degree of Campbell's characteristic feeling. One line delights me, & I must mention it; because I admire it myself, & because it seems to be admired by no one else!

"With a SLOW smile that touched him to the heart".[1]

I think the epithet exquisite!–

We long to hear thro' Mama, that all the dear Travellers have reached Cheltenham, in safety, & well doing. Henrietta, Bro, (who leaves this place shortly for school) Granny & Trippy tell me to say every thing affectionate from them to you!

Believe me, dearest James,
Yours always affectionately
E B Barrett.

I open my letter to tell you with Granny's love . . "that October is past, & the needful is wanted."[2]

Addressed and franked by EBB's uncle on integral page: London Nov.ʳ twelve 1825 / James G. Clarke Esq / Fenham House / Newcastle on / Tyne / S M Barrett / [and in EBB's hand on reverse when folded] James G Clarke Esq.ʳ / Fenham.

Docket, near foregoing addresses, in James Graham-Clarke's hand: Ans^d 8th Decr 1825.
Publication: None traced.
Manuscript: Edward R. Moulton-Barrett.

1. *A Tale of Paraguay* (1825), canto 4, v. 47.
2. Mrs. Moulton had been left an annuity by her brother, George Goodin Barrett (1760–95). His executor was his partner, Leonard Parkinson (John Altham Graham-Clarke's father-in-law). After Parkinson's death, responsibility for the payment of the annuity passed to the Graham-Clarkes.
Two paragraphs follow in the hand of Henrietta (SD543).

---

222. MARY MOULTON-BARRETT TO EBB

[Hope End]
Tuesday Nov. 23^d [1825][1]

My beloved Ba: I am full of anxiety to hear whether dearest Papa's letter, was intended to prevent Bro's going to school, or whether he was gone before it arrived. *Today,* I trust this anxiety may be satisfied, & that also, respecting my dear Mother from whom I have never heard for three weeks, tho' she purposed setting off in that following the date of her last letter. There lies your wonderful letter before me, containing a mystery, which Papa & I in vain endeavour to solve; *he* suspects you have had some proposal, (not of a *matrimonial* nature) from Mr Duncan, while I have suggested that it might be from Mr Blaquiere, to which he answers, "the Pope is as likely"[2]—so to prevent further conjugal discord, & more necessarily, to satisfy that torment Curiosity, *common I* maintain, to *man* & woman, pray let us further into y^r secret as soon as you may see it fitting. I can only say, that nothing can be more desireable than the *lucre* you mention, save & except health & comfort, but I own, I should grieve to see you fagging to the destruction of both, at some periodical publication, which *may* be the subject, of this *"imposing"* proposal—but you are launched on the world as Authoress, & must I suppose be contented to purchase fame at the Common Cost.– I like the prospectus of your new *nurstling,* as far as I can see of it, & so does Papa. Our greater interest turns however to that immediately forthcoming: I trust it must speedily now be emancipated from Mr D. & his Devils; are there to be any advertisements? We are grieved to hear of dearest Granny's asthma: has she tried the 13 cloves of garlic in a pint of spring water; buried 3 or 4 days, & a cup full taken night & morn^g– it *has* done much good. Your acc^t of all her affection, & the unceasing kindness you receive, went to our hearts: it is indeed, dearest Ba, *passing words!* Let me see what I have to tell you in return for all the gratification of *mind & heart* afforded by your dear letter! Nothing I believe but that I walked thro' the mud to Church on Sunday, accompanied by Ann,[3] who was much smarter than *me*—as you will have little difficulty in believing— M.[r] Hockin[4] was full of enquiry after you & Hen[tta] & did duty in his *best* manner: The Sunday before, E. Pew had left poor M[rs] Mutlow[5] as well as usual, when she got up: & having lighted the fire, she returned & found that the poor sufferer had got up to put on her stockings, & in the act of putting on her garter, had dropped down dead! A happy release I trust from extraordinary suffering— M[rs] Barker is really greatly better— On Sunday she came here in time to hear the morning service, dined merrily with Minny, came in to Evening prayers, & as it was a bad Even[g], slept here, as happy as possible, & really quite well— She is so delighted with hearing Papa, that she begs she may sometimes be allowed to come on Sundays— I wish you could see Arabel *pasting* up the school room windows, & hear her exclamations of delight at the *9* cock pheasants parading their beautiful plumage on the lawn! A note from Miss Commeline today tells me Laura[6] has been in bed some days with the influenza, & all their servants have been ill— She is still anxious to pay her visit here, so long talked of, when you return— She says of "Judah"[7] that the lines are very beautiful, written with great power, very unlike female poets!! They seem hopeless of poor James C.[8] ever recovering his power of hearing— I am over head & ears in debt in the visiting way (*morning*) duty, I mean, particularly to the Cliffes,[9] who have been here several times— Miss C. continues all her religious activity & is as great a favorite with Papa as ever— I am glad to hear Mazzochetti is in London where his talents must be estimated, & ensure him prosperity— We grieve at your acc.[t] of Louisa B[utler]—pray give my love & kind wishes to them— No letter from Bro today, induces us to suppose he is not gone to school— No letter too from Fenham!– E. Ridley[10] gives a better acc.[t] of herself & Mother—they are at Abinger[11]—go to their Cottage at Hertingfordbury in Feb[y].– Miss Clives[12] Husband has their stall at Glouc.[r] We are talking of *walking* over to call on M[rs] Trant some fine frosty morning, tho' it is easier to talk of than to *execute 9 miles*. Daly[13] wants to know "when he is to see his *friends*, Miss Barrett & Hen[tta] he is afraid they'll be forgetting him". Every body here seems to have the measles but us—they are very bad in Ledbury– All are quite well here thank God– Our quiet & early hours seem to agree to admiration with dearest Papa—I never saw him look better in my life—last night we sat in the Drawing Room for the purpose of having Music, but he had no sooner begun to sing than he found out it would not do without Audience, & more warmth– We are indeed more cozy in the Library—this cold weather– I am so beset with

talkers, that I know not what I am writing, & had better come to a close—
I must however tell you of Seppy's sweetness tonight, in giving up his
pencil, that Alfred might draw, tho' he was watching him anxiously, to
take his turn when he was tired— there never was such a Chesterfield in
petticoats.[14] A letter from Ann Surtees[15] gives a tolerable acc[t] of the
poor girls— I know not yet what they are to do.

Dominic T[rant]— we hear is at Malvern. Our united loves & kisses
to you all, Granny & Treppy ever included in our dearest affections.

Your own Mother

Addressed and franked by EBB's uncle on integral page: London Nov[r] twenty five 1825 /
Miss Barrett / M[rs] Moulton's / Hastings. / S M Barrett.
Publication: None traced.
Manuscript: British Library.

1. This is how the letter was dated, although Tuesday was the 22nd, not 23rd. The year
comes from the postmark.
2. James Duncan had undertaken to publish EBB's *An Essay on Mind*, although he
did not do so until 25 March 1826. Mr. Blaquiere is thought to be the Edward Blaquiere
who was an ardent advocate of Greek independence, as was EBB. He had published
several works on this subject.
3. A maid at Hope End.
4. The Rev. John Pearce Hockin, Rector of Coddington since 1810.
5. These two ladies have not been identified; presumably they were local residents.
6. Daughters of the Rev. James Commeline, Sr., Vicar of Redmarley D'Abitot, 6 miles
S.E. of Ledbury. The family were friends of long standing; a letter of 19 February 1815
(SD221) speaks of their being house-guests.
7. We have not been able to identify this poem. The word "Judah" does not appear in
Gladys Hudson's concordance of EBB's published works. Also see SD541.
8. The son of James Commeline, Sr.
9. The Allen Cliffes of Mathon. The eldest daughter, Mary, later married Thomas Best,
and published several works of a religious nature.
10. Elizabeth Ridley (d. 1867) was the only daughter of Henry Ridley, D.D. (1753–
1825), Prebendary of Gloucester and Rector of Hertingfordbury, and his wife Frances (*née*
Surtees). She was the niece by marriage of Mary Moulton-Barrett's aunt, Mary Surtees
(*née* Altham). EBB gave her a copy of *The Battle of Marathon* (now at Yale, *Reconstruction*,
B6).
11. At this time, the Rector of Abinger was Henry John Ridley (1778–1834), Elizabeth
Ridley's brother.
12. The daughter of Edward Bolton Clive, former M.P. for Hereford.
13. Groundsman and dairyman at Hope End.
14. A reference to Philip Stanhope, 4th Earl of Chesterfield (1694–1773), politician
and man of letters.
15. EBB's great-aunt, Mary Altham, had married Aubone Surtees. Ann Surtees is
thought to be Mary Anne (*née* Hawkins), the wife of their nephew John Surtees.

not like, but still sacred —

Mary Moulton-Barrett

My dearest Henrietta

You ordered [me] to [send] now & then ... so [that] you shall receive a few lines ... to assure [you] that I am quite as well as can be expected — which is [very] little. My first introduction was much more awkward than I anticipated ... [for] I was shown into the library, where sat, or stood (I did not know which,) one unknown gentleman soliloquizing — or at least solilo- quizing. This was worse than the [Rickey] scene!

I am, as yet, the only stranger in the family circle — so that I

Letter 240

223. EBB TO JAMES GRAHAM-CLARKE

2. Paragon Place Hastings
Dec^{ber} 13.th 1825.

My dearest James,

This ragged bit of paper is certainly a much too shabby representive [*sic*] of what I must needs say in behalf of our affectionate & grateful feelings towards you. Your letter is very kind & gratifying; gratifying as proceeding from *you*, & kind as vouchsafed to *us*. I assure you there was not one amongst us, from Granny *down to Bro*[1] (who is quite well now) to whom the expression of your kind feelings did not give pleasure, & who were not ready to return them with ten per cent interest. So much for ourselves.

We hear every thing good from all at home, who make as yet no advances in the way of getting us there. Christmas will most probably see us at Hastings, &, but for the Almanack, we might mistake it for April! We open the windows to let in the air, & draw down the blinds to keep out the sun; finding it quite unnecessary to improve a slight acquaintance with the fire who holds a sinecure. Were I inclined to be ill natured in respect to your dear coterie (& that, for my credit's sake, I am not) I might draw "COMPARISONS" which, as the writing master's copy says, "are odious."[2] But after all you have Newcastle coals, & the "yule log", & merry hearts to keep the rest 'alight.'

Give our very best love to every body near you, for without shrewdness I may conclude 'every body' so close in your neighbourhood to be 'somebody' beloved by me. Congratulate them on your recovery which delights us all so much; as to your Bachelorship I cant for my womanly credit say a word. You may make the best of it, but you will want an Eve after all. Granny desires me to compliment you on your anti-matrimonial propensities, & if you were of the 'amiable' sex I might be inclined to do so—otherwise it "sticks in my throat."[3] Your professorship is quite a PROFESSION. You take your *degrees*, in so slovenly a manner, that it seems highly probable that you should change your mind . . in a DEGREE; & instead of sitting down contented with a Bachelorship, be Master of ARTS[4] according to our Herefordshire aspiring pronunciation: i.e. "hearts"!

I say all this a little spitefully, inasmuch as I was fairly taken in by the preamble of your letter, & actually expected on the turning of the leaf to be in possession of the name of your betrothed. In return you deserve a little malice from *me*.

Sam the younger has gone home for the Christmas Holidays; & I write to Sam the Elder much seldomer than I think of him. Neither of us have time enough for the renewal of our ancient correspondance. *So* we both say, but there is a little scepticism on my side.

You ask me about my book. I can only say that it has been in the press nearly five months, & thro' the weekly calls on me for proof-correcting, is a constant source of annoyance. If Mr Bayford's friendliness had not encouraged and assisted me I should have been quite wearied of the whole business before this. But he has shown me much kindness, & his interest procured me valuable observations from other of his friends. I suppose we shall be done now in a few weeks, & shall advertise when the last sheet is in the press. Do you know any body who could be induced to notice it in the way of Criticism . . *Averce* [sic] would do as well as any thing, to produce a sale!–[5]

Granny suffers from her cough in spite of this UNseasonable weather. She & Trippy with Bro Henrietta & myself unite in best of loves to dear Grandmama, & *that* never forgotten Bummy together with little Arabella & Louis d'or![6]

Believe me always my dearest James
Your gratefully affectionate
E B Barrett.

Money recieved with many thanks!——
Henrietta hopes you wont change your intentions respecting her.

Addressed and franked by EBB's uncle on integral page: London December fifteen 1825. / James Graham Clarke Esq / Fenham House / Newcastle on Tyne / S M Barrett.[7]
Publication: None traced.
Manuscript: Edward R. Moulton-Barrett.

1. EBB placed an asterisk here. A related asterisk and the word "cool" appear at top of page 1.
   2. John Donne's "Elegies" (1633), No. 8 (later titled "The Comparison").
   3. Cf. *Macbeth*, II, 2, 30.
   4. Underscored three times.
   5. This whole paragraph refers to the protracted business of getting *An Essay on Mind* into print.
   6. Although the gender here is clearly masculine, we take this to be a punning reference to Arabella Butler's younger sister, James Graham-Clarke's niece, Louisa Charlotte.
   7. On reverse when folded, in EBB's hand, is the address: "James G Clarke Esqr / Fenham." It was crossed out, presumably by her uncle when he addressed and franked the letter.

224. MARY MOULTON-BARRETT TO EBB

Hope End–
Decr 30.th 1825.

My own dearest Ba:

It is not only on the plea that I have a letter of yours to answer, that I now propose to devote to you some of my dulness, but that I also long to tell you with how much satisfaction of heart I heard of your receiving the Sacrament. May it be now, & *ever* to my beloved child, her strength in weakness, her comfort in sorrow, & her *health* in joy, as it ever must be to those who take it in faithful remembrance, as long as sin & suffering belong to humanity. Since your dear letters are next best to seeing you, I need scarcely say that they are more valued than even mince pies, plum cake, or any other festivities of the season & much more greedily devoured—there would be a regular, or rather irregular scramble for them amongst the *juniors*, if I did not generally take it upon me to deliver them, with due emphasis to the public ear. First let me tell you, how much we like your motto:[1] it is selected not only with "*modesty*", but with much good taste; we think it a bold poetic licence to make poor Riga *sing* from the scaffold,[2] but have no doubt that his strain is appropriate, with more in it, even than that of the dying swan: the additions to the fugitive pieces, must encrease their interest & importance: I hope the last sheet is actually come & gone; as to *the mystery*, I begin to think it must be impenetrable. Time seems to have no effect in unravelling it: I have only one word to say about it, & that is an entreaty that you will not bind yourself to any laborious undertaking without letting us know, for we cannot help entertaining more vulgar solicitude about your precious health, than either wealth or fame: The mind indeed cannot retain its powers, if the casket which contains it, be injured or weakened, & you cannot encrease your hours of study, without sacrificing your health: You may think this "stale & unprofitable"[3] but it is the anxiety of our hearts dearest Ba!– There is another subject very near mine just now, tho' it is one of such delicate texture that I scarcely know how to touch upon it, sensible as I am, that all your fears will vibrate to the idea of leaving dearest Granny! that day however MUST come, & from a hint of Papa's yesterday, I have felt an apprehension that it may come *too* suddenly to admit of your going to Walthamstow, which I should dread Sam would consider unkind, as they took you from hence,[4] & have expressed so much *certainty* on the subject of your going to them– I know not how to suggest any escape from this danger, as it is only a surmise of my *own*, (tho' a *very strong* one), that Papa's cogitations run upon Bro's being your escort home, before he goes to C[harter]. House. As this however is a mystery almost as dark as your own, (saving that some time ago he mentioned *that* as the only means he could think of for getting you home) I can suggest only, the expediency of your expressing *speedily*, your desire to spend if only a *week*, with Sam on your way, whenever you return: I am sure Granny will be of my opinion, that this *pleasure*, is an incumbent *duty* also– I would not for worlds have any sort of neglect shewn to that kindest of Uncles & of Friends– he deserves much more than we can ever do for him—& as a fortnight of the holidays only remain from next Tuesday, I own I rather dread your receiving some sudden mandate: Consult with dearest Granny & Tippy on this subject; for my own part, believe me, my beloved children my only wish is that the plans may be altogether such as may best suit your own wishes, & my own selfish feelings, are all directed to entire sympathy with yours– Say nothing of all this when you write, further than any allusion you may think right to Walthamstow– We were *all* pleased to hear of Tippys kindness in taking you to the play, which to your strong *dramatic* tastes, must have been a great treat. We do not *hear* even, of M.ʳ Foleys scenic fêtes this year:⁵ trees heavy in wreaths of snow, pheasants feeding above the rock, & smiling faces round the Xmas board, & yule log, stand in lieu of all the histrionic display of *talent* which distinguished our Christmas sports last year; I must however add, the sport which greeted my eyes from the school room window this moment of the five eldest rolling an immense *roll* of snow, which their united strength can scarcely move, up the coach road, with many exulting shouts of delight ⟨★★★⟩

Publication: None traced.
Manuscript: British Library.

   1. On the title page of *An Essay on Mind* appeared Tasso's line, "Brama assai, poco spera, e nulla chiede." For the whole stanza, with a translation, see letter 226.
   2. Konstantinos Rhegas (1757?–98), Greek patriot and poet executed by the Turks, was the subject of EBB's "Riga's Last Song," published with *An Essay on Mind*.
   3. Cf. *Hamlet*, I, 2, 133.
   4. The previous summer EBB's uncle Sam and his wife Mary were visiting Hope End. When they departed, they took EBB and Henrietta with them to their residence at Walthamstow, near London, and later to Hastings.
   5. Probably E.T. Foley, a patron of the local library, whose seat was Stoke Edith.

225. UNIDENTIFIED CORRESPONDENT TO EBB

[   ]
[ca. 1826]¹

To
Miss Barrett
on reading her "Essay on Mind"

Enchantress welcome! Poesy's young child,
    That with bold hand hath seized Apollo's Lyre,
    Mingling in sweetest concord words of fire,
I welcome with a votary's transport wild
Thy lay, so pure—so lofty—modest—mild—
    Hail Intellectual Fair, sent to inspire
Our duller day! sure on thy birth Heaven smil'd
    And gave us thee to gaze at and admire—
Thy Seraph muse wings her bright meteor flight
    Above thy sex's far as Byron's harp
Sounds o'er his brother's, or Day outshines Night.
    Ye Fateful Sisters, long forbear your warp
And woof to weave for her! Guard her ye Nine!
    And Thou Great God of Song, for *Barrett* she is Thine!

To
The Same
On reading her poem of "MARATHON"

But if my heart with ecstasy oerflow'd
    When on my wondering, ravished senses fell
    Thy Intellectual Song, how may I tell
The heightened rapture in my soul that glow'd
When "MARATHON" and Greece the lov'd abode
    Of heroes charm'd my spirit like some spell
    To see thy eaglet muse scarce from the shell
Burst, spurning sonnet, epigram or ode,
    And soaring mount the Epic sky to gain!
When thus Mind, Virtue, Genius, Beauty twine
The laurel wreath, as all in thee combine,
    Who feels and owns not thy heaven gifted strain?—
Then onward—nor dread Critic's venom'd dart
Thy fame may well defy his blackest art

[ca. 1826] No. 225

Publication: None traced.
Manuscript: Berg Collection.

1. Dated by the fact that *An Essay on Mind* was published in March 1826. A copy of these verses, in the hand of Mary Moulton-Barrett, is with Mary V. Altham.

---

226. MARY MOULTON-BARRETT TO EBB

[Hope End]
Sunday– [8 January 1826]¹

Canto 2ᵈ Stanza 16.

Colei Sofronia, Olindo egli s'appella;
D'una Cittate entrambi, e d'una fede,
Ei che modesto è si, com'essa é bella,
Brama assai, poco spera, e nulla chiede
Nè sa scoprirsi, o non ardisce; ed ella
O lo sprezza, o nol vede, o non s' avvede
Cosi finora il misero ha servito
O non visto, o mal noto, o mal gradito.²

I should really be sorry if you see it necessary to abandon your pretty motto, & hope you will agree with me, that it may serve as well in the 3ᵈ as first person, tho' of that you will best judge– I am glad however that you used the precaution of referring to the line, much as the commodities in that well filled *store house* of yours may be depended upon to be of sterling value– All your assurances of love on the birth of *1826*, delighted our hearts *dearest* Ba.– May it shower on your own dear head every blessing! We rejoice in the reports of dearest Bro's mirth-stirring disguises, as sources of amusement to dear Granny & you all, & as proofs of his being *really* in health & spirits– hearing of all this revelry & happiness, reconciles me to the diminution in our sports, & Xmas joy, in missing three of the dear faces, which have ever been the leaders & promoters of it all: Arabel & Sam, have been your active substitutes, & I fancy her pen is now employed in reporting the excellence of the cake, which was most gratefully enjoyed, a subject likely to elicit so much eloquence, that I can only presume to make a slight allusion to the beauty of Septimus & Octavius³ dressed in the Grecian finery, which once shone upon you & Bro, with the rather *un*classical additions of wreaths of flowers, & seated upon the table in the drawing room, with the dazzling cake before them, Seppy brandishing the carving knife! Mʳ Moncrieff amuses us extremely, & I hope we shall hear more of him.[4] As to his dismal prognostics, I am as little inclined to pin my faith on them, as on the 500£ for two songs—he must be of a very romantic turn of mind!– it is forming too low an estimate of this "thinking people," to deny all prospect of success to a poem on such a subject & to make a silly song, a mine of wealth, tho' it cannot be denied, that but too large a portion of this wise nation *may* lean to the song– I long to see the lines which charmed the black-holed critic, into more gentle bearing.– A most kind letter from dear Mary last night, gave me infinite pain, by mentioning the necessity for her consulting Dr Babbington about her little ailments as she calls them.[5] I find from Sam, he does not wish much allusion to be made to them to *her*– God grant they may speedily be removed: as she assures me Dr B. promises they shall but that she must remain immediately under his inspection for some little time, & her kind proposal is, that yours & Hen^{tta's} return home, should not be thought of, till she can bring you— & hopes you may *first*, go to W——[6] this I think *will be* the plan, dearest Ba, for tho' no words can tell how much I long to see you both & beloved Bro, I really think it no way desirable that he should make this long journey so near the close of the holidays, as it would be at the risk of his catching cold, when he will, I fear want all his strength, to exchange his present kind care & comforts for the *roughnesses* of that seat of learning– You will too, I suspect, be better pleased to linger a little longer, near dearest Granny, & to warm yourself at Sam's *well heaped* hearth, ere you return to your snow clad hills, & elevated bed room[7]—& for my part, I comfort myself with the hope that sweet Marys better health & your return, will not be long delayed.— Even *I* must acknowledge it to be *bitter* cold.– We have had snow all this week, & it seems little likely to leave us– With such weather, holidays have been limited to three days, with rather shorter lessons on others– Do tell Hen^{tta} how well Mary Brimmel officiated in churning & cleaning the dairy, since poor Mary has been obliged to return home—she is a *handy* little thing– Rebecca is come to see us from Cheltenham, grown quite fat, & a blaze of fashion– she does not seem to rest in any place since she left us—C[heltenham]. she says, is not full[—]houses in the Crescent, let at 3 guineas & ½– We have invitations to Mr Foleys plays next week. ["]She stoops to Conquer", & ["]Roland for an Oliver," with "Charles 2" but vain his histrionic talents to *us*, this year! Miss Commeline comes for a few days on the 12.th— the fair Maria fears her sore throat must prevent her– it is Miss C.^s own proposal, & she *hopes* to find you! hopes in vain– James C.[8] hears much better– Bell seems unusually gay, & all quite well– I think I told you of Emma

H[eseltine]'s arrival– I am anxious to receive acc.^{ts} of Fanny– *Many* loves
& kisses– I will write Henrie^{tta} soon–

Ever my beloved Ba's
Most affec.^{te} Mother

How anxious we are to have your acc.^{t} of the blooming bride!

Address, on integral page: Ba.
Publication: None traced.
Manuscript: British Library.

1. Mary Moulton-Barrett's thanks for greetings "on the birth of *1826*," suggest that the
letter was written after 1 January 1826. She also mentions that Miss Commeline plans to
visit on the 12th. The only Sunday between 1 and 12 January in that year was the 8th.
2. Torquato Tasso (1544–95), *Gerusalemme Liberata* (1581):
"Sophronia she, Olindo hight the youth,
Both of one town, both in one faith were taught,
She fair, he full of bashfulness and truth,
Lov'd much, hop'd little, and desired nought;
He durst not speak, by suit to purchase ruth,
She saw not, mark'd not, wist not what he sought;
Thus lov'd, thus serv'd he long, but not regarded,
Unseen, unmark'd, unpitied, unrewarded."
(Edward Fairfax's 1817 translation)
The fourth line of the Italian text was used by EBB as the "motto" mentioned by her
mother. It appeared on the title page of *An Essay on Mind.*
3. Octavius Moulton-Barrett, born 11 April 1824.
4. Probably William Thomas Moncrieff (1794–1857). Although prominent primarily in
the theatre, he did write articles for various magazines. His "dismal prognostics" may refer
to *An Essay on Mind*, but we cannot clarify.
5. Probably William Babington (1756–1833), well-known London physician.
6. Walthamstow, home of Mary and Samuel Moulton-Barrett, 6 m. N.E. of London.
7. EBB's bedroom and sitting-room were in the highest part of the house.
8. In letter 222, Mary Moulton-Barrett had expressed doubts about James Commeline's
recovering his hearing.

---

227. EBB TO SAMUEL MOULTON-BARRETT (UNCLE)

[Hastings]
[ca. January 1826]^{1}

My dearest Sam,

I should certainly excommunicate you did not my conscience
reproach me as not quite deserving an apotheosis myself so I shall even
let this Epistle wash out my own offences before I say any thing more
of yours. To help this merciful disposition of mine out of the ruts,
Marys note last Night very much assisted, in which she mentioned your
intention of finally leaving Town next week. I am heartily glad of it as
your vanity may lead you to suppose and although you have remained
away a week longer than I intended you should yet your promised LONG

visit here must pay a hundred p!̠ cent on my angel-like patience; which payment (without a pun or with one, as you please) will be a FUND of joy to us all.

My "purpureus pannus"[2] by way of exordium may give you room to guess that the anxious fears I some time ago entertained about Bro's coming have to a considerable degree subsided. So far we know from James Trant, for Papas thoughts on the subject are to us as inscrutable as if we had all been truants and adhered to the fourth form. There is a great difference between yourself, & him, at least in *one* respect—for if *your* reveries are *upon* a rose *his* are *under* it. ⟨* * *⟩

Publication: None traced.
Manuscript: Armstrong Browning Library.

1. Dated by reference to "fears . . . about Bro's coming." Normally EBB would have welcomed a visit from Bro, but her fear was that he might come to take her away from Hastings too soon. However, the preceding letter indicates that he would not be making the journey.
2. "Purple patch"—a brilliant or ornate passage in a literary composition (Horace, *De Arte Poetica*, 15–16).

---

228. MARY MOULTON-BARRETT TO EBB

School Room: with a wretched pen &
no time to mend it:—Feby 28.th [1826][1]

My own dearest:

The news ran like lightning last night thro' the nursery to me, that a brown, paper parcel was come for Papa from Worc!̠ which "*felt* very much like books," but in all my anxiety, I was obliged to labor thro' the duties of the toilette for dinner, (not very mighty to be sure) & then while Lane, with his usual grace, stood at right angles with napkin in his hand, & the boiled leg of mutton & mince veal, nearly smoked their last, was I doomed to find patience as I could, till Papa entered, with the welcome words, "there is your poem"!̠[2] No joy could be greater, save from seeing the beloved Authoress herself, & vain the temptations of our "rich repast," till I had peeped into those pieces which had not yet delighted our eyes—nor did Papa, taste any thing, till he had found the paper cutter, so that between every two or three mouthfuls, we had "Riga's" dying strain, or a "dream," or something which made us feel too much to do the usual justice to M!̠̠ Treherns cookery,[3] & soon Seppy bounced in, to say he wanted "Ba's *pome*, for Arabel & *them* in the Drawing room": When I retired to the literary party, Arabel, who had read the fugitive pieces & some of the Essay to the listening circle, told me she thought the former beautiful, but that she did not understand a word of the former;[4] which is more honesty than all its readers will observe, & Henry who was indulging in turning "*clean*" over head & heels, after his intellectual treat, declared he thought "every word of it, was very nice indeed." After these learned critics had betaken themselves to bed, Papa & I, each with a precious little vol: in our hands, drew close to the fire, & conned over every word from the pretty neat title page, to that word of five letters, which none of its readers will reach without regret.[5] As I know how much, "More dear than all the world beside" is, *indeed* the approbation of

"The best Mæcenas of *your* strain".[6]

I wish my beloved Ba, that I *could* tell you all he said in commendation, of this wond'rous little book; The preface he says is equal to any thing he ever read, & would do honor to any man, whatever his pretensions– With the notes too he is particularly delighted & dwells much on f: Book 2^d h:d^o b:d^o e: Book 1, & f:d^o– e.b:1. he thinks preeminent in elegance, & in moral:[7] On a first reading, he selected "the prayer" as his favorite, but on becoming better aquainted with the mystery of Fame, & highly poetic beauty of "The Dream," he owns, that he cannot decide which to prefer amongst the novelties– There is a tone in "the prayer" which so instantly found its way to my heart, that none of the high claims of its competitors, can ever dislodge it– Next with me, comes "the Dream," ["]Fame" I certainly do not like so well, but I believe one does not become immediately acquainted with it; surely, of all mundane things, justly deserved literary fame, is the most lasting, as your own note e. book 1: declares, & tho' I much admire the *humility* of the last musical stanza, I think there is more of melancholy in it, than the subject justifies– & it must be acknowledged, that throughout the vol: you leave no corner, wherein poor Earthly Vanity can comfort herself, from the generally denounced close to her career: Nothing certainly can be more true, yet nothing less acceptable, to many of your readers– What is become of the line about *Judge* Jeffries,[8] & tell us the whole sense of "*Pan was not*"[.][9] The song, is a little gem, & some of the stanzas very striking in "The Past" but none of these can vie, both to my taste & feelings, with the beautiful lines to Bro, & to Papa, which I rejoiced to welcome, leading the fugitives– it is a powerful recommendation of the Author, to hearts of sensibility, & a just tribute to her beloved Father!—— Whether it be that the time elapsed since we saw the essay, gives it the additional charm of novelty, or that it comes in a more imposing form from the press, it is certainly true that it has gained amazingly upon us: There are some delightful passages in the 1st book, that beginning "Thou thing of light!["] for its severity, & for *effect*, Niagara & the Avon; & the sweet lines to

Campbell;[10] but from the 2ᵈ book, it seems *impossible* to make a selection: I had indeed, no just idea of its merits: its interesting variety, extensive allusions, & harmony of numbers– you have done well, to close with what cannot fail to charm all ears awake to poetry, or hearts alive to affecᵗᵉ & generous feeling in the passage beginning "I love my own dear land"–to the end– Papa is *enchanted* with it:–[11] Beloved Ba! ought I, to have assumed the critics frown, & told you of faults & failings? in truth if such there are, they are far beyond my *ken*, & did I look into this little vol: with any other, than a Mothers eyes, I should read it with delight; how then, with my heart filled as it is, with the dearest, tenderest, & most affecting associations, can I speak or think of it, but with the most unqualified praise! There never was any circumstance, in the existence of your dearest Father or my own, that could afford us the same gratified feelings, as this strong evidence that our beloved child, has so well applied, & cultivated the talents with which she is gifted: Oh! long may they be thus devoted to great & good purposes, that she may continue to bestow happiness & thankfulness on those who love her, & be enabled to give a good account of them at the last!– A word must be said for Mʳ Duncan, who has *got it up*, elegantly & neatly: it is singularly correct, as one seldom sees a book, without the necessity for an erata: we wish the paper had been thicker, & think you *very* humble & moderate in your charges;[12] but it is a comfort to think that all purchasers, have good reason to be contented with these bargains: it is impossible to be otherwise than sanguine as to its success, tho' time must be necessary to make it known, & it is thrown naturally, into many channels, North, South, & West– I hope Dʳ Batty, & Miss Clarke[13] cannot fail of seeing it—they will both appreciate it. What will be most exposed to censure, is the bold freedom of contempt, for those "brittle" things, monarchs: but you do not mind that, & on the Greek cause, you will gain many warm adherents– By the bye, I have never said a word of the spirited & pathetic stanzas of Demetrius:[14] & Rigas last song: Papa cannot get over, the *circumstance* of the latter, tho' he much likes the poetry: What papers is it advertized in? I hope the London booksellers have copies: would that we could get it reviewed, I shall try if James[15] has any means– Papa pleases himself with thinking how much dearest Granny must be gratified, as must all those, who love you in any proportion, as she does: dear kind T, is the most munificent patroness we have yet heard of–[16] We have only two copies as yet– Col: Money heard of the poem for the first time today, & with *clergy* Hill,[17] left Papa in haste to see if Mʳˢ Thackway[18] had any copies left– Dearest Henᵗᵗᵃ letter to Papa & dear Trepsacks to Arabel are just arrived, & have afforded infinite satisfaction to us *all*– Henᵗᵗᵃ's has been on its way since Thursday I think—& one of mine to you must have been longer, but it is no wonder in Sam's perplexity of business: he is *very* kind to be so plagued by our letters—[19] Mathews has been here today, looking perfectly recovered from his accident— They are all going on well— Hannah has left her excellent place, & taken one in Manchester to be near her parents, which is rather a pity— Emma has served her time at a Mantua Makers, & thinks of setting up for herself; The children are all at the national school: he says the distress at Manchester is not nearly so great as represented: The manufactories act more from caution than necessity—but that there are many robberies committed.[20] I was out till six o'clock this lovely (*first*) Spring Even͛! Arabel sends a thousand thanks to dear T. for her letter which delights her so much—tell her I will write to her soon which I am shocked not to have done, but—my two *encroaching* correspondents, leave me so little to say—— I am glad my sweet Addles had a quadrille— her *lawn* will soon be gay in lillies, & [her] cottage looks well— Seppy says he means to make her garden *"twite booful"*— May God bless, my loved children & Granny & Trippy—

Ever their most fondly attached

MB –

Papa sends Granny a kiss, & loads from the Jun[rs]— all well —
Give my love to the Blaydes:[21] & remember me to Miss Clarke—

Addressed and franked by EBB's uncle on integral page: London March three 1826 / Miss Barrett / M[rs] Moulton's / Paragon / Hastings. / S M Barrett.
Publication: None traced.
Manuscript: British Library.

1. Year provided by frank.
2. Advance copies of *An Essay on Mind*, published 25 March 1826.
3. "The Dream" and "Riga's Last Song" appeared on pp. 139–145. The cook was probably the wife of John Treherne.
4. Mary Moulton-Barrett apparently meant to use "former" and "latter" in this sentence, but instead used "former" twice. The first is the one probably intended as such, because at that spot she first wrote "latter," then crossed it out.
5. "Finis," p. 152.
6. The first of the miscellaneous poems is "To My Father on His Birth-day" (pp. 109–111), where she writes (lines 38–44):

Thought only how to win thy smile—
My proudest fame—my dearest pride—
More dear than all the world beside!
And now, perchance, I seek the tone
For magic that is more its own;
But still my Father's looks remain
The best Mæcenas of my strain;"

See letter 192 for the original version of the poem.
7. EBB wrote elaborate notes for *An Essay on Mind* (which is in two books), and gave alphabetical call-outs. Mary Moulton-Barrett indicates the father's preference for notes f, h and b from book 2; e and f from book 1. Note e appears on page 91, and refers to line 229: "That hail 'th' eternal city' in their pride." It reads as follows: "'Imperium sine fine

dedi,' says Virgil's Jupiter. How little did the writer of those four words dream of their surviving the Glory, whose eternity they were intended to predict! Horace too, in the most exulting of his odes, boldly proclaims that his fame will live as long as 'Capitolium Scandet cum tacitâ virgine Pontifex.' Yes! his fame *will live!*—but where now is the Pontifex, and the silent vestal? where now is the Capitol? Such passages are, to my mind, pre-eminently more affecting than all the ruins in the world!"

The first of the Latin passages quoted by EBB ("I gave them empire without end") is taken from the *Æneid* (I, 279). The second ("So long as the Pontiff climbs the Capitol with the silent Vestal") is from Horace's *Odes* (III, 30, 8–9).

8. Perhaps Mary Moulton-Barrett read hurriedly, and overlooked line 113: "Let Jeffrey's praise, our willing pen, engage." As a letter from John Ramsey makes clear (SD565), this reference was to Francis Jeffrey, Lord Jeffrey (1773–1850), critic and sometime editor of *The Edinburgh Review*.

9. The final three lines of "The Dream" (p. 145) are:
"For a God came to die, bringing down peace—
'Pan *was not;*' and the darkness that did wreathe
The earth, past from the soul—Life came by death!"

10. The passage beginning "Thou thing of light!" starts in Bk. I, line 19; that relating to Niagara and the Avon is Bk. I, 46–54, and the reference to Campbell appears in Bk. I, 78ff.

11. Bk. II, pp. 80–88.

12. The book was priced at five shillings.

13. Reference to "Dr. Batty's beautiful drawings" in a letter from Mary Moulton-Barrett to Henrietta (SD550) identifies Robert Batty (1763?–1849), a well-known amateur artist, who spent his last years in Hastings. Miss Clarke has not been identified.

14. The stanzas on pp. 126–128 are prefaced by the explanation "Occasioned by a passage in Mr. Emerson's Journal, which states, that on the mention of Lord Byron's name, Captain Demetrius, an old Roumeliot, burst into tears."

15. James Graham-Clarke.

16. This reference to Miss Trepsack as a "most munificent patroness" suggests that it was she, rather than EBB's father, who helped defray the costs of printing *An Essay on Mind*.

17. Probably the Rev. Charles Hill from Bromesberrow, a village about 5 miles S.S.E. of Hope End.

18. Mrs. Thackway was one of two booksellers on High Street in Ledbury.

19. i.e., for franking.

20. Cutbacks in the output of weaving mills, owing to increased competition from foreign mills, had resulted in extensive unemployment and unrest. *The Times* of 26 January 1826 reprinted an article from *The Manchester Mercury*, which spoke of a "deep and general feeling of depression amongst commercial men . . . In the woollen branches we hear the most appalling accounts of the dismissal of work-people . . . In the silk-trade there is a most serious degree of stagnation and distress . . . and in the cotton-trade the state of things is daily becoming more serious."

21. Hugh Blaydes (1777–1829) and family. They were from the North of England (seats in Yorkshire and Nottinghamshire), in Hastings for his health. Miss Trepsack wrote to Henrietta 25 December 1826: "The Blaydes enquire constantly after you all, they have been very attentive, coming frequently to see us" (SD572).

229. MARY MOULTON-BARRETT TO EBB

[Hope End]
Tuesday night April 3 ^d [*sic* for 4] [1826]¹

My beloved Elizth As I have but a poor opinion of words, when they are expected to set down very faithfully matters of the heart, I will not impose upon them, the whole burden of the pleasure & interest your letter afforded me: You Poets know enough of the eloquence of silence to make you most useful correspondents to dull writers like me, who perhaps can feel, better than they can speak. You need not check your imaginings on the topics of my gratification from the affec^{te} spirit of your letters. My admiration of the wise & moderate reception of L^y M's observations,² & above all, of my gratitude, & surprize at dearest M^{rs} M[oulton]'s affec^{te} generosity towards you: for tho' her acts of generous affection are indeed too many to admit of *ordinary* wonder at any of them, yet this is of so serious a magnitude, that it cannot but make us feel more strongly than ever, that there can scarcely be such another Grand Mother in the world—& we have the comfort of believing, that there cannot be a more grateful Grandchild, which is the only *just* recompense she *can* receive for all her disinterested love in this world!– What have I to tell you in return for this truly delightful letter, my darling Ba! only I believe the cheering tidings that we are at length *thawed* by this first delightful day of spring, as Arabel & I experienced as we toiled over Wellington Heath,³ she in her plaids, & me, in my pilgrims suit of grey, & lined gloves, all which, ungrateful as we are for the debts we owe them, we vowed to discard, in this first sunny hour of prosperity! Would it not be very possible for you & dearest Addles to enjoy the luxury of bathing now, for the probably short remainder of your happy visit! Indeed it seems an advantage that it would be a great pity to lose, & I believe it is a very desirable season to bathe, particularly on that warm shore, & when the weather is fine: if Granny & Treppy should not disapprove, pray try it—if only a *few dips*, they would be of use to you, if not to Hen^{tta} I must say that you acquit yourself most satisfactorily on the score of Lord Byron– & I wish your answer could be *put in*, in your own words, wherever the objection may be made which doubtless it will in many cases, tho' not with L^y M's sincerity⁴– *She* certainly should have seen it, only that they are gone to London– Papa met Mrs Drummond yesterday, who said she had only just been able to procure *her* poem, & that she was going to send out two copies immediately to Malta to Lord Hastings Sisters *or* Daughters, who are very literary⁵– Col: & Mrs Money called here the other day, & spoke of it in high eulogium; *something more*, I might have extracted from Col: M. who is not only capable of forming an opinion, of his

own, but has candor enough to avow it, only Mrs Watson was here at
the same time, & as she has a good deal to say, & sat next the Colonel, I
could not penetrate him further– Mrs W. spoke with great anxiety of
Mrs Simpson who is to be confined again in July, & the dangerous
symptoms of her former confinements, are so certain to occur again,
that every apprehension is entertained for her– she has two boys, & a
most kind Husband– (I am in hopes the poem will fall into |Millonans|
hands, thro Mr Boissier who is his Curate)^6^– that is par paranthese–
now to return to M^rs^ W: she told me that M^rs^ S— constantly sees poor
Mrs R. Scarlett– five weeks ago, no hope was entertained for Robert, &
his own spirits were dreadfully affected by the prospect– he is however
a little better again;^7^ The little Blissets & their Father^8^ are with M^rs^ S—
lovely children, tho' not like the Mother. This is a gala day—Mr Daly's
grand annual party—tea at four, & the milk in the Dairy, invited with
the company, to assist in the crumpets– Nothing can exceed Seppe's
important bustle of preparation, but Octavius lowers the dignity of the
assembly extremely by persisting in it that he is going to drink tea with
"pigs farm!"– Arabel bustled thro' her music lesson in all speed, that
she might adjourn to her toilette, but you will have sufficient
recollections of the enchanting fête– Mrs Trant & Henry are coming
today for a day or two, (*Lent being over*), so that there is altogether an
extraordinary sensation here– I rejoice to hear that Mrs T. has had a
letter from James, giving an excellent account of himself, of the crops,
& of his happiness in Mont Serrat,^9^ with which he is delighted–
Dominic is still in the Reading gay world—he seemed to think Malvern
deplorably dull—— Pray write to Sam more at length; he complains of
your letters being short, tho' you must not for the world, hint to him
that I told you so—— I do not hear any thing more of dearest Papa's
journey^10^—thank God he is well & cheerful—— I fear Mary is not
stronger: They are going directly to Tunbridge I fancy, I trust with
benefit to her– after that Sam seems uncertain where to go—but I trust
here: Hen^ttas^ dear Mrs Lennard, is going abroad, pour s'amuser:^11^ The
Ernle Moneys are in London, & come some day this week to Marcle–
Expectation is on tiptoe to see the girls, & divers are the conjectures
how far they may be reconciled to their quiet parsonage, after seeing
the world & collecting all its most attractive accomplishments— I must
manage to go to see them, & will give you all details– Poor Mrs Webb is
a little better—— Great is our surprize to hear that Mrs Wakeman^12^ has
let Malvern for a year to a Mr Burns a Catholic, because she is too *poor*
to keep up both houses: he comes in May, & she goes to Sarnsfield–
poor Miss Harper is to occupy a room at Mr Jenkin's *opposite*– she is
much the same, never likely to be well– it is sad to think that the good
old lady must be so imposed upon by her steward & people about her,

as to be so straigthened [*sic*]– I send you poor Miss Price's kind note, which is *we* think very gratifying with regard to the poem, tho' most painfully descriptive of her own heart rending anxieties!– Dominic has presented his Mother with his Grand Mothers little poney carriage & poney, in which we are to take a drive tomorrow– M^{rs} T– has taken her house at M[alvern]— for another year, & says she would not live in London for the world! She is looking very well & happy—& Henry quite agreeable– James says he found Trants like a cullender, but he has made it as *tight as a bottle*, & has established himself comfortably for two years– I finish while Jane curls & brushes my hair, so do not wonder at the strange variety in my letters– The united loves from all here, to all your loved circle–

My own dear Ba's & Hen^{tta's} fondly affec^{te}
Mother

Take care of Miss P's note because I want to preserve *all* opinions I can collect of THE[13] poem.

Addressed and franked by EBB's uncle on integral page: Tunbridge Wells. April nine / 1826. / Miss Barrett / Mrs Moulton's / Paragon / Hastings / S M Barrett / [and in Mary Moulton-Barrett's hand, on reverse when folded] Ba–
Publication: None traced.
Manuscript: British Library.

1. Year determined from frank. If Mary Moulton-Barrett correctly named the day as Tuesday, it was 4 April.
2. Lady Margaret Maria Cocks (1792–1849), daughter of the 1st Earl Somers of Eastnor Castle, and herself a poetess.
3. Two miles N. of Ledbury, bordering the Hope End estate and within walking distance of the main house.
4. Apparently a response to Lady Margaret's criticism of EBB's "Stanzas on the Death of Lord Byron," recently republished in *An Essay on Mind* (pp. 117–119).
5. Francis, 1st Marquis of Hastings (1754–1826), was at this time Governor and Commander-in-Chief of Malta. Although he had two sisters still living, both were married and unlikely to be in Malta; it was probably his four unmarried daughters who were "very literary."
6. Probably the Rev. Peter Edward Boissier of Malvern Wells. The other clergyman mentioned (Millonan?) has not been identified.
7. Robert Scarlett (1794–1861) was the eldest son of James Scarlett (later Lord Abinger) and his wife Louise. Mary Moulton-Barrett wrote to Henrietta on 11 April 1826 (SD550) that she had had "a most distressing account of poor Robert Scarlett who is in a state of hopeless decline & general decay ... His doating Parent is distracted with her grief."
8. Joseph Blisset lived with his family at Letton Court, Hanmer's Cross, between Hereford and Hay-on-Wye.
9. The Trants had an estate in Montserrat, in the West Indies.
10. According to family letters, he was in London.
11. "To enjoy herself." Mrs. Lennard has not been identified.
12. James Best, in *A Description of Malvern* . . . (1825), identified Mrs. Wakeman as a Roman Catholic who had the gift of one of the local ecclesiastical livings (Little Malvern). Because of her faith, she was able to make a nomination, but the formal presentation of the living had to be made for her by Earl Somers (p. 175).
13. Underscored five times.

230. EBB TO EDWARD MOULTON-BARRETT (FATHER)

[Hastings]

My beloved Papa's birthday.
May 28th 1826.[1] Hope End

A Joy was pulsing at my heart,
As I looked o'er the sea,—
For dearest eyes were gazing there,
And *they* were close to *me!*

Nathlesse gone Time did visit me,
And Memory bared his face—
To tell me of the absent love,
And of the absent place!

So thought I, in my secret thought,
Of those I see today—
Of those who, at the fair hill's side,
Were dearest . . . & *away!!*

So thought I of familiar brows,
Which smiles so often find!
Yea! of the voices which breathe out
The tender words & kind!

And thus, while Joy pulsed at my heart,
Sorrow that Joy did woo!
Belovëd ones were near to *me*—
But *I*[2] not near to *you!*

Lo! now, the voices, that I wished,
Give me their gentle sound–
The dear home faces turn on mine,
And *mine* looks fondly round—!

This say I, while beside me clings
Full many, a bright-haired boy—
—Love, when we *part*, is only LOVE—
But, when we *meet*, tis JOY!!–

Then let no thought come ⟨to⟩ me
Unfitted ⟨to⟩ beguile
And let no word rise to the lips,
Unspoken with a smile.

We meet to bless this blessing day,
Whereon such mirth must be;

We meet in Joy where Erst we met;
We meet in love to THEE!
    Dearest Papa's attached child
    Ba–

Publication: Marks, p. 349 (in part).
Manuscript: Wellesley College.

1. His 41st.
2. Underscored twice.

---

231. EBB TO MARY MOULTON-BARRETT

[Hastings]
[ca. June 1826][1]

I cant afford you many lines beloved Mama for Trippy Henrietta Bro Sam & myself are on the wing for the races. And yet as I have not written three or four days to you I wont let it occasion any omission to make you dream of neglect in one who loves you dearly and constantly. We did not think the Boys looking well in town, and when desperately wet and blue they made their appearance here from the London stage we certainly did not think them looking better. They now nevertheless begin to "repair", beneath the influence of these mild refreshing gales—and Sam is enchanting with his gadding tongue, black silk stock, & couleur de rose garters.

Sam and Mary cannot come down here, from pressure of business so I think it unlikely that my Boulogne reverie should be realized. There is a rumour afloat of going for a few days to Brighton which seems more *palpable*, but you must not mention it either in your letters here or to Hope-End. We are all most happy and have indeed reason to be so!

Docket, on page 4, in EBB's hand: Not finished or sent, I cannot burn it now.
Publication: None traced.
Manuscript: British Library.

1. Probably written shortly before EBB left Hastings, ca. June 1826.

---

232. ELIZABETH MOULTON TO EBB

[?Hastings]
[ca. June 1826][1]

Papa when on board the ship Elizabeth sailing for England, in the year 1892[2]—gave this glove, wet with his tears, to Doctor Archer,[3] with strict charge to deliver it into Bessey's own hands– This same *Bessey* was Granny—who has hitherto preservd it as a mark of affection—but now, as the child of this same papa, not long since, expressd a wish to possess this glove, it is here given up to her– may every trifle & all that concerns so good a parent, be ever dear to the hearts of his children——

EM——

Publication: None traced.
Manuscript and enclosure: Berg Collection.

1. EBB was with her grandmother for eleven months in 1825–1826. It is possible that this letter and its enclosure were handed over to her at the conclusion of that visit.
2. 1892 (for 1792) underscored twice. *Felix Farley's Bristol Journal*, dated 29 September 1792, reported the recent arrival of the ship *Elizabeth* in Bristol from Jamaica. Evidence shows that EBB's father Edward and his brother Samuel were on board, and probably also their sister Sarah. Since an "S" is embroidered on the glove, it must actually have belonged to Samuel or Sarah. Nevertheless it is wrapped, with the letter, in a plain sheet of paper on which EBB has written: "My beloved Papa's glove."
3. Possibly James Archer, D.D., who was a chaplain in London in 1791 and the author of several volumes of sermons.

---

233. EBB TO UVEDALE PRICE

Hope End
June 1826.

My dear Sir,
    Tho' I recieved your sheet of observations[1] at Hastings more than a fortnight ago, travelling from thence & settling here after an eleven months absence have induced me to delay writing until this morn͇ Giving your observations their due consideration occupies more time than feeling their kindness; and I was anxious to speak to you of my convictions as well as of my obligation. It hardly seems *real* to me that my unworthy little book should recieve M͇ Price's toleration much less his approval, and thus human frailty secures my exercise of a virtue—I am too *proud* not to be *grateful.*
    Dare I rely on your indulgence, or will you think me very presumptuous if I intrude on you the few remarks which occured to me

while reading your criticism?– You object to my Expression 'Aonian rhyme' (used in reference to Cowleys Pyramus & Thisbe)[2] on the ground of "*Aonian* leading one to suppose that in our native clime he first wrote in Greek or latin." Why in *latin*? & *if* in latin, why not in *English*; since we apparently have as much right to call our verse *Aonian* as the Romans had? The inspirers of our national poetry are the Muses—the sacred Nine,—the veritable AONIDES. Gray who seems positive as to their identity, says that they

> "in Greece's evil hour
> Left their Parnassus for the Latian plains."

&

> ["]When Latium had the lofty Spirit lost,
> They sought oh Albion! next, thy sea encircled coast."[3]

Surely if the *Aonides* be the inspirers, Aonian is the inspiration— besides, as old Sir John Denham says

> "as Courts make not kings but kings the court,
> So where the Muses & their train resort–
> Parnassus stands."   COOPER'S HILL[4]

With respect to the word "*illustrate*" which I have made a dactyl "contrary to usage"[5] I must build my defence rather on analogy than on any precedent immediately in point. I think it may be observed that among our old Poets—Spenser especially—the established accent of a word is often changed with its position in a line. In the following line from the Faerie Queen "Envy" has its present trochaic accentuation—

> "Ne wicked ēnvy̆, ne vile gealosy"—

directly afterwards it is a spondee—

> "Each other does ēnvȳ with deadly hate"—

Here 'courage' is a trochee—

> "One day when him high cōurăge did emmove"

afterwards a spondee—

> "His stout cōurāge to stoupe & shew his inward paine."[6]

Instances of this license are to be found in Milton, tho' more rarely, as in "*aspèct*" &.c You object to my conversion of *illustrate* also because "to make a vowel short before three consonants as *str* must be injurious to euphony & articulation." We have however an instance of this in the recieved accentuation of the word *circumspect* among others.

To my expression "Science' soaring sons"[7] you say in objection– "such an elision as this . . & afterwards '*prejudice*'[8] . . I do not remember to have seen made use of, except in proper names, as *the wrath of Peleus' son.''* I believe a similar elision may be found in the Dunciad—

"On Dulness' lap the sacred head reposed"[9]

To your other instructive criticisms I thankfully accede; & if the remarks I have ventured to make in these instances, be thought by you presumptuous (& they almost seem so to myself) let me beseech you to forget them,—only remembering what I^{10} must always remember with pleasure,—that I am,

dear Sir,
Most gratefully yours
EBB –

Address, on integral page: Uvedale Price Esq[re]
Publication: None traced.
Manuscript: British Library.

1. On EBB's *An Essay on Mind.*
2. Line 137.
3. *The Progress of Poesy* (1757), lines 77–82.
4. Lines 5–7 of Sir John Denham's *Cooper's Hill*, in the revised text of 1655.
5. Line 267: "And use the truth to illustrate a lie!"
6. These four lines from *The Faerie Queene* are, respectively, bk. I, canto 12, v. 41; bk. II, canto 2, v. 19; bk. II, canto 1, v. 50 and bk. II, canto 1, v. 42.
7. Line 510.
8. Line 571: "But, lest contracting prejudice mislead."
9. Bk. III, line 2, slightly misquoted.
10. Underscored twice.

---

234. UVEDALE PRICE TO EBB

Foxley
June 12.th 1826

Dear Miss Barrett

I had heard with much satisfaction, from M[rs] Barrett's letter to my daughter, how favourably you had received my remarks & criticisms; but have great pleasure in receiving the same intelligence under your own hand, & in your own words. I am in general very apt to put down what remarks occur to me, whenever I am much pleased with any work: & in the present case I was interested in the work, in the writer, & in all that belongs to her.

You have very candidly acquiesced in the greater part of my criticisms; & have done right in defending yourself against those that did not carry conviction: *I,* again shall do right in defending my criticisms where I still think them well founded; & the discussion may not be useless, tho' it should fail to alter your opinion. With regard to *aonian*, I agree with you in all you say of it; & am much pleased with your illustrations & quotations, particularly that from Gray: I agree with you that we have as good a right to the inspiration of the Aonides, Pierides or whatever name they may be called by, as the Romans had; & certainly full as good a one as the French have to Boileau's "Chastes Nymphes de Permesse,"[1] but all this does not meet my objection, or, at least what I meant to object; which is to *any* Epithet as superfluous, & to such as one as *Aonian* as tending to mislead. If I mistake not, you could only intend to say that Cowley's first productions were in rhyme or verse, simply as distinguished from prose: yet when I first read the passage I thought you intended some discrimination by the epithet: *Aonian* fills up the verse & the rhythm very harmoniously; but your verses are remarkably free from any thing like *remplissage*,[2] & that is one of their many excellencies: I think you will see, on looking at the passage, that, leaving out the epithet,—"made his first essay in rhyme," is all that is wanting for the *sense.* When Milton says that his "adventurous song"

intends to soar
Above th' Aonian Mount, while it pursues
Things unattempted yet in prose or rhyme.[3]

He simply distinguishes the two modes of writing; & had he transferred the epithet from the mount, & said "in prose or in Aonian rhyme," would you not have thought the epithet superfluous, or meant to convey some sort of discrimination? I may be mistaken, but the two cases seem to me much alike.

No defence of īllŭstrăte, in respect to usage, could at all satisfy me short of the word itself having been employed as a dactyl by some poet of reputation: & I should then say that it never ought to be so employed again. The instances you have given from Spencer [sic] & Milton, of the established accent having been changed by them, do not appear to me exactly in point. In the first place, there is no objection to *ēnvý couráge* or *aspéct*, on the score of cadence & articulation, especially when compared with īllŭstrăte: & secondly, the accent on the last syllable of those words, & the consequent change or their cadence was not a new creation, but a restoration: a restoration of what had been the established mode from the time of the Conquest, to Chaucer's time, & thence to that of Henry 8th Almost all the words that we now accent on the first, as *honoúr* [sic for hónour] vírtue were then accented on the last as

Saw I Conquést sitting in great honoúr.[4]

If you accent this, & Chaucer's verses in general, as we accent Dryden's & Pope's they have neither metre, nor rhythm. The same accent prevails in ancient proper names as

Fairest of fair O Lady mine Venús[5]

- - - - - - - - -

Thy Æneás is come to paradise.[6]

on this point, & on the pronunciation of Latin in those early days, I shall have a great deal to say in a work upon which I am now employed. The old accent I believe, lasted till about the middle of Henry 8[ths] reign, & then only *began* to give way to the new; which was but just established, & perhaps not completely, in his daughter Elizabeth's time, when Spencer flourished: he was extremely fond of Chaucer, & used many of his antiquated words, & often his mode of accenting; Milton more sparingly.— I am still inclined to think that such elisions as *Science', prejudice',* tho' they would be very convenient, are seldom, if ever, used, except in proper names: & your quotation from Pope tends to confirm me in my opinion. If *dulness* had been, as it usually is, the name of a quality, & spelt accordingly with a small *d*, the elision would have been decidedly in your favour; but the quality is personified, having a lap, on which a head reposes: it is written, as you have written it with a large *D*, which bespeaks rank, &, in the present case the highest of all—that of a Goddess; which she bears throughout the Dunciad. She therefore has the same right to an elision as Venus or Thetis.— I hope you are going on with some new work, & that you will soon give me an opportunity, as you liked the sheet I took the liberty of sending you, of sending you another of the same kind: remember however, that I am in my 80th year, & that by any long delay you may lose an admirer & critic.

With all our best regards to M[r] & Mrs Barrett, believe me

Most sincerely & faithfully yours

U Price

Address, on integral page: Miss Barrett / Hope End / Ledbury.
Publication: None traced.
Manuscript: Armstrong Browning Library.

1. Line 3 of "Ode sur la prise de Namur" (*Œuvres de Boileau Despréaux*, 1821, II, 468).
2. "Padding."
3. *Paradise Lost*, I, 14–16.
4. "The Knight's Tale," line 2028.
5. *Ibid.*, line 2221.
6. Chaucer's *The Legend of Good Women* (III, "The Legend of Dido," line 1103).

235. EBB TO EDWARD MOULTON-BARRETT (BROTHER)

[?Hope End]

[26 June ca. 1826][1]

alphabetic address.

Admit an alphabetic address, actively abetting affection, and advancing admiringly as an agrestic agent. Because beloved Brother, Ba being Behemoth-like,[2] "biggest born," bearing brains bastinadoed by birthday befoolings, blesseth brachygraphically: besides—could commonplace complimentary courtesy compass complicated considerations, content crabbed critics? Doubtlessly, delightfully dedicated days ⟨d⟩emand debonair devices: every eccentric ⟨en⟩deavour excites entertainment: fantastic ⟨ful⟩ly forgeth festive fetters for free feet, glibly ⟨gil⟩d! *Hot*herwise how Hindrances have ⟨ho⟩nour's heritage—*h*and *h*all's h.up!!!!! ⟨in⟩consequence I, if indeed it is incumbent, ⟨jus⟩tify jovial jestings! Judge, kind kindred! ⟨Le⟩t "lacklustre" Love labor laughing; lugging ⟨le⟩tters leisurely! May many manly marks make ⟨m⟩y minor marvellous! May no nonsenses nor naughtiness narrow nature! Owning openess, overreach odiousness! Practising patience, perpetuate peace—quoting quiddities, quiet quarrellings—regarding religion, regulate reason—saying sagely, sit safely—take things temperately—venture valiantly—undecieved, understand —*und*— weighing warning, wax wise!

With wonted wishes,—you yawning youth,

Yours Zealously——

Publication: None traced.
Manuscript: Berg Collection.

1. Probably in lieu of a birthday ode to Bro; the year conjectured by the handwriting. This was his 19th birthday.
2. Cf. Job, 40:15–24; probably a hippopotamus.

---

236. UVEDALE PRICE TO EBB

Foxley

July 1st 1826

Dear Miss Barrett

This very amicable controversy, may, I think, be of use to us both; for you are well furnished with arms, & dextrous in the use of them. The line from Lucretius is aptly quoted in favour of your repeatedly attacked & defended *Aonian*; I think, however, there is a clear distinction between the two cases; you will form your judgment when I have given my reasons. You ask me very pertinently, whether I think the epithet—*pierio*[1]—superfluous? I do not; tho' it might be called without any disparagement super-abundant. It seems to have been the poet's intention in this & other places, strongly to impress on Memmius,[2] the dryness, obscurity, & novelty of the subject & the difficulty of treating it in Latin

Propter egestatem linguæ et rerum novitatem.[3]

& his earnest wish & endeavour to allure his patron's attention by all the charms of poetry; he therefore adds *pierio* to *suaveloquenti*[4] & immediately afterwards *dulci* to *Musæo*

Et quasi Musæo dulci contingere melle.[5]

That he was well satisfied with what he had done we learn from what he had just said

Primum, quod magnis doceo de rebus & arctis [*sic*, for artis].[6]

- - - - - - - - - -

Deinde quod obscura de re tam lucida pango
Carmina, Musæo contingens cuncta lepore.[7]

He therefore in the pride & fulness of his heart abounds in epithets, & the whole of the context plainly shews the meaning & force of *pierio*. Now I must own, & I believe have already confessed, that when I read

Lisp'd his first accents in Aonian rhyme[8]

I said to myself (knowing nothing of Cowley's early productions, or in what metre, or language they were written) in *what* rhyme? The reason of my asking such a question,—for I should be sorry to think it sheer dulness of apprehension—I take to be this, that *Aonian pierian, heliconian,* & such epithets, if used singly & simply, do not, in my judgment suggest the idea of *excellent,* or *inspired by the Muses,* but require—at least in English—something with them to guide us to such a signification: on that ground therefore, I should object to *Aonian,* even supposing the early verses of Cowley to be equal to the finest of Lucretius; that is, to some of the finest in all poetry. With regard to the epithets themselves *pierian* does not occur in Milton, *aonian* but once, & applied to a sensible object, to the Mount itself: neither of the words occur in Shakespear; Pope in his well known line

Drink deep, or taste not the Pierian spring.[9]

also applies it to a sensible object. As there is unluckily no index to his or Dryden's works, I have no means of knowing how often, or in what manner such epithets may have been used by them; you are very likely to ferret them out: till you do, & can shew me some instances in your favour, I may be allowed to keep my opinion. The next question regards the verses themselves: I have never seen them; for they are not in the only edition I have of Cowley published by Spratt in 1680;[10] but he says,—speaking with praise of it's contents,—"in the 13th year of his age a little book came out under his name" these last words seem to imply a sort of doubt whether the contents were really his; however that may be, the fact is, that although by his own account the editor was publishing "what was extant," & collecting whatever more he could find, he has not thought fit to insert them: it may therefore naturally be suspected, either that he had some doubts of their authenticity, or, notwithstanding his praise, that he did not think them aonian enough to be inserted among his later productions. You at once allow that the epithet would be superfluous & ill-placed in Milton, because he simply distinguish'd the two modes of writing; "Now" you add "the passage in question in my book does not mean to draw any discrimination between the departments of prose & poetry, *but* to shew at what various times, & by what various causes Genius asserts his being in the soul: Cowley's aonian inspiration is given as an instance of it." No doubt it is: but what if the little book had contained nothing but prose? would you have noticed it at all? probably not; for it was only curious as shewing that Cowley's genius for poetry, as distinguished from prose, was in his soul at an early age: & if the book had been in prose, & you had thought fit to notice it, you still must have made the distinction, & have shewn that Cowley did *not*, like Pope & others "lisp in numbers,"[11] as his first productions were in prose.— You have very candidly confessed that *illūstrăte* is very untuneable; & therefore, I will add, very unworthy of your poetry: on the other hand there are many words that you would have improved by changing the accent; & tho' I should have thought it my duty to remonstrate, I should have done so, gently & unwillingly; if, for instance, you had laid the accent on the 2d syllable instead of the 1st of *chăracter*, & have used it as *charácter* throughout your poem, you would then have changed a bad dactyl into a good amphibrach; have given it an easier articulation, & a better cadence, & in both respects much nearer to the ancient pronunciation: still you would not have been justified in making the alteration, tho' for the better: because it not only is contrary to present usage, but to that of former poets, whose verses would be spoilt in recitation were the new mode to be generally adopted: how much stronger the case when a good amphibrach in constant use, is changed to a bad dactyl! But although you give up this particular word, you are unwilling to give up your belief in the licence of changing the accentuation of words according to their position, & you refer to your quotations from Spencer [*sic*], & to my remarks on them: & then say "Now I find in Chaucer the same variety of accent tho' in a less degree than in Spencer: we have *pérfect* accented as a trochee & as a spondee with only a few intermediate lines; thus

> Living in peace & pārfĭte charitee.[12]
> - - - - - - - - - - -
> For he was Epicurus' owen son
> That held opinion that plein delit
> Was ver* aily felicité pārfīte[13]

From all I have observed in respect to the pronunciation in Chaucer's time, & I have paid no slight attention to it, *parfite* was a spondee in both places; as true a one in the first quoted line, as the following spondees are in two lines with which you are well acquainted,

> Thinkst thou in vain while pāle Tīme glides away
> She rakes cōld grāves, & chronicles their clay.[14]

These monosyllabic spondees (we have scarcely any others) give so much variety & expression to the rhythm, such a relief from the perpetual recurrence of trochees & iambi, that we may well regret our having none, or next to none, of the dissyllabic kind. Pope would have been very glad of them when he was painting slowness of motion; but when he wished to give something of a spondaic cast to the well known line

> When Ajax strives some rock's vast weight to throw[15]

he could only do it by two such monosyllables as *vāst weīght*, for we make *sŏme rōck's* an iambus; &, in defiance of position, & ancient prosody, *Ājăx* a trochee! Our habits of pronouncing are so trochaic, & so anti-spondaic, that you very naturally pronounced & considered *parfyte* in the first quoted line as a trochee, though in the last as a spondee: the difference is, that in the last it *must* be a spondee (for such an iambus as *părfīte* is out of the question) in the first it *may* be either a trochee or a spondee: but Chaucer, & the poets of those ages were as little inclined to trochees as we are to spondees. The fact is, that the accentuation from the Conquest to Henry 8th was purely Norman, & nearly what the french is at present; & a Frenchman (as far as metre & rhythm are concerned) would recite Chaucer with great propriety; while an Englishman, who followed our usual accentuation, would per-petually disfigure the metre & the rhythm. Chaucer, I have no doubt, in all places (with regard to quantity) pronounced *parfite*, as the French now pronounce *parfaite*, & my belief is that he made *living* nearly, if not quite a spondee, & pronounced the verse also very much as a Frenchman would

Vivant en paix, & parfaïte unité!

The last word I was obliged to change, as in french verse the *e muet* must *always* be. a syllable before a consonant, as it *frequently* is in Chaucer's. My belief is (tho' I speak with diffidence on on [*sic*, for a] subject to which I have not paid particular attention) that the licence you contend for, tho' a very convenient one was seldom made use of; & I am now inclined to think, what I was not when I wrote to you, that Spencer in both the places meant *envý* & *couráge* to be accented on the last, for a spondee will agree with the metre in both places: Chaucer, I will venture to say, in point of quantity, *certainly* pronounced them both as the French do *envie* & *courage*; & Spencer *probably* did. Milton, as you observe, laid the accent on the last of *aspéct*, contrary to our present usage; whether to that of his own time I know not, as I do not recollect seeing the word in Dryden or any contemporary poet: Milton, however, religiously keeps to the same accent, having used the word no less than ten times in the Paradise lost: Shakespear, I believe always accented it on the last, & has used the word very often. As a further proof how truly french the accentuation was in Chaucer's time, you may observe that *opinión*, instead of having only three syllables, must like the french word have four, opinion. I will add two lines of Chaucers so thoroughly french as to be quite burlesque with our present accents

To make it somewhat agreáble
Tho' some words fail in a sylláble.[16]

A few last words on Elisions: If my notion—for it is little more—be just; i.e. that proper names only have a good right to those in question, *prejudice* can hardly have a claim on that score: *Science* has preferred what sounds a very odd one: that of being placed on the same footing with Dulness & admitted *ad eundem.*[17] Were I to make a distinction—& no one can be more *en train*, I should say the Dulness in the Dunciad is a person; Science, in Mind, little more than a personification: the Goddess Dulness acts & speaks, as it is right & proper she should, a[s] much as any Goddess in the Iliad: Science—also very properly—acts & speaks very little: she does however, make one very short speech, & as you so humbly recommend her to my mercy I will answer like ancient Pistol

As I suck blood I will some mercy shew.[18]

I must indeed be a most sanguinary & pitiless critic if I did not: especially as she is so often in the elided genitive, that it would be very troublesome to get her out of it.— I shall now quit my office of Aristarchus[19] till you call me to it again by a new work: & then, should it be your wish, shall willingly resume it. The subject you have thought of I approve highly & am confident it will *devellop genius*.[20] With all our best regards to M[r] & M[rs] Barrett, believe me

Most sincerely & faithfully yours
U Price

Addressed and franked by Robert Price on integral page: Hereford July one 1826 / put in the office on the second / Miss Barrett / Hope End / Ledbury / Robert Price.
Publication: None traced.
Manuscript: Armstrong Browning Library.

1. "Pierian," pertaining to the Muses.
2. Gaius Memmius, Roman orator and poet, tribune (66 B.C.), friend of Lucretius and Catullus. Lucretius addressed *De Rerum Natura* to him.
3. "Because of the poverty of language and the novelty of my subject" (*De Rerum Natura*, I, 139).
4. "Sweetly speaking" (*op. cit.*, I, 945).
5. "And as it were to touch it with the Muses' delicious honey" (*op. cit.*, I, 947).
6. "First, because my teaching is of high matters and difficult" (*op. cit.*, I, 931).
7. "Next, because the subject is so obscure and the songs I write so clear, as I touch all with the Muses' grace" (*op. cit.*, I, 933–934).
8. *An Essay on Mind*, line 137.
9. Pope's "Essay on Criticism" (1711), line 216.
10. Thomas Sprat (1635–1713), Bishop of Rochester, friend and biographer of Cowley.
11. "I lisp'd in Numbers, for the Numbers came" ("Epistle to Dr. Arbuthnot," 128).
12. Line 532 of the Prologue to *The Canterbury Tales*.
13. *Ibid.*, lines 336–338.
14. *An Essay on Mind*, 216–217.
15. Line 370 of "An Essay on Criticism."
16. "The House of Fame," III, 7–8, slightly misquoted.
17. "Similar to it."
18. *Henry V*, IV, 4, 64.
19. Aristarchus of Samothrace (*fl.* 156 B.C.), curator of the library of Alexandria, was held to be the greatest critic of antiquity.
20. See letter 242, note 17.

---

237. JOHN KENYON[1] TO EBB

Malvern Wells.
July 12 [1826][2]

My dear Miss Barrett.

I had scarcely quitted you, when I thought that I had been very injudicious, to say the least, to beg your book– Probably enough, you may not have another in the house.

I am going to London too where I shall have an immediate opportunity of furnishing myself at Duncan's– I shall therefore redress as much as may be my faux pas by leaving the book for you at Mrs Trants, ere we go on Saturday.

Your work has not afforded solitary pleasure—Mrs Kenyon has shared it with me, and Mr Philipps[3] is making himself acquainted with it.

For myself, claiming a cousin-ship in some degree or other, I have read it with pride as well as pleasure——

Your Essay on Mind is a bold attempt– It is always hard to reconcile didactic with poetic excellence– I say Excellence– The levels are more easily combined—but the lofty points—the real summits always appear to me to spear up in opposite directions.

If this is true even in Ethical didactics, as I think even Pope has proved—it is yet more so I think in Metaphysical– It would be easier to poetize Paley[4] than Condillac[5]–

What however you have boldly attempted, you seem to my judgment to have considerably succeeeded in– I cannot but admire the thought and reading and power you have brought to your task—as well as the clearness & force & fancy with which you have often explained & compressed and illustrated your sometimes reluctant materials.

I could point out many passages that have much pleased me—a great deal in the second book, for instance that treats of the poetical faculty—perhaps more particularly that passage, which may have given you very little trouble, in Page 61 beginning—"Oh breathes there" and ending "and Prostrate Israel[''][6] &c.– But the smaller pieces, I must confess are my more particular delight.– More or less, all of them– The verses to your Father—the sweet ones to your Brother—those page 123—To Somebody—all these please one both for moral and poetical merit—but I hardly know how to praise sufficiently the "Past", which combines pensive feeling with originality—the Dream—Every Stanza of it—the ancient Lands—Paradise—the Deluge—all is excellent—and most of all—to my taste I mean—the three Stanzas called "the prayer[']—which in tenderness of thought—and in expression harmonizing with the thought throughout, seems to me all that one could desire.

I wish you to consider this as the sincere expression of my opinion—as far as it may have any value & not as the mere compliments one makes in return for a book.

Fame, I hope if you should persevere seeking her, will not turn out to you what you have so poetically described her, and what in truth she has turned out to so many–

—But you have plenty of time before you– You have not been long choosing and beginning late– Those who are interested for you have told me that you do not at all times spare yourself enough– Consider that at your time of life, all need not be done in a day– I think myself bound to say this to you, because I am aware that the very thanks I have been giving you for what you have been doing are likely enough to stimulate you to be doing still more—and more than is good for you–

You see I am taking more than a cousin's liberty—but you are docile—and I knew your Father before he was as old as you now are– Without fixing the degree of relationship I beg leave to subscribe myself–

Your affect^{ate} Cousin
John Kenyon.

Mrs Kenyon turns from your book to add her acknowledgment to mine.

Address, on cover sheet: Miss Barrett, / Hope End, / near Ledbury.
Publication: None traced.
Manuscript: Wellesley College.

1. John Kenyon was born in Jamaica, distantly related to the Moulton-Barretts (his great-grandmother was the sister of EBB's great-grandfather). Although he was an old friend of EBB's father, he is, strangely, not mentioned in any of EBB's or other extant family letters prior to this time. Doubtless he sought EBB out after the publication of *An Essay on Mind*.
2. Year provided by the publication of *An Essay on Mind*.
3. Caroline Curteis (d. 1835), who married Kenyon in 1823, was his second wife. Mr. Philipps has not been identified.
4. William Paley (1743–1805), English theologian and philosopher. His best-known work is probably *A View of the Evidences of Christianity* (1794).
5. Étienne Bonnot de Condillac (1715–80), French philosopher. He held that it was possible to apply logical reasoning in metaphysics and morals with the same precision as in geometry.
6. Pages 61–63; the beginning phrase is actually "Oh! beats there . . ."

---

238. EBB TO UVEDALE PRICE

Foxley.
October—1826.

Mr Price's desire that I should read these sheets[1] with the design of remarking on them I have obeyed with much deference to him, & distrust of myself. I have read them with deep interest & attention—& have been greatly struck by the original chain of argument, consolidating a powerful body of facts—by the vanquishing of possible objections—the *meta fervidis evitata rotis.*[2] It would lie rather hard on my veracity to be obliged to cavil for the mere sake of cavilling; & M^r

Price's system as explained in the Ictus metricus[3] & very original chapter on Elisions has left a strong impression on my mind. I have been made satisfied that if, as scriptural commentators concieve, *light* represent order or consistency, the present established system of accentuation is one *"cui lumen ademptum"*.[4] And I am convinced that, of the two systems, Solomon's judgement would not acknowledge a relationship to poetry in that system, whose object it is to destroy the *animal life* of poetry . . the harmony. Having this conviction it is extremely pleasing to me to own it. I have so much satisfaction in thinking that Horace's hexameters may be read with *an ear* & yet with luxury. And I have so much more than *satisfaction* in thinking that we may grasp at the celebrated harmony of Homer, & find no longer a mere κεινη τρυφαλεια[5]—the pleasant sound of Greek words without the music of their disposition. This satisfaction I am indebted for to M.[r] Price. The doubts which offered themselves to my mind in the course of reading what I have read of his, I either found dispelled as I went on, or a little consideration on my part dispelled them. To speak in Homers own style, which may be applied to many objections (& objectors) to this system, the *Cranes* are only formidable to the *Pygmies.*

With regard however to the chapter on hexameters as compared to modern heroic metres, MY *cranes*, as they have been flatteringly asked to do so, will have the boldness to say something. They are inclined to think that maugre the decided truth as well as wit of M.[r] Price's Greek pun, a degree more variety than he has allowed to our heroics is due to their structure. I will write down, under correction, his statements, & my reasons for doubting them!

M.[r] Price's assertion that "we cannot in strictness have any dissyllabic spondee" seems to be controvertible. I think we have several examples to the contrary in Milton whose '*os magna sonaturum*'[6] is very partial to the spondaic structure. I cannot recall to my mind any line which the ancients have left us of much grander construction than the following—710. book 3.[d] of Paradise Lost.

> Cŏnfūsi̅on he̅ard hĭs voĭce, & wĭld ūpro̅ar
> Sto̅od ru̅led.

Now I certainly feel strongly that if the spondaic claim of "Uproar" be not admitted—if it be converted into a trochee, or left an iambus, the grandeur of sound will be sensibly diminished. I feel strongly the exquisite effect of the first amphibrach & subsequent trochees—like the heaving of the half formed elements.

> "Cŏnfūsiŏn he̅ard hĭs voĭce ănd["]—

And I feel no less strongly the sudden cessation of confusion, the sudden firmness, & "standing fast" produced *by* what appear to me the five successive long syllables—when

"wīld ūprōar

Stōōd rūled".

I think that in this instance as in a great many others, there is a poetical necessity for the acknowledgment of the existence of English dissyllabic spondees—& that this necessity may be exemplified by the unconscious accentuation of any unlearned reciter who has feeling & a correct ear. For '*uproar*' is surely in this place as true a spondee as the Italian *virtù*, or Pope's monosyllabic one "vast weight".

On the line
"When Ajax strives some rocks vast weight to throw"[7]—

there is among others, the following observation—"That Ajax is really a trochee will be felt by putting it in the place of *vast weight*, where a trochee would evidently injure the metre & rhythm." Putting '*Ajax*' in the place of *vast weight* certainly proves it to be a trochee from the peculiar change which takes place in the construction of the line. But I do not *think* a trochee in that place *injures* the metre any more than an iambus would. It has appeared to me that a trochee introduced before the last foot (supposing the last foot to be an iambus) produces an agreable relief from the monotony of the usual heroic structure. The following examples from Chaucer's Knight's tale are among the most melodious I can recollect—

"Ånd sōlĭtāire hĕ wās ĕvĕr ălōne
Ånd wāiling āll the nīght māking hĭs mōne".[8]

Also Milton's.

Fŏr Lȳcĭdās ĭs dēad, dēad erĕ hĭs tīme.[9]

That "our heroics seldom begin with a dactyl." This must from the context allude to trissyllabic dactyls, which however I had concieved not rare at the beginning of English heroics.

With regard to dactyls monosyllabically composed they give I think a *frequent* charm to the beginning of our heroics. Mʳ Price quotes from Milton

Light as the lightening glimpse, they ran they flew.[10]

and observes upon it—"This beginning—a trochee followed by a short syllable, that by a long one, & forming a choriambus, is frequent in Hexameters & hardly less so in our heroics". Now I do not see why the trochee with its subsequent short syllable should be made perforce part of a choriambus instead of being permitted to hold, by courtesy at least, independant rank as a dactyl. I will take the commencing part of the dactylic Greek Hexameter, quoted immediately below, and I will write it in the place of the commencement of what M! Price calls rather strongly, our *anti-dactylic* heroic verse. If, after having done this, the accentuation or tune of the line suffer no alteration, I believe a fair conclusion may be drawn that the two commencements have a ressemblance in character—that the character of each is dactylic.

"Light as the lightening glimpse, they ran they flew."

" 'Ἄνεϱες ῆδε[11] glimpse, they ran, they flew."

One word in favour of a poetical prejudice.

"Shakespeare Milton Ariosto and Tasso have done all that was possible in less perfect languages & metres". I regret that, in this enumeration of modern great Poets, Dante should be omitted—for the cause of the omission is any thing but clear. I acknowledge a strong feeling of preference for Dante in his rugged grandeur, to Tasso "tra i fiori e l'erba"[12]—I dont say "*estinto*"[13]—and setting aside sublimity of conception, which I certainly have little to do with here, it appears to me that on mere metrical grounds he has a claim to the honor of being named by M! Price, & associated with Milton. Not having studied the Divina Commedia with immediate reference to the present subject, & not having it by me to refer to, many splendid examples must necessarily remain unremarked. But one instance of metrical felicity occurs to me, singularly expressive, which M! Price will recall without an effort—

"E caddi come corpo morto cade".[14]

It is almost superfluous to observe what a different character is here given to the iambi—(no longer *celeres*[15])—by the monotony of consonants & vowels— How much heaviness & falling & stiffness we have instead—how much of the "corpo morto". Dante has at least "done all that was possible in a less perfect language & metre".

Publication: HUP, II, 64–70.
Source: EBB's fair copy at Huntington Library.

1. Apparently, while EBB and Henrietta were visiting Uvedale Price at Foxley in October 1826, he asked her to read and criticize the proof sheets of his book (*An Essay on the Modern Pronunciation of the Greek and Latin Languages*, published in the following year). After discussing her comments in person, Price wrote a more reflective response (letter 241).
2. "The turning-post avoided by furious wheels" (Horace, *Odes*, I, i, 4–5).
3. On pp. 37–38 of his *Essay*, Price defines the *ictus metricus* as "a stroke or stress given to certain syllables in metrical compositions . . . always on a long syllable" and calls it "the surest and most approved guide in recitation."
4. "Deprived of sight" (Vergil, *Æneid*, III, 658).

5. "Empty helmet" (*Iliad*, III, 376).
6. "Tongue of noble utterance" (Horace, *Satires*, I, vi, 43–44).
7. "An Essay on Criticism" (1711), line 370.
8. "The Knight's Tale," lines 1365–66.
9. "Lycidas," line 8.
10. *Paradise Lost*, VI, 642.
11. The substitution of the Greek words ("men and") is only to make a point; they have no meaning in this context.
12. "Through the flowers and the grass." Variations on this phrase are found both in Dante's *Purgatorio* and Tasso's *Rime sparse*.
13. "Dead, extinct."
14. "And fell as a dead body falls" (*Divina Commedia*, I, 5, 142).
15. "Rapid."

---

239. SAMUEL MOULTON-BARRETT (BROTHER) TO EBB

13, Charterhouse Squ.
Sunday. Oct. 1.ˢᵗ [1826]¹

My ever dearest Ba

I recieved your kind letter on Wednesday and I dare say you were surprised at not hearing ⟨fr⟩om me on Sunday, but I did not know if I was going out for I put my name down on Friday expecting a ⟨n⟩ote and I suppose that Tippy forgot to write so I could not go. I have got Bro's books and I do not know if they are right or not; so I will send you a list of some of them, I have got. Three vol of Sophocles, two volumes of Heroditus [sic] and a map of Heroditus, Essay on mind, two small Virgils; I shall keep one, the Batle [sic] of Marathon, A Gradus, Lempreyre [sic] classical Dict, A Cicero, Eae moralia, Bible; and some other small books. All that I do not want I shall send to Granny and she will send them to you the first opportunity. We had at Peneys to day Geese, and apple pudden, that is more than the Watkieytes have had. I am surprised at not hearing from Henrietta, I think she has left off writing to me for I have not heard from her for a week and more, tell her she must write before I write again. I was examined by Russell on Friday and I got second. I thought Papa would have been down here by this time as hop-picking is over. It is raining now as hard as ever it can. Just like London. I had a letter from Hartley² on Friday to ask me out on Saturday but I refused as I expected a letter from Granny to ask me out do not you tell her when you write though. I had a box on Saturday evening from Devonshire filled with stones and rotten apples, and I cannot find out who it is. There is know [sic] news for I wrote so lately that I told you all the news that is within these smokey walls. I will write soon again but not till I hear from some of you. Give my very best love to them all. This is not Peneys own house it is belonging to all the masters they have all paid so much towards it. I think the newgate calender[3] is given up for we cannot get any of them, is not that a *pity.* Mind I shall not write till some of you do.

Your ever
affectionate
Sam.

Address, on integral page: Miss Barrett / Hope-End / Nr Ledbury / Herefordshire.
Publication: None traced.
Manuscript: Edward R. Moulton-Barrett.

1. 1826 was the only year of Sam's attendance at Charterhouse in which 1 October fell on Sunday.
2. Perceval Hartley (1814–91) was a pupil at Charterhouse from June 1826 to December 1831.
3. *The Newgate Monthly Magazine, Or, Calendar of Men, Things and Opinions* ceased publication in August 1826.

---

240. EBB TO HENRIETTA MOULTON-BARRETT

[Eastnor Castle]
[ca. November 1826][1]

My dearest Henrietta,

You desired to know how I got on, so you shall have a few lines to assure you that I am quite as well as *can be expected*—which is *very ill.* My first introduction was even more awkward than I anticipated, for I was shewn into the Library where sat, or stood (I did'nt know which) one unknown gentleman soliloquizing—or at least solitudinizing. This was worse than the *Foxley scene!*

I am, as yet, the only stranger in the Family circle—so that I am both *in* the way, & out of my way. There are here M.[r] & M.[rs] Waddington,[2] Miss Cocks[3] & *the* gentleman, whose name I dont know yet, & whose capabilities I dont know yet—Further than his playing on the flute, & being ycleped *Joe* by his intimates. Lord Somers was so unwell last night, that he retired to M.[r] Selwyn.[4] Lady Margaret is very kind & *silencieuse.*[5] The Dinner was formal enough, & when we went to bed at Eleven I thought it was at least four in the morning. Nevertheless we had music; for M.[rs] Waddington had her guitar on which she plays very well—& she gave us several overtures on the piano, accompanied by M.[r] Joe. The Conversation was down five degrees below *freezing.* Every body thinking what to say next—except M.[rs] Waddington who does not seem to think *at all.*

Tomorrow we are to have an accession of company of some kind— but I dont know of what. NOT THE Commelines I fear. M.ʳ Blizzard is mentioned. Dearest Henrietta! I thought of you this morning, as I told you I should—: I would give any thing to be back again; but I hope we shall *improve* a little before Tuesday. Tuesday's Dinner I think of more than I ever thought of any dinner—because I shall then see Papa & Mama again.

God bless you beloved Henrietta.

Post is going without my note.

Your own Ba–

I was *obliged* to sing Kathleen last night— Pray pity me–

A Capital Fire!——

Publication: None traced.
Manuscript: R.J.L. Altham.

1. The visit described here probably came after EBB's visit to Foxley in October, and before the Eastnor visit discussed in letter 249.

2. The Rev. George Waddington was Rector of Northwold in Norfolk. In 1817, he had married Jane Cocks, Earl Somers' cousin. After Waddington's death in 1833, at the age of 43, his widow became the second wife of Earl Somers, on 3 June 1834.

3. Probably Earl Somers' sister, Harriet Cocks.

4. Congreve Selwyn, surgeon, in charge of the Dispensary in Ledbury.

5. "Still."

---

241. UVEDALE PRICE TO EBB

Foxley

Nov.ʳ 17.ᵗʰ 1826

As I have taken the liberty of calling you *Ba*, I shall not be more ceremonious in writing than in speaking; & therefore in this, & in all future letters, unless you forbid me, shall quit dear Miss Barrett, for dear Ba.– I have read your paper with more attention than I could give it in a hasty reading; & now, after repeating how much pleased I am with your approbation of the main part of what I have written, & with the very gratifying & ingenious manner in which you expressed it, I shall go to your remarks on what I have said of the pre-eminence of the hexameter. "M.ʳ P's position, that we cannot in strictness have any dissyllabic spondee, appears to me controvertible: I think we have many examples of the contrary in Milton. I cannot recall to my mind any line that the ancients have left us of a more sonorous construction than

> Confusion heard his voice, & wild uproar
> Stood rul'd;"

Your comment on this striking line & on its spondaic rhythm is very just & impressive;– I agree with you that *uproár* is in that place as true a spondee as *virtù*, but not so true a one as vast weight; a nice, yet, I believe, not a fanciful distinction. The Italians,—I speak, however, with diffidence of what relates to a foreign language,—do not make *virtù* an iambius *though* accented on the last syllable; they do not pass quickly over the first syllable, as in *ferì, tremò,*[1] but—giving more length & stress to the accented syllable—pass on to it *adagio, ma non troppo*, as "Cáde virtù dall'infiammate stelle",[2]—not dwelling equally on both syllables as might be indicated by *vir'tù*, yet not hurrying over the first as in Cáde valòr. So I should do with the word in question: not make it, as many readers, on seeing that the accent was in this case shifted from the first to the last, might be apt [to] do,—*ŭprōar*, yet still give the chief length & stress to the last syllable; & I should do it on account of the expression. The emphatic syllables are *wild* & *roar*; *up*, is much less so, tho' a useful augmentative; & therefore I should not pass rapidly, but move, as it were, leisurely over it, & rest fully on *roar*.– In fact, as it appears to me, the word is not changed from a trochee, as we now pronounce it to a spondee, but, as I said before, the accent is merely shifted from the first to the last, & therefore, according to the usual mode of pronouncing would be an iambus; but, from what you very truly & ingeniously term "a poetical necessity", the voice ought to well upon it more than it would according to the common rule, yet less than on the accented syllable, & in a tone of voice less marked & decided. This instance then, though very well adduced, & perhaps as good a one as you will be able to get, does not at all affect my position—namely that we have not in strictness any dissyllabic spondee in our language, every dissyllable having an accent either on the first or the last,—& accent (you must give me credit till I can bring my full proofs) always making the accented syllable the longest. One experiment you may easily & in various cases try yourself: place the ancient mark of long, in greek, latin, or english verses on the syllables upon which we lay our accent, & the mark of short on the *un*accented, & it will guide you exactly to our pronunciation of them whether right or wrong; if right, as in

Αὖτῐς ἔπε'ιτᾰ πεδόν'δε κῠλῖν'δετ̆ο λᾱ'ᾰς ἀνᾰ'ῑδης[3]

accent & true quantity,—as you see—coincide, while in

Sῐ pē'tĕrĕt pĕr ā'mῐcῐ'tῐăm pā'trῐs ā'tqŭe suᾰm nῑl[4]

accent & our false quantities equally coincide. But again, to shew the lengthing power of accent, & it's useful guidance when properly applied, place an accent on ALL the long syllables, & on those only of this piece of wretched prose, & it will guide you to the true rhythm of an hexameter; &,—what no one could suspect from our recitation—to a dactylic, tho' not a very harmonious rhythm: the accentual marks will indicate the exact quantity; those of the Ictus the syllables on which the ancients laid a stress

> Sí peterét per amícitiam' patrĭs átque suám, níl uñquám próficerét.

On the other hand, place the ancient marks of long & short on all the syllables of an english verse & it will as truly indicate the pronunciation as the accentual: as

> Gōddĕss ăwāke ărise, ălās mў fēars.[5]

Our accent then & ancient quantity are hereby identified; for I do not conceive how any clearer proof of their identity can be given than the convertibility of the marks. If this be so—to return to the foot in question—no dissyllable in English can strictly be a spondee; for a spondee with one accented or long, & one *un*accented or short syllable, is a contradiction. Among the dissyllables proposed as spondees, *amen* (not a very english one) is most frequently mentioned: & when pronounced solemnly, on solemn occasions, an equal length is given to the two syllables: but the strong bent of our pronunciation is to accént, that is to lengthen one of the syllables in every disyllable. In the responses, you often hear the *a* hurried over: & this is more likely to take place where the word is introduced into compositions that are any thing but solemn; as in the old ballad of Qⁿ Eleanor

> Amen amén quoth earl Marsháll[6]

where the second *amen* would naturally be made an iambus, were it only for the rhythm. In Greek, setting the *eta* at defiance, we make it a trochee, accompanying it with two others: α'μην α'μην λε'γω υ'μιν.[7] *Finite* is another word claiming to be a spondee & with as good a claim as any: Johnson accents it on the first, but gives no example from poetry: it is not used by Shakespear, & only once by Milton,

> will he draw out,
> For anger's sake, finite to infinite?[8]

& there, with little difference to the metre or the rhythm, it may be made a trochee, an iambus, or a spondee: such is the licence in our prosody & pronunciation! *Julý* has also pretentions, & not ill founded, tho' our propensity inclines us to make it an iambus: I remember it's being made a trochee in some ludicrous verses of Mʳˢ Greville's:

> Bút you in the month of Júly
> Grew so frisky & unruly.[9]

I am well persuaded from all that I have observed, that there is no dissyllable in English, to the two syllables of which we habitually give an equal length, as the Greeks, & as the Romans must have done; who certainly did not make their proper name *Jūlī* so frisky, as to appear in the character of a spondee, a trochee, or an iambus according to the wish & fancy of the poet. To the ancients, spondees, molossi & dispondees, were familiar in their strict quantity; our speech is so decidedly trochaic & iambic, that it requires something of effort & reflection to make us give an equal length even to two syllables in the same word. We trochaize the french language, as [we] do these of the ancients; & when a Frenchman says of an Englishman, "il a beaucoup," or, "tres peu d' accent,"[10] it is not, I believe, merely on account of the difference in the *tones*, but in the *quantity*; thus, for instance, when in the "François a Londres," *Le Milor* says to his model & instructor in french manners & graces, "Mōnsiĕur le Mārquĭs, ăprēnĕz mŏi lĕs airs & lĕs făcŏns,"[11] he makes all the dissyllables trochees; raising at the same time the pitch of his voice on the first syllable: what then is called our *accent* in French, is compounded of accent, in the ancient sense, & of quantity; of elevation & of duration; & nearly as much of the one as of the other: these, in truth, are the two main distinctions in all human speech.—— In Pope's line,

When Ajax strives some rocks vast weight to throw,[12]

I have said, in order to shew the proper name to be really a trochee, that if you transpose *Ajax & vast weight*, the trochee would evidently injure the metre & rhythm; this you object to; not to the proof of its being trochee, but to the injury that would be done to the metre & rhythm: I shall alter the passage something in the way you have suggested, by calling it "the peculiar change made by a trochee so situated in the cadence of the line." I might have said that, so placed, a trochee checks the usual flow of the rhythm by an unusual pause, although as you observe, it would produce an agreable relief from the *monotony* (an avowal very much in favour of my general position) of the usual heroic structure. . Your expression "a *peculiar* change" shews it not to be frequent, & I cannot call to mind any instance of the sort, tho' there probably must be several: those you have given & marked from Chaucer

And solitaire he was ēvĕr alone
And wailing all the night, mākĭng his mone[13]

are exactly in point as we now pronounce the words, but not (I might almost say certainly) as Chaucer did: I am persuaded that *evér* & *makíng* were then as much spondees as *toujours* & *faisœnt*, or, at least, that the accent was on the final. The line from Milton has better pretentions; still I think the trochees doubtful

For Lycidas is dead, dead ere his prime.[14]

ere is a very long syllable to the ear, & moreover is contracted; & tho' we have no scruple or difficulty in vaulting over the longest syllables, yet *dead ere his* makes but an indifferent dactyl, & there seems to be no objection on the score of expression to laying *some* stress on "*ère* his prime"; for the affecting circumstance is, that with such high promise of future excellence he died *before* it was realized: as Homer, & after him Virgil, mentions the pathetic circumstance of the parent birds being robbed of their young while yet unfledged,

ʿοισι τε τεϰνα

Αγϱοται εξειλοντο, παϱος πετεεινα [*sic*, for πετεηνα]

γενεσθαι[15]

I have spoken of the beginning of Miltons line

Light as the lightening glimpse, they ran they flew,[16]

as forming a choriambus; & improperly: for tho' it does form one, it is with the first of a dissyllable: upon this you say "I do not see why the trochee with its subsequent short syllable, should be made perforce part of a choriambus, instead of being permitted, at least by courtesy, to hold independent rank as a dactyl." This is a very lively, & good-humourdly sarcastic attack: I acknowledge the *perforce*, & readily give up the choriambus: but you must allow me to say that your independent dactyl, will on more than one account require a good deal of courtesy: "Light as the" compared with true ancient dactyls is just such a one as Των πας θε . . , or, Tum fas de . . , a bad dactyl with the addition of a subsequent long syllable must make a bad choriambus, and "Light as the light" answers exactly to Των πας θεων[17] or Tum fas deum: the dactyl, if pronounced by itself & made independent, would not be in favour of the dactylic character of our language; for besides *as*, which does not promote rapidity, *the*, which, on such occasions, we pronounce with a sort of *e muet*, as the French do *te*, & *me*, is neither an harmonious nor a very articulate termination: & the second & third monosyllable, ought, I think, for the sake of euphony & connection, to be joined at once to the object of comparison. In reciting the line, I should lay a strong emphasis on the first word; &, after a very slight pause should pass on, without any other stoppage, to the fifth word. Light, as the lightning glimpse; the greek beginning of a verse join'd to the english word—"Ανεϱες ηδε glimpse" as you have joined them, certainly answers to it, as far as a perfect dactyl & trochee, can answer to such very opposite specimens of those feet; & the junction shews the extreme difference between the character of the hexameter & that of our heroic verse both in metre & rhythm: the greek dactyl & trochee absolutely require a subsequent short syllable, as "Ανερες ηδε γυναικες,"[18] when the rhythm goes off with quite another spring & elasticity from "Light as the lightning glimpse," where the rapidity is checked by the long monosyllable (after a trochee, not quite so rapid as the thing signified) just as it would be in "Ανερες ηδε γην." A second dactyl, as

"Light, as the lightning of heaven,"

tho' more rapid, would hardly accord with our style of versification; I never, indeed, observed an instance of even two successive dactyls in our heroics; whereas in hexameters, three & four often succeed one another, & not unfrequently five, as they do in the greek line. I therefore think myself justified in calling our heroic metre, as compared with that of the ancients, anti-dactylic; tho', compared with that of the French, it may be called dactylic; for Marmontel says "nous n'avons pas de dactyles, nous n'avons que des anapestes."[19] In our heroic metre the dactyl is not consider'd as a foot, it must always, I believe, be resolvable into dissyllabic feet, or the verse will not scan; just as, in hexameters, trochees, iambi, anapæsts &cæ must form part of dactyls or of spondees: most of our english dactyls, especially when compared with those in Greek or in Latin are very imperfect, & defective; numbers of them end on two consonants: on *nt*, as *Fir'mament*; some with two likewise in the middle, as *Gov'ernment*; numbers on *ng*, that being the termination of our participles present; & of a most retarding kind, as *clustering murmuring*: compare this last—not one of our worst—with *murmura* or μερμερα. In this set also there are sometimes two consonants in the middle as *comforting*, or—the termination being different—with three, as *comfortless*, yet, being accented on the first syllable, they all pass muster as dactyls. *Harmony*, is among the most perfect in the language, & a word in every way pleasing: so likewise is *Victory*: in each of them,—the consonant in the first syllable being followed by one of a different kind,—we are obliged to separate them in pronunciation: the *o* is followed by a single consonant, & the *y* has the vowel sound of our *e*, not, as in many cases the diphthongal & long sound of our *i*. *Melody*, considered as a dactyl, is imperfect from having a short accent: Minstrelsy with the same termination, is clogged in the centre. In *magnify glorify*, & other words of the same sort, the two first syllables are as we could wish them; but the *y* has the diphthongal sound of *i*, & the words were formerly pronounced as amphimacers, *mag'nify*. *satisfy* has a short accent at the beginning, &

two consonants in the middle; & this I believe is a fair account of the mass of our trissyllabic dactyls. In the ancient languages, besides the trissyllabic, a number of excellent dactyls were formed by trochees with a subsequent short syllable; but as our trochees so often end on two consonants, & begin with a short accent, the dactyls formed by them must have the same defects & imperfections. Numerous & excellent greek & latin dactyls are formed by means of an iambus followed by a pyrrhic: our iambi are perfect; but (begging pardon of Bro & the Charterhouse), we have no dissyllabic pyrrhic; nor, as we pronounce them, is there a single on[e] in Greek or in Latin; that fruitful source of dactyls is therefore cut off altogether: it may easily be reproduced in Greek & Latin; it cannot be produced in English (nor, I may add in Italian) without destroying the established character of the language. These statements, tho' not made with that view, convincingly shew, what you, indeed, neither want to be informed nor convinced of, the various reasons why the attempt to make a poem in english hexameters is the idlest of all attempts: it is attempting to build a palace without proper or sufficient materials. Voltaire, who cannot be accused of want of partiality to the french language & to french poetry, used to say, when any one spoke in raptures of his verses, & promised them immortality, "hélas! Monsieur, nous bâtissons en brique!"[20] & tho' he spoke immediately of his own, he probably meant to include modern languages in general. He called the Greek, & most truly, "la plus belle langue que les hommes ayent jamais parlé"[21] The Latin, as the Romans themselves felt & acknowledged, is much inferior: yet had the Greek never existed, who could read the best latin writers of the best ages both in prose & in verse without being tempted to pay it the same compliment? or at least that of its' being the best adapted to the various styles of composition. By selecting what is choicest in the materials we possess, & studying how they may be most happily disposed & arranged, much has, & much may be done; but there is no giving to them the higher quality, & superior splendour of the ancient marbles.—— You have given me a good scold for my omission of Dante; & well deserved, & thank you for it: I believe what carelessly passed in my mind was, that Shakespear & Ariosto, Milton & Tasso lived about the same time,

Ουτος δε προτερης γενεης, προτερων τ' ανθρωπων.[22]

even prior to Chaucer. This is but an idle excuse for the neglect of such a man; he shall be placed, where on every account he ought to be placed, at the head of his countrymen.

⟨As there will be three Italians, I must have three English,—were it only for the sake of symmetry,—to oppose to them: & after Shakespear

& Milton (following the order of Gray) shall come, "Dryden's less presumptuous ear."[23] I hope you admire his ode as much [as] I do; tho', probably, as I do, with some few drawbacks: we had no conversation on the subject; but I trust that if you had felt any material objections to what I had advanced on the versification, & the various metres, you would have mentioned, or put them down in writing.

Believe me most truly yours
U Price⟩[24]

Publication: None traced.
Manuscript: Armstrong Browning Library.

1. In this and later letters discussing scansion, numerous foreign words are cited as examples of particular accent or rhythm. As their meaning is not relevant in the context in which they are used, we do not translate them.
2. "Virtue falls from the flaming stars." It is likely that Price, relying on memory, misquoted Petrarch's "Cade virtù dall'infiammate corna" ("Virtue falls from the burning brows"; line 4 of Sonnet 9, *Rime di F. Petrarca*, 1821, I, 11).
3. "And again earthward rolls the pitiless stone" (Homer's *Odyssey*, XI, 598).
4. "If he should beg him by his father's friendship and his own, no [headway could he make]" (Horace's *Satires*, I, iii, 5).
5. Thomas Gray (1716–71), "Hymn to Ignorance" (1742), line 25.
6. Line 43 of "Queen Eleanor's Confession" in Thomas Percy's *Reliques of Ancient English Poetry* (1765).
7. "Amen, amen, I say unto you."
8. *Paradise Lost*, X, 801–802.
9. We have been unable to locate the source of this quotation. Presumably it was by the Fanny Greville (*née* McCartney) whose "Prayer for Indifference" (ca. 1753) appears in many anthologies.
10. "He has a lot" or "very little accent."
11. "Monsieur Marquis, teach me airs and graces."
12. "An Essay on Criticism," line 370.
13. "The Knight's Tale," lines 1365–66.
14. "Lycidas," line 8.
15. "From whom farmers take their young before they can fly" (*Odyssey*, XVI, 217–218).
16. *Paradise Lost*, VI, 642.
17. "All of the gods."
18. "Men and women."
19. "We have no dactyls, we have only anapæsts." An inaccurate quotation from *Éléments de Littérature*. Marmontel's observation was "the French language has few dactyls and many anapæsts" (I, 154 in the 1846 edition).
20. "Alas, Sir, we build in brick!" This appears to be a paraphrase of Voltaire's observation "Les anciens travaillaient en marbre et nous en pierre" ("The ancients worked in marble and we in stone"; *The Complete Works of Voltaire*, ed. Theodore Besterman, 1968, II, 516).
21. "The most beautiful language that men have ever spoken" (letter of 6 May 1768 to Étienne de La Montagne; Besterman's edition of Voltaire, letter no. 14051).
22. "But this one is of a former age and of earlier men" (*Iliad*, XXIII, 790).
23. Gray's "The Progress of Poesy," line 103.
24. The passage within angle brackets appears immediately after page six of the manuscript and Price added this headnote: "This page I very giddily skipped over; as you must, & return to it after the two next."

242. EBB TO UVEDALE PRICE

[Hope End]
[ca. December 1826][1]

As you have permitted me to express opinions on more important subjects, you must let me assure you, dear Sir, that "Ba" is *much* better pleased to hear from you than "Miss Barrett" *could* be. I have been deeply interested by your letter—almost as much as I have been gratified! For the distinction & encouragement which I recieve from you, I *feel* my thanks, trusting that for the *feeling's* sake, you will forgive the imperfect expression.

I acknowledge the justice of your position "that there is in English no dissyllable, to the two syllables of which we habitually give an equal length", but, tho' I have reconsidered the subject with great attention & with the assistance of your remarks, I do not yet feel inclined to acknowledge that there is in English heroic verse no dissyllable, to the two syllables of which we are not induced by position to give an equal length. In my quotation from Milton you excommunicate "uproar" from the trochaic, spondaic, & iambic pale! & leave it if with "a *local* habitation", at least without "a *name*".[2] "Uproar", however, I will own, does partly deserve this hard usage on account of the inconvenient consonant on its first syllable, which we must rest on, if we rest at all, & which we gladly leave for "*roar*", taking advantage of the new accent. But I still think that this organic preference should be surmounted as much as possible, in deference to the *expression*. The expression appears to me to depend entirely on *contrast*—on the distinct preservation of the different characteristics of the first & second parts of the line: the first representing the restlessness of startled confusion by the heaving of the voice—the second representing the firmness of order by the firmness & decision of the voice. Now I cannot help thinking that by making "wild" & "roar" the emphatic syllables, & by considering "up" "much less so", as you propose doing, you make the distinct characteristics less distinct, & therefore injure the expression of the line. Your *adagio non troppo* does not quite satisfy my ambition for "*up*": I should prefer a *largo con espressione.* "Uproar" suffers in good company—with the Italian virtù—&, not to be too national, virtù shall have the benefit of an "*in forse*"[3] before I go on to our English spondees. It seems to me very clear that in the line you quote

"Ca'de virtù dall'infiammate stelle"—[4]

virtù has little spondaic pretension; but I am doubtful whether it may not have, from position, the same spondaic rank which I would grant to some English dissyllables. I submit it to you whether in the following line from Francini's Ode to Milton

"Sol virtù rintracciando il tuo pensiero"–[5]

the metre is contented with an *adagio non troppo* on *virtùs* first syllable. To my ear the dissyllable is, in that place, a true spondee. To return to English spondees, I do not think that your able statement of the identity of what we call *accent* & the ancient quantity, bears very hard on my opinions, because, as in the case of 'uproar', I would not *shift* but *multiply* the accent. In some instances indeed the accent is merely *shifted*, as with the words 'triùmphing' for the usual 'trïumphing', & ŭntō for the usual ūntŏ—so that Herrick says properly—

> Thus, Julia, let me woo thee,
> Thus, thus, to come unto thee—[6]

but all this seems very different from what I am contending for– Since I acknowledged that there existed a little organic disinclination to mark equally the two accented or long syllables of *uproar*, I must hazard an opinion that, in a line which I shall take from Comus,

"Amongst the ēnthrōñed Gods on sainted seats"—[7]

there exists a greater degree of organic disinclination to do *otherwise* than mark equally the two accented or long syllables of *enthroned*. For the inclination of the organs pleads strongly for a resting upon *throned*, & the metre *necessitates* us to rest on the "en", & thus, between the organic preference & the metrical necessity, the spondee prefers its claim. In the following line (from Comus again)

> "their way
> Lies thro' the pērplēxed paths of this drear wood"–[8]

I think our organs would be a little 'perplexed',—tho', as you observe, they are seldom scrupulous about such matters, to know how to shorten the last of the dissyllable, while the metre would be equally 'perplexed' if we attempted to shorten the first. There are some dissyllabic words compounded of monosyllabic ones, which are I believe, spondees—as in the Arcades—

> Under the shady roof
> Of branching elm stār-prōof;[9]

where the expression obliges us to rest on *star*, the metre on *proof*! In these predicaments what recourse have we but the acknowledgement of spondees? I find that pĕrspēctĭve has been recieved as a molossus by some poets—a discovery only agreable to me as it supports an argument

that, if, with "our trochaic & iambic habits of speech,["] we can
manage a word of three long syllables, we may at least aspire to the
management of a word of *two*. My first example of this practice, I take
from the Night thoughts—

"Joy behind joy in endless p͞ersp͞ec͞tive."[10]
"By p͞ersp͞ec͞tive devised, beholding now"–
                              Drayton's Barons' Wars.[11]

"All our good deeds & bad—a p͞ersp͞ec͞tive
That shows us hell–"   Websters *Duchess of Malfi*.[12]

You murmur a little against the "licence in our prosody &
pronunciation", & triumphantly refer to the practice of the Greeks &
Romans, which was far from authorizing a word's appearance in the
character of a spondee trochee or iambus, "according to the wish &
fancy of the poet". I am not desirous of comparing our poetical habits
with the "severiores muras"[13] of the ancients—tho' the latter were by
no means Dracos,[14] being remarkably good-humoured to certain words
in certain positions. Of this good humour we have many instances, as in
the line,

A'υταϱ 'επειτ' 'αυτοισι βελο͞ς 'εχεπευχες εφιεις
βαλλ.[15]

where βε̆λο̆ς the pyrrhic becomes βε̆λο͞ς the iambus, without the foreign
aid of consonants. By an artifice of the understanding to conceal its
subjection to the ear, we pronounce the *cæsura* to have effected the
change. But if we *reason* instead of *calling names*—if we *analyze* the
cæsural line, we shall, I believe, find, that we have much the same
motive for lengthening the last syllable of "βελος" as for lengthening
the first syllable of 'enthroned' or 'perplexed'–

                    Cynthius *aurem*
            Vellit et admonuit–[16]

The desire which at the conclusion of your letter, you in kindness
express, & the promise which you make: (being in every way suited to
gratify my ambition) must act as a strong stimulus to exertion. I have
been thinking of late that *genius developped by circumstances &
developped tardily* might make a fine subject for a narrative Poem: but
I have proceeded no further with my plan than the outworks.[17] If the
extraordinary history of Alfieri's mind, as given in his memoirs,[18] occur
to you, you will know at once the character of my design.

                    Believe me
              Most truly & gratefully yours
                    E B Barrett.

Publication: None traced.
Manuscript: Armstrong Browning Library.

1. This letter is a response to letter 241.
2. *A Midsummer Night's Dream,* V, 1, 17.
3. "In doubt."
4. See letter 241, note 2.
5. "Virtue alone seeking your thought." This is line 44 of an 84-line ode addressed "Al Signor Gio. Miltoni Nobile Inglese" by Antonio Francini of Florence. The ode was included at pp. 5–9 of *Joannis Miltoni Londinensis Poemata,* 1645.
6. "The Night-Piece. To Julia" in *Hesperides* (1648).
7. Line 11.
8. Lines 36–37.
9. Milton's "Arcades," lines 88–89.
10. Line 171 of "Night the First" in Edward Young's *The Complaint: or Night Thoughts on Life, Death, & Immortality* (1742).
11. Canto VI, line 279 in the revised text of 1603; however, it reads "prospective" not "perspective."
12. IV, 2, 386–387.
13. Literally "more severe walls," meaning stricter rules.
14. Draco, an Athenian of the 7th century B.C., whose code of laws gave birth to the phrase "of Draconian severity."
15. "Thereafter on the men themselves he let fly the sharp-pointed darts" (*Iliad,* I, 51–52).
16. "Cynthius pulled his ear and warned" (Vergil, *Eclogues,* VI, 3–4).
17. This remark dates the genesis of "The Development of Genius," published in *HUP,* II, 99–133. No extant manuscript carries either date or title; the editor of *HUP* gave it the title by which it is now known, adapting the phrase used by EBB in this letter.

EBB had obviously forgotten that she had mentioned this project before—Price commented approvingly on her choice of subject at the end of letter 236.

18. *Memoirs of the Life and Writings of Victor Alfieri* (1810).

---

243. UVEDALE PRICE TO EBB

Foxley
Decb^{er} 20.th 1826

Dear Ba.

When Luxmoore[1] was with us, a little before he called at Hopend [*sic*], I shewed him what I had just been writing on the Charter-house mode of pronouncing, chiefly that of their passing over the vowel to the consonant in iambi & pyrrhics but continuing to accent them, as we do, on the first syllable: He read it with more interest than he is apt to feel on such subjects, & wished me to go on with it; having as great a dislike to *eg'o* πυϱ'ι *fug'e, pig'er*[2] &ca as I have; & being convinced by what I shewed him, that the trochaic cadence & the shortened finals (two principal objects of reform) are much the same in μεγ'α δ' αμ'φι πυλ'αι μυκ'ον as in με'γα δ' αμ'φι πυ'λαι μυ'κον, but with a much worse sound; & that the dactylic rhythm, & four out of the five dactyls in

βϱιθοσυνη μεγᾰ δ' αμφι πυλαι .. μυκόν ουδ αϱ οχηες[3]

were for want of the long finals & the true cadence of the pyrrhic, equally destroyed in both modes. He is not acquainted with Dr Russell, but thinks from what is said of him that he is a very liberal man, & one who would like to discuss a subject of this sort; of course, if he thought the remarks worthy of his attention. I have now finished my little dissertation & have had a fair copy made of it: & as it may be conveyed in a few covers I shall venture to send it you & probably in the course of this week: & if on reading it you & your brother should think the statements well founded, & the sheets altogether not unworthy of Dr Russell's notice, your Brother perhaps, from his charter house connections might know some one sufficiently acquainted with D^r R to mention to him that such a letter (for it is in that form & addressed to you tho' without your name,) had been written & by whom, & to ask him whether he would like to look at it: if he should you might perhaps contrive to send it to him before the vacation is over. The undisguised freedom of my attack on the change I have just spoken of will be no slight trial of his candour & liberality, tho' I have given the praises they so well deserve to two other changes; that of stopping on the vowel before a *single* consonant, as a'ridus, e'met, Th'lyre, o'mine, & to that of separating two consonants of the same kind, as in ter'ruit, ir'ritus. These two changes were made,—indeed necessarily, in consequence of the first, but might, & ought to remain, should the first, as I earnestly wish it may, be abandoned. I hope you & your Brother will both of you examine my ms. with a critical eye, & let me know if you should discover any material errors in any of my positions: I heartily wish, on every account, that we were near neighbours, & could talk over the whole viva voce.——

I have a good deal to say to you in reply to *your* reply; but I have lately had some visits from my arch-enemy that arch-fiend Dyspepsia, & have had hard work to finish the ms. I am going to send you: She acts in various ways sometimes by extreme irritation, at others by stupor & lethargy under the influence of which last, with a little mixture of the first, I am now writing; I will ask you however while I am half awake, whether you have read the Subaltern? It is said, by military men to be a very exact as well as lively account of the D. of Wellington's campaign in the Pyrenees from the taking of St Sebastian to the surrender of Bayonne: a great part of it is interesting even to so unmilitary a man as myself, but the whole account of the attack & capture of St Sebastian at the beginning of the work, is most striking in all its circumstances & all its detail: the dreadful sublimity of such a scene is likewise enhanced & rendered more awful, by a most impressive description of a thunderstorm that on the very morning when the attack was to be made appeared to be slowly collecting its terrible ammunition: the close oppressive heat of the atmosphere, the lowring sulphureous clouds, the preternatural stillness, the silence, the apparent alarm felt by all animals, seem to be the vivid, but true & unexaggerated images of what he really witnessed. As the day passed on the hour of attack drew near, the clouds gradually collected into one black mass directly over the devoted city & almost at the instant when the troops began to march into the trenches the storm burst forth: still it was comparatively mild in it's effects.[4] I am very much persuaded from the general style & character of the work that all this singular coincidence did take place just as it is related, & should be very sorry to think otherwise for if I could suppose any thing to have been invented or arranged for the purpose of effect, it would completely defeat it's purpose. Admitting the exact truth it is a most striking combination, & the grandest contest ever exhibited between the

> mortal engines whose hoarse throats
> Th' immortal Joves dread thunders counterfeit[5]

& the thunders themselves: as to Salmoneus, his exhibition was not much better than playhouse thunder & lightning.[6] What makes me inclined to think that the author did not sacrifice truth to effect is that he mentions the first burst of the storm as comparatively mild; then leaves it & goes on with the attack to the end of it & of the chapter; & after such mighty preparation I felt a little disappointed that so little had been produced. In the next chapter, not having chosen to interrupt his narrative of the attack, he returns to the particular movement of his own corps a few days previous to it: they were ordered to advance up in the mountains, but were suddenly recalled to join the besiegers, & were with them when the attack began. He then resumes his account of the thunder-storm where he had left off: "this," he says "went on increasing every minute, so that at the moment when our leading files emerged from their cover (it was *mild* when they marched *into* the trenches) one of the most fearful thunder-storms to which I ever listened had attained its height": & then after a little interval, & a little suspense to the reader, the full combination & grand chorus is restored. I have been trying to recollect the descriptions of thunder-storms in poetry & the circumstances mentioned: the *sulphureous* clouds, & any indication of sulphur, I only remember in Homer who in two passages mentions the smell of it with an epithet, which shewed that he thought it terrible, & therefore on the same principle with Burke, sublime.

ως' δ' οθ' υπ'αι ριπης πατρος Διος εξερι'πη δρυς
Προρρι'ζος δεινη δε θεειου γινεται οδμη[7]

You will certainly have observed the five successive trochees in the first verse, either in the old or the Charter-house mode, & the miserable ending of the line: in fact, there is neither dactyl nor spondee, metre nor rhythm, connection, expression nor harmony till you come to the adonic at the end of the second line. The other instance is where Jupiter darts his thunderbolt at the feet of Diomeds horses

Δεινη δε φλοξ ωρτσ θεειου καιομενοιο[8]

The stillness is noticed, & in the most striking manner by Shakespear; but I cannot recollect an example in poetry, tho' I dare say you will, of the alarming impression of the storm, while yet collecting, on all animals. I have been writing a great deal in my sleep, & will now return to my armchair. Believe me with our best regards to you all

Most truly yours
U Price

Publication: None traced.
Manuscript: Armstrong Browning Library.

1. Probably Charles Scott Luxmoore (1794?–1854), Prebendary of Hereford and eldest son of John Luxmoore (1756–1830), who had been Bishop of Hereford 1808–15.
2. See letter 241, note 1.
3. ["The stone fell by its own] weight, and the gates grated loudly around" (*Iliad*, XII, 460).
4. *The Subaltern* (1825) by George Robert Gleig (1796–1888). The passage describing the storm occurs in chapter 3.
5. *Othello*, III, 3, 355–356, slightly misquoted.
6. Salmoneus, son of Æolus, pretended to be a god, making thunder by dragging kettles behind his chariot, and hurling torches to simulate lightning. He was struck dead by Zeus.
7. "As by the stroke of Father Zeus a tree is uprooted, and there comes the terrible smell of sulphur" (*Iliad*, XIV, 414–415).
8. "And there shot up the terrible fire of burning sulphur" (*Iliad*, VIII, 135).

---

244. EBB to Uvedale Price

Hope End
December 30.th 1826.

My dear Sir,
    I have defered writing to you, in the hope of being enabled to communicate D.r Russells *resolutions* respecting your m.s. which was sent to him very soon after its arrival here. My brother is not well acquainted with any person in the habit of regular communication with D.r Russell, of whom he could make use as an intermediate agent in the business. But he had no difficulty in applying to D.r R. personally both

because he had been under his immediate instruction some months before he left Charterhouse, & from a feeling that no *intimacy* was necessary to justify the mention of your name to a literary man. Losing time, in this case, would have been losing opportunity. Without delay therefore Bro forwarded your m.s. alleging, as a motive, that its statements had appeared to some Persons likely to interest D.ᶠ R. & adding that its writer, who had given much attention to the subject of accent generally, was not only open to discussion but desirous of it. D.ᶠ Russell's reply reached us last night. He begins by expressing himself gratified by "the communication of M.ᶠ Price's letter which has certainly interested tho' it has not convinced him". He goes on to regret that want of leisure renders it quite impossible for him to enter on any discussion of this kind. He "will however just remark that he concieves sounds in language to be perfectly arbitrary, but that we approve most of those to which the ear has been habituated. Could we persuade all the nations of the Continent to agree with England in any pronunciation of Latin & Greek, it would be worth while to alter our habits, & conform. But as that can never be the case, the main point to which he looks, as teacher of those languages, is the best mode of communicating a knowledge of the Quantity at the same time with the word itself. If M.ᶠ Price, or any other gentleman, will point out a more ready & sure mode than that which the Charterhouse pronunciation supplies, he, D.ᶠ Russell, will have little hesitation in adopting it. As to accent & Quantity tho' they be the same in our own language, they are not the same in the Greek & Latin. A modern Greek, it is well known, reads the Iliad according to accent only, neglecting Quantity; most Englishmen read it according to Quantity only, neglecting accent. What if it were possible to find a mode of reading it, observing *both*?"

I regret extremely, for the sake of the Charterhouse, this termination to a negociation from which I expected so much. The advantage, derivable from the knowledge of your system, can however only be deferred till that knowledge be made more public—for when light is general, no one can say "It is dark"—except the blind!— In the meanwhile I am surprised at D.ᶠ Russell's not shewing more eagerness on a subject which we should have thought one naturally interesting to a man of his peculiar avocation, & reputed classical tastes: & I am still more surprised at the character of his few observations. His first objection that it would not be worth while to alter our habits of pronunciation unless we could persuade all nations of the Continent to agree with us may surely be used by an opponent to the Charterhouse System—which *has* altered our habits of pronunciation without consulting "all nations of the Continent"— By your adoption of the

Italian pronunciation of the vowels, *you* come much nearer conformity. With regard to the best mode of communicating a knowledge of Quantity, you would hardly allow that D! R. has hit upon it—& he strives with a shadow of his own conjuring when he contends that accent & Quantity are not the same in the ancient languages.

It is very disinterested in me to regret your having troubled yourself about this subject without the desired result, for my brother & I were much gratified by reading your m.s. before we dispatched it—as you permitted us to do. You desired Bro to mention any part of your statement relating to the Charterhouse which seemed to him doubtful. He thinks that in the words *rub´us Cur´ius χυν´ε*, you must concieve the *u* to be pronounced by Charterhouse scholars much as the *u* in '*cunning* or *curry*'—which is not the case. The *u* preserves its usual sound, & has only less stress bestowed on it. For my own part, from what I have been allowed to read of yours & to hear from you in conversation, the substance of the m.s. was not new to me. But you have concentrated on the disjecta membra[1] in so powerful a manner, & placed them in so luminous a point of view, that it would be my own fault if my convictions were not strengthened. Your proofs are indeed "armati del piu fin metallo[2]—" "from HEAD to *foot*" I may add—for I like your attack on the Acephalous Monsters. I am delighted with all you say respecting *Expression*—especially with your comment on Virgil's "vale valĕ". It is a most poetical discovery.[3]

Your letter of the 20ᵗʰ pleased me so much—everywhere but where it spoke of your indisposition—that I hardly know how I have waited till now to thank you for it– I have not yet read the Subaltern, & your very animated comment on what must in itself be so striking, will add greatly to my interest when I do– The principal circumstance—i.e. the coincidence of the storm & the battle reminded me strongly of a passage, in the Supplementum Lucani, which represents a storm during a sea fight.

Nec jam remorum sonitus, clangorve tubarum,
Audiri poterant: hominum clamore premuntur:
Sed remos voces que hominum sonitumque tubarum
Bacchantes venti, tempestatesque sonoræ
Exsuperant.[4]

The Author of the Supplement evidently remembered his Master's

Innumeræ vasto miscentur in æthere voces;
Remorumque sonus premitur clamore: nec ullæ
Audiri potuere tubæ.[5]   Pharsalia. Lib. 3.

but I think rises above him, not only on account of the tempest, but on

account of the fine moral climax which gradually elevates the mind—
allowing it to dwell upon the dashing of the oars & the clang of the
trumpets, before they are lost in the shouts of the combatants—& on
the shouts of the combatants before the "Bacchantes venti,
tempestatesque sonoræ" swallow all. In Lucan the climax is inverted;
&, if I may judge by my own experience, the mind is rather startled
than elevated. There is undoubtedly a new combination of striking
circumstances in your Capture of St Sebastian. The Author of the
Supplementum Lucani has a tempest & a sea fight, but no thunder.
Hesiod in his Combat of the Immortals—I can hardly acknowledge any
thing finer in poetry—adds to the βελεα στονοεντα[6] and the μεγαλω
ἀλαλητω[7]—the

$$βροντη'ν \ τε \ στεροπη'ν \ τε \ και \ ἀιθαλοεντα \ κεραυνον[8]$$

but not a word about sulphur. I wish there were!– I cannot however
allow that sulphur is only mentioned in *Homer* when I find this
expressive passage in Petronius Arbiter—

quum sulfure rupta corusco
Intremuit nubes, elisosque abscidit ignes".[9]

The following fine lines are from Chamberlayn's Pharonnida

Th' imprisoned flame
When the clouds' stock of moisture could not tame
Its violence, in *sulphury* flashes broke
Thorough the glaring air; the swoln clouds spoke,
In the loud voice of thunder.[10]

besides Beattie's

When *sulphurous clouds* roll on th' autumnal day[11]–

& Shakespeare's

"cracks
Of sulphurous roaring"[12]–

After some searching, I have only found "the alarming impression of
the storm, while yet collecting, on all animals" mentioned in
Chatterton's Excellent Balade of Charitie,—which I am sure you must
think poetically excellent—

"The coming ghastness doth the cattle pall"[13]—

but here the cattle have had a more ordinary indication of the
approaching storm than your awful circumstances of close oppressive
heat, præternatural stillness & silence—for "the bigg drops fall"–[13]

Your description has sunk me so deeply into gunpowder & sulphur, that you must forgive my proving my interest in a manner very unequivocal & perhaps very tiresome. The more I know of your indulgence, the more liberties I take with it! I anxiously hope to hear that you have no continuation of uncomfortable feelings to complain of—& beg you dear Sir, to believe me always

Most gratefully yours

E B Barrett.

Publication: None traced.
Manuscript: Armstrong Browning Library.

1. "Dismembered limbs" (Horace, *Satires* I, iv, 62).
2. "Armed with the finest metal" (Ariosto's *Orlando Furioso*, VII, 3, 1).
3. "Farewell, farewell" (*Eclogues*, III, 79). Price's comment (p. 235) was "When the last syllable of the iambus has its due length and stress . . . and when we appear to linger on it, and then connect and blend it with the pyrrhic nearly as one word—vale-vale—the last farewell, being breathed out in a weaker and lower tone, seems a faint echo of the first; and, in my mind, is very happily suited to the expression."
4. "Now neither the splash of the oars nor the sound of the trumpets could be heard, they were drowned by the shouts of men; but the Bacchantian winds and the loud storm overcame the sounds of oars and voices and trumpets" (Thomas May, *Supplementum Lucani*, VI, 33–37).
5. "Innumerable voices were mixed together in the vast sky; the sound of oars was concealed by shouting, nor could any trumpets be heard" (Lucan's *Pharsalia*, III, 540–543).
6. "Mournful shafts" (*Theogony*, 684).
7. "Great war cries" (*Theogony*, 686).
8. "Dazzling thunder and shining lightning" (*Theogony*, 707).
9. "When a cloud shook and was riven by shining sulphur, and shot forth a burst of flame." EBB must have been quoting from memory; in all the editions of *Satyricon* we have checked, ranging from 1709 to 1912, the reading (cap. 122) is "fulgere" ("to flash" with lightning), not "sulfure."
10. *Pharonnida, an Heroic Poem* (1659), III, canto 3, by William Chamberlayne (1619–89). EBB's copy of the 1820 edition sold as Lot 562 of *Browning Collections* (see *Reconstruction*, A610).
11. *The Minstrel* (1771), I, verse 54, by James Beattie (1735–1803).
12. *The Tempest*, I, 2, 203–204.
13. *An Excelente Balade of Charitie* (1777), verse 5, by Thomas Chatterton (1752–70).

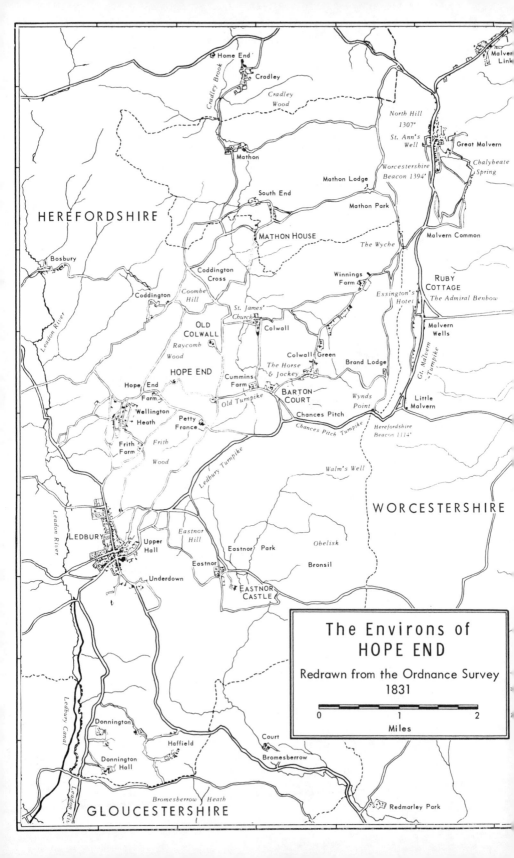

The Environs of
HOPE END

Redrawn from the Ordnance Survey
1831

0   1   2
Miles

Appendices

APPENDIX I

Biographical Sketches of Principal Correspondents and Persons Frequently Mentioned

THE MOULTON-BARRETT FAMILY

ELIZABETH MOULTON (1763–1830)

EBB's beloved paternal grandmother was born on 1 October 1763 in Jamaica at the vast Cinnamon Hill estate of her parents, Edward and Judith Barrett. She married Charles Moulton on 28 August 1781, but the union was not successful. Most of her time in Jamaica was spent at Cinnamon Hill—the birthplace of her four children. These were: Sarah (1783); Edward, EBB's father; Samuel, her favourite uncle; and George (1789), who died in infancy. Sarah, known as "Pinkie," died in England at age 12, shortly after having been immortalized in Thomas Lawrence's now-famous portrait, which can be seen at the Huntington Art Gallery, San Marino, California. When Sarah, Edward and Samuel were sent to England for schooling in 1792, their mother did not accompany them (see letter 232). She went to England before long, however, and remained there, together with her lifelong companion, Mary Trepsack ("Treppy"). She resided for the most part in various leased quarters in the London borough of St. Marylebone, where over the years other members of her extended family had elected to live. (Barrett Street, near Portman Square, was named for a family member.) William Surtees Cook noted that in 1827 Mrs. Moulton's "residence was in Baker Street which was then much considered, there being no Belgravia, no Tiburnia, above all no 'buses!'" Until her son Samuel married, he made his London home with her when Parliament was in session. She enjoyed the numerous visits of EBB's father, in town from Hope End on business, occasional visits of his growing family, and the weekly visits of her two grandsons, Edward and Samuel, during their schooling at Charterhouse. There was deep love between Elizabeth Moulton and her namesake, which sometimes prompted grandmotherly advice: "Now My darling Child you must allow me to say I think you are too BIG to attempt fighting with Bro . . . He is strong & powerful– I have seen him very rude & boisterous to you & Harry [Henrietta]" (see letter 45). She and Treppy were, on occasion, distressed by EBB's scholarly pursuits at the expense of more feminine activities, and to the detriment of her health. When Elizabeth Moulton died, 29 December 1830, her son Edward found a letter assigning £4,000 "to my darling Elizabeth with all my trinkets I wish it were more for her sake."

MARY MOULTON-BARRETT (1781–1828)

She was born 1 May 1781 at Newcastle-upon-Tyne, daughter of John and Arabella Graham (later Graham-Clarke). Her father was a wealthy merchant who, through involvement in West Indies trade, had developed ties with the Barrett family. As a result of this connection, Mary Graham-Clarke and Edward Moulton-Barrett became acquainted and, on 14 May 1805, were married. She is consistently described as very beautiful. At the time of marriage, she was twenty-four years old and Edward was not quite twenty. At first Edward's guardian, James Scarlett, opposed the match, possibly because of the age difference, but after becoming acquainted with her he reportedly said: "I can hold out no longer—she is far too good for him." The couple leased and settled at Coxhoe Hall, where EBB and Bro were born. By 1809, after a temporary stay in London, they had moved south to the Hope End estate in Herefordshire. From 1806 to 1824, Mary Moulton-Barrett gave birth to twelve children. Only one (Mary, at age three) died before reaching maturity, in a period when childhood deaths were common; this testifies to the good care that the Moulton-Barrett children apparently received. The mother took pride in her children's accomplishments, especially those of EBB, and spent much time copying their poems and other literary endeavours. Undoubtedly they were helped along by her own writing talents. While she did not write professionally, she expressed her thoughts capably in long and chatty personal letters. A journal which she kept during an 1815 trip to France and a subsequent letter to her mother (SD235 and SD236) show her as a keen observer and commentator. She was an accomplished artist. Comments in EBB's childhood writings leave no doubt that Mary Moulton-Barrett gave careful attention to the children's schooling, at home on the Hope End estate. It appears also that she played a sort of game with EBB, serving as "publisher" for some of the latter's juvenilia. But despite the satisfaction with her children, Mary Moulton-Barrett's family situation was not entirely a pleasant one. Family correspondence shows her as somewhat subservient to her husband, who did not always consult her about his plans. (See for instance letter 224.) In a letter to RB dated 27 August 1846, EBB wrote of her as follows: "A sweet, gentle nature, which the thunder a little turned from its sweetness—as when it turns milk—One of those women who never can resist,—but, in submitting & bowing on themselves, make a mark, a plait, within, .. a sign of suffering. Too womanly she was—it was her only fault." Mary Moulton-Barrett lived only about four and a half years after the birth of Octavius, her youngest child. Her health was failing by the mid-1820's; rheumatoid arthritis was a contributing factor. In the autumn of 1828 she felt well enough for a trip to Cheltenham to take medical treatment (see letter 321), but she died there on 7 October. She was buried in a vault near the altar of the Parish Church of St. Michael and All Angels, Ledbury, with her daughter Mary.

EDWARD BARRETT MOULTON-BARRETT (1785–1857)

Born on 28 May 1785 at the Cinnamon Hill estate of his maternal grandfather, Edward Barrett, in Jamaica, he was the second child and first son of Charles and Elizabeth Moulton. The parents apparently did not for long have any household of their own, and Edward's relationship with his father was never very satisfactory. Grandfather Edward Barrett, one of Jamaica's wealthiest and most influential planters, was determined to preserve his plantation "empire" and his family name.

By the time he reached an advanced age, however, his only legitimate male heirs were Elizabeth's two sons, Edward and Samuel. Their surname, of course, was Moulton, but in 1798, under Royal Licence and Authority, it was changed to Moulton-Barrett. The grandfather died later in that year, and the two boys inherited the bulk of his estate. By then they were in England for schooling, having crossed the Atlantic with their older sister, Sarah, in 1792. Edward briefly attended prestigious Harrow school, but reportedly "received there so savage a punishment for a supposed offense ('burning the toast') by the youth whose 'fag' he had become, that he was withdrawn from the school by his mother, and the delinquent was expelled." At the age of sixteen he was sent to Trinity College, Cambridge, by his guardian, James Scarlett. Before reaching his majority, he married in 1805 Mary Graham-Clarke, daughter of John Graham-Clarke, a wealthy and influential businessman residing near Newcastle-upon-Tyne. The couple leased and settled first at Coxhoe Hall, where EBB was born in 1806. Three years later the impressive Hope End estate, near Ledbury, Herefordshire, was purchased, and in the ensuing years greatly altered to the Turkish designs of Loudon.

Much has been said and written about the character of Edward Moulton-Barrett. He was devoutly religious, a loving but dictatorial husband and father, a reserved man who kept his feelings to himself, a "country gentleman" much occupied with business and community affairs. He was twice elected, in 1812 and 1814, as Sheriff of Herefordshire. Starting in the mid-1820's, his life was darkened and embittered by misfortune: financial reverses in Jamaica (including adverse legal decisions), which eventually caused the loss of Hope End; the death of his wife in 1828; the death of his brother Sam in 1837; and the deaths of his sons Sam and Edward in 1840. Losing the Hope End Mansion and Park in 1832 (the woodland was still in his possession at his death), he took his family first to Sidmouth and then to London, finally settling in 1838 at 50 Wimpole Street, where he resided until his death. As is well known, he promptly disinherited all three of the Moulton-Barrett children—Elizabeth, Henrietta and Alfred—who married during his lifetime. In fairness to him, however, it must be realized that his objections, especially when viewed against the background of Victorian parental attitudes, were valid. RB was not a "gentleman" according to the accepted code and neither EBB's nor Henrietta's husband was financially able to provide the kind of comfort to which the girls were accustomed. As to Alfred's bride, shortly after her birth her mother became mentally unbalanced and incapacitated. Edward's feelings toward his children were summarized in a single sentence by his son George in a letter to RB, 24 December 1888: "[Our] father was kind & tenderly attached to his children, in excess indeed as he could not bear the idea of a profession or a marriage that would lead to separation."

William Surtees Cook's entry in his diary (*Reconstruction*, L4) under 17 April 1857 reads: "My dearest Henrietta's poor father died at his house, 50. Wimpole Street, London at half-past eleven o'clock this night. He had been long ill, from having broken his leg some years ago, by being thrown down by a cab, besides other causes of suffering. His dissolution was finally accelerated by going to Epsom to vote for a member for the county. The fatigue and excitement were too much for him—and it brought on an attack of erysipelas—which weakened him so much that he gradually sunk. Edward Moulton-Barrett was in the 72^d year of his age." From his will Edward omitted EBB, Henrietta and Alfred. Charles John, the eldest living male issue, received the Jamaican properties and family portraits. The other five living children—Arabel, George, Henry, Septimus and Octavius—received equal shares of the English estate, which came to a total of £63,695.12.1¼. Charles John, not concurring with his father, chose to give £5,000 to each of his disinherited sisters from his own inheritance. Alfred was given a like sum from the English estate. Edward Moulton-Barrett was buried on 24 April, at the Parish Church of St. Michael and All Angels, Ledbury, in the same vault as his wife and daughter Mary, located near the altar in the north-east corner. Reportedly every shop in Ledbury was closed in his honour, though he had been gone from that vicinity for many years.

SAMUEL BARRETT MOULTON-BARRETT (1787–1837)

Born on 31 March 1787 at the Cinnamon Hill estate of his maternal grandfather, Edward Barrett, in Jamaica, he was the third child and second son of Charles and Elizabeth Moulton. The biographical sketch of his elder brother Edward (EBB's father) describes the childhood of both, their taking of the name Barrett, being sent to England for schooling, and inheriting the bulk of their grandfather's estate. Sam had little or no formal schooling but did receive tutoring, including that of William Lewis Rahm, with whom he spent time in Scotland and on the Continent. He was in Denmark at the time of Britain's 1807 bombardment of Copenhagen. There was a special relationship between Sam and EBB from the beginning of her life. In the first letter she is known to have received, from her father, this uncle is mentioned as "your Sam" (letter 1). There was no formality between them: she never called him anything but just "Sam." He reportedly claimed to love her more than did even her father. He was with her during a substantial part of her stay, for health reasons, at the Spa Hotel, Gloucester, in 1821 and 1822. In 1824 there apparently was a serious quarrel between Sam and his brother, EBB's father, and there is evidence that she played a key role in patching it up (see letters 195 and 196). Sam is generally described as a person whose friendships were genuine and lasting, a person far more outgoing and congenial than his brother Edward. In comparing the two, EBB wrote to Sam (letter 227), "There is a great difference between yourself, & him, at least in *one* respect—for if *your* reveries are *upon* a rose *his* are *under* it." His amiable instincts may sometimes have gone too far. On 19 September 1808, shortly after Sam's coming of age, James Scarlett wrote to Edward Moulton-Barrett as follows: "... he is very popular. I wish we could prevail upon him to be less liberal in making *gifts*. It is not the value of the money that I should care about; but it is the character it gives him of carelessness & extravagances. He will always find people to receive his presents, but they will laugh at him & others will join them. ... I have reason to believe that many respectable persons who would be very glad to court his society are rather afraid of doing so lest they should be either thought to have their own interest in view, or be put to the necessity of refusing his presents. At present this is the only fault I have to find with Sam" (SD114).

    Sam's seat was Carlton, an estate located in Yorkshire, near Richmond, and about seven miles south of Darlington. Sam entered the British Parliament, representing the Borough of Richmond, North Riding, Yorkshire, in 1820, and remained its member until 1828. While the House was sitting, the Moulton-Barretts took full advantage of his privilege of franking letters, so that they could be sent free of postal charges. Bundles of letters would be sent to him by various members of the family for franking; as Mary Moulton-Barrett said in letter 228, "he is *very* kind to be so plagued by our letters." Until his marriage, he used his mother's London residence in Baker Street while sitting in the House. His marriage to Mary Clementina Cay-Adams occurred at Gloucester, 20 March 1823. Their residence while in the south was at Walthamstow.

Growing British agitation against slavery in the colonies must have been deeply troubling to Sam as a member of Parliament. The Moulton-Barretts recognized the evils of slavery, yet their family empire in Jamaica had been built upon it. Sam himself was to leave England for Jamaica before the issue was resolved. He and his wife went there in 1827 in an effort to untangle problems on the Moulton-Barrett plantations. They took Cinnamon Hill as their chief residence. Biographers note the kindness and compassion shown by Sam and Mary toward the Jamaican slaves. This treatment is credited with helping the Moulton-Barretts to weather storms of slave revolt far better than did most planters. Mary Clementina died in 1831. Two years later Sam married Ann Eliza Gordon, who survived him (and whom EBB did not particularly like). Sam died at Kingston, 23 December 1837, while involved with government business at Spanish Town, leaving a legacy of several thousand pounds and shares in the ship *David Lyon* to EBB. His burial place is Cinnamon Hill. The death of this favourite uncle was among those deeply mourned by EBB.

EDWARD BARRETT MOULTON-BARRETT (1807–40)

Born at Coxhoe Hall, 26 June 1807, a country estate leased by his father south of Newcastle-upon-Tyne, he was the second child and first son of Edward and Mary Moulton-Barrett. An early nickname "Buff" soon gave way to "Bro," by which he was known thereafter. On 1 August 1807, not long after the birth of this first son, his father wrote to Jamaica (SD79) and suggested a holiday for the plantation slaves. There is no evidence of any similar suggestion in the previous year when EBB was born. Most of Bro's childhood was spent at Hope End, where EBB eagerly participated in Greek and Latin lessons that she received from tutor Daniel McSwiney. Bro possessed artistic and poetic talent, but artist William Artaud wrote from Hope End on 29 March 1818 (SD283) that "tho by no means deficient" this brother had "no chance in competition" with EBB. Whatever his abilities may have been, Bro's chief claim to fame is as EBB's favourite brother— perhaps her favourite of all people. The hero of her *Aurora Leigh* is thought by some to have been modelled after him. The two were separated during Bro's stay at Charterhouse, the prestigious London boarding school, from 1820 to 1826, but he kept her amply supplied with humorous and needling letters, which give an interesting picture of English schoolboy life in that period. Bro was away in Jamaica for a while in the mid-1830's, helping his uncle Sam with readjustment problems relating to the emancipation of plantation slaves. When EBB went to Torquay for health reasons in 1838, Bro accompanied her. It was not intended that he should stay, but, because of EBB's urgent pleading, he was allowed to. Reportedly he had a romance there, but was frustrated by the well-known family pressures against marriage. On 11 July 1840 Bro went on a cruise in Babbacombe Bay in *La Belle Sauvage* belonging to Carter Godfrey. With him were Capt. Clarke, Mr. Vanneck, and a boatman, William White. When two or three miles off Teignmouth the boat capsized in a squall, all being drowned. The bodies of all but Vanneck were recovered. On 6 August they were buried in Torre Church-yard, but the graves cannot now be identified. Bro's death was a shattering event in the life of EBB; she could never put this tragedy out of her mind. Moreover, feeling that it would not have happened had she not insisted on his staying with her, she never ceased to blame herself. She was scarcely able to mention the event—or Bro as an individual—even to RB. She became extremely upset when the episode was described in an 1852 book, *Recollections of a Literary Life*, written by her friend Mary Russell Mitford.

HENRIETTA BARRETT MOULTON-BARRETT (1809–60)

Born on 4 March 1809 at 10 Upper Berkeley Street, London, she was the third child and second daughter of Edward and Mary Moulton-Barrett. Nicknames included "Addles," "Daddles," "Harry" and "Ta." Of the young Moulton-Barretts who survived early childhood, Henrietta ranked just above Sam in age, while EBB and Bro came first and second. The close ties which developed between Henrietta and Sam were somewhat like those between the elder two. So just as Bro bombarded EBB with letters during his 1820–26 Charterhouse school years, Sam did much the same with Henrietta while he was at the same school from 1822 to 1828. Henrietta has been described as one of the most religious of the Moulton-Barrett children, yet she was also fond of music and dancing, and, while with EBB in the resort town of Torquay, greatly enjoyed its social opportunities. She met the usual family obstacles in efforts at romance. In a letter to RB dated 15–16 January 1846, EBB describes "dreadful scenes" between Henrietta and her father. Ironically, it was Henrietta who had to give Mr. Moulton-Barrett his first news of EBB's elopement. Finally, in 1850, four years after EBB's marriage, Henrietta married a cousin, Army Captain William Surtees Cook (usually called Surtees), and was of course immediately disowned by her father. (It is believed that the pair had been secretly engaged for some time.) Henrietta was more fortunate than EBB, receiving, in general, the sympathy of the other Barrett children. EBB kept in contact with Henrietta through correspondence, and the Brownings visited the Cooks' Taunton home while in England in 1856. Two sons and a daughter were born to Henrietta and Surtees through the years 1851 to 1856. In 1857 the family moved to Thurlbear, Somersetshire. There Henrietta, after prolonged suffering, died of cancer at their home, Stoke Court, on 23 November 1860. She was buried at Thurlbear Parish Church. Her illness and death deeply distressed EBB and may well have contributed to the latter's final decline in health and her own death in 1861.

SAMUEL BARRETT MOULTON-BARRETT (1812–40)

Born at Cheltenham on 13 January 1812, he was the fifth child and second son of Edward and Mary Moulton-Barrett. Generally known as Sam, he apparently lacked a nickname. He was not quite three years younger than Henrietta, and a special closeness existed between them. He showered her with talkative letters during the times when they were apart. As was the case with his brother Edward, his formal schooling was at prestigious Charterhouse in London, Sam's stay there extending from 1822 to 1828, during which time he advanced from the twelfth to the sixth form. Written evidence depicts him as personable and mischievous. EBB was fond of Sam, though not so close to him as to Bro. His early death spared him from having to take sides in the family upheaval over her marriage to RB. During the late 1830's, Sam spent much of his time in Jamaica, involved in management of the Moulton-Barrett plantations. He was there with his uncle Sam at the time of the latter's death in December 1837. (Sam received £1,000 under the uncle's will.) In 1838 Sam visited the United States, making several stops along the eastern seaboard, including New York City. He was active in Jamaican public affairs, reporting, for instance, in a letter to Henrietta dated 24 October 1839 (SD1065): "I attend the quarter Sessions on Tuesday next and take my seat as Magistrate." Sam died of a tropical fever at the Cinnamon Hill estate in Jamaica on 17 February 1840, and was buried at Cinnamon Hill. His death, at the early age of twenty-eight, was a severe blow to the Moulton-Barretts, especially to EBB, ill at Torquay. By just under five months it preceded another family tragedy—Bro's drowning.

ARABELLA BARRETT MOULTON-BARRETT (1813–68)

Born at Hope End, 4 July 1813, Arabella was the sixth child and fourth daughter of Edward and Mary Moulton-Barrett. She was named after her grandmother, Arabella Graham-Clarke. Her ties with EBB were extremely close. On 4 July 1831 EBB wrote (*Diary*, p. 42): "Dearest Arabel's birthday. She is 18; and an interesting intelligent amiable feeling girl. I should love her even if she were not my sister; & even if she did not love me." The two were, however, separated during part of Arabella's childhood, because she spent considerable time with Minny Robinson from early 1817 through 1820, first at Ramsgate and then at Worthing, both seaside resorts, where she took cures for an illness caused by a leech being placed on an artery. In family letters written during this early period, she was often referred to as "Babes." When EBB herself lived at Torquay for health reasons, Arabella was present during much of the time. There, according to a hint in a letter by EBB to their brother George, dated 17 June 1840, she was involved, at least briefly, in a romance. Be that as it may, she never married, devoting herself instead to artistic interests, religion, the care of her father, and social service. EBB and RB helped her with efforts on behalf of the poor by contributing a sixteen-page pamphlet, which was sold at a bazaar for sixpence a copy. Entitled *Two Poems*, it was their only joint production. EBB's poem was "A Plea for the Ragged Schools of London"; RB's, "The Twins." In the mid-1840's at the Wimpole Street house, Arabella became quite aware of her sister's clandestine courtship, though she—along with others—was kept in the dark as to wedding plans. After the marriage and the flight to Italy, intensive correspondence developed between these two sisters. In fact, EBB's letters to Arabella surpassed in total volume those sent to any other person. (She wrote *more* letters to Mary Russell Mitford, but those to Arabella were *longer*.) On EBB's trips to London after her marriage, she sometimes visited Arabella at the Wimpole Street house. That is where the latter continued to live until the household was broken up after the 1857 death of her father, from whose estate she received about £11,000. She then took up residence at 7 Delamere Terrace. She was nurse and companion to her sister Henrietta during the latter's fatal illness in 1860. When RB and Pen returned to London after the death of EBB, they settled near Arabella. Her Delamere Terrace home served as a gathering place for the Moulton-Barrett clan. Deeply devoted to RB, she died in his arms on 11 June 1868. She was buried at Kensal Green Cemetery.

CHARLES JOHN BARRETT MOULTON-BARRETT (1814–1905)

Nicknamed "Stormie" or "Storm" because of his arrival in the midst of one, he was born at Hope End, 28 December 1814, the seventh child and third son of Edward and Mary Moulton-Barrett. He was named after his paternal grandfather upon whose death he was left £1,000 because of this. With a timid and nervous disposition and with a frequently-mentioned speech impediment, he nevertheless is characterized as gentle, loving, honest, and generous—perhaps overly so. RB, in a letter to Isabella Blagden dated 19 December 1863, told how Charles John offered "to make an immense sacrifice" to pay a cousin a supposed debt which was not legally valid. As to Stormie's relationship with EBB, she always wrote endearingly of him, though she never won his total acceptance of her marriage to RB. To some extent, he shared in her poetic ability. Along with his brother George, Charles John matriculated at Glasgow University, but, on account of his speech impediment, he did not take a degree. In 1844, he and his brother Henry left on a sea voyage to Egypt. By then, Stormie had also begun shuttling back and forth between England and Jamaica, and Jamaican plantation interests were to take up most of his attention for the remainder of his life. Upon the 1857 death of his father, as oldest surviving son, he was the principal inheritor of the Moulton-Barrett fortunes, acquiring from his father's estate all the vast Jamaican properties and the family portraits. From his inheritance he gave £5,000 each to his sisters EBB and Henrietta. After his father's death, Stormie returned to Britain for the first time in ten and a half years. In 1858 he leased from cousins (the Williamses) an estate called Bryngwyn, near Oswestry, Shropshire, to be used when he was on that side of the Atlantic. Charles John was the last family member to reside on the estates in Jamaica. When the decline in Moulton-Barrett fortunes took away the last one, Retreat Penn, he continued to live in Jamaica—at Clifton, near Falmouth. Charles John married Anne Margaret (née Young) in Jamaica in 1865, where he died on 21 January 1905, survived by a daughter, Arabella. He was buried at Retreat Penn.

GEORGE GOODIN BARRETT MOULTON-BARRETT (1816–95)

He was born at Hope End on 15 July 1816, eighth child and fourth son of Edward and Mary Moulton-Barrett. "Georgie" was the nearest he had to a nickname; the given name "Goodin" came from the family of his great-grandmother Judith Barrett (née Goodin). Taking a degree at the University of Glasgow in 1835, he practised as a barrister at the Inner Temple from 1838 until an early retirement in 1860, brought on in part by a hearing impairment. He was also on the Oxford Circuit with the Assize Court. His occupation was openly scorned by EBB, who had little respect for such worldly matters as law practice. After the death of her favourite brother Bro, however, George was the one to whom she most frequently turned and in whom she confided. Like all the other surviving brothers, he broke sharply with EBB after her marriage, but he was the only one who became fully reconciled to it. In 1847 he sent a note saying that he forgave her but not RB, but after calling on them when they first returned to England in 1851 he was on friendly terms with both. A lively correspondence developed between George and the Brownings, and it continued between him and RB after EBB's death. RB relied on him for unofficial legal advice, and referred to him as a "useful brother." George and Charles John were joint executors of their father's will, but the settling of the properties was primarily done by George. He received nearly £11,000 from his father's estate. After the breaking-up of the Wimpole Street establishment, it appears he shared with Arabel until he retired in 1860, when he established a base at Warnicombe House, near Tiverton, Devonshire. He spent much time travelling in England and on the Continent. In later years he moved his residence frequently—Weymouth, Ilfracombe, and Tenby. Never marrying, George died at Tenby, 11 August 1895, and was there buried. In his will he released Charles John of his indebtedness, gave bequests to his brothers Henry and Octavius and to his nieces and nephews, and presented the balance of his estate to his brother Alfred.

HENRY BARRETT MOULTON-BARRETT (1818–96)

Born at Hope End on 27 July 1818, he was the ninth child and fifth son of Edward and Mary Moulton-Barrett. Family members frequently called him "Harry" and "Henny," names they also applied to his sister Henrietta. As a child, he was tutored in Latin by EBB. Henry apparently had a restless nature, and was more independent of his father than were most of his brothers. Family correspondence contains frequent reference to his restlessness. In a letter to brother George dated 17 June 1840, EBB wrote: "Has Henry made up his mind to some occupation which is *not* insurmountably objectionable to Papa? I am sure he is too kind, & I hope he is too wise, to cleave any longer to military or naval fancies." In another letter to George, dated 1 August 1843, she mentioned Henry's "passion for pilgrimages." By that time, starting in the autumn of 1836, Henry had already spent about two years studying in Germany with a companion-tutor. In 1844 he and Charles John left on a sea voyage to Egypt. Along with various others in the family, Henry took part in negotiations to ransom Flush from dog-stealers in the 1846 episode shortly before EBB's marriage. Henry opposed that marriage, as did the other Moulton-Barrett brothers, but there was a reconciliation. In 1860, Henry married a widow, Amelia Morris (*née* Holland), at Torwood Church, Newton Abbot. They had three sons and two daughters, born between 1862 and 1870. From his father's estate Henry received nearly £11,000. He eventually acquired a home at Combe Head near Bampton, Devonshire. Later he took up residence at Dunsland, North Devonshire. Surtees Cook describes this in his Diary (*Reconstruction*, L4), in an entry dated 5 December 1878, as "a grand old place—a most imposing mansion with splendid hall, dining & drawing rooms & bedrooms to match." By the time of his death, Henry was, in the words of his will, at "Arcott Sidmouth in the County of Devon." (In this will, the name "Harry" rather than "Henry" is used.) He died on 17 May 1896 and was buried at Sidmouth. Also buried there is his wife, who had died at Dunsland on 13 September 1887. By English laws of primogeniture, the eldest son, Harry Peyton Moulton-Barrett, became the head of the Moulton-Barrett family upon the death of Charles John.

ALFRED PRICE BARRETT MOULTON-BARRETT (1820–1904)

Nicknames were commonplace in the Moulton-Barrett family. The origin of Alfred's, "Daisy," and his feelings about it, are not known. Born at Hope End, 20 May 1820, he was the tenth child and sixth son of Edward and Mary Moulton-Barrett. He was the godson of Miss Caroline Price of Foxley. The year of his birth was also that in which EBB's *The Battle of Marathon* appeared. In disposition as well as age, a sizeable gulf existed between the boisterous Alfred and the scholarly EBB. He is said to have been largely in the background of EBB's life. While the latter was in Torquay, from 1838 to 1841, most members of the Moulton-Barrett family visited her. Alfred may have gone, but there is no record of his having done so. It should be noted, however, that he was at University College, London, during at least a part of this time. He didn't lack artistic and literary talent. A number of his sketches of family members survive, as does a seventy-two-stanza epic concerning his sister Henrietta's 1850 elopement. Living as an accepted member of the Moulton-Barretts' Wimpole Street household was Elizabeth Georgiana Barrett, a close cousin, thirteen years younger than Alfred. (Her nickname, "Lizzie," was more conventional than Alfred's.) He became attracted to her, and they were married in Paris on 1 August 1855. EBB and other family members objected to the marriage on account of the mental instability of Georgiana's mother, plus the poor state of Alfred's finances. He was immediately disinherited, as EBB and Henrietta had been after their earlier marriages. He did, however, eventually receive £5,053.12.5 from his father's English estate, most going to settle debts. It is interesting to note that in the 1840's Alfred was a close friend of Surtees Cook, the cousin who married Henrietta. There is evidence of considerable contact between EBB and Alfred in the 1850's. In a letter to Alfred dated 23 June 1855, EBB quoted her son, Pen, as having told her that he liked Alfred "nearly as much as you & papa." Details on Alfred's occupational activities are hazy. Jeannette Marks lists him among the five Moulton-Barrett sons present in Jamaica at one time or another. He was at the offices of the Great Western Railway in the 1840's, though his connection with that company and his time of leaving it are not clearly known. He went to France "on Her Majesty's Service" early in 1855, possibly in connection with Crimean War troop movements. He travelled to Madeira, presumably on government business, in 1856. In a letter to Arabella Moulton-Barrett dated 4 October of that year, EBB reported that he was hoping to receive a consulship. There was also a trip to Hong Kong in 1857. In the absence of a steady occupation during Alfred's later years, the family lived mainly by borrowing against Lizzie's inheritance, in trust for her mother who lived to an advanced age, although incapacitated shortly after Lizzie's birth. As this situation developed, relief was finally provided by Lizzie's brother, Edward George Barrett, who gave them an annual income from his Jamaican estates, in lieu of her inheritance. Edward George never married, and willed his estates to his nephew, Edward Alfred Moulton-Barrett, son of Alfred and Lizzie. Alfred had no close association with RB after EBB's death, and—despite earlier affection—his later feelings toward Pen are indicated by a caricature depicting the latter as a pig (reproduced in *Tragi-Comedy*, p. 102). Lizzie and Alfred had two sons and two daughters, born in the years 1859 through 1867. Their financial situation improved in 1895 on account of a bequest by Alfred's brother George. Alfred died at St. Jean-de-Luz, France, on 24 May 1904, and was buried there. Georgiana survived until 18 April 1918, when she died in London.

SEPTIMUS JAMES BARRETT MOULTON-BARRETT (1822–70)

Born at Hope End on 11 February 1822, he was the eleventh child and seventh son of Edward and Mary Moulton-Barrett. Nicknames included "Sette," "Seppy," and "Set." Septimus was a special favourite of his father, with whom he slept as a child. In a birthday letter to "Papa" dated 28 May 1827 (SD625), he wrote: "You are a very funny old fellow." In a letter to Julia Martin dated 28 August 1832, concerning the family's departure from Hope End, EBB tells that her father, staying behind to clear up final details, could not bear to part with Sette, and kept the boy with him. When the family was in London, Septimus studied at the University of London and at the Middle Temple. He is cited in the diary of Surtees Cook (*Reconstruction*, L4) as having been "a barrister at law." He performed an important service for EBB in 1846 by ransoming Flush from the notorious London dog-stealers. This was just before EBB's marriage, of which Septimus, like the other brothers, disapproved. He sent her an unfriendly letter in 1847, but met with her during the Brownings' visit to London in 1851. Septimus spent the last part of his life in Jamaica. In a letter to brother George dated 12 October 1860, EBB wrote of his going there and said: "I hope he may be qualified to manage the estates." Evidence indicates that he wasn't. He did serve there, however, as Custos Rotulorum (principal Justice of the Peace), and as a member of the colonial Legislative Council. Whatever may have been his activity in political affairs, his extravagances and mismanagement are blamed for the final loss of the Moulton-Barrett estates in Jamaica. This loss did not occur, however, until after his death. His last days were spent at Cinnamon Hill, where he died on 17 March 1870, and where he was buried.

OCTAVIUS BUTLER BARRETT MOULTON-BARRETT (1824–1910)

He was born at Hope End on 11 April 1824, the twelfth (and last) child and eighth son of Edward and Mary Moulton-Barrett. Octavius' nicknames included variations such as "Occy" and "Occyta." EBB, in some of her letters, called him "Joc." As oldest and youngest of the Moulton-Barrett children, EBB and Occy were 18 years apart in age. Octavius was only four years old at the time of his mother's death. EBB tutored him in Greek and made many endearing references to him in her writings. On 15 November 1831, for instance, she wrote: "Dearest little thing! ... he sate on my knee, & I told him stories." (*Diary*, p. 180). Despite all this, Octavius stood with his brothers in opposing the marriage between EBB and RB, but indications are that by 1856 he had become friendly toward both. In the mid-1840's Octavius studied architecture, and he was recalled by a niece—Mary Altham—as "a clever artist" (*Reconstruction*, p. xviii). He is frequently mentioned in the diaries of Henrietta's husband, Surtees Cook (*Reconstruction*, L4). An entry for 9 February 1858 tells of his sailing for Jamaica with Charles John and Septimus. Unlike these other two, however, he did not spend a substantial part of his life there. On 19 March 1859 Octavius married Charlotte Mackintosh. She died on 6 October 1861 and was buried in Thurlbear Churchyard, near the grave of Henrietta. An infant son was buried at the same time. Octavius and Charlotte had one other son, born in 1860. Octavius' second wife was Maria Elizabeth Morris and they were married 17 April 1865. They had three daughters and two sons, born between 1866 and 1874. From the estate of his father, who died in 1857, Octavius received a payment of nearly £11,000. In 1872 his wife's grandmother died and they received a much larger inheritance. Octavius lived in various homes after the break-up of the Wimpole Street household. Entries in Surtees' diary for 1863 mention "his place Trefnanny Hall, near Welshpool,

Montgomeryshire" as a "quiet country gentleman's seat." By 31 October 1864 his residence was cited as Combe House, near Dulverton, Somersetshire. In 1868 his home was The Holt, near Winchester in Hampshire. Eventually he went to Westover, near Calbourne, Isle of Wight. He died there on 11 November 1910, and was buried at Calbourne. To the Isle of Wight residence he had taken books and furniture acquired as his share from the Wimpole Street household, and most of the items remain in the hands of his descendants. The family has given to the British nation a portfolio of his drawings of the Houses of Parliament, made while they were under construction, and while he was studying architecture under Sir Charles Barry.

THE GRAHAM-CLARKE FAMILY

JOHN GRAHAM-CLARKE (1736–1818)

EBB's maternal grandfather was born at Hull with his surname simply Graham. He was educated at Penrith Grammar School, which his father—also named John Graham—had attended. He went to Newcastle-upon-Tyne as a young military officer in the 1760's and remained there for the rest of his life. In January 1786 he added the name Clarke to his own in compliance with the will of Thomas Mowld, a relative and a Clarke descendant from whom he inherited property. The name was added by Royal Licence, and this was one of the early uses of such a process. It is worth noting that John Graham-Clarke later played a key role in securing similar permission for the Moulton brothers, Edward and Samuel, to add Barrett to their family name. He became a wealthy businessman and merchant, and Jeannette Marks (p. 279) refers to his "commercial and social influence" as "beyond exaggeration." He had extensive industrial interests, plantations in Jamaica, and ships employed in West Indies trade. His West Indies involvement brought him into close association with the Barretts. His first marriage was to a wealthy widow, Mrs. Rutter, who died in 1771. Through this marriage he acquired a profitable brewery business. His second marriage, all-important in relation to Moulton-Barrett family history, was to Arabella Altham—daughter of Roger Altham—on 12 June 1780. They had nine children, two of whom (Jacob and Henry) died in infancy. The first was EBB's mother, Mary [q.v.], born 1 May 1781 in Newcastle. The other six who lived to adulthood are discussed below. John Graham-Clarke had luxurious homes, including Fenham Hall near Newcastle-upon-Tyne, which he acquired shortly after his daughter's marriage to Edward Moulton-Barrett. A favourite summer home was Kenton Lodge, three miles outside Newcastle. He died at Newcastle on 7 August 1818 and was buried there at St. Andrew's Church, as was his wife.

ARABELLA GRAHAM-CLARKE (1760?-1827)

EBB's maternal grandmother was a daughter of Roger Altham, a Proctor in Doctors' Commons, London, and she was related to the Surtees family, from whom came Henrietta Moulton-Barrett's husband, Surtees Cook. It is through her, moreover, that EBB's ancestry is traced to King Edward I. Arabella was considerably younger than John Graham (later Graham-Clarke), whom she married in 1780. She had literary ability, as indicated by a birthday poem written to daughter Mary (see SD43). EBB was fond of this grandmother, but the attachment does not seem to have been quite so close as that with Elizabeth Moulton. After the death of John Graham-Clarke, Arabella continued to live, accompanied by her daughter Arabella (Bummy), at Fenham Hall until her own death, which occurred on 10 November 1827. She was buried at St. Andrew's Church, Newcastle-upon-Tyne.

JOHN ALTHAM GRAHAM-CLARKE (1782-1862)

EBB's uncle. Born at Newcastle-upon-Tyne on 3 October 1782, he was the second child and first son of John and Arabella Graham (later Graham-Clarke). He married Mary Elizabeth Parkinson, daughter of Leonard Parkinson of Kinnersley Castle, near Hereford, whose activities included a partnership with George Goodin Barrett in the Jamaican slave trade. The couple made this same place their principal home, and it was often visited by members of the Moulton-Barrett family. John is recorded as having been a magistrate for the counties of Gloucester and Hereford. John and Mary had two sons, John and Leonard. In 1843 the latter married a first cousin, Isabel Butler, daughter of his father's sister Frances. Isabel, however, died at an early age. Family correspondence provides evidence of extensive business dealings between John Altham Graham-Clarke and the Moulton-Barretts. It also indicates that he was sometimes in financial difficulties. In a letter to EBB's father dated 19 June 1828 (SD 659) he wrote: "I assure you on my word that I have not Ten pounds in the World." He died at Frocester Manor on 22 January 1862, and was buried locally.

ARABELLA SARAH GRAHAM-CLARKE (1785-1869)

This frequently-mentioned aunt of EBB was known by the nicknames "Bell," "Bummy," and "Bum." Born at Newcastle-upon-Tyne on 27 June 1785, she was the fourth child and second daughter of John and Arabella Graham (later Graham-Clarke). She was an accomplished harpist and avid reader. Never marrying, she devoted much of her time and attention to Graham-Clarke and Moulton-Barrett relatives. As did other family members, she engaged in a great deal of travelling and visiting. For a number of years, her principal base was the family home, Fenham Hall, where she lived with her mother until the latter's death in 1827. In the following year, 1828, she accompanied her sister Mary Moulton-Barrett to Cheltenham, where Mary died on 7 October. After that, Bummy became of great service to the surviving Moulton-Barretts, spending much time with them at Hope End and elsewhere. There were, however, some clashes of will between her and EBB. Letters by EBB to Hugh Stuart Boyd and entries in her diary, written during the period just before the loss of Hope End, tell of Bummy's being there at that time. Much to EBB's exasperation, Bummy apparently knew what was going on, but helped the father to keep his unpleasant secret. When Bummy's sister Charlotte Butler died, in 1834, Bummy took responsibility for Charlotte's two daughters. (They were Cissy, who died in 1843, and Arlette, who married in 1847.) She was present during much of EBB's stay at Torquay, taking care of her own expenses there. She was among various family visitors staying at 50 Wimpole Street—and causing complications for EBB—in the summer of 1846 shortly before the elopement with RB. Close as had been Bummy's usual relationship with EBB, she sided against the latter when facts of the elopement became known. Bummy visited EBB in London in 1851, but reportedly was not friendly. Her late years were spent mainly at Frocester Manor, Gloucestershire and 32 Imperial-Square, Cheltenham. In the diary of Surtees Cook (*Reconstruction*, L4) there is an entry for 31 December 1869 reporting the death of "aunt Bell" on the previous morning "at her residence at Cheltenham. She is to be buried at Frocester." In her will she made substantial specific bequests to a number of relatives, and left the remainder of her estate to nephew John Altham Graham-Clarke, Jr., who was appointed her executor.

CHARLOTTE BUTLER (1787–1834)

Born at Newcastle-upon-Tyne, she was the fifth child and third daughter of John and Arabella Graham-Clarke. Church records tell of her baptism on 28 August 1787. She was often called "Lotte." She reached adulthood at Fenham Hall, the luxurious family home. Niece EBB wrote to Charlotte's sister Bummy (letter 62), mentioning various members of the Fenham household, and she spoke of imagining "Charlotte with a grave face & a pair of spectacles painting or at that *much admired* loom." On 13 June 1822 she married the Rev. Richard Pierce Butler (1784–1855), whose eldest brother, Sir Thomas Butler, had previously married Charlotte's sister Frances. Richard was Vicar of Trim, in Ireland, and their home was the Garryhundon estate, near Carlow. They had two daughters: Charlotte Mary ("Arlette"), who married Army Captain Charles William Reynolds on 24 June 1847; and Cissy, who died while in her teens. Charlotte died at Dieppe in August 1834 during a family sojourn in France. Her husband, Richard, lived until 1855, spending much time on the Continent.

FRANCES BUTLER (1790–1868)

Born at Newcastle-upon-Tyne on 3 March 1790, she was the sixth child and fourth daughter of John and Arabella Graham-Clarke. In family letters she is generally mentioned as "Fanny." She was the subject and recipient of a teen-age poem by EBB entitled "To dearest Fanny on receiving from her an apron" (see *Reconstruction*, D953). She grew to adulthood in the Graham-Clarke family home, and on 30 January 1812 married Thomas Butler (1783–1861). He was a brother of the Rev. Richard Pierce Butler, who later married Frances' sister Charlotte. The residence of Thomas and Frances was Ballin Temple, County Carlow, Ireland. In 1817, upon the death of his father, Thomas became the 8th Baronet of Cloughgrenan, and Frances thereby acquired the title of Lady Butler. They had a large family, consisting of at least five sons and six daughters.

Substantial efforts were made toward their education. In a letter of 14 December 1830 (SD733), Aunt Bummy wrote to Henrietta: "from all accounts their house is filled all the day by Masters from *every* Country & I hope the great anxiety to have the poor children accomplished will not deprive them of the essential necessity of air and exercise." A tragedy occurred in Frances' family on Good Friday, 1831, as reported by Bummy in a letter to Henrietta dated 8 April of that year (SD740). One of the sons, Tom, accidentally shot and killed his brother John. Bummy commented: "This is indeed a grievous & great trial for poor Fanny, & Sir T. . . . I trust dearest Bro will be more than ever careful where he places his gun." Living seven years after the death of her husband, Frances died on 30 August 1868 at Westwood Park, Scarborough.

JAMES GRAHAM-CLARKE (1791–1859)

Born at Newcastle-upon-Tyne on 27 September 1791, he was the seventh child and third son of John and Arabella Graham-Clarke. He had literary talent, as indicated by two lengthy verse letters written to his sister Mary Moulton-Barrett in April 1812 (SD160 and 162). EBB sometimes chided him for not making more use of this talent. James grew to adulthood at Fenham Hall, the Graham-Clarke family home. A letter from his sister Charlotte to Henrietta Moulton-Barrett dated 5 October 1820 (SD354) gives evidence of his being there and refers to his "well stocked menagerie." He did considerable travelling—visiting relatives in Ireland and elsewhere—and was a frequent visitor at Hope End. A letter to him from EBB's father, 9 October 1828 (SD675), indicates that he was visiting Hope End at the time of Mary Moulton-Barrett's death in Cheltenham. Later family correspondence shows him to have been much involved in Graham-Clarke and Moulton-Barrett business interests, including those that involved Jamaica. For many years, and with great efficiency, he conducted the business at Newcastle-upon-Tyne. He never married. A letter from him to EBB's uncle Sam dated 20 December 1827 (SD638), shortly after the death of his mother, shows that he was still living in the family home at Fenham. He wrote: "I cannot make up my mind to leave it, altho' it is rather too large." Eventually, in 1833, he did sell the property and made his home at Benwell Lodge, near Newcastle. Upon retirement, some years later, he moved to the Continent. In the late years of his life he caused family concern with an undefined illness, which appears to have given rise to severe paranoid tendencies. He died at Tours, France, at the end of 1860.

JANE ELIZABETH HEDLEY (1796–1877)

Jane was born at Newcastle-upon-Tyne, ninth and youngest child, and fifth daughter, of John and Arabella Graham-Clarke. She was baptized on 7 June 1796. She grew to adulthood in the family home and married Robert Hedley (ca. 1794–1862) on 18 October 1821. The latter is almost always mentioned in family correspondence as "Uncle Hedley." A letter (139) from Mary Moulton-Barrett to EBB dated 28 November 1821 tells of their honeymoon on the Continent. They were living at Torquay when EBB went there for health reasons in 1838, and she stayed with them for a while. Uncle Hedley was one of her favourite people. Jane and Robert Hedley had three sons and five daughters. One of the daughters, Elizabeth, was apparently a very beautiful child and is frequently mentioned as "Ibbit" in EBB's letters. Family correspondence indicates that the Hedleys moved from Torquay to Southampton in the summer of 1839. Later they took up residence in France. They came from France to London in the summer of 1846 for the elaborate wedding of their daughter Arabella to J.J. Bevan. This was just before EBB's marriage to RB, and the Hedleys' presence as visitors at 50 Wimpole Street created a problem for EBB. All indications are that Jane was not a tactful person; she sensed what was going on, and did not hesitate to make pointed remarks. Jane was somewhat critical when the marriage finally took place, but Uncle Hedley sided with EBB. Robert Hedley was a man of considerable wealth. He had £20,000 invested in a French railway and was understandably alarmed by the revolution which occurred in France in 1848. The Hedleys left their residence in Tours and went to live for a time at Tunbridge Wells, England. By 1851 they were back in Paris, where the Brownings visited them. A Hedley son—Robert, generally called Robin—visited Casa Guidi with his bride in the early 1850's. In the summer of 1856, Jane Hedley and EBB's friend Julia Martin made a final effort to persuade Edward Moulton-Barrett to "forgive" the three children—EBB, Henrietta, and Alfred—who had married without his approval. (He replied to Mrs. Martin that he "had forgiven" them, but he never communicated with them.) The Hedleys went back to England before the husband's death, which occurred at West Monkton, Somersetshire. He was buried there on 15 April 1862. Jane died in London on 1 May 1877 and also was buried at West Monkton.

OTHER PRINCIPAL PERSONS

DANIEL McSWINEY

This teacher and Moulton-Barrett family friend came from Ireland, but his birth and death dates are not known. He was engaged as a tutor in 1817 to instruct Bro in Latin and other subjects necessary for entry into Charterhouse school. It is thought he spent eight months with the family at Ramsgate and then went to Hope End. EBB eagerly joined with Bro in studies of Latin and Greek. When Bro went to London in 1820, McSwiney left Hope End, but correspondence dating through the 1820's shows that he frequently visited Bro and other family members in London. Existing contemporary documents carry many interesting comments on McSwiney's characteristics. In a letter to Henrietta dated 1 July 1820 (SD346) EBB's father wrote: "Mr. McSwiney has had an application to go to a gentleman in Somersetshire as a Tutor and among the many Queries put to him is asked whether he is of an uniformly mild Temper which I have advised him to answer in the Affirmative with the remark, that he is peculiarly so, except when made angry, and then he will not answer for the consequences." EBB in 1819 wrote a poem entitled "Visions" (*Reconstruction*, D1096), which surfaced despite her intention to keep it hidden, in which she referred to him as "Paddy." Among other things, she said that he "does not, *quite detest* a glass of wine" (see letter 91, including notes 1 and 2). See also letter 198, dated August 1824, in which Bro mentions McSwiney's appearing on the scene at Charterhouse "as great a dandy as ever." The same letter tells of his being comfortably settled at

Brighton. A letter from Samuel Moulton-Barrett to his sister Henrietta dated 17 June 1830 (SD727) mentions McSwiney's still being at Brighton teaching seventeen scholars. This is the latest available reference concerning him. McSwiney made literary efforts, which included a novel, although its fate is not known. EBB was apparently less than complimentary about some of his writing, and in letter 125 he called her "Miss Sauce-box." For an example of his poetical work see SD353.

UVEDALE PRICE (1747–1829)

This classical scholar, a member of the English aristocracy and longtime friend of the Moulton-Barretts, was born in 1747. The family estate was Foxley, near Hereford. Besides classical studies in Greek and Latin, and Italian poetry, his interests included music and landscape gardening. The poet Wordsworth is mentioned as a visitor at his home. He published *An Essay on the Picturesque* in 1794, arguing in favour of natural beauty in landscaping as opposed to the formal and artificial. He became interested in EBB and her work when she published *An Essay on Mind* in 1826. This interest led to an intensive correspondence between the two, mostly concerning accent, metre, and the pronunciation of classical languages. He wrote a book on this subject, published in 1827, entitled *An Essay on the Modern Pronunciation of the Greek and Latin Languages.* EBB helped him with the proof sheets of this work and he incorporated many of her comments and suggestions in the final text. In 1826 and early 1827, EBB struggled with a long poem, "The Development of Genius" (see *Reconstruction*, D731). She showed it to her father in early February 1827 and he ridiculed it (see Appendix III, item 4), but Price encouraged her. However, it was not published in her lifetime. Price was married to Lady Caroline (*née* Carpenter, 1754–1826). They had two children, Caroline and Robert. The latter served in Parliament 1818–41 and 1845–56. Uvedale Price received a baronetcy on 12 February 1828. EBB obviously knew of this honour in advance and mentioned it in a letter to Hugh Stuart Boyd dated 24 December 1827 (letter 282). Sir Uvedale died at Foxley on 14 September 1829. He was eulogized in a poem by EBB entitled "To the Memory of Sir Uvedale Price, Bart." (*Reconstruction*, D1046).

MARY TREPSACK (1768?–1857)

She was the daughter of an impoverished Jamaican planter, William Trepsack, and a female slave. Orphaned early in life, she became the ward of Samuel Barrett, a younger brother of Edward Barrett of Cinnamon Hill. When Samuel died in 1782, Mary came to the Cinnamon Hill estate. From then on, she was the constant friend and companion of Elizabeth Moulton, EBB's paternal grandmother. She is generally referred to in family correspondence as "Treppy" or "Trippy." She evidently had some private funds and underwrote the publication expenses for EBB's *An Essay on Mind with Other Poems*, 1826. EBB wrote endearingly of her to RB in a letter dated 2 June 1846: "She has nursed . . tossed up . . held on her knee—Papa when he was an infant; the dearest friend of his mother & her equal, I believe, in age—so you may suppose that she is old now."

Yet she can outwalk my sisters." Treppy lived with Elizabeth Moulton until the latter's death in 1830. Mrs. Moulton left her £2,000 plus numerous personal effects. From then on, Treppy lived at various London addresses in the St. Marylebone Parish, and was a regular visitor at the Wimpole Street home of the Moulton-Barretts. Indications are that she was well aware of the situation between EBB and RB. After the marriage and flight to Italy, EBB sent letters to her sisters in care of Treppy, rather than sending them directly to Wimpole Street where they might have been intercepted by the father. The Moulton-Barretts carried out Elizabeth Moulton's final wish that Treppy be well cared for. In later life she grew deaf and became paranoid and thought the Wimpole Street people were trying to poison her. Eventually, most of her money was lost through unwise speculations by John Gordon (brother-in-law of EBB's uncle Sam) and she became largely dependent on EBB's father. Her place of residence at the time of her death on 9 March 1857 was in Welbeck Street, London. Her legacies included a parrot for EBB's son Pen, which was kept for him by Arabella. Furniture and linen were given to Henrietta and Surtees. The silver, which had belonged to Elizabeth Moulton, went to EBB (for a list see *Reconstruction*, pp. 615–616, items 1–23). Mary Trepsack was buried 11 March 1857 at Kensal Green Cemetery.

APPENDIX II

Checklist of
Supporting Documents

IN EDITING THIS volume of the Brownings' collected correspondence, we have studied all known original items of Browningiana during the period it covers. Besides primary sources (listed in *The Browning Collections: A Reconstruction*) there exists an extensive body of significant secondary source material, most of it relating to the Barrett and Moulton-Barrett families.

Among early documents are those dealing with the extensive Jamaican properties of Edward Barrett and his descendants, Edward Moulton-Barrett's difficulties as an absentee landlord, and the litigation that greatly affected his financial status and led ultimately to the sale of the Hope End mansion. Other material, less abundant, sheds light on early Browning family backgrounds.

These supporting documents have been invaluable in editing the correspondence. In numerous cases they helped us assign dates; and, even more, they have helped with notes to enhance the meaning of the letters. We have decided, therefore, to provide a listing of such items—thus sharing them with others contemplating in-depth Browning studies.

Listed below is the supporting material for the period covered by this volume. Subsequent volumes will carry similar appendices of material parallel to their primary-correspondence contents.

Relevant extracts are given where the material includes comments directly pertaining to EBB or RB, or comments impinging on events covered in the primary correspondence. Following the practice established for our *Checklist*, in cases where the writer, recipient, or any part of the date is conjectured, and no extracts appear, we give the first phrase for positive identification. This is also done in cases where there are two letters of the same date to the same recipient. Location of the document is given, as a cue title or abbreviation, in square brackets at the right-hand margin.

SD1]   21 October 1771. Deed of Agreement. Between William Nicholson, Benjamin Wells and Robert Browning (grandfather).   [ABL]

SD2]   12 April 1774. Copy of Indenture. Between Edward Barrett (1734–98) and Thomas Reid, Jr., concerning the conveyance of land near Palmetto Point, Jamaica. Filed 7 December 1774.   [ERM-B]

SD3]   13 April 1774. A.D.s. Between Thomas Reid, Jr. and Edward Barrett (1734–98), concerning the conveyance of land near Palmetto Point, Jamaica. Filed 9 July 1774.   [ERM-B]

SD4]   25 February 1779. A.L.s. Thomas Browning to Robert Browning (grandfather). Published: *BSN*, 4 (March 1974), 23–24.   [Collings]

SD5]   17 December 1782. Copy of Letter. Edward Barrett (1734–98) to Samuel Barrett (1765–94).   [ERM-B]

SD6]   11 May 1784. Bond for loan. Between Robert Browning (grandfather) and Thomas Ayrton. Accompanied by payment receipts signed by Ayrton.   [ABL]

SD7]   11 May 1790. A.L.s. George Goodin Barrett (1760?–95) to Elizabeth Barrett Williams.   [ERM-B]

SD8]   21 May 1793. A.D.s. Schedule of Title Deed, respecting John Cook's Estates.   [Altham]

SD9]   16 November 1793. A.L.s. Judith Barrett to Elizabeth Barrett Williams, asking her to commission a portrait of Sarah Moulton (Pinkie).   [ERM-B]

SD10]   3 April 1794. Lease Agreement. Between Robert Browning (grandfather) and Catherine Abbott, on his leasing a house at 7 Great Cheyne Row.   [ABL]

SD11]   6 November 1794. A.L.s. Judith Barrett to Elizabeth Barrett Williams, concerning portrait of Sarah Moulton (Pinkie).   [ERM-B]

SD12]   8 December 1794. A.L.s. George Goodin Barrett (1760?–95) to Elizabeth Barrett Williams, concerning death of Samuel Barrett (1765–94).
                                                                            [ERM-B]

SD13]   9 December 1794. A.L.s. Henry Waite Plummer to Elizabeth Barrett Williams, concerning death of Samuel Barrett (1765–94).   [ERM-B]

SD14]   13 December 1794. Newspaper. Supplement to *Cornwall Chronicle*, Montego-Bay, Jamaica, containing report on death of Samuel Barrett (1765–94).
                                                                            [ERM-B]

SD15]   12 January 1795. A.L.s. Judith Barrett to Elizabeth Barrett Williams, concerning portrait of Sarah Moulton (Pinkie), and death of Samuel Barrett (1765–94).   [ERM-B]

SD16]   14 May 1795. A.L.s. George Goodin Barrett (1760?–95) to Elizabeth Barrett Williams.   [ERM-B]

SD17]   1 July 1795. A.L.s. George Goodin Barrett (1760?–95) to Elizabeth Barrett Williams.   [ERM-B]

SD18]   25 August 1795. A.L.s. George Goodin Barrett (1760?–95) to Elizabeth Barrett Williams.   [ERM-B]

SD19]   12 October 1795. A.L.s. George Barrett Plummer to Elizabeth Barrett Williams, concerning death of George Goodin Barrett (1760?–95) and portrait of Sarah Moulton (Pinkie).   [ERM-B]

SD20]   30 November 1795. Statement of Account. Watt and Walker to Elizabeth Barrett Williams, with appended letter signed by Richard Watt.   [ERM-B]

SD21]   6 December 1795. A.L.s. Edward Moulton-Barrett (father) to Elizabeth Moulton. *Newca*[*s*]*tle / Dear Betsy / We are much obliged to our Friends for the good things they sent us. We are going to have Holidays and to be merry at Christmas. / I remain, dear Betsy, Your affectionate / E. Barrett.* Docket, in EBB's hand: *My dear dear Papa's letter given to me* [*by*] *my beloved Granny who is now with* God.   [BL]

SD22]   31 March 1797. A.L.s. Edward Barrett (1734–98) to Elizabeth Barrett

Williams.   [ERM-B]
SD23] 1798–1819. Collection of papers in two boxes, relating to addition of "Barrett" to surnames of Edward and Samuel Moulton, and permissions to bear Moulton and Barrett Arms. *Box 1:* 2 January 1798. Licence for additional surname of Barrett, signed by George III; 21 February 1798. Grant to bear Barrett Arms; Ms. Pedigree. Descendants of Samuel Barrett (1689–1760); 2 March and 21 March 1798. 2 A.Ls.s. George Harrison to John Graham-Clarke. *Box 2:* 4 July 1815. Grant to bear Moulton Arms; 24 December 1813. A.L.s. William Radclyffe (Rouge Croix Pursuivant) to Charles Moulton who appended A.L.s. (27 December 1813) to Edward Moulton-Barrett (father); 16 September 1814, 8 July and 3 August 1815. 3 A.Ls.s. William Radclyffe to EM-B; 28 July 1819. A.L.s. Mr. Moore to EM-B.
                                                                  [ERM-B]
SD24] 11 August 1798. A.L.s. Elizabeth Moulton to John Graham-Clarke.
                                                                  [ERM-B]
SD25] 23 October 1798. A.L.s. Robert Moulton to John Graham-Clarke.
                                                                  [ERM-B]
SD26] 13 November 1798. Copy of Document. Will of Edward Barrett (1734–98), proved 21 August 1799.   [Berg]
SD27] 20 November 1798. A.L.s. Robert Moulton to John Graham-Clarke, concerning death of Edward Barrett (1734–98).   [ERM-B]
SD28] [1799]. Copy of Verse. "An irregular ode, addressed to Miss D. Heseltine, by a sincere friend [John Bayford] . . ."   [Berg]
SD29] 20 March 1799. A.L.s. Elizabeth Moulton to John Graham-Clarke.
                                                                  [ERM-B]
SD30] 14 May 1799. A.L.s. Judith Barrett to John Graham-Clarke, concerning Elizabeth Moulton's intention of leaving England for Jamaica.   [ERM-B]
SD31] 22 June 1799. Copy of Letter. James Robertson to George Innes.
                                                                  [ERM-B]
SD32] 25 February 1800. Receipt for Payment. "One New Negroe Woman." Messrs. Flash & Cohen to Patty Cook.   [ERM-B]
SD33] 29 March 1800. A.L.s. Edward Moulton-Barrett (father) to John Graham-Clarke.   [ERM-B]
SD34] 17 June 1800. A.L.s. Henry Waite Plummer to Elizabeth Barrett Williams.   [ERM-B]
SD35] 13 October 1800. A.L.s. Eliza Plummer to Elizabeth Barrett Williams.
                                                                  [ERM-B]
SD36] [ca. 1802]. Verse signed with initials. "Mary Clarke! What a treasure untold," by Elizabeth Ridley.   [Berg]
SD37] 20 September 1802. A.L.s. Elizabeth Moulton to Leonard Parkinson.
                                                                  [PG-C]
SD38] 19 February 1803. A.L.s. Elizabeth Moulton to [Leonard Parkinson]. *I wrote to you some time since . . .*   [PG-C]
SD39] 16 May 1803. A.L.s. Eliza Plummer to Elizabeth Barrett Williams.
                                                                  [ERM-B]
SD40] 6 December 1804. A.L.s. Robert Moulton to Charles Moulton, including financial reports.   [ERM-B]
SD41] [ca. 1805]. Statement of Account. "An Account of the Annual Crops of Cinnamon Hill, Cornwall, Cambridge, and Oxford Estates," 1799–1804.
                                                                  [ERM-B]
SD42] 21 February 1805. A.L.s. Henry Waite Plummer to Leonard Parkinson.   [PG-C]

SD43] 1 May [ca. 1805]. Birthday Verse unsigned. [Arabella Graham-Clarke (grandmother)] to Mary Moulton-Barrett.   [Berg]

Winter no more with Storms & piercing Cold
Presides o'er Natures comfortless domain
No more each object drooping we behold
No more with Snow is white each hill & plain!

The trees which frost o'erhung with Icy Spires
Shoot forth in buds & form a leafy Seat
Involving warblers from the feathered choirs
To join harmonious in their carol sweet

Well pleased his verdant fields the farmer Views
That promise fair to yield the grateful corn
While round the Sheperd [sic] play his tender Ewes
And play as if more blyth by his return

Tied to the rural Scenes & flowing Meads
By gentle Spring is Every infant band
Oh happy throng! Tis you that pleasure leads
With Mirth bestowing health now hand in hand—

And say Maria, say dear little Fair
If Kenton's trees & shrubs of various hues
Its chearful breezes & its fragrant Air
Which give delight to All can fail with you

Oh No– Each View that pleasure can impart
And each delight that Nature has to give
Each gen'rous plant, which warms a feeling heart
Improved in yours must flourish, shoot, & live

Then haste to Kenton form a little group
And take two Brothers sprightly as they're young
Who taught by you to cull each sweet shall stoop
And note each beauty as they trip along!

Yet well yon flower may hang with modest bend
That you Maria, little think how faint
Appears its bloom, unequal to contend
With cheeks whose blushes baffle Flora's paint.

Sweet girl thus blessed with every Native grace
While days succeeding yet new graces bring
Still your mind grow lovely as your face
With both may every season prove a spring!

Then shall a Father gaze with glistening Eye
His Wifes loved Image yours shall then display
The Mother fond, but justly Vain, shall cry
Exalting, Welcome happy First of May! ——

SD44] 13 December 1805. A.L.s. James Scarlett to Edward Moulton-Barrett (father).   [ERM-B]

SD45] 20 December 1805. A.L.s. James Scarlett to Edward Moulton-Barrett (father).   [ERM-B]

SD46] [28 January 1806]. A.L.s. James Scarlett to Edward Moulton-Barrett (father). *I am but just returned from Manchester. . . .*   [ERM-B]

SD47] [February 1806]. A.L.s. James Scarlett to Edward Moulton-Barrett (father). *Enclosed is a letter which my brother . . .*   [ERM-B]

SD48] 4 February 1806. File Copy of Letter. Edward Moulton-Barrett (father) to John Graham-Clarke.   [ERM-B]

SD49] [30 March 1806]. File Copy of Letter. Edward Moulton-Barrett (father) to Robert Moulton. *I have enclosed this in a letter to Mr. S. . . .*   [ERM-B]

SD50] 30 March 1806. File Copy of Letter. Edward Moulton-Barrett (father) to Philip Scarlett.   [ERM-B]

SD51] 20 April 1806. Copy of Letter. Raymond B. Waite to Elizabeth Barrett Williams.   [ERM-B]

SD52] [May 1806]. A.L.s. James Scarlett to Edward Moulton-Barrett (father). *. . . I certainly never will advise you to put your name to any bills . . . It would be hard upon you that you should not have the benefit of your own fortune when you come of age & still more injurious to your family if you should deprive them of it. . . .*   [ERM-B]

SD53] 9 May 1806. A.L.s. Raymond B. Waite to Elizabeth Barrett Williams.   [ERM-B]

SD54] [July 1806]. A.L.s. James Scarlett to Edward Moulton-Barrett (father). *I beg you would not think . . .*   [ERM-B]

SD55] 11 August 1806. A.L.s. James Scarlett to Edward Moulton-Barrett (father).   [ERM-B]

SD56] [ca. September] 1806. Copy of Document. Valuing Cambridge Estate at £119,012.17.6. on 11 September 1806. [ERM-B]

SD57] [ca. September] 1806. Copy of Document. Valuing Oxford Estate at £95,820 on 12 September 1806. [ERM-B]

SD58] 18 September 1806. A.L.s. James Scarlett to Edward Moulton-Barrett (father). [ERM-B]

SD59] 1 October 1806. A.L.s. James Scarlett to Edward Moulton-Barrett (father). [ERM-B]

SD60] 15 October 1806. A.L.s. James Scarlett to Edward Moulton-Barrett (father), about overspending by Samuel Moulton-Barrett (uncle). [ERM-B]

SD61] 20 October 1806. A.L.s. James Scarlett to Edward Moulton-Barrett (father). [ERM-B]

SD62] 8 November 1806. A.L.s. James Scarlett to Edward Moulton-Barrett (father). [ERM-B]

SD63] [3 December 1806]. A.L.s. James Scarlett to Edward Moulton-Barrett (father). *I recd. this just now* . . . [ERM-B]

SD64] 26 December 1806. A.L.s. James Scarlett to Edward Moulton-Barrett (father). [ERM-B]

SD65] 30 December 1806. A.L.s. James Scarlett to Edward Moulton-Barrett (father). [ERM-B]

SD66] [?1807]. A.L. (third person). Edward Moulton-Barrett (father) to Leonard Parkinson. *Mr. Barrett presents his Compliments* . . . [PG-C]

SD67] 4 January 1807. File Copy of Letter. Edward Moulton-Barrett (father) to Philip Scarlett. [ERM-B]

SD68] 10 January 1807. A.L.s. Martin Williams to Elizabeth Barrett Williams, concerning transfer of a slave. [ERM-B]

SD69] 27 January 1807. A.L.s. James Scarlett to Edward Moulton-Barrett (father). [ERM-B]

SD70] 13 February 1807. File Copy of Letter. Edward Moulton-Barrett (father) to Charles Moulton. [ERM-B]

SD71] 28 February 1807. File Copy of Letter. Edward Moulton-Barrett (father) to Philip Scarlett. [ERM-B]

SD72] 15 March 1807. File Copy of Letter. Edward Moulton-Barrett (father) to Charles Moulton. [ERM-B]

SD73] 29 March 1807. File Copy of Letter. Edward Moulton-Barrett (father) to Philip Scarlett. [ERM-B]

SD74] 30 April 1807. File Copy of Letter. Edward Moulton-Barrett (father) to Philip Scarlett. [ERM-B]

SD75] 1 May 1807. File Copy of Letter. Edward Moulton-Barrett (father) to James Robertson [ERM-B]

SD76] 29 June 1807. A.L.s. James Scarlett to Edward Moulton-Barrett (father). . . . *Mr Rham has been here this instant to apprize me of the addition to your family upon which I heartily congratulate you & Mrs. Barrett. I am glad to hear you have a son.* . . . [ERM-B]

SD77] 8 July 1807. A.L.s. James Scarlett to Edward Moulton-Barrett (father). *I am this moment favoured with your letter. I am very sensible of the Compliment you pay me in desiring me to be one of the Sponsors for your boy. I shall be happy to oblige you in this, & as I cannot be personally present, I must beg the favour of you to represent me on the occasion. Under such tuition as he*

will receive from his mother & you I think I may safely venture to answer for his
sins till he is fourteen, & I sincerely wish he may ⟨long⟩ live to be the delight of
both his parents. . . .   [ERM-B]
        SD78]   30 July 1807. File Copy of Letter. Edward Moulton-Barrett (father)
to Charles Moulton.   [ERM-B]
        SD79]   1 August 1807. File Copy of Letter. Edward Moulton-Barrett (father)
to Philip Scarlett. . . . *I have the satisfaction of informing you that I was blessed*
on the 26th June last with a Son he and his Mother are [d]oing well, the Negroes
ought I think to have a holiday and some money distributed among the Principals
You will however do as you please. . . .   [ERM-B]
        SD80]   16 August 1807. File Copy of Letter. Edward Moulton-Barrett (father)
to Mr. Harrison.   [ERM-B]
        SD81]   1–17 September [1807]. A.L.s. Samuel Moulton-Barrett (uncle) to
Edward Moulton-Barrett (father). . . . *Tell that dear Sister of mine, that I bought*
her yesterday 2 Indian Gowns, 1 Plain, the other figured. I have sent them with
young Stanhope . . . *As for you I shall think you very well off if you get a very*
large fur pelisse which I have bought you. I merely give you this to prevent you
from grumbling, & from reeking your vengeance upon that hopeful family of yours.
I hope to God little Elizabeth is christened, and that she still promises as well as
when she was under my direction. Mary allowed that she was an Angel, & I thought
her so much like her Uncle that I gave my assent. . . .   [Wellesley]
        SD82]   1 September 1807. A.L.s. James Scarlett to Edward Moulton-Barrett
(father).   [ERM-B]
        SD83]   11 September 1807. A.L.s. James Scarlett to Edward Moulton-Barrett
(father).   [ERM-B]
        SD84]   4 October 1807. File Copy of Letter. Edward Moulton-Barrett (father)
to [Philip Scarlett]. *Not having much to communicate* . . .   [ERM-B]
        SD85]   [November 1807]. Incomplete File Copy of Letter. Edward Moulton-
Barrett (father) to [Philip Scarlett]. . . . *order the Clerk of the Estate* . . .   [ERM-B]
        SD86]   10 November 1807. File Copy of Letter. Edward Moulton-Barrett
(father) to [Philip Scarlett]. *This morng. received a packet* . . .   [ERM-B]
        SD87]   14 November 1807. A.L.s. James Scarlett to Edward Moulton-Barrett
(father).   [ERM-B]
        SD88]   25 November 1807. File Copy of Letter. Edward Moulton-Barrett
(father) to [James Scarlett]. *I received a letter some days ago* . . .   [ERM-B]
        SD89]   30 November 1807. File Copy of Letter. Edward Moulton-Barrett
(father) to [Philip Scarlett]. *In case my letters to you* . . .   [ERM-B]
        SD90]   12 December 1807. A.L.s. James Scarlett to Edward Moulton-Barrett
(father).   [ERM-B]
        SD91]   19 December 1807. Newspaper. *The London Gazette.*   [ERM-B]
        SD92]   1808. A.D. unsigned. Admeasurement of Hope End Estate by
G. Clark in 1791, valuation made in 1808. Bears annotations by Edward Moulton-
Barrett (father).   [Hereford]
        SD93]   [ca. 1808]. A.D. unsigned. Statement of births and deaths of Negroes
and stock on Cambridge and Oxford Estates, from 1 January to 31 December 1807.
                                                                            [ERM-B]
        SD94]   [ca. 1808]. A.D. unsigned. Statement of Negroes and Stock on
Cambridge and Oxford Estates as of 1 January 1808.   [ERM-B]
        SD95]   6 January 1808. File Copy of Letter. Edward Moulton-Barrett (father)
to Boddington, Philips Sharpe & Co.   [ERM-B]

SD96]   6 January 1808. File Copy of Letter. Edward Moulton-Barrett (father) to Philip Scarlett.   [ERM-B]

SD97]   14 January 1808. File Copy of Letter. Edward Moulton-Barrett (father) to Boddington, Philips Sharpe & Co.   [ERM-B]

SD98]   17 January 1808. A.L.s. James Scarlett to Edward Moulton-Barrett (father).   [ERM-B]

SD99]   22 January 1808. File Copy of Letter. Edward Moulton-Barrett (father) to James Scarlett.   [ERM-B]

SD100]   26 January 1808. File Copy of Letter. Edward Moulton-Barrett (father) to Mr. Moore.   [ERM-B]

SD101]   1 February 1808. File Copy of Letter. Edward Moulton-Barrett (father) to Mr. Forster.   [ERM-B]

SD102]   2 February 1808. File Copy of Letter. Edward Moulton-Barrett (father) to Philip Scarlett.   [ERM-B]

SD103]   25 February 1808. File Copy of Letter. Edward Moulton-Barrett (father) to Mr. Macnamara.   [ERM-B]

SD104]   April 1808. File Copy of Letter. Edward Moulton-Barrett (father) to Philip Scarlett.   [ERM-B]

SD105]   12 April 1808. File Copy of Letter. Edward Moulton-Barrett (father) to Boddington, Philips Sharpe & Co.   [ERM-B]

SD106]   17 April 1808. File Copy of Letter. Edward Moulton-Barrett (father) to Mr. Moore.   [ERM-B]

SD107]   3 May 1808. File Copy of Letter. Edward Moulton-Barrett (father) to Robert Moulton.   [ERM-B]

SD108]   3 May 1808. File Copy of Letter. Edward Moulton-Barrett (father) to Philip Scarlett.   [ERM-B]

SD109]   3 May 1808. File Copy of Second Letter. Edward Moulton-Barrett (father) to [Philip Scarlett]. *I sincerely thank you for your kindness . . .*   [ERM-B]

SD110]   11 May 1808. File Copy of Letter. Edward Moulton-Barrett (father) to Mrs. Harrison.   [ERM-B]

SD111]   26 May 1808. A.L.s. John Cook to Elizabeth Cook (*née* Surtees).   [Altham]

SD112]   22 June 1808. A.L.s. John Cook to Elizabeth Cook (*née* Surtees).   [Altham]

SD113]   5 September 1808. Printed Broadside. Entitled "Heads of Agreement. Barrett, &c. versus Plummer, &c." Sent to Charles Moulton, 9 December 1808.   [ERM-B]

SD114]   19 September 1808. A.L.s. James Scarlett to Edward Moulton-Barrett (father).   [ERM-B]

SD115]   2 October 1808. Deed. Relating to a marriage settlement between William Smith and Hannah White. Signed by Robert Browning (grandfather), Jane Browning and Margaret Morris Browning.   [ABL]

SD116]   7 October 1808. A.L.s. H. W. Melvin to Elizabeth Barrett Williams.   [ERM-B]

SD117]   [ca. 1809]. Plat. Estate of Retreat Penn as established by resurvey in 1809.   [ERM-B]

SD118]   [ca. 1809]. Copy of Plat. Estate of Retreat Penn as established by resurvey in 1809.   [ERM-B]

SD119]   9 January 1809. A.L.s. James Scarlett to Edward Moulton-Barrett (father).   [ERM-B]

SD120]   20 January 1809. Receipt. To Elizabeth Barrett Williams for purchase of stock.   [ERM-B]

SD121]   1 May 1809. Copy of Conveyance. Henry Ashmeade to Alexander Kidston entered 2 June 1809.   [ERM-B]

SD122]   11 May 1809. A.L.s. James Scarlett to Edward Moulton-Barrett (father).   [ERM-B]

SD123]   12 May [1809]. A.L.s. Mary Moulton-Barrett to Arabella Graham-Clarke (grandmother). ... *With respect to* Hope End *we are just as when I last wrote— They have not agreed in the price—tho' the treaty is still on foot—and I still think will end to Edwards wishes he is delighted with the place— There are deer in the Park, & it is surrounded with fine hills covered with wood— A Stream runs through it—forming a Cascade— Nothing in short* Ever was *so picturesque & beautiful—there are 475 Acres— £27.000 asked—Including house,* furniture, (which is old) *as it stands— Edward offers £24.000— I think they may meet* half *way, tho' it is at present the plan to* stand firm— *Another Gentleman I believe in the mean time is gone to see it—& his determination, may bring things to a quick decision— Thus it stands Exactly, at present, & it may continue so for some days longer, or I should not have Given you an Account so correspondent to my last— I shall not write again till I can do so, more to your Satisfaction; Anxiously &* Ardently *dearest Mother, as I have wished Nothing to intervene with the delightful plan of seeing you this year, I must admit, & so must you, that if Edward makes this purchase, & takes immediate possession, wh[i]ch he must do! that to go into the North this year, would not be practicable—it will be right & necessary that he should get established there directly, & Even I, who have thought of a journey to the dear North, as the* Summit *of* happiness, *would not undertake it with half the pleasure; knowing we should be so limited for time, as we inevitably must be, if he makes the purchase. ...*   [ERM-B]

SD124]   17 May 1809. A.L.s. James Scarlett to Edward Moulton-Barrett (father). ... *I hope you will find your Estate in herefordshire answers. I am very anxious that you shd. get fixed to your satisfaction, any where* ...   [ERM-B]

SD125]   [ca. June 1809]. Statement of Account. To the credit of Henry Ashmeade.   [ERM-B]

SD126]   1 September 1809. Copy of Conveyance. Alexander Kidston to Henry Ashmeade entered 3 October 1809.   [ERM-B]

SD127]   26 October 1809. Copy of Letter. James Robertson to Shawes & Le Blanc.   [ERM-B]

SD128]   24 November 1809. A.L.s. Shawes & Le Blanc to Edward Moulton-Barrett (father).   [ERM-B]

SD129]   28 December 1809. Receipt. For Henry Ashmeade's taxes paid to Public of Jamaica and Parish of Saint Ann.   [ERM-B]

SD130]   [ca. 1810]. Statement of Account. Estate of Edward Barrett (1734–98) in account with James Scarlett, from 1 January 1809 to 24 February 1810.   [ERM-B]

SD131]   [ca. 1810). Verse, unsigned. Entitled "The Peacock. A Fable after the Manner of Gay."   [ERM-B]

SD132]   17 February 1810. A.L.s. James Scarlett to Edward Moulton-Barrett (father). ... *By those entries it will appear that the mortgage of 10,000. upon your Hope End Estate which I hold is to secure the repayment to me of so much of the funds which I claim as trustee in case I should hereafter be called upon to make any further disbursements on account of the trust on your grandfathers Estate. In*

other words you will be intitled to have a release or an assignment of that mortgage from me as soon as all the charges upon your grandfathers estate are satisfied ⟨by y⟩ou & your brother, & upon your giving me a release of indemnity against all further claims upon me as Executor or trustee. It being understood between us in the meantime that so long as you pay your portion of those demands to which I can hold on account of your grandfathers will & which may exceed the interest of the personal Estate now in the funds I am not to call upon you either for interest or principal upon that mortgage. . . . I looked eagerly in your letter for some account how you & Mrs Barrett liked Hope End—the neighbourhood—& compy. I hope you are satisfied. You promised to write to me soon after you were fixed. . . .
                                                                    [ERM-B]
    SD133] 6 March 1810. Copy of Letter. Edward Moulton-Barrett (father) to Shawes & Le Blanc.   [ERM-B]
    SD134] 9 March 1810. A.L.s. Mary Surtees to Elizabeth Cook (*née* Surtees).
                                                                    [Altham]
    SD135] 12 March 1810. Copy of Letter. James Robertson to Shawes & Le Blanc.   [ERM-B]
    SD136] 14 March 1810. A.L.s. Robert Shawes to Edward Moulton-Barrett (father).   [ERM-B]
    SD137] 25 March 1810. Copy of Letter. Edward Moulton-Barrett (father) to Shawes & Le Blanc.   [ERM-B]
    SD138] 4 April 1810. A.L.s. Shawes & Le Blanc to Edward Moulton-Barrett (father).   [ERM-B]
    SD139] 16 April 1810. A.L.s. James Robertson to Edward Moulton-Barrett (father).   [ERM-B]
    SD140] 16 April 1810. A.L.s. Shawes & Le Blanc to Edward Moulton-Barrett (father).   [ERM-B]
    SD141] 27 April 1810. Copy of Letter. Edward Moulton-Barrett (father) to [Shawes & Le Blanc]. *The only reply I can give you to your letter . . .*   [ERM-B]
    SD142] 30 April 1810. Statement of Account. Plummer Barham & Co. to Elizabeth Barrett Williams.   [ERM-B]
    SD143] 11 May 1810–23 March 1816. Collection of 38 A.Ls.s. Various correspondents to George Goodin Barrett (1792–1854), concerning his military career.   [ERM-B]
    SD144] [2 October 1810]. A.L. unsigned. [Mary Trepsack] to Elizabeth Barrett Williams. *. . . We are now at Hope End– Mary has another Girl to the great disappointment of every one, they are both doing well– I never saw more lovely children– Ba particularly clever, reads extremely well, writes very prettily indeed—& Edward as happy as possible—quite delighted with his purchase—it is a Beautiful place– Nature has been bountiful in the scenery—which is grand & extensive—this situation is rather retired, too much so for most young men, but just the thing for the present owner who is up to his chin in brick & mortar—when the improvements which are intended to be made are finished it will be very handsome—the House is very Indifferent Society they can have as much as they like—being a very centrical situation to many gay places—Bath—Gloucester— Worcester—Cheltenham & their own. I hear the roads are not so good as cou'd be wishd owing to the Country being so Hilly. the Capt has been here & thinks this place resembles St Ann's very much—he was well when we left Town—Sam has been at Mr Clarkes for some weeks & I understand on his leaving there will bend his steps this way– . . .*
                                                                    [ERM-B]

SD145]   1811. Copy of Document. Plaintiff's case in lawsuit of Edward Moulton-Barrett (father) against Mary Lane.   [Hereford]

SD146]   1 April 1811. A.L.s. Elizabeth Barrett Williams to George Goodin Barrett (1792–1854). . . . *your Aunt M. & Trip remains at Cheltenham with Edwards Family, but I hope to see them in Town soon.* . . .   [ERM-B]

SD147]   29 May 1811. Receipt. James Newby to Henry Ashmeade for a rent payment.   [ERM-B]

SD148]   22 June 1811. A.L.s. Richard Barrett to Elizabeth Barrett Williams.   [ERM-B]

SD149]   8 August 1811. A.L.s. Richard Barrett to Elizabeth Barrett Williams.   [ERM-B]

SD150]   1 October 1811. A.L.s. James Scarlett to Edward Moulton-Barrett (father).   [ERM-B]

SD151]   2 October 1811. A.L.s. John Altham Graham-Clarke to Edward Moulton-Barrett (father).   [ERM-B]

SD152]   30 October 1811. Receipt. John Pownall to John Altham Graham-Clarke for a payment made by Edward Moulton-Barrett (father).   [ERM-B]

SD153]   2 November 1811. A.D.s. Notice of Inquiry in lawsuit of Edward Moulton-Barrett (father) against Mary Lane.   [Hereford]

SD154]   19 November 1811. A.L.s. Richard Barrett to Mary Barrett Lockhead.   [ERM-B]

SD155]   19 November 1811. A.L.s. Richard Barrett to Elizabeth Barrett Williams.   [ERM-B]

SD156]   1 January 1812. A.D.s. Thomas Blundell to Martin Williams, John Graham-Clarke, and Charles Nicholas Pallmer concerning the estate of George Goodin Barrett (1760?–95). With two enclosures dated 3 January 1812.   [ERM-B]

SD157]   6 January 1812. A.L.s. Edward Barrett (1791–1819) to George Goodin Barrett (1792–1854).   [ERM-B]

SD158]   [19 January 1812]. A.L.s. John Altham Graham-Clarke to Edward Moulton-Barrett (father). *I know not how to thank* . . .   [ERM-B]

SD159]   22 March 1812. Promissory Note. George Goodin Barrett (1792–1854) to A. Müller. Bears acknowledgment of repayment, 8 April 1812.   [ERM-B]

SD160]   [April 1812]. Verse Letter signed. James Graham-Clarke to Mary Moulton-Barrett et al. *And was my lay, to feeling true* . . .   [Berg]

SD161]   April 1812. Verse unsigned. "On the breaking up of a most agreeable party at Cheltenham," by [James Graham-Clarke]. Accompanied by copies of two responses on one leaf, one signed "Revd. H. Parsons."   [Berg]

SD162]   [18 April 1812]. Verse Letter signed with initials. James Graham-Clarke to Mary Moulton-Barrett, with note added by Edward Moulton-Barrett (father). . . . *Mrs. Moulton appears a good deal better, and begs you will send one of Ba's Shoes up immediately.* . . .   [Berg]

SD163]   20 May 1812. A.L.s. Charles François Dumouriez to Robert Browning, Sr. Offered for sale by Myers & Co., London, undated catalogue entry, clipping in editors' files.   [   ]

SD164]   14 February 1813. Copy of Letter. Unidentified Correspondent to Mr. Moore. Concerning Edward Moulton-Barrett (father) taking office as Sheriff of Herefordshire. *Mr. Barrett has done me the honour* . . .   [Hereford]

SD165]   [31 March 1813]. A.L.s. Edward Moulton-Barrett (brother) to Edward Moulton-Barrett (father). *My dear Papa I love* . . . Bears docket in hand of

Mary Moulton-Barrett: "Bro's first attempt to write with pen & ink— On Sam's birth day—March 31st 1813." [Berg]
    SD166]   3 April 1813. A.L.s. William Osbourne to Edward Moulton-Barrett (father). [Hereford]
    SD167]   [9 June 1813]. A.L.s. James Scarlett to Edward Moulton-Barrett (father). . . . *Next October is the month when I shall be most at leisure & if you could come to town, or what would be much more agreeable to me bring Mrs Barrett & your family to Abinger for some days in that month I shd. be very happy. . . . When the next legacy is paid I shall present a release of my mortgage on your Herefordshire Estate or assign it to any person you think fit.* . . .   [ERM-B]
    SD168]   7 October 1813. A.L.s. Edward Moulton-Barrett (father) to Rickards & Hankins. [Hereford]
    SD169]   29 October 1813. A.L.s. T. Lane to Rickards & Hankins. [Hereford]
    SD170]   31 October 1813. A.L.s. T. Lane to Samuel Rickards. [Hereford]
    SD171]   14 November 1813. A.L.s. T. Lane to Rickards & Hankins. [Hereford]
    SD172]   14 December 1813–1817. Collection of 2 A.Ls.s. and 13 Documents. Concerning land transactions made near Hope End by Edward Moulton-Barrett (father). [Hereford]
    SD173]   [ca. 1814]. Statement of Account. In hand of Edward Moulton-Barrett (father), for January 1811–November 1813. [ERM-B]
    SD174]   [1814]. A.L.s. Edward Moulton-Barrett (father) to Samuel Rickards. *Enclosed I send you Copies of the Indictments* . . . [Hereford]
    SD175]   [1814]. A.L.s. Edward Moulton-Barrett (father) to Samuel Rickards. *I shall be obliged to you* . . . [Hereford]
    SD176]   [1814]. A.L.s. Edward Moulton-Barrett (father) to Samuel Rickards. Relating to EM-B's work as Sheriff of Herefordshire. *The Bearer John Brown has applied* . . . [Hereford]
    SD177]   [1814–1815]. Approximately 21 Bills & Receipts. Relating to service by Edward Moulton-Barrett (father) as Sheriff of Herefordshire. [Hereford]
    SD178]   [1814–1815]. Five Statements of Account. Relating to service by Edward Moulton-Barrett (father) as Sheriff of Herefordshire. [Hereford]
    SD179]   [ca. February 1814]. A.L.s. James Scarlett to Edward Moulton-Barrett (father). *I have seen Messrs. Shawes & Le Blanc* . . . [ERM-B]
    SD180]   1 February 1814. A.L.s. Edward Barrett (1791–1819) to Unidentified Correspondent. *I would thank you to forward* . . . [ERM-B]
    SD181]   March 1814. Draft of Document. Edward Moulton-Barrett (father) to Inhabitants of Ledbury. Relating to his duties as Sheriff of Herefordshire. [Hereford]
    SD182]   3 March 1814. Copy of Letter. S. Moore to Unidentified Correspondent. Concerning Edward Moulton-Barrett (father) taking office as Sheriff of Herefordshire. *I saw Mr. Barrett only just before he left town* . . . [Hereford]
    SD183]   3[–5] March 1814. A.L.s. Edward Moulton-Barrett (brother), Henrietta Moulton-Barrett and Mary Moulton-Barrett to Arabella Graham-Clarke (grandmother). . . . *Edward has been in Town a fortnight today, when I expect him & Sam at dinner for the last four days I have been treated with Mr. Hiltons Society, whose visit here has been long expected. he is good natured Man, & bears patiently the Childrens Noise all day, & playing backgammon with me in the Evengs—him excepted I have not seen a single soul, since E's departure, so that news I have*

none *to tell you– Elizth Ridley wrote to offer herself to come tomorrow & stay a few days, & I dread to hear that she will not be acceptable to the beaux, particularly as we have not any room but* this *to dine & sit in the library being painted. Some of the brass ballustrades are put up, & the Elegance of the hall, really reminds one of the Arabian nights tales. I think it is beautiful & unique– The Drawing Rooms, now, are the only part of the house that exhibits* brick *walls* interior. . . .

[ERM-B]

SD184]   18 April 1814. A.L.s. Edward Moulton-Barrett (father) to Samuel Rickards.   [Hereford]

SD185]   [20 April 1814]. A.L.s. Samuel Barrett (1788–1824) to Elizabeth Barrett Williams. *I have this Evening received* . . .   [ERM-B]

SD186]   7 May 1814. Copy of Verse. Edward Moulton-Barrett (brother), copied by Mary Moulton-Barrett and headed "Edward Barrett's first Poetic Effort."

[Huntington]

SD187]   31 May 1814. A.L.s. T. Lane to Rickards & Hankins. Includes list of fees.   [Hereford]

SD188]   [ca. June–September 1814]. A.N. unsigned. [Mary Moulton-Barrett] to Edward Moulton-Barrett (father). *It is painful for me to ask you, but* . . . Reply by EM-B is added.   [ABL]

SD189]   2 June 1814. A.L.s. Edward Moulton-Barrett (father) to Samuel Rickards.   [Hereford]

SD190]   22 June 1814. A.L.s. T. Lane to Edward Moulton-Barrett (father).

[Hereford]

SD191]   3 July 1814. A.L.s. Edward Moulton-Barrett (father) to Samuel Rickards.   [Hereford]

SD192]   9 July 1814. Copy of Letter. Samuel Rickards to T. Lane.   [Hereford]

SD193]   19 July 1814. A.L.s. T. Lane to Samuel Rickards.   [Hereford]

SD194]   14 September 1814. A.L.s. T. Lane to Samuel Rickards.   [Hereford]

SD195]   26 September 1814. A.D.s. Richard Waite to Martin Williams, John Graham-Clarke, and Charles Nicholas Palmer concerning the estate of George Goodin Barrett (1760?–1795). With two enclosures dated 13 October 1814.

[ERM-B]

SD196]   [29 September] 1814. Printed Receipt signed. M. Cove to Edward Moulton-Barrett (father). Relating to a rent payment.   [Hereford]

SD197]   12 October 1814. Printed Document. Order by Edward Moulton-Barrett (father) as Sheriff of Herefordshire, concerning property of Benjamin Pullen.   [Hereford]

SD198]   13 October 1814. A.L.s. T. Lane to Samuel Rickards. Includes financial statement.   [Hereford]

SD199]   13 October 1814. A.L.s. James Scarlett to Edward Moulton-Barrett (father).   [ERM-B]

SD200]   14 October 1814. A.L.s. Edward Barrett (1791–1819) to [Elizabeth Moulton]. *The enclosed half note* . . .   [ERM-B]

SD201]   26 October 1814. A.L.s. T. Lane to Samuel Rickards, with docket by Edward Moulton-Barrett (father).   [Hereford]

SD202]   5 November 1814. A.L.s. T. Lane to Samuel Rickards.   [Hereford]

SD203]   7 November 1814. A.L.s. Edward Moulton-Barrett (father) to Samuel Rickards.   [Hereford]

SD204]   14 November 1814. Two Draft Copies. Projected Agreement between Bishop of Hereford et al and Edward Moulton-Barrett (father).   [Hereford]

SD205]   16 November 1814. A.L.s. T. Lane to Samuel Rickards.   [Hereford]
SD206]   9 December 1814. Receipt. T. Lane to Edward Moulton-Barrett (father), for rent payment.   [Hereford]
SD207]   9 December 1814. A.D.s. Relating to land acquisition by Edward Moulton-Barrett (father).   [Hereford]
SD208]   10 December 1814. A.L.s. T. Lane to Rickards & Hankins.
[Hereford]
SD209]   [10 December] 1814. Draft Copy of Document. Agreement between Edward Moulton-Barrett (father), Dr. Cove, and Bishop of Hereford, concerning land.   [Hereford Cathedral]
SD210]   10 December 1814. A.D.s. Agreement between Edward Moulton-Barrett (father), Dr. Cove, and Bishop of Hereford, concerning land.   [Hereford]
SD211]   10 December 1814. Fair Copy of Document. Agreement between Edward Moulton-Barrett (father), Dr. Cove, and Bishop of Hereford, concerning land.   [Hereford]
SD212]   [1815]. A.L.s. Edward Moulton-Barrett (father) to Samuel Rickards. *Will you look into the Corners of your Office . . .*   [Hereford]
SD213]   16 January 1815. A.L.s. T. Lane to Rickards & Hankins.   [Hereford]
SD214]   21 January 1815. A.L.s. T. Lane to Hankins.   [Hereford]
SD215]   1 February 1815. A.L.s. T. Lane to Rickards & Hankins.   [Hereford]
SD216]   8 February 1815. Copy of Receipt. T. Fulljames to Edward Moulton-Barrett (father).   [Hereford]
SD217]   10 February 1815. Draft Notice of Trespass. Concerning damage to lands of Edward Moulton-Barrett (father).   [Hereford]
SD218]   11 February 1815. Statement of Account. T. Lane to Edward Moulton-Barrett (father).   [Hereford]
SD219]   11 February 1815. A.L.s. T. Lane to [Edward Moulton-Barrett (father) and Samuel Rickards]. *Inclosed I send Dr. Cove's authority . . .*   [Hereford]
SD220]   16 February 1815. A.D.s. Notice from Edward Moulton-Barrett (father) to Thomas Croft and James Gregg.   [Hereford]
SD221]   19 February 1815. A.L. signed with initials. Mary Moulton-Barrett to Arabella Graham-Clarke (grandmother). . . . *—poor dear Jane thought she was going away for two or three days, & has staid a Month: I was particularly sorry she was not here last Monday as we had a party to dinner,—& there is no parallel for this Event in the records of Hope End for the last 4 Years. Lord Somers, Mr Higgins, The Kearneys, The Commeline family and with them Mrs. Weller, & Mr. Parkhurst, a friend of James'—the Commelines & friends staid all night—most lavish they all were of admiration of the house & its furniture, which are indeed very unique & striking: I long for you to see them: Ld. S. did not go away till two in the Morng—he was in the Country only for a day or two— This glimpse at society, has left us since as quiet & contented as usual. . . . Dear Jane Enclosed to us your Dear Notes to the Children, which were great delights to them, & kept them up an hour later than usual to decipher them. James' was very amusing, tho' Hentta pronounced it to be "Shamefully written, & all blots"—I long to see John to have a more particular Acct of you all— Ba has not written much poetry since we came home— Milton had not always the faculty, nor can we Expect it in this humble little Votary— I send you one to little Sam on his birth day Jany. 13th 1815 . . .* [See Letter 22.]   [ERM-B]
SD222]   4 March 1815. A.L.s. T. Lane to Rickards & Hankins. Including copy of letter from Lane to T. Fulljames.   [Hereford]

SD223] 21 March 1815. A.D.s. Bond granted by George Goodin Barrett (1792–1854) to Samuel Barrett (1788–1824) in the amount of £800. With attached verification dated 4 April 1833.   [ERM-B]

SD224] 21 March 1815. Copy of Document. Bond granted by George Goodin Barrett (1792–1854) to Samuel Barrett (1788–1824) in the amount of £800. With attached verification dated 4 April 1833.   [ERM-B]

SD225] 22 March 1815. A.L.s. Edward Moulton-Barrett (father) to Samuel Rickards, asking that this letter be considered as his "discharge from office" as Sheriff of Herefordshire.   [Hereford]

SD226] 12 May 1815. Copy of Notice. Rickards & Hankins to Robert Solloway.   [Hereford]

SD227] 18 May 1815. Copy of Notice. Rickards & Hankins to Thomas Allen.
                                                                    [Hereford]

SD228] 22 May 1815. Receipt signed. T. Lane to Edward Moulton-Barrett (father), acknowledging payment for stamps and fees.   [Hereford]

SD229] 30 June 1815. Copy of Certificate. By W. Smith, concerning a payment to James Steers.   [Hereford]

SD230] 13 July 1815. A.L.s. Edward Barrett (1791–1819) to Mary Barrett Lockhead.   [ERM-B]

SD231] 9 August 1815. A.L.s. T. Lane to Rickards & Hankins. Enclosing receipt for a payment by Edward Moulton-Barrett (father).   [Hereford]

SD232] [October 1815]. Sketch. By [Charles John Moulton-Barrett], showing a house.   [Berg]

SD233] 3 October 1815. A.L.s. Richard Barrett to Edward Barrett (1791–1819).   [ERM-B]

SD234] 3 October 1815. A.L.s. Richard Barrett to Elizabeth Barrett Williams.   [ERM-B]

SD235] 17 October–31 December 1815. Journal. Recording a journey to Paris made by EBB and her parents; in the hand of Mary Moulton-Barrett.   [Berg]

SD236] 25 October 1815. A.L. signed with initials. Mary Moulton-Barrett to Arabella Graham-Clarke (grandmother). *On the 17th we left London at 5 in the Eveng. and after the carriage was ordered dear Ba seemed so unhappy at our going that it invented my idea that it would be a material improvement to her to do so, and she jumped into the ⟨Ca⟩rriage with us. Mr. M. Wyatt, who is an excellent artist, was also acceptable addition to our party– We slept that night at Rochester & the night following at Calais, having performed our Voyage in two hours and half—an excellent passage Ba and I suffering only very little from sickness and that I think more from hunger than any thing else– You cannot concieve the effect of the French boats coming out to meet us, the noise they made and the uproar of the fights—walking into the Sea to meet us, to have the honor of carrying us on Shore—all of them half naked & quarrelling for the freight. Edward was rath⟨e⟩r rebellious, however it was all in vain they hoisted him off on their shoulders, and away we all went, set down on the very fine sands, from whence we had to climb a ladder to the magnificent pier– After going to have our passports examined at the Customs, we went to Quillacs hotel ... On the 20th we slept at Boulogne, on the 21st at Abbéville a most magnificent and excellent Inn, (The Arch Duke of Austria had slept in our room there the night before on his way to England) on the 22d. at Clermont, that day we breakfasted at Chantilly ... That Eveng. we reached Paris seeing the superb church of St. Denis, ⟨where⟩ the Kings are buried– We drove to six or seven Hotels before we could find apartments at any. .... Ours,* *the only we could get, is the* fifth *story. Three pretty bed rooms, a Kitchen Anti room & Sitting room, with French windows opening on a balcony which looks upon the Thuillerie Gardens, & Palace–* ... *We have taken this* house *for a fortnight from the 23d. I fancy then we shall take our departure.* ... *The people seem all happy & idle Paris is like one splendid fair. No severe anxious business faces as in London– Ba enjoys every thing as much as we do– E. waits to take me out. They both unite with me in kind⟨es⟩t love to you* ... *Mad[a]m[e] Catalani is living here & performs– I shall certainly visit her.*   [ERM-B]

SD237]   10 November 1815. A.L.s. John Harris to Samuel Rickards. With account relating to service by Edward Moulton-Barrett (father) as Sheriff of Herefordshire.   [Hereford]

SD238]   27 November 1815. A.L. signed with initials. Mary Moulton-Barrett to Arabella Graham-Clarke (grandmother). *Last night we arrived here,* alive *& well, & thankful to be again in dear old England* ... *We left Paris this day week, Edward Ba & I in the open barouche, at three in the Eveng. & slept that night at St. Germain, where our King James was confined, the next night we slept at Vert Galant, where we were to stop from the rainy darkness of the night but found the accommodation so wretchedly bad, that we sat up all night, in a cold & gloomy apartment, the fit abode of ghosts, & made Ba sleep on chairs– the next night we reached Rouen. Nothing can be finer than the situation of the Town, in a Valley, thro' which the Seine Expands into a lake adorned by wooded Islands romantic mountains rising behind the Town, a filthy place, but ornamented by a very magnificent Cathedral .. at six in the Morng. we departed, & at 9 in the Eveng. reached Abbeville the best Hotel in France, travelling without alarm of any kind– we reached Boulogne the following Eveng, & at five the next Eveng. we sailed for England* ... *Your letter in Paris was a great comfort to me– Ba is delighted with her journey & with your* old *letter today–* ...   [ERM-B]

SD239]   29 November 1815. Six Notices of Trespass, signed. Rickards & Hankins to Thomas Cook, Thomas Hammond, John Hollings, Charles King, William Lucy and John Skipp.   [Hereford]

SD240]   4 December 1815. Notice of Trespass, signed. Rickards & Hankins to William Henry Brydges.   [Hereford]

SD241]   26 December [1815]. A.L. unsigned. [Mary Moulton-Barrett] to Arabella Graham-Clarke (aunt). *This Elegant Scratch* ...   [Berg]

SD242]   [19 May 1816]. Incomplete A.L.s. George Goodin Barrett (1792–1854) to Edward Barrett (1791–1819). ... *happiness and for so small* ...   [ERM-B]

SD243]   28 May 1816. Birthday Letter signed. Henrietta Moulton-Barrett to Edward Moulton-Barrett (father).   [Berg]

SD244]   [ca. 1817]. A.D. unsigned. Statement of Negroes on Cambridge Estate from 1 January 1806 to 1 January 1817.   [ERM-B]

SD245]   [ca. 1817]. A.L.s. Charlotte Butler to Edward Moulton-Barrett (brother). *As I daresay you* ...   [Berg]

SD246]   [1817]. A.L.s. Arabella Moulton-Barrett to Mary Moulton-Barrett, with note added by Mary Robinson. *I hope you and dear Papa* ...   [Berg]

SD247]   1817. Rhymed Riddles. Addressed to Mary Moulton-Barrett.   [Berg]

SD248]   11 January 1817. Printed Document. Oath, sworn by Edward Moulton-Barrett (father), upon becoming a Burgess and Freeman of the City of Gloucester.   [ERM-B]

SD249]   14 January [?1817]. A.L.s. Mary Robinson to Henrietta Moulton-Barrett. *I hope you will Pardon me* ...   [Altham]

SD250] [17 January 1817]. A.L.s. John Altham Graham-Clarke to Edward Moulton-Barrett (father). *I have this morning sent off the four cows . . .*   [ERM-B]

SD251] [4 February 1817]. A.L.s. John Altham Graham-Clarke to Edward Moulton-Barrett (father). *I have delayed answering . . .*   [ERM-B]

SD252] [4 March 1817]. Birthday Letter signed. Edward Moulton-Barrett (brother) to Henrietta Moulton-Barrett. *I congratulate you . . .*   [Berg]

SD253] 5 April 1817. Receipt. Bank of England to Elizabeth Barrett Williams.   [ERM-B]

SD254] 7 April 1817. A.L.s. John Harris to [Samuel Rickards]. Relating to service by Edward Moulton-Barrett (father) as Sheriff of Herefordshire. *You sent me the enclosed Acct instead of the . . .*   [Hereford]

SD255] [1 May ?1817]. Birthday Letter signed. Henrietta Moulton-Barrett to Mary Moulton-Barrett. *I hope you will . . .*   [Berg]

SD256] 14 May 1817. A.L.s. James Scarlett to Edward Moulton-Barrett (father).   [ERM-B]

SD257] 22 May 1817. A.L.s. Edward Moulton-Barrett (father) to Samuel Rickards.   [Hereford]

SD258] [28 May ?1817]. Birthday Letter signed. Henrietta Moulton-Barrett to Edward Moulton-Barrett (father). *I wish you many . . .*   [Berg]

SD259] [ca. 4 July] [1817]. Birthday Letter signed. Henrietta Moulton-Barrett to Arabella Moulton-Barrett. *I hope you will be . . .*   [Berg]

SD260] [4 July 1817]. Birthday Verse unsigned. Edward Moulton-Barrett (brother) to [Arabella Moulton-Barrett]. *Dear Baby! thou whose dark blue eyes . . .*   [Berg]

SD261] [15 July ?1817]. Birthday Letter signed. Henrietta Moulton-Barrett to George Goodin Moulton-Barrett. *You must excuse me writing . . .*   [Berg]

SD262] 14 September [?1817]. A.L.s. Henrietta Moulton-Barrett to Unidentified Correspondent. *How much pleasanter it is . . .*   [Berg]

SD263] [20 September 1817]. Copy of Letter. [Edward Moulton-Barrett (brother)] to Arabella Graham-Clarke (aunt). *I trust my beloved Bum will not . . .*   [Berg]

SD264] 9 November [1817]. A.L.s. Mary Robinson to Mary Moulton-Barrett. *There is very Little Alteration . . .*   [ERM-B]

SD265] [23 December 1817]. A.L. unsigned. [Edward Moulton-Barrett (brother)] to Mary Moulton-Barrett. *The cheerful season of Christmas is almost . . .*   [Berg]

SD266] 27 December 1817. A.L.s. with illegible signature, in French. To George Goodin Barrett (1792–1854).   [ERM-B]

SD267] 29 December [?1817]. A.L.s. Arabella Moulton-Barrett to Edward Moulton-Barrett (brother). *My dear Bro I hope you have . . .*   [Berg]

SD268] 29 December 1817. Birthday Letter signed. Edward Moulton-Barrett (brother) to Charles John Moulton-Barrett.   [Berg]

SD269] 31 December 1817. Statement of Account. Retreat Penn in account with Philip Scarlett.   [ERM-B]

SD270] [ca. 1818]. A.D.s. Statement of Negroes on Cinammon Hill Estate from 1 January 1817 to 1 January 1818.   [ERM-B]

SD271] [ca. 1818]. A.D.s. Statement of Negroes on Retreat Penn from 1 January 1817 to 1 January 1818.   [ERM-B]

SD272] [ca. 1818]. A.L.s. Edward Moulton-Barrett (father) to Samuel Rickards. *The Bearer of this is Mr. Postring . . .*   [Hereford]

SD273]   [1818]. A.D. unsigned. Statement under Oath by Edward Moulton-Barrett (father). *Edward Moulton Barrett of Hope End in the parish of Colwall . . .*
[Hereford]

SD274]   [1818]. Two Riddles. By Edward Moulton-Barrett (brother), in the hand of Mary Moulton-Barrett. *Why is a wise man, like a looking glass?*   [Berg]

SD275]   January 1818. Five A.Ls.s. From various correspondents to George Goodin Barrett (1792–1854), concerning a duel in which he was involved. With his statement of the affair and a newspaper dated 26 January 1818.   [ERM-B]

SD276]   12 January 1818. A.L. signed with initials. Samuel Barrett (1788–1824) to George Goodin Barrett (1792–1854).   [ERM-B]

SD277]   23 January 1818. Statement of Account. Retreat Penn from 31 December 1816 to 31 December 1817.   [ERM-B]

SD278]   [30 January 1818]. A.L.s. James Martin to Edward Moulton-Barrett (father). *I hope you feel with . . .*   [ERM-B]

SD279]   14 February 1818. A.D.s. Will and Testament of Mary Barrett Lockhead.   [ERM-B]

SD280]   [4 March ?1818]. Birthday Letter unsigned. [?Samuel Moulton-Barrett (brother)] to Henrietta Moulton-Barrett. *My dearest Tar me wish . . .*   [Berg]

SD281]   [6 March 1818]. Birthday Verse signed. Edward Moulton-Barrett (brother) to Henrietta Moulton-Barrett. *Hail dearest Addles at thy joyful birth . . .*
[Berg]

SD282]   14 March 1818. A.D.s. Examination of John Badley before Edward Moulton-Barrett (father), Justice of the Peace. With three related documents concerning the same case.   [Hereford]

SD283]   29 March 1818. A.L.s. William Artaud to Wager Tayler. *. . . . I am now painting for Mr. Barret a picture of the dimentions of what is called a Bishops half length, containing a compisition of four of his children, whole lengths and the size of life, the eldest not quite six years old. . . . I expect also to paint a companion to it, of the same size, to consist of a group of children more advanced in age and reason and of course their countenances more decidedly marked and more capable of suffering the restraint of sitting with some degree of patience. The eldest of these is a girl of about eleven years old, and possessing an extraordinary genius. She has a command of language and ideas that is quite marvellous and her versifycation is sufficiently varied and harmonious. She absorbs the learned languages as freely and as rapidly as chalk does water, and yet with all the power of application. She has all the engenuous simplicity and airy volatillaty of spirits of the most sprightly of her age and sex. Her brother tho by no means difficient has no chance in competition with her She is idolized by her parents and yet such is the excellence of her disposition that I think she is not in the least danger of being spoilt. Indeed she bids fair to be one of those sublimatics of the sex which to the cordial satisfaction of Mary and her little coterie of independent females, may stand up and fairly defy those imperious and boisterous creatures called men; to produce with all their lofty pretentions one among them of superior spiritual endowments. . . .*   [Tayler]

SD284]   28 April 1818. Copy of Document. Statement of Negroes on Cambridge and Oxford Estates as of 28 June 1817.   [ERM-B]

SD285]   1 May 1818. Birthday Verse signed. Edward Moulton-Barrett (brother) to Mary Moulton-Barrett.   [Berg]

SD286]   [1 May ?1818]. Birthday Letter signed. Henrietta Moulton-Barrett to Mary Moulton-Barrett. *I am allways happy to see . . .*   [Berg]

SD287] [28 May ?1818]. Birthday Letter signed. Samuel Moulton-Barrett (brother) to Edward Moulton-Barrett (father). *My dear kind Papa I wish you ...*
[Berg]
SD288] 10 June 1818. Printed Document. John Smith, General Surveyor, to Edward Moulton-Barrett (father), concerning road work.   [ERM-B]
SD289] [15 July ?1818]. Birthday Letter signed. Edward Moulton-Barrett (brother) to George Goodin Moulton-Barrett. *Though in a great hurry ...*   [Berg]
SD290] 21 July 1818. A.L.s. William Artaud to Wager Tayler. ... *I am still at Hope End, but am very near the conclusion of that part of my labours which I can accomplish there. The final touches to the pictures must be given in London. ...*
[Tayler]
SD291] [ca. August 1818]. Statement of Account. Rickards & Hankins to Edward Moulton-Barrett (father) for period of 11 March 1812–11 August 1818. With two additional entries in the hand of Edward Moulton-Barrett, 8 June 1823 and 10 November 1829.   [ERM-B]
SD292] [November 1818]. Music Score. By [Charles John Moulton-Barrett].
[Berg]
SD293] [26 December 1818]. Birthday Letter signed. Arabella Moulton-Barrett to Charles John Moulton-Barrett, with note by Mary Robinson. *I wish you many happy returns ...*   [MM-B & RAM-B]
SD294] 28 December 1818. Birthday Verse signed. Edward Moulton-Barrett (brother) to Charles John Moulton-Barrett.   [Berg]
SD295] [28 December 1818]. Birthday Letter signed. Henrietta Moulton-Barrett to Charles John Moulton-Barrett. *Your birthday is again ...*   [Berg]
SD296] [28 December 1818]. Birthday Letter signed. Samuel Moulton-Barrett (brother) to Charles John Moulton-Barrett. *I am glad that I can write ...*
[Berg]
SD297] [ca. 1819]. A.D. unsigned. Statement of Negroes and stock on Cornwall Estate from 28 December 1817 to 28 December 1818.   [ERM-B]
SD298] [ca. 1819]. A.D. unsigned. Statement of value of Negroes on Cambridge and Oxford Estates as of 22 February 1819.   [ERM-B]
SD299] January 1819. Printed Riddle, with rhymed solution. Addressed to Mary Moulton-Barrett.   [Berg]
SD300] [13 January ?1819]. Birthday Letter signed. Charles John Moulton-Barrett to Samuel Moulton-Barrett (brother). *I wish you ...*   [Berg]
SD301] [13 January ?1819]. Birthday Letter signed. Henrietta Moulton-Barrett to Samuel Moulton-Barrett (brother). *I have long wished for ...*   [Berg]
SD302] 27 January 1819. A.L.s. Richard Barrett to Elizabeth Moulton, concerning death of his brother Edward Barrett (1791–1819).   [ERM-B]
SD303] 2 March [1819]. Birthday Letter signed. Arabella Moulton-Barrett to Henrietta Moulton-Barrett. *I wish you many ...*   [MM-B & RAM-B]
SD304] [3 March 1819]. A.M.s. "A Fragment," by Edward Moulton-Barrett (brother), addressed to EBB. *T'was morn and the red sun reflected brilliancy ...*
[Berg]
SD305] [4 March 1819]. Birthday Letter (third person). Charles John Moulton-Barrett to Henrietta Moulton-Barrett. *Storm kisses ...*   [Berg]
SD306] 4 March 1819. Birthday Verse signed. Edward Moulton-Barrett (brother) to Henrietta Moulton-Barrett. Draft copy with Altham.   [Berg]
SD307] [4 March 1819]. Birthday Letter signed. Samuel Moulton-Barrett (brother) to Henrietta Moulton-Barrett. *I hope you will ...*   [Berg]

SD308] 22 March 1819. A.L.s. Samuel Hilton to Samuel Moulton-Barrett (uncle), concerning Jamaican estates. [ERM-B]
SD309] 31 March 1819. Birthday Letter signed. Henrietta Moulton-Barrett to Samuel Moulton-Barrett (uncle). [Berg]
SD310] [ca. May 1819]. A.L. signed with initials. Samuel Moulton-Barrett (uncle) to Mary Moulton-Barrett. *It is only necesssary to say that* . . . [Morgan]
SD311] [1 May 1819]. Birthday Verse signed. Edward Moulton-Barrett (brother) to Mary Moulton-Barrett. *Ye Muses nine* . . . [Berg]
SD312] 6 May [1819]. A.L.s. Arabella Moulton-Barrett to Mary Moulton-Barrett, with note by Mary Robinson. *I arrived at Worthing last night* . . . [Berg]
SD313] 28 May 1819. Birthday Letter signed. Henrietta Moulton-Barrett to Edward Moulton-Barrett (father). [Berg]
SD314] [15 July 1819]. Birthday Letter signed. Charles John Moulton-Barrett to George Goodin Moulton-Barrett. *I love you too much* . . . [Berg]
SD315] [15 July] 1819. Birthday Letter signed. Edward Moulton-Barrett (brother) to George Goodin Moulton-Barrett. *I cannot help offering* . . . [Berg]
SD316] 17 July 1819. Copy of Document. Will & Testament of Charles Moulton, paternal grandfather of EBB. [ERM-B]
SD317] [27 July 1819]. Birthday Letter unsigned. [Henrietta Moulton-Barrett] to Henry Moulton-Barrett. *We were all surprised* . . . [Berg]
SD318] 1 August 1819. A.L.s. J. P. Aitten and J. L. Hilton to Edward Moulton-Barrett (father), concerning death of Charles Moulton. [ERM-B]
SD319] 21 August 1819. A.L.s. Edward Moulton-Barrett (father) to Samuel Rickards. [Hereford]
SD320] 23 August 1819. Printed Document. Oath, sworn by Edward Moulton-Barrett (father) upon becoming a free Citizen and Guild-Merchant of the City of Hereford. [ERM-B]
SD321] 30 October 1819. File Copy of Letter. Edward Moulton-Barrett (father) to Messrs. Aitten & Hilton, concerning death of Charles Moulton. [ERM-B]
SD322] 1 November [1819]. A.L.s. Arabella Moulton-Barrett to Henrietta Moulton-Barrett. *My dear Henrietta I hope you* . . . [Altham]
SD323] 7 November 1819. A.L.s. Henrietta Moulton-Barrett and Mary Moulton-Barrett to Arabella Moulton-Barrett. [Wellesley]
SD324] 27 December 1819. A.L.s. Robert Dewer to Elizabeth Barrett Williams. [ERM-B]
SD325] [28 December 1819]. Birthday Letter with Verse signed. Henrietta Moulton-Barrett to Charles John Moulton-Barrett. *I must again* . . . [Berg]
SD326] [ca. 1820]. Verse signed with initials. "Comparisons," by Daniel McSwiney. [GM-B]
SD327] [ca. 1820]. Verse signed with initials. "To the Harp," by Daniel McSwiney. [GM-B]
SD328] 13 January 1820. Birthday Letter signed. Charles John Moulton-Barrett to Samuel Moulton-Barrett (brother). [Berg]
SD329] 13 January 1820. Birthday Verse unsigned. [Edward Moulton-Barrett (brother)] to Samuel Moulton-Barrett (brother). *From Heaven's ethereal regions I implore* . . . [Berg]
SD330] 13 January 1820. Birthday Letter with Verse signed. Henrietta Moulton-Barrett to Samuel Moulton-Barrett (brother). [Berg]
SD331] 9 February 1820. A.L.s. Freemen of the City of Hereford (James Child, Jr., Secretary) to Edward Moulton-Barrett (father). [ERM-B]

SD332]   9 January [*sic* for February] [1820]. A.L.s. T. Jones to Edward Moulton-Barrett (father). *I hope you will prove* . . .   [Berg]

SD333]   17 February 1820. Copy of Letter. Edward Moulton-Barrett (father) to [Freemen of the City of Hereford (James Child, Jr., Secretary)]. *In consequence of my absence* . . .   [ERM-B]

SD334]   [ca. March 1820]. A.L. signed with initial. Mary Trepsack to Henrietta Moulton-Barrett. . . . *My best love to dear Ba & say I shall expect her puzzle & she must send me one of her first poem, Battle of Marathon* . . .   [Altham]

SD335]   3 March [1820]. Birthday Letter signed. Arabella Moulton-Barrett to Henrietta Moulton-Barrett, with note by Mary Robinson. *It is with great pleasure* . . .   [MM-B & RAM-B]

SD336]   4 March 1820. Birthday Letter signed. Charles John Moulton-Barrett to Henrietta Moulton-Barrett.   [Berg]

SD337]   4 March 1820. Copy of Birthday Letter. Edward Moulton-Barrett (brother) to Henrietta Moulton-Barrett.   [Berg]

SD338]   [4 March ?1820]. Birthday Letter (third person). Henry Moulton-Barrett to Henrietta Moulton-Barrett. *As Henry cannot speak* . . .   [Berg]

SD339]   4 March 1820. Birthday Letter signed. Samuel Moulton-Barrett (brother) to Henrietta Moulton-Barrett.   [Berg]

SD340]   [22 March 1820]. A.L.s. Arabella Graham-Clarke (grandmother) to Mary Robinson. *I received your letter only a few days* . . .   [Wellesley]

SD341]   [22 March 1820]. A.L.s. Mary Moulton-Barrett to Arabella Moulton-Barrett. *How will you jump for joy* . . .   [Wellesley]

SD342]   [1 May ?1820]. Birthday Letter signed. Samuel Moulton-Barrett (brother) to Mary Moulton-Barrett. *My dear Mama I hope that we will be* . . .   [Berg]

SD343]   28 May 1820. Copy of two Birthday Verses. Edward Moulton-Barrett (brother) to Edward Moulton-Barrett (father). One is in Latin, the other with a note.   [Berg]

SD344]   [28 May ?1820]. Birthday Letter signed. George Goodin Moulton-Barrett to Edward Moulton-Barrett (father). *Pway wove ou's seet George.*   [Berg]

SD345]   [28 May ?1820]. Birthday Verse signed. Henrietta Moulton-Barrett to Edward Moulton-Barrett (father). *We must skip and we must play* . . .   [MM-B & RAM-B]

SD346]   1 July [1820]. A.L. signed with initials. Edward Moulton-Barrett (father) to Henrietta Moulton-Barrett. . . . *Ba & Stormy's letters have just been sent us to read–* . . .   [Altham]

SD347]   [4 July ?1820]. Birthday Letter signed. Henrietta Moulton-Barrett to Arabella Moulton-Barrett. *As I am quite sure* . . .   [Berg]

SD348]   4 July [1820]. Birthday Letter signed. Samuel Moulton-Barrett (brother) to Arabella Moulton-Barrett. *I hope you* . . .   [Berg]

SD349]   [15 July ?1820]. Birthday Letter signed. Charles John Moulton-Barrett to [George Goodin Moulton-Barrett]. *Come play with me* . . .   [Berg]

SD350]   August 1820. Copy of Birthday Verse. Edward Moulton-Barrett (brother) to Henry Moulton-Barrett.   [Berg]

SD351]   18 August 1820. Copy of Document. "Extract from one of the pen books . . .", concerning Retreat Penn, by Richard Barrett.   [ERM-B]

SD352]   [ca. September 1820]. Statement of Account. Rickards and Merrick to Edward Moulton-Barrett (father) for 27 June 1819 to 13 September 1820.   [ERM-B]

SD353]   19 September 1820. Verse signed by Daniel McSwiney. Dedicated
to EBB.   [GM-B]

Lines produced by the scenic beauties of Hope End
to Miss Elizabeth Barrett Barrett

The shades of night are hastening down
To steep in blue the mountains brown
The sky is cloudless and serene:
The winds are pillowed and the scene
So beautiful, so wild, so sweet
When forests, fields, and waters meet,
Is bathed in such delicious hues,
Beneath the twilights falling dews,
That man afar from sorrows sphere
Might muse away his anguish here:
While o'er his erring thoughts subdued
That quiet tranquillizing mood,
That tone of harmony would steal
Which Poets feign and Angels feel.
Lo, in the south a silver star
With amber radiance shines afar
The eldest daughter of the night
In glory warm in beauty bright
Thou diamond in the pathless dome
Of azure, whither dost thou come?
Far, far within the orbless blue
A tiny lustre twinkles thro'
With distant and unsteady light
To catch the eyes then mock the sight

Till as the shades of darkness frown
And throw their viewless curtains down
The very veil that mantled earth
Awakens thee to brighten birth
And bids thee glow with purer ray
A Lily on the tomb of day.
The blue horizon circles round
This silent spot of fairy ground
So hushed, that e'en my very breath
Intrudes upon the still of death
No trace of mind or man is here
The sight to win, or heart to cheer;
Like him who on Fernandy sate
Lamenting o'er his lovely fate
While in the hush of winds, the roar
Of ocean thundering on the shore
Was heard, the only living sound
To break the deep and dull profound—
So here I rest in tempests roll
Above my head or in my soul
Amusing heart a watchful eye
Conversing with the earth and sky
              Daniel McSwiney
              Septr. 19. '20.

SD354]   5 October 1820. A.L.s. Charlotte Graham-Clarke to Henrietta
Moulton-Barrett. . . . *James has lately added a ring tailed monkey to his already
well stocked menagerie which I think would very soon become a grand favorite
with my friends Sam Storm and George—it is precisely like a little old man and
full of mischievous tricks—then there would just be a* very little *farming for your
tiresome Pap⟨a &⟩ Mama could* toddle *about* any & everywhe⟨re⟩ *Ba must h⟨ave⟩
her* sanctum & you *may appropriate as large a space as you can find in my* snuggery
*for your various employments—in short I think we might contrive to spend our
time very* cannily *with nice rides, walks, & drives in the jaunting car.* . . .   [Altham]

SD355]   3 December 1820. A.L.s. Lord Grey to Samuel Moulton-Barrett
(uncle).   [ERM-B]

SD356]   11 December 1820. A.L.s. Fanny Bowmaker to Henrietta Moulton-
Barrett.   [Altham]

SD357]   [28 December ?1820]. Birthday Letter signed. Arabella Moulton-
Barrett to Charles John Moulton-Barrett. *I wish that* . . .   [MM-B & RAM-B]

SD358]   28 December 1820. Copy of Birthday Verse. Edward Moulton-
Barrett (brother) to Charles John Moulton-Barrett.   [Berg]

SD359]   28 December 1820. Birthday Letter with Verse signed. Samuel
Moulton-Barrett (brother) to Charles John Moulton-Barrett.   [Berg]

SD360]   31 December 1820. A.L.s. Charlotte Graham-Clarke to Henrietta Moulton-Barrett.   [Altham]

SD361]   [?1821]. A.L.s. Mary Moulton-Barrett to Henrietta Moulton-Barrett. *... Ba has been very comfortable all day, quite as much so as yesterday– I have been sitting drawing all day at the bottom of her bed, & she has been talking merrily, & enjoying a poor* wood pigeon *for dinner– ...*   [Altham]

SD362]   [?1821]. A.L. unsigned. [Mary Moulton-Barrett] to Henrietta Moulton-Barrett. *... Sam will tell you how well our dear Ba is going on– Thank my kind Sam for his note today & kiss all the dear little tribe for me– I anxiously hope to hear my beloved Storm is going on well, & that he will follow the excellent example you have all set him in getting so soon well– ...*   [Altham]

SD363]   [?1821]. A.L.s. Samuel Moulton-Barrett (uncle) to Henrietta Moulton-Barrett. *... I beleive that I shall go to Carlton in a very few days, which I shall do without much regret, as it will be only for a very few days, & Ba is so much better today. ... Ba desires her affectionate love to Arabella & is much obliged for her letters & entreats a repetition of them.*   [Altham]

SD364]   [ca. 1821]. A.L.s. Rosa H. to Henrietta Moulton-Barrett. *I was glad to have the pleasure ...*   [Altham]

SD365]   13 January 1821. Birthday Verse signed. Edward Moulton-Barrett (brother) to Samuel Moulton-Barrett (brother).   [Berg]

SD366]   18 January 1821. A.L.s. Samuel Moulton-Barrett (uncle) to Henrietta Moulton-Barrett. *... I have ordered two cloaks similar to Ba's, for yourself & Arabella. ...*   [Altham]

SD367]   17 February 1821. Copy of Document. Will and Testament of Mary Roderick. Entered 5 December 1827.   [ERM-B]

SD368]   27 February [?1821]. A.L.s. Henrietta Moulton-Barrett to Charles John Moulton-Barrett. *How goes on the farmers ...*   [Berg]

SD369]   [ca. March 1821]. A.L.s. Charles John Moulton-Barrett to Mary Moulton-Barrett. *I saw Bro ...*   [Berg]

SD370]   4 March 1821. A.L. signed with initial. George Goodin Barrett (1792–1854) to Elizabeth Turner.   [ERM-B]

SD371]   [4 March ?1821]. Birthday Letter signed. George Goodin Moulton-Barrett to Henrietta Moulton-Barrett. *I hope I will be good ...*   [Berg]

SD372]   4 March 1821. A.L.s. Mary Moulton-Barrett to Charles John Moulton-Barrett, with notes added by Arabella Moulton-Barrett and [Samuel Moulton-Barrett (brother)].   [Berg]

SD373]   4 March 1821. Birthday Letter signed. Samuel Moulton-Barrett (brother) to Henrietta Moulton-Barrett.   [Berg]

SD374]   16 March 1821. A.L.s. Samuel Moulton-Barrett (brother) to Charles John Moulton-Barrett.   [Berg]

SD375]   1 May 1821. Birthday Verse with Note signed. Arabella Moulton-Barrett to Mary Moulton-Barrett.   [MM-B & RAM-B]

SD376]   [1 May ?1821]. Birthday Verse unsigned. [?Charles John Moulton-Barrett] to Mary Moulton-Barrett. *Do you love me ...*   [Berg]

SD377]   [1 May ?1821]. Birthday Letter signed. Henry Moulton-Barrett to Mary Moulton-Barrett. *I hope you love ...*   [Berg]

SD378]   1 May 1821. Birthday Verse signed. Samuel Moulton-Barrett (brother) to Mary Moulton-Barrett.   [Berg]

SD379]   8 May 1821. A.L.s. Dr. I. Carden to Edward Moulton-Barrett (father). *Your clear detail of the symptoms of the disorder still affecting your* daughters, though considerably mitigated, induces me to entertain the same opinion of the nature & treatment of the malady as I form'd on witnessing it for the first time. The only variation I am inclined to suggest in the medicine, is to make the Bark draught a little stronger with Bark & add to each dose half a teaspoonful, a little more to the eldest & rather less to the youngest, of the volatile Tincture of Valerian. The cold shower bath for Miss B. I entirely approve of. The system of exercise in the open air must be pursued as much as possible, & if the rides could be varied the advantage wd be greater. In this way I hope & expect you will see a progressive amendment in their complaints, & that in a few weeks I shall have the pleasure of hearing of their being free from this harrassing malady. Should it prove however more tedious than I anticipate, an entire change of air would be desirable, & the choice of place, if dry, would be less material than the change itself. Before I conclude I would suggest the trial of a tight flannel roller around the abdomen by day only. With cordial good wishes to Mrs Barrett & your young people . . .   [Morgan]

SD380]   [?20 May 1821]. Birthday Verse signed. Arabella Moulton-Barrett to [?Alfred Price Moulton-Barrett]. *My dear Baby* . . .   [MM-B & RAM-B]

SD381]   [?20 May 1821]. Birthday Verse unsigned. [?Charles John Moulton-Barrett] to [?Alfred Price Moulton-Barrett]. *This is your birthday what fun* . . .

[Berg]

SD382]   [20 May 1821]. Birthday Verse with Note signed. Henrietta Moulton-Barrett to Alfred Price Moulton-Barrett. *My Alfred my affectionate sweet* . . .   [Berg]

SD383]   21 May 1821. Birthday Verse signed. Edward Moulton-Barrett (brother) to Alfred Price Moulton-Barrett.   [Berg]

SD384]   [28 May ?1821]. Birthday Verse with Note signed. Arabella Moulton-Barrett to Edward Moulton-Barrett (father). *This is your beloved birthday*
. . .   [MM-B & RAM-B]

SD385]   [28 May ?1821]. Birthday Verse signed. Charles John Moulton-Barrett to Edward Moulton-Barrett (father). *As it is your birthday* . . .   [Berg]

SD386]   28 May 1821. Birthday Verse signed. Edward Moulton-Barrett (brother) to Edward Moulton-Barrett (father).   [Morgan]

SD387]   [28 May ?1821]. Birthday Letter unsigned. [?George Goodin Moulton-Barrett] to Edward Moulton-Barrett (father). *Many appy turns* . . .   [Berg]

SD388]   [28 May ?1821]. Birthday Verse signed. Samuel Moulton-Barrett (brother) to Edward Moulton-Barrett (father). *I hope that you will* . . .   [Berg]

SD389]   24 June 1821. A.L.s. William Coker to [Edward Moulton-Barrett (father)] with a copy of Coker's letter to Dr. Nuttall concerning illness of EBB. *Dear Sir— I have thought you might derive some satisfaction from knowing what communication I made to your friend Dr. Nuttall– I have therefore taken the liberty of sending you a copy of it—any mis-statement or omission which may have inadvertently occurred you will be enabled to correct and supply—that the Doctors mind may not be misled in its conclusions by a want of precision and fact, in the details of this interesting case—for the removal of which you have my most hearty wishes. I am Dear Sir, / Your most obedient servant / William Coker / N.B. I trust Mr. S. Barrett will excuse my sending this under cover to him.*
[Dr. Coker's letter to Dr. Nuttall is as follows.]
Sir, / You will probably have been prepared by your friend Mr. Barrett to expect a letter from me, which in the hope of soothing a highly interested, and interesting family I gladly undertook to write to you– The subject on which I have to communicate upon, is not new to you—the case of Miss Barrett—that

prodigy in intellectual powers and acquirements! I saw her in consequence of some of our mutual friends having known that I had been successful in removing some painful affections of the nerves which assume the intermittent shape– This case unfortunately differs materially from them and is one of essential importance, both to the lady herself and to her friends– Though you have had a description of it from her own eloquent pen, I shall, as briefly as I can recapitulate it's history and state its present symptoms– It began with pain in the head, which continued at intervals for seven weeks—the pain then attacked various parts of the body, for a considerable period—and for the last month it has permanently seated itself on the right side, that is about the centre of the angle formed by the greatest projection of the ribs, the umbilicus, and the anterior superior spinous process of the os ilium– The pain commences here is carried to the corresponding region of the back, up the side to the point of the right shoulder, and down the arm. The suffering is agony—and the paroxysms continue from a quarter of an hour to an hour and upwards—accompanied by convulsive twitches of the muscles, in which the diaphragm is particularly concerned– The attack seems gradually to approach its acme, and then suddenly ceases—during it's progress the mind is for the most part conscious of surrounding objects but towards it's close, there is generally some, and occasionally, very considerable confusion produced by it– There are generally three attacks in the day and none during the night—very considerable debility and consequent nervous irritation, producing smallness and feebleness of the pulse—pain, and weakness in the back, which will not allow her sitting up, without support by pillows, and she is always rendered worse by exercise– The feet are generally cold—the pupil appeared much dilated, but contracted on the stimulus of light— She sometimes awakes in the night in great fright; and says that in the morning there is a sensation as though a cord were tied round the stomach (i.e. the part affected) "which seems to break", to use her own expression. She is unable to rest on the right side—the tongue clean, and the stomach and bowels (aperient medicine is required) seemed to be so little affected, as to have excited my surprise, though she has only a relish for highly seasoned food– She has shrunk so much as to have produced in the minds of her friends great anxiety, though her countenance does not indicate to a stranger any cause for alarm– The mind has ceased in a great degree to engage in those investigations and pursuits which formerly constituted it's greatest delight, and there appears to be a degree of listlessness perceptible to those around her, even where the affections are concerned–

I understand she has taken a variety of powerful medicines without any permanent benefit– Opium at one time relieved the spasms but it has ceased to have that effect– I examined the side, the spinal column as accurately as I could– In the side I should have remarked that she feels the sensation of its being swolen, which by no means appears to be the fact– There is too great irritability in the abdominal muscles to allow of much pressure being made upon them—but nothing like visceral accretion is to be inferred from the case itself or from the best examination I could make, nor could I detect any thing obviously wrong about the spine– I should state that two of the sisters of this young lady had some time since, the same kind of pain, or nearly so, which occupied the second stage of this malady. They were all suffering at the same time, which created a suspicion that they had taken something deleterious—they both however soon recovered, without much, if any, medical treatment– For

*what remains for me to add, I shall have to make some apology– I trust you
will excuse my giving you the views I entertain of this case, and I hope you will
with the same candour give me yours– I am greatly assisted in this subject, by
having witnessed some years since in a young lady, a strikingly similar, though
much more aggravated case, which terminated at length in decided affection of
the spine—from which she has recovered and is the mother of three children–
When I first saw this lady in Hampshire, she was suffering from the same kind
of spasms, as I observed in Miss Barrett (the left side being here affected) and
they were most vividly recalled to my recollection on this occasion– She was
at this time relieved by bleeding &c. though her debility was infinitely greater
than Miss Barrett's. I did not see any reason at this period to imagine there
was disease of the spine, nor had it entered into the contemplation of the
physician and surgeon who attended her– After some three or four weeks, she
was enabled to travel home to Salisbury a distance of 40 miles—where I again
saw her in consultation. I had no doubt the vertebral column was now affected—
the surgeon who attended her concurred with me in opinion, and she ultimately
recovered– You will agree that it is difficult to remove the effect which an
impression of this kind, must make upon the mind of a medical man– Keeping
therefore this case in view, and for reasons which shall be stated below, I should
recommend, generally, the treating Miss Barretts case as for diseased spine,
upon the plan recommended by Baynton—giving only such medicine as might
assist the operations of nature or as its exigencies would require—bleeding
might also be employed if necessary to mitigate the spasms, and the Unguentum
Antimonii Tartarisati applied to the side, would prove some counter irritation—
proper attention should be paid to the ingesta– Medicine seems to have, and
to have had no effect, and the worst as it appears to me that can result from
the adoption of this measure, will be the loss of time if it should even be proved
to have been injudiciously recommended– The reasons I alluded to above, are
the history of the case—no relief having been obtained from the variety of well
directed attempts to remove its' influence. The increasing debility—loss of
locomotive power—pain in the back—its' requiring support in the erect posture—no attack during the night—constant inconvenience from exercise, together with the state of the nervous and sanguiferous systems, indicating a high
degree of sympathy, and most probably referable to derangement in some highly
important organ– The uterine system is not materially affected– At the same
time that I confess, the positive proofs are wanting of the existence of diseased
spine, I must say that this is the best inference, I could draw of Miss Barretts
from the opportunity I had of enquiring into its nature and of witnessing her
sufferings– Being more anxious for the welfare of the sufferer, than for the fate
of my own opinion, I shall again request you to use every freedom in commenting
upon this communication, and beg to remain, Sir, Your most obedient servant*
                                                                Wm. Coker
*N.B. You will probably have thought me tedious but it is impossible to see such
a patient without feeling a lively interest in her recovery.*   [Morgan]

SD390]   [4 July ?1821]. Birthday Letter signed. Charles John Moulton-Barrett
to Arabella Moulton-Barrett. *If you will not take the cherries . . .*   [Berg]

SD391]   8 July [1821]. A.L.s. Samuel Moulton-Barrett (uncle) to Henrietta
Moulton-Barrett. *Your present of a rose was like yourself very sweet & pretty, &
I cherished it the more coming from you– Where the Cake is which you threatened
to send Ba, I cannot guess, excepting that your Papa eat it unconsciously. I wish*

*my dear chicken all Ba's pains could be as easily releived, as your lamentations
about the Dove. . . .*   [Altham]

SD392] 23 July [1821]. A.L. signed with initials. Samuel Moulton-Barrett
(uncle) to Henrietta Moulton-Barrett. *Though you must have suffered unendurable
. . .*   [Altham]

SD393] [ca. August 1821]. A.L.s. Rosa H. to Henrietta Moulton-Barrett. *I
am truly happy indeed to find that Miss B. is so much improved in health lately
and I hope she will be perfectly recovered by the time I come over into that Country
which shall be before long. . . . I suppose Master Barrett is at Home from School
as his Sister is so ill. . . .*   [Altham]

SD394] [August 1821]. A.L.s. Arabella Moulton-Barrett to Charles John
Moulton-Barrett. *Have you heard . . .*   [MM-B & RAM-B]

SD395] August 1821. A.L.s. Edward Moulton-Barrett (brother) to Henrietta
Moulton-Barrett. *According to promise I sit down to write you a line, to tell you
of dearest Ba's illness to day, she is certainly bett⟨er⟩ her po⟨or pu⟩lse is more
regular and her spirits very good she has been free from pain to day except during
her spasms the first of which was very long, three hours all but a quarter, though
mild, the second sixty four minutes and as mild the paroxism of the last was
particularly so, the third has not yet come on I will write again soon . . .* [Altham]

SD396] 9 August 1821. A.L.s. Edward Moulton-Barrett (brother) to Henrietta Moulton-Barrett. *I am delighted to have an opportunity of giving you a good
account of dearest Ba She is certainly considerably better within these two days,
though her pains and paroxisms are very much the same. Her pulse is however
lower and much more regular, her spasms or catchings much less frequent, and
her eyes as strong as ever they were, her apetite is most capital and it is with the
greatest difficulty she can be prevented from talking. Jane recommended as a
certain cure for all such disorders, a good mutton pie well seasoned. . . .* [Altham]

SD397] [ca. 9 August 1821]. A.L.s. Mary Moulton-Barrett to Henrietta
Moulton-Barrett. . . . *—you will I know be pleased with Bro's acct. of our dear
Ba, who is very comfortable today, & delighted with her letters which arrived
unexpectedly, as she thought she had had today's share yesterday— Indeed my
sweet Addles she is always so happy to hear from you, that I had much rather have
you write to her, so never think about me, excepting to love me always as dearly
as I love you, which is Mama's greatest blessing. . . .*   [Altham]

SD398] 11 August 1821. A.L. signed with initials. Samuel Moulton-Barrett
(uncle) to Henrietta Moulton-Barrett.   [Altham]

SD399] 24 August 1821. A.L.s. Edward Moulton-Barrett (brother) to
Henrietta Moulton-Barrett. *Many many thanks for your beautiful letters, the disap-
pointement of not hearing from you before is fully made up for. Ba is much the
same to day as yesterday but certainly upon the whole considerably improved, the
attack of this morning was very short, only 64 minutes but excessively violent, her
pulse is very quiet and regular and her eyes perfectly well. I went this morning,
to see his Majesty but was deprived of that* supreme *pleasure by his not stopping
a moment . . . he disappointed poor Mr Dowling most dreadfully for he had a grand
repast prepared for him . . .*   [Altham]

SD400] [24 August 1821]. A.L.s. Mary Moulton-Barrett to Henrietta
Moulton-Barrett. *Your pretty letters please our darling Ba more than any of her
little enjoyments— She slept very well last night, & has been very comfortable
today—the pain in the ribs I am sorry to say, still follows the spasms, but it does
not last long. . . . The Aldermen tried to comfort themselves for the affront by*

*Eating up the royal Collation, & the disappointed crowd by Abuse– Dear Bro was
of the latter Class—& tho' Ba allowed him to go, she said very indignantly, it was
what she would not do herself.* . . . *Ba Eat the breast of a partridge today &
enjoyed it very much.* . . .   [Altham]
 SD401] 27 August 1821. A.D.s. Marriage Certificate of George Goodin
Barrett (1792–1854) to Elizabeth Jane Turner. With a memorandum giving their
three children's birth dates.   [ERM-B]
 SD402] [ca. September ?1821]. A.L.s. Mary Moulton-Barrett to Henrietta
Moulton-Barrett. . . . *I must first tell my Hentta. that our dear Ba's first spasm
today, was, Trepsack says, the mildest she has seen—the second has not been so
mild, but with neither has there been the slightest pain in the ribs, so that we trust
that evil is gone—in all other respects, she is going on as favorably as possible,
slept well last night, & has been very comfortable today– Enjoying her pudding
& roast partridge– Bro met Mrs. O. in the street, & was just passing her when
the two baskets caught his eye & he recognised them as old friends—great was
Bas surprise when Mrs. O. appeared at her bed side, with the brace of partridges
in one hand, & the little live prisoner in the other, which she did not discover till
she took the little basket in her hand, & peeking thro its wires, she saw the brilliant
yellow plumage– Never was delight greater than hers, than when she saw this
proof of her dearest Addles love, and never indeed was there a more beautiful little
bird—during the warm part of the day it was set in its pretty new cage (which Sam
sent her directly) in the open window & when Eveng. drew on, it was put on the
drawers where dearest Ba could see all its little movements till it fell asleep—it
does not seem to have suffered at all from its journey, & it is grown so beautiful
that I could not have recognised the bare little thing I left–* . . . *Ba desires me to
give you twenty kisses & as many thanks for your lovely present & amusing letter,
both of which she values, as she knows they came from her dear Addles heart!–*
. . . *Never mind writing to me. I make all my rights over to Ba.*   [Altham]
 SD403] [ca. September ?1821]. Incomplete A.L. unsigned. [Samuel
Moulton-Barrett (uncle)] to Henrietta Moulton-Barrett. . . . *I mean to send tomorrow . . . two lockets for yourself & Arabella, the latter contain a capital proof of
Ba's recollection of you, by way of stimulating your recollection of her. If not of
the most fashionable manufacture, nor of the most choice ornaments, you will feel
great indifference about the exterior in consideration of the interior. This induced
me to look about for something very plain, Ba feasted last night on a second edition
of wedding cake, which was universally admitted to be much better than that from
Newcastle.* . . .   [Altham]
 SD404] [September 1821]. A.L.s. Mary Moulton-Barrett to Henrietta
Moulton-Barrett. *Tho' you will hear so good an Acct. from dearest Papa of Ba, I
know it may be some little pleasure to have a line from me to assure you how well
she is going on, & how comfortable she has been all today, Excepting when the
tiresome spasms came on—the pain in the ribs is a great deal better & she is as
merry tonight as can be– Make yourself Easy & happy about her, my dearest
Hentta. & I will write every day to you.* . . . *We have got a new lodger here, who
they say is crazy, & Ba is quite delighted at this little variety!* . . . *I am desired by
Ba to say with her best love that the silver medal is for Arabel. She is quite pleased
you like them so much.* . . . *Bro has been at the Cathedral today, & afterwards
took a ride—he amuses himself very comfortably; you will see him I daresay soon,
but it is so great a pleasure to poor Ba to have him here that I know my kind
Henta. does not grudge it.* . . .   [Altham]

SD405]   [25 September 1821]. A.L.s. Mary Moulton-Barrett to Henrietta Moulton-Barrett. . . . *Ba has been very easy all today excepting in the paroxysm, which is the same– Mrs. Pitt kindly sent her a partridge, the breast of which she enjoyed for her dinner with bread sauce & then took two hours comfortable sleep– Bro has been suffering from eating too many plums—two of Ba's pills, not being sufficient, a dose of the water was added this Morng— & that a good black dose, at Dr. Barons recommendation, so that he has had a very* BUSY *day of it . . . Ba & Bro desire loves & kisses in abundance–* . . .   [Altham]

SD406]   [ca. October 1821]. Incomplete A.L. unsigned. [Samuel Moulton-Barrett (uncle)] to Henrietta Moulton-Barrett. *Though I am not commissioned by Ba, I venture to say that had she been able she would have addressed to you a few lines, as it is, I must be her substitute (a poor one I am conscious of) to express to you her best thanks for the great pleasure your letters afford her. . . . Were it not that your visit here would be prejudicial to yourself, we should* all *heartily desire your presence; & none more than Ba whose affection for you is of that better stamp, that seeks your profit & interest rather than it's own. . . . Ba sends you a cloak, grey, to protect your dear self least the Winds of Heaven should visit your cheek too roughly. She adds likewise two handkerchiefs for the benefit of your little ones between whom & their patroness or rather Parent, so great a difference of age exists. . . .*   [Altham]

SD407]   [2 October 1821]. A.L. signed with initials. Edward Moulton-Barrett (father) to Mary Moulton-Barrett. *Ba has just recovered from her second attack which has not been quite so long as that of yesterday neither was the first this Morning, and both tolerably easy in the conclusion– She has had some little difficulty in making Water and to assist her nerves of the Bladder it was thought necessary to put on a small Blister on the very bottom of the Back; of course this created some uneasiness, but she is now quite comfortable– I trust it will have the affect in stimulating the Parts to do their proper office. . . .*   [Altham]

SD408]   2 October 1821. A.L.s. Edward Moulton-Barrett (brother) to Henrietta Moulton-Barrett. . . . *your last letter was particularly capital and excited bursts of laughter and applause from all, it certainly deserved it abounding with wit and eloquence, and remarkable for the choiceness of its expressions, and the elegance of its language, Ba was in raptures, so were we all. Ba has not been in such good spirits today in consequence of a blister which was put on last night and which gives her some uneasiness, however her appetite has not suffered in the least. Yesterday the two first spasms were long but they went off quietly, the last was only twenty minutes and by no means violent, the first this morning was shorter than that of yesterday, and not more violent, she has just awoke out of a sound sleep, with the second spasm on her. Nothing seems to diminish these horrible attacks and sleep itself is broken in upon, time and patience will I hope overcome what doctors and physic cannot destroy. . . .*   [Altham]

SD409]   4 October 1821. A.L.s. John Harris to Samuel Rickards. Relates to service by Edward Moulton-Barrett (father) as Sheriff of Herefordshire. [Hereford]

SD410]   [ca. 10 October ?1821]. A.L.s. Mary Moulton-Barrett to Henrietta Moulton-Barrett. *Having with some difficulty penetrated the fog, we arrived about an hour ago, & while our dearest Ba & Storm are devouring a pheasant between them, I must impart some of the happiness which I feel to my sweet Addles, in the great improvement which I observe in our precious Invalid since I saw her last, she is perfectly cool, in great spirits, her head quite free from pain & the spasms have been for the last two days very mild—they all seem to consider her, consid-*

erably better,—& my own observation happily convinces me of it– I write this with a thankful heart my beloved Child, & I am sure you will read it with the same– ... *Ba read her letter the* instant *we came with great impatience, & desires her best love & thanks for this amusement they have afforded her—she has got* Ellens portrait *pinned up at the bottom of her bed & thinks it very like– I left all my darlings this* Morn *with a heavy heart but hope to return to them with a happy one, if our dear Ba continues to go on so well–* ... *Ba says she asked for you to come, but was contented for this time to give it up, as Papa wished it, & depends on seeing you very soon–*   [Altham]

SD411] [14 October 1821]. A.L.s. Mary Moulton-Barrett to Henrietta Moulton-Barrett. *Our darling Ba slept well last night, and has been very comfortable in all respects but the spasms, which however have been mild– She had a chicken for dinner today, & for some days has drunk milk Whey for breakfast & tea, & with her dinner– She likes it* much, *and it agrees very well with her– We have not heard from Bro today as we expected, but Ba has had a letter from Bum with Accts of more* bridal gifts *& the certainty of Jane's marriage on Thursday–* ... *Ba made me tell her all* you *said & did while I was at home, & seemed better amused by it than any other subject– I read her prayers to her today in the bible, & she has altogether been very comfortable– I was surprized to find a* fire *in her room; the whole house seems very clean & comfortable now* ... *Ba begs you will go to the school & examine for her the* petticoats *& Stockgs of Ann Hooper, & Elizth Harford. Ba is getting some things to send, & wishes you to let her know the exact State of their wardrobes–* ...   [Altham]

SD412] 13 November 1821. A.L.s. Charlotte Graham-Clarke to Henrietta Moulton-Barrett. ... *my next pleasurable subject is our beloved Ba's improved health, of which you speak so certainly and so affectionately—that it does my heart good—indeed my sweetest Henrietta I do sanguinely hope each day now, will bring successively some increase of amendment, and that the next time we have the happiness of meeting we may all be blessed with our usual good share of health and spirits to enjoy every moment of each others agreeable society, a circumstance which seems lately to have been of rare occurrence.* ...   [R.J.L. Altham]

SD413] 28 December 1821. Birthday Verse signed. Edward Moulton-Barrett (brother) to Charles John Moulton-Barrett.   [ERM-B]

SD414] [28 December ?1821]. Birthday Verse signed. Samuel Moulton-Barrett (brother) to Charles John Moulton-Barrett. *Who was born on this day* ...   [Berg]

SD415] [ca. 1822]. A.L.s. Samuel Moulton-Barrett (brother) to Mary Moulton-Barrett. *I am so very sorry that I did not write before but as I have time I will write to you and Henrietta I hope that Ba is better* ...   [Berg]

SD416] [ca. 1822]. A.L.s. Mary Trepsack to Charles John Moulton-Barrett. *I sent you my dear Stormy* ...   [Berg]

SD417] [13 January ?1822]. Birthday Verse with Note signed. Edward Moulton-Barrett (brother) to Samuel Moulton-Barrett (brother). *As twelfth night king one morning lay* ...   [ERM-B]

SD418] [4 March ?1822]. Birthday Verse with Note signed. Arabella Moulton-Barrett to Henrietta Moulton-Barrett. *Come forth my lay* ...   [Altham]

SD419] [4 March ?1822]. Birthday Letter signed. George Goodin Moulton-Barrett to Henrietta Moulton-Barrett. *I hope you have* ...   [Altham]

SD420] [4 March ?1822]. Birthday Letter signed. Henry Moulton-Barrett to Henrietta Moulton-Barrett. *I like nothing better* ...   [Berg]

SD421] [4] March 1822. Birthday Letter signed. Samuel Moulton-Barrett (brother) to Henrietta Moulton-Barrett. *As your birthday is come I must write to you I hope that you will have a very happy party in the cottage I suppose ⟨that⟩ Stormy will be your butler and Ge⟨orge⟩ your footman. Ba said that she would have a ball on her birthday I sup⟨pose you⟩ will have one. I shall write to her. I ⟨know⟩ what fun you will have on your birthday. . . .* [Altham]

SD422] 22 April 1822. A.L.s. C. Robertson to Edward Moulton-Barrett (father). [ERM-B]

SD423] 22 April 1822. A.L.s. Milligan Robertson & Co. to Edward Moulton-Barrett (father). *In consequence of your having . . .* [ERM-B]

SD424] 22 April 1822. A.L.s. Milligan Robertson & Co. to Edward Moulton-Barrett (father). *We have the pleasure . . .* [ERM-B]

SD425] 26 April 1822. Copy of Letter. Edward Moulton-Barrett (father) to [Robertson & Co.] *By your desire I have put my name . . .* [ERM-B]

SD426] [1 May 1822]. Birthday Verse signed. Arabella Moulton-Barrett to Mary Moulton-Barrett. *Come, and celebrate this happy day . . .* [MM-B & RAM-B]

SD427] [1 May 1822]. Birthday Verse unsigned. [Charles John Moulton-Barrett] to Mary Moulton-Barrett. *What shall I say . . .* [Berg]

SD428] 1 May 1822. Birthday Verse signed. Edward Moulton-Barrett (brother) to Mary Moulton-Barrett. [Berg]

SD429] [1 May 1822]. Birthday Letter signed. George Goodin Moulton-Barrett to Mary Moulton-Barrett. *You are kind to me . . .* [Berg]

SD430] [1 May 1822]. Birthday Verse unsigned. [Henrietta Moulton-Barrett] to Mary Moulton-Barrett. *. . . And may she have her hearts desire / Which fills her eyes with sparkling fire / And puts new harp strings to her lyre / Which is to see dear Ba once up again / Breathing the fresh air that breathes the Wren* [Berg]

SD431] [1 May 1822]. Birthday Letter signed. Henry Moulton-Barrett to Mary Moulton-Barrett. *I wish you many . . .* [Berg]

SD432] [1 May 1822]. Birthday Verse signed. Samuel Moulton-Barrett (brother) to Mary Moulton-Barrett. *My Dear Mama I must intreat . . .* [Berg]

SD433] (20 May ?1822). Birthday Verse unsigned. [?Charles John Moulton-Barrett] to Alfred Price Moulton-Barrett. *May you live long . . .* [Berg]

SD434] [20 May ?1822]. Birthday Letter signed. Henry Moulton-Barrett to Alfred Price Moulton-Barrett. *Sweetest boy Daisy happy turns . . .* [Berg]

SD435] [?28 May 1822]. Birthday Letter signed. Charles John Moulton-Barrett to [?Edward Moulton-Barrett (father)]. *I hope you will have . . .* [Altham]

SD436] [28 May ?1822]. Birthday Verse signed with initials. Edward Moulton-Barrett (brother) to Edward Moulton-Barrett (father). *When morning, clad in lustre bright . . .* [Berg]

SD437] [17 June 1822]. Verse signed with initials. "While here forlorn & lost . . . ," by Henry Trant. [ERM-B]

SD438] [26 June ?1822]. Birthday Letter signed. Henry Moulton-Barrett to Edward Moulton-Barrett (brother). *Dearest Borzy's birs-day . . .* [Berg]

SD439] [4 July ?1822]. Birthday Letter signed. George Goodin Moulton-Barrett to Arabella Moulton-Barrett. *How glad I am . . .* [Berg]

SD440] 19–20 July 1822. Two exercises. Entitled "English History" and "Romans," in an unidentified hand. [Altham]

SD441] 20 July 1822. A.L.s. Samuel Moulton-Barrett (brother) to Mary Moulton-Barrett. *I am very sorry to see Papa is gone away tell Ba not to be so witty. . . .* [Berg]

SD442] 27 September 1822. Copy of Document. Baptismal record of Edward George Barrett. [ERM-B]

SD443] [2 November 1822]. A.L.s. Samuel Moulton-Barrett (brother) to Mary Moulton-Barrett. *There is a boy at Cha[r]terhouse ...* [ERM-B]

SD444] [19 November 1822]. A.L.s. Samuel Moulton-Barrett (brother) to Mary Moulton-Barrett, with note by Mary Trepsack. *Jane came to dine with Granny but she did not bring her little boy with her. I hope that Ba will be able to play with us in the Holidays. ... I am glad to hear that Ba is so much better. ...* [Berg]

SD445] [28 December 1822]. Birthday Verse with Note signed. Arabella Moulton-Barrett to Charles John Moulton-Barrett. *My dearest boy ...*
[MM-B & RAM-B]

SD446] [28 December ?1822]. Birthday Verse signed with initials. Edward Moulton-Barrett (brother) to Charles John Moulton-Barrett. *Hail wreathed snows, hail winter's icy chains ...* [Berg]

SD447] 28 December 1822. Birthday Letter signed. George Goodin Moulton-Barrett to Charles John Moulton-Barrett. [Berg]

SD448] 18 January 1823. A.L.s. Richard Barrett to Mary Barrett Lockhead.
[ERM-B]

SD449] 4 March 1823. Birthday Letter (third person). Alfred Price Moulton-Barrett to Henrietta Moulton-Barrett. [Altham]

SD450] 4 March 1823. Birthday Letter signed. Henry Moulton-Barrett to Henrietta Moulton-Barrett. [Altham]

SD451] 6 April [1823]. A.L.s. Samuel Moulton-Barrett (brother) to Mary Moulton-Barrett. *... we are not going to have Holidays till the seventh of May. I hope that Ba will be well by that time. I am so sorry to hear that her ancle is bad. ...*
[Berg]

SD452] 8 April 1823. A.L.s. Hackey Plummer & Blanc to George Goodin Barrett (1792–1854). [ERM-B]

SD453] 1 May 1823. Birthday Letter signed. Arabella S. Butler to Mary Moulton-Barrett. [Berg]

SD454] 1 May 1823. Birthday Letter signed. Louisa C. Butler to Mary Moulton-Barrett. [Berg]

SD455] 1 May 1822 [*sic* for 1823]. Birthday Verse with Note signed with initials. Henrietta Moulton-Barrett to Mary Moulton-Barrett. *Hail lovely May! ...*
[ERM-B]

SD456] [1 May 1823]. Birthday Letter signed. Henry Moulton-Barrett to Mary Moulton-Barrett. *I hope you will let me ...* [Berg]

SD457] 9 May 1823. Copy of Letter. Edward Moulton-Barrett (father) to Samuel Hilton. [ERM-B]

SD458] [20 May ?1823]. Birthday Verse with Note signed. Arabella Moulton-Barrett to Alfred Price Moulton-Barrett. *Let us enjoy this happy day ...*
[MM-B & RAM-B]

SD459] 20 May 1823. Birthday Verse signed. Charles John Moulton-Barrett to Alfred Price Moulton-Barrett. [Berg]

SD460] [20 May ?1823]. Birthday Verse signed with initials. Edward Moulton-Barrett (brother) to Alfred Price Moulton-Barrett. *No tones sublime, no lofty strains of fire ...* [Berg]

SD461] 20 May 1823. Birthday Letter signed. George Goodin Moulton-Barrett to Alfred Price Moulton-Barrett. [MM-B & RAM-B]

SD462] 20 May [1823]. Birthday Verse signed with initials. Henrietta Moulton-Barrett to Alfred Price Moulton-Barrett. *Apollo strike thy lyre again ...*
[Berg]

SD463] 20 May 1823. Birthday Verse signed. Samuel Moulton-Barrett (brother) to Alfred Price Moulton-Barrett. [Berg]

SD464] [28 May ?1823]. Birthday Verse signed. George Goodin Moulton-Barrett to Edward Moulton-Barrett (father). *How happy am I ...*   [Berg]

SD465] [28 May ?1823]. Birthday Letter signed. Henry Moulton-Barrett to Edward Moulton-Barrett (father). *Many many happy turns ...*   [Berg]

SD466] [ca. 1824]. Incomplete A.L. unsigned. [Samuel Moulton-Barrett (uncle)] to Henrietta Moulton-Barrett. *. . . I have long had it in view to give you a bit of my mind, but as a fair opportunity was wanting to me, I unwillingly deferred it until such time as such should present itself—a passage in your letter affords me the Peg, so excuse me if with your leave or without it I hang my hat on it— Before beginning, by way of Dedication, let me announce to you that "my bit of mind" is wholly & exclusively for yourself, Mama & Ba—now to proceed—the text upon which I mean to comment is the passage in your letter in which you allude to Bro's & Sams application for cloathes to their Father—Bro has no excuse for making this application, for* first *he had cloathes in December last, & secondly I have at various times asked him whether he required any, & his answer was always in the negative—I excuse however any thing from Bro, he neither knows better, nor can he do better. But I trust you do, & that you will reflect well, & act cautiously in avoiding any thing which may add to your Fathers expenses, as well as avail yourself of every means of saving him even an application. The result of the late law suit has most unfortunately made it absolutely necessary to consult his pocket as anxiously as an affectionate Child like yourself would consult his feelings— Charity being most required at home, must not travel so much abroad as it used to do— I say this now especially to you dearest Addles, not to reproach, but to guide you that you may know that not until you shall have supplied your own wants, as well as those about you, can you be said to be as likely to assist others. As my own means are of late much improved I hope to be able (not so much out of affection for* YOU ALL) *as out of regard to my Brother, to lighten the burden of providing for your immediate expenses—you will I hope consider this as exclusively applicable for necessaries & not to be laid out otherwise, whilst Ba will I hope,* RELIGIOUSLY *apply her spinsters mite to the same purpose. Unless this be so understood & so applied my object is not gained, & you continue as great a burden upon ...*   [Altham]

SD467] 2 January 1823 [*sic* for 1824]. A.L.s. Victoire to Henrietta Moulton-Barrett. *Voulez vous bien ma très chère et très aimable henriette ...*
          [R.J.L. Altham]

SD468] 11 February 1824. Birthday Letter signed. Henrietta Moulton-Barrett to Septimus Moulton-Barrett.   [Berg]

SD469] 11 February 1824. Birthday Letter signed. Henry Moulton-Barrett to [Septimus Moulton-Barrett]. *My sweet old ...*   [Berg]

SD470] [4 March ?1824]. Birthday Letter signed. Edward Moulton-Barrett (brother) to Henrietta Moulton-Barrett. *. . . Sam desires me to tell you to tell Ba as your letter will be at Hope End before hers that he will be at Gloucester on Thursday. . . .*   [Altham]

SD471] [28 March 1824]. A.L.s. Samuel Moulton-Barrett (brother) to Henrietta Moulton-Barrett. *. . . We never hear how Ba's Poetry is going on I keep thinking it will be published every day for I always look in the newspapers to see. I wish she would let us know. . . .*   [Altham]

SD472] [1 May ?1824]. Birthday Letter signed. Alfred Price Moulton-Barrett to Mary Moulton-Barrett. *Mama not peacock but Mama ...*   [Berg]

SD473] 1 May 1824. Birthday Verse with Note signed. Arabella Moulton-Barrett to Mary Moulton-Barrett.   [Berg]

SD474] [1 May ?1824]. Birthday Verse signed. Charles John Moulton-Barrett to Mary Moulton-Barrett. *My dear mama I hope you are well today* . . .   [Berg]

SD475] [1 May ?1824]. Birthday Letter signed with initials. George Goodin Moulton-Barrett to Mary Moulton-Barrett. *I hope we shall have* . . .   [Berg]

SD476] 1 May 1824. Birthday Letter signed. Henrietta Moulton-Barrett to Mary Moulton-Barrett.   [Berg]

SD477] [1 May 1824]. Birthday Letter signed. Henry Moulton-Barrett to Mary Moulton-Barrett. *indeed I love you* . . .   [Berg]

SD478] 20 May 1824. Birthday Verse signed. Arabella Moulton-Barrett to Alfred Price Moulton-Barrett.   [MM-B & RAM-B]

SD479] [20 May ?1824]. Birthday Verse signed with initials. Edward Moulton-Barrett (brother) to Alfred Price Moulton-Barrett. *Tis spring! the sun with renovating ray* . . .   [Berg]

SD480] [20 May ?1824]. Birthday Letter signed. Henry Moulton-Barrett to Alfred Price Moulton-Barrett. *I wish you* . . .   [Berg]

SD481] [28 May ?1824]. Birthday Letter signed. Alfred Price Moulton-Barrett to Edward Moulton-Barrett (father). *me wish ou* . . .   [Berg]

SD482] 28 May 1824. Birthday Verse with Note signed. Arabella Moulton-Barrett to Edward Moulton-Barrett (father).   [MM-B & RAM-B]

SD483] 28 May 1824. Birthday Verse signed. Charles John Moulton-Barrett to Edward Moulton-Barrett (father).   [Berg]

SD484] 28 June [*sic* for May] 1824. Birthday Letter signed. Henrietta Moulton-Barrett to Edward Moulton-Barrett (father).   [Berg]

SD485] 28 May [1824]. Birthday Verse signed. Samuel Moulton-Barrett (brother) to Edward Moulton-Barrett (father). *O, t' is the twenty eighth of May* . . .
                                                                        [Berg]

SD486] 14 June 1824. A.L.s. Michael White Lee to George Goodin Barrett (1792–1854), concerning death of Samuel Barrett (1788–1824).   [ERM-B]

SD487] [29 June 1824]. A.L.s. Samuel Moulton-Barrett (brother) to Henrietta Moulton-Barrett. . . . *There is no news I can tell for there has been no flogging for a long time, tell Stormy he must come to be flogged, or Ba, as she wants to come so much.* . . .   [Altham]

SD488] [29 June 1824]. A.L.s. Samuel Moulton-Barrett (brother) to Mary Moulton-Barrett. *I beg your pardon for not writing* . . .   [Altham]

SD489] [15 July ?1824]. Birthday Verse with Note signed. Arabella Moulton-Barrett to George Goodin Moulton-Barrett. *Come Muses come, and aid my lay* . . .
                                                            [MM-B & RAM-B]

SD490] 15 July 1824. Birthday Verse signed. Charles John Moulton-Barrett to George Goodin Moulton-Barrett.   [Berg]

SD491] [15 July 1824]. Birthday Letter signed. Henry Moulton-Barrett to George Goodin Moulton-Barrett. *I wish you many happy returns of your day* . . .
                                                                        [Berg]

SD492] [30 July 1824]. A.L.s. Samuel Moulton-Barrett (brother) to Mary Moulton-Barrett, with note by Mary Trepsack. . . . *the holidays begin next Thursday so you must get Ba and Henrietta from Cheltenham.* . . .   [Berg]

SD493] [28 December ?1824]. Birthday Verse unsigned. [Edward Moulton-Barrett (brother)] to Charles John Moulton-Barrett. *How vain the attempt* . . .   [Berg]

SD494] [ca. 1825]. Birthday Letter signed. Ann to Mrs. Ogle. *Now as it is your birthday . . .*   [Berg]

SD495] [ca. 1825]. A.L.s. A. E. Biddulph to Henrietta Moulton-Barrett. *We send a loaf of very . . .*   [Altham]

SD496] [ca. 1825]. A.L.s. Frances Butler to Henrietta Moulton-Barrett. *You should I assure you . . .*   [Berg]

SD497] [ca. 1825]. A.L.s. Mary Clementina Moulton-Barrett to Henrietta Moulton-Barrett. *The frames for the . . .*   [Altham]

SD498] [ca. 1825]. A.L. unsigned. [?Samuel Moulton-Barrett (brother)] to Edward Moulton-Barrett (father). *I write to you this day . . .*   [Berg]

SD499] [ca. 1825]. A.L.s. Samuel Moulton-Barrett (brother) to Henrietta Moulton-Barrett. *. . . I hope that Ba is better as I should very much like to hear. I hope that you will very soon write to me to tell me how she is. . . .*   [Altham]

SD500] [ca. 1825]. Cover Sheet. Addressed in unidentified hand to Arabella Graham-Clarke (aunt), bearing juvenile comments by Moulton-Barrett children.
                                                                                [RAM-B]

SD501] 3 January 1825. A.L.s. Selina Graham to Henrietta Moulton-Barrett.
                                                                                [Altham]

SD502] [13 January ?1825]. Birthday Letter signed. Edward Moulton-Barrett (brother) to Samuel Moulton-Barrett (brother). *. . . I would have adressed you in verse but I did not know this pleasing day would have arrived so soon (in which I am most agreably surprised) and I not being so intimate with my Muse as Ba is with hers I am obliged to submit to my hard fate which I do very reluctantly but I hope you will not think me less sincere by it as indeed I am not. . . .*   [Berg]

SD503] [?February 1825]. A.L.s. [Arabella Graham-Clarke (aunt)] to Henrietta Moulton-Barrett. *Your letter charmed me and I should . . .*   [Altham]

SD504] [10 February 1825]. A.L.s. Mary Clementina Moulton-Barrett to Henrietta Moulton-Barrett. *I must thank you . . .*   [Altham]

SD505] 11 February [?1825]. Birthday Letter signed. Alfred Price Moulton-Barrett to Septimus Moulton-Barrett. *I wish you many . . .*   [Berg]

SD506] 11 February 1825. Birthday Verse signed. Arabella Moulton-Barrett to Septimus Moulton-Barrett.   [MM-B & RAM-B]

SD507] 11 February 1825. Birthday Verse signed. George Goodin Moulton-Barrett to Septimus Moulton-Barrett.   [Berg]

SD508] 23 February 1825. A.L.s. Samuel Moulton-Barrett (brother) to Henrietta Moulton-Barrett.   [Altham]

SD509] 27 February 1825. A.L.s. Samuel Moulton-Barrett (brother) to Henrietta Moulton-Barrett.   [Altham]

SD510] [3 March 1825]. Birthday Letter signed. Mary Clementina Moulton-Barrett to Henrietta Moulton-Barrett, with note by Samuel Moulton-Barrett (uncle). *Pray accept this little . . .*   [Altham]

SD511] 6 March 1825. Incomplete A.L. [Samuel Moulton-Barrett (brother)] to Henrietta Moulton-Barrett. *You must really forgive my impertinent [letter] I wrote yesterday for I really was in such I rage I was determined to give it to you I did not suspect you but Ba for I know it was her for it was just in her stile so I immediatly wrote and gave it to her. . . . You must excuse me for not writing to you on your Birthday for you know how busy I always am in the week days but however I wish you many happy returns of your birthday now and Ba's to for I believe it is her's to day. . . . I could not prevent Monies from reading your letter he said he was very much pleased with it how he laughed when he saw the shilling instead of the sovereign he said he was certain Ba had changed it do not let her*

have your letter again if it was her but it was very wise of her to keep nineteen
shillings and send me one I have sent it . . .   [Altham]
SD512] [April ?1825]. A.L.s. Samuel Moulton-Barrett (brother) to Henrietta
Moulton-Barrett. *I received your letter . . .*   [Altham]
SD513] [11 April 1825]. A.L.s. Mary Clementina Moulton-Barrett to
Henrietta Moulton-Barrett. . . . *Pray tell your dear Mother and Ba that I am*
grateful for their kind letters, which I only delay to answer according to the dictates
of my heart; but will not do so at this moment ⟨that⟩ another post may carry my
letters, & thus increase the frequency of my giving you intelligence of dear Mrs.
M and Trepsack whille I am with you. . . .   [Altham]
SD514] 1 May 1825. Birthday Verse with Note signed. Arabella Moulton-
Barrett to Mary Moulton-Barrett.   [MM-B & RAM-B]
SD515] 1 May 1825. Birthday Verse with Note signed. Charles John
Moulton-Barrett to Mary Moulton-Barrett.   [Berg]
SD516] 1 May 1825. Birthday Verse with Note signed. George Goodin
Moulton-Barrett to Mary Moulton-Barrett.   [Berg]
SD517] 1 May 1825. Birthday Letter (in Italian) signed. Henrietta Moulton-
Barrett to Mary Moulton-Barrett.   [Berg]
SD518] 1 May 1825. Birthday Letter signed. Henry Moulton-Barrett to Mary
Moulton-Barrett.   [Berg]
SD519] 1 May 1825. Birthday Letter unsigned. [?Septimus Moulton-Barrett]
to Mary Moulton-Barrett. *Dear Mama this is you's birthday . . .*   [Berg]
SD520] [28 May ?1825]. Birthday Verse unsigned. [?Arabella Moulton-
Barrett] to Edward Moulton-Barrett (father). *Roused from her hallowed haunts no*
Muse I pray . . .   [Berg]
SD521] 28 May 1825. Birthday Verse with Note signed. Charles John
Moulton-Barrett to Edward Moulton-Barrett (father).   [Berg]
SD522] [28 May] 1825. Birthday Verse unsigned. [Edward Moulton-Barrett
(brother)] to Edward Moulton-Barrett (father). *Beauteous and bright again the rosy*
spring . . .   [Kelley]
SD523] [28 May] 1825. Birthday Letter signed. George Goodin Moulton-
Barrett to Edward Moulton-Barrett (father). *I hope this day may . . .*   [Berg]
SD524] [28 May 1825]. Birthday Letter signed. Henry Moulton-Barrett to
[Edward Moulton-Barrett (father)]. *I hope by your next birthday . . .*   [Berg]
SD525] 28 May 1825. Birthday Verse with Note signed. Samuel Moulton-
Barrett (brother) to Edward Moulton-Barrett (father).   [Berg]
SD526] [28 May ?1825]. Birthday Letter signed. Septimus Moulton-Barrett
to Edward Moulton-Barrett (father). *This is ous birthday . . .*   [Berg]
SD527] [ca. June 1825]. A.L.s. Arabella Graham-Clarke (aunt) to Henrietta
Moulton-Barrett. *As I have only a moment . . .*   [Altham]
SD528] 3 June 1825. Receipt. William Braess to George Goodin Barrett
(1792–1854), concerning funeral of Mary Barrett Lockhead.   [ERM-B]
SD529] [July 1825]. A.L.s. Arabella Moulton-Barrett to Mary Moulton-
Barrett. *J'espère que vous avez arrivè en parfaite . . .*   [MM-B & RAM-B]
SD530] [July 1825]. Incomplete A.L. [Henrietta Moulton-Barrett] to
Arabella Moulton-Barrett. *I will not lose a post in thanking you for your amusing*
letter, & at the same time assuring you of my inveterate anger for your unpardonable
saucy hint to me in your epistle to Ba, I give you warning Arabel if you attempt
again to transgress I shall not forgive you so quickly. . . .   [Wellesley]
SD531] 15 July 1825. Birthday Verse with Note signed. Arabella Moulton-
Barrett to George Goodin Moulton-Barrett.   [MM-B & RAM-B]

SD532] 15 July 1825. Birthday Verse with Note signed. Charles John Moulton-Barrett to George Goodin Moulton-Barrett.   [Berg]

SD533] 15 July 1825. Birthday Letter signed. Henry Moulton-Barrett to [George Goodin Moulton-Barrett]. *You are a nice chap ...*   [Berg]

SD534] [ca. August 1825]. A.L.s. George Goodin Moulton-Barrett to Mary Moulton-Barrett. *I am very sorry for not writing ...*   [Berg]

SD535] [ca. August 1825]. A.L.s. Mary Moulton-Barrett to Henrietta Moulton-Barrett. *I really am uneasy not to have had a line from you or Ba so long—tell her to remember, that two or three lines on a half sheet is all. I have [not] heard from her for a month not a line too from Hope End! If tomorrow does not bring me letters, I think I shall* set off home *which I should indeed have done with James yesterday,* if I could, *but letters demanded his return so speedily that he was obliged to hurry by Liverpool, & set off at 11 last night— ...*   [BL]

SD536] [August 1825]. A.L.s. Charles John Moulton-Barrett to Mary Moulton-Barrett. *I hear you have arrived at Garryhundon. ...*   [Berg]

SD537] [August 1825]. A.L.s. Charles John Moulton-Barrett to Mary Moulton-Barrett. *I hope you will ...*   [Berg]

SD538] 2 August 1825. A.L.s. Richard Barrett to Elizabeth Barrett Williams.   [ERM-B]

SD539] 13 August 1825. A.L.s. Charles John Moulton-Barrett to Mary Moulton-Barrett.   [Berg]

SD540] 18 August [1825]. A.L.s. Henrietta Moulton-Barrett to Arabella Moulton-Barrett. *As Ba has usurped my Quill, to write to our dearest Papa, I must console myself by writing to you ... Ba you may suppose is delighted at the permission that our dearest Papa has given her to bathe, I am particularly pleased about it, as in my opinion I think it will be of great service to her– ...*   [Wellesley]

SD541] [ca. November 1825]. A.L.s. Mary Clementina Moulton-Barrett to Mary Moulton-Barrett. *... I have delighted Mama by reading to her dear Ba's beautiful lines on Judah—and am much obliged to Mr. Barrett for affording her that pleasure. I have directed the paper on to dear Mrs. M. ...*   [UCLA]

SD542] [10 November 1825]. Incomplete A.L.s. Mary Clementina Moulton-Barrett to Mary Moulton-Barrett. With note in the hand of Mary Trepsack. *... went with their party to a launch yesterday—Sam having ...*   [Scripps]

SD543] [12 November 1825]. A.L.s. Henrietta Moulton-Barrett to James Graham-Clarke. *I cannot refrain from adding a few lines to Ba's despatch ...*   [ERM-B]

SD544] [ca. 1826]. A.L.s. Alfred Price Moulton-Barrett to Edward Moulton-Barrett (father). *I love you nearly as well ...*   [Berg]

SD545] [ca. 1826]. A.M. unsigned. Lullaby by [?Henrietta Moulton-Barrett] to Mary Moulton-Barrett. Includes musical score. *hushabye baby ...*   [Berg]

SD546] [ca. 1826]. Incomplete A.L. [?Mary Clementina Moulton-Barrett] to Arabella Moulton-Barrett. *... But now to answer Mama's Queries must be my first undertaking—tell her. There is but little hope of Granny going to Hope End this winter she is immoveable– That our beloved Bro if he continues as he is now will be able to adjourn to the Charter House in a very few days & that Ba & Henrietta never say any thing about returning home as such is Granny's particular desire– ...*   [Wellesley]

SD547] 29 January 1826. A.L.s. John Altham Graham-Clarke to Edward Moulton-Barrett (father).   [ERM-B]

SD548] 30 January 1826. A.L.s. Lord Petre to John Cook.   [Altham]

SD549] 10 March 1826. A.L.s. Lord Petre to John Cook.   [Altham]

SD550]   11 April [1826]. A.L. unsigned. [Mary Moulton-Barrett] to Henrietta Moulton-Barrett. . . . *How little did I think when I saw you drive away in Mary's barouche, that I was not to see those dear faces again for* 10 *long months. They are indeed gone, & yet no certain means arranged for your return! but indeed this* must *be thought of.* . . . *Dear Grandmamma has I fear been suffering a good deal, from the shaking hand in which her letter of yesterday was written—from* her cough—*she has had Dr. Ramsay, but she assures me that she is better, in proof of which she was to have a large dinner party the next day.* . . . *She says the poem has caused quite a sensation in the North—nearly* 50 *copies were sold in NC & more ordered. Dr. Ramsay, who is a* very *clever man, said that he considered it so extraordinary a production that he did not doubt its being reviewed—that he should have some conversation about it with Mr Losh who is one of the illuminati of the North, & well acquainted with the learned in Edingh. Mr. Daniell was spreading its fame in Durham, that County which is bound to take a lively interest, seeing that the authoress drew her first breath there. My mother had sent a copy into Scotland to Mrs. Waldie, a person highly qualified to appreciate it, & having known me from my birth, & having many literary friends, my mother thought it might be the means of introducing it favourably into Scotland, & therefore made* this *one exception to her rule of never lending or giving it. I trust a great deal will be done there for the loved authoress's fame & pocket, for however base & low, the latter may be in competition with the former, it is not to be despised. After Church on Sunday, a shower of rain induced us to accept the shelter of Mr. Hockin's room, where he said with some pique, that he had heard for the* first *time of the poem at Mr. Dean's dinner & that he should certainly purchase it immediately, particularly as Papa had* bought *his sermon—* . . . *I do envy you the sight of Dr. Batty's beautiful drawings, & wish he would lend you one to copy, tho' I suppose it could scarcely be* asked, *prints are engraved from many of them: he has an accurate knowledge of music too, & is altogether a man of such good taste, that I entirely depend not only on his purchasing, but also on his greatly admiring our precious Essay. Hentta Farrer writes in wonder of it, no one, she says, would believe it to be the work of a female, much less, so young a one.* . . . *Mrs. Deffell tells me she is in some respects better, in others worse since I saw her.* . . . *Mrs. Campbell & her lovely children quite well. They all have* the *poem. Mrs. D says it has been her amusement &* study *& however incapable she may be of judging of a literary work, nature & the feelings of the heart she can appreciate as well as the learned, therefore she is delighted with the Essay, tho' the subject be dry & deep—"it exhibits in its pages the purity, the piety of the Author's mind. Extensive reading & the power of carefully separating, as she proceeds in the study of dangerous writers, the tares from the wheat, it seems to me a wonderful production." She begs that you & Ba will not omit to let them see you as you go thro' London* . . . *Daly has condescended to put the flower garden in beautiful order sowing seeds &c* . . . *Georgy has taken possession of one of Ba's curved beds, & is doing more for it, than ever the proprietor would.* . . .   [BL]

SD551]   26 April [ca. 1826]. A.L. (third person). Mr. Morgan to Mary Moulton-Barrett. *Mr. Morgan presents* . . .   [Scripps]

SD552]   16 May 1826. A.L.s. Angela Bayford to Henrietta Moulton-Barrett. . . . *As to Ba, I hardly dare offer my congratulations to her, as excepting the pleasure she must undoubtedly derive from seeing those so dear to her, I doubt whether she is much charmed with the removal from a Town where she may have free, and continual access to a Library—and a* Pastry-Cooks! *I am also afraid, she will not relish the greek and latin lessons, which are again, I suppose to be*

*under her control. But beg her to weigh against these disadvantages, the great
delight of being able to regale at pleasure on the strawberries, and cherries, which
will soon begin to ripen. . . . We sent a copy of Essay on Mind, to Papa who is
still in the Netherlands, and he has lent it to my uncle James, who thinks some
parts of it most* exquisite, *and is* astonished & delig⟨hted⟩ *with it* ⟨al⟩*together,
and he thinks a copy of it ough⟨t⟩ directly to be sent from the Author to each of
the principal Reviews, and he has no doubt but the Quarterly will notice it. Papa
highly approves of this plan, and begs that Ba will adopt it without loss of time.
Emily lent the Essay on Mind to John Cumberlige who read it attentively and
returned it, marked in* several *places, but only* once *in* disapprobation. *At the corner
of what page this 'Qu' is placed I dare not tell, and I fear even Emily will not
venture, without some encouragement from Ba. . . .*   [Altham]

   SD553] [28 May ?1826]. Birthday Letter signed. Alfred Price Moulton-
Barrett to Edward Moulton-Barrett (father). *Many happy return . . .*   [Wellesley]

   SD554] [28 May ?1826]. Birthday Verse signed. Arabella Moulton-Barrett
to Edward Moulton-Barrett (father). *This is the pleasant month of May . . .*
                                                                    [MM-B & RAM-B]

   SD555] 28 May 1825 [*sic* for 1826]. Birthday Verse signed. Charles John
Moulton-Barrett to Edward Moulton-Barrett (father). *Hygeia come, and give us
health . . .*   [Wellesley]

   SD556] [28 May ?1826]. Birthday Verse unsigned. [Edward Moulton-Barrett
(brother)] to Edward Moulton-Barrett (father). *If ere pure thoughts inhabit mortal
breast . . .*   [Wellesley]

   SD557] 28 May 1826. Birthday Verse unsigned. [?George Goodin Moulton-
Barrett] to Edward Moulton-Barrett (father). *May old Saturn give me time . . .*
                                                                        [Wellesley]

   SD558] [28 May ?1826]. Birthday Verse signed. Henrietta Moulton-Barrett
to Edward Moulton-Barrett (father). *Returned to Home, returned to thee . . .*   [Berg]

   SD559] [28 May ?1826]. Birthday Letter signed. Henry Moulton-Barrett to
Edward Moulton-Barrett (father). *What shall I say . . .*   [Wellesley]

   SD560] [?28 May 1826]. Birthday Note signed. Octavius Moulton-Barrett
to Edward Moulton-Barrett (father). *Most witty will you like Ockys . . .*   [Wellesley]

   SD561] [15 July ?1826]. Birthday Letter signed. Alfred Price Moulton-
Barrett to George Goodin Moulton-Barrett. *my dear george how glad I am . . .*
                                                                            [Berg]

   SD562] [ca. August 1826]. A.L. signed with initial. Mary Trepsack to
Henrietta Moulton-Barrett. . . . *You quite astonish me in expressing so much anxiety
about a certain little gentleman, who you know I vowed vengeance against. I cannot
account for it, but there is a something in his ugly face which disarms you the
moment you see him, & sends anger flying from him. We sent for a place as soon
as we got Ba's letter begging he might not be kept, at the same time was in hopes
none wd be had. I know he is anxious, altho he appears perfectly contented. It
certainly is more natural that he shd prefer being with such lovely set as you all
are, than with us who have nothing to amuse him with. . . . I agree with you that
Ba has a sweet voice, If she wd only forget any one was listening to her, but a
little practice wd. soon make her get the better of that nervousness. See what it is
to work hard my dear henny, by so doing you find the pleasure it has given to your
father & mother, for we have been delighted to hear they think you look very much
improved in your musick. I wish you were both here that you might have a few
lessons whilst we remain. . . .*   [Altham]

SD563]   27 September [1826]. A.L.s. Samuel Moulton-Barrett (brother) to Henrietta Moulton-Barrett. *I hope I shall have a letter from* [*you*] *soon for I have written twice to your once; I had a letter from dearest Ba this morning, you cannot think how delighted I was to have a letter from her as it was the first I ever had. I hope she will not be offended at my not answering her letter sooner but tell her I will promise to answer it on Saturday. . . .*   [Altham]

SD564]   5 October 1826. A.L.s. Samuel Moulton-Barrett (brother) to Henrietta Moulton-Barrett. With a continuation in the hand of Mary Trepsack. [By Sam]: *. . . I have not heard from you for more than a week and I have written so often, but I must forgive you as I know you cannot help it for you are so busy with the children hearing them their lessons, and making that little girl Ba walk out, . . . Tell Ba that Tippy will send her books, I mean to say Bro's books, the first opportunity. I shall keep as many as I think proper. . . .* [By Treppy]: *. . . say to Ba, never to talk to me again about Campbell, I am in a rage whenever I hear his name mentioned. I enquired about the New Monthly on Monday & was disappointed. The advertisement in one of the papers say Miss LEL is to enrich the Literary Gazette with another of her poems. I hope when our dear authoress is as well known we shall see her name blazoned in the public press. I wish we could ascertain the number of her copies sold—she must pick up her spirits. Merit will meet with its due reward. I hope she will spend a pleasant time with her old friend Mr. Price, she has already found one disinterested admirer. . . .*   [Altham]

SD565]   14 October 1826. A.L.s. John Ramsay to James Graham-Clarke. *Pilgrim St. N. Castle / Dear Sir / Some time ago I sent a Copy of the little work of your highly-gifted, elegant-minded Niece to a literary character in Edinburgh well known to Jeffrey. I did not hear from him till yesterday.– Now tho' he does not approve of the book being sent to Jeffrey yet as he enters pretty fully upon the* subject of Mind *and into the reasons that unfit it to be compressed into didactic poetry I shall transcribe parts of his letter to me.*

"I perused with much pleasure the Essay on Mind &ca. The whole I consider an excellent production when the age of the Author is taken into account. But I have hesitated to present the book to the Edinr Reviewers– They who remember how Byrons early productions were treated by that Corps *will not be surprised that I should entertain doubts on the subject. You know there is no friendship in trade, and if reviewed at all the book must be treated in the usual style of that work—that is it must be left to the poetical department which I believe* is not Jeffreys. *If read by himself from politeness to me he would either have taken no notice of it, or treated it with that perfect freedom which from the constitution of his mind he can scarcely relinquish, but which I am convinced must in this case have produced painful feelings in the mind of the young author, & which must have proved hurtful to the future progress of her talents.– The subject "Mind" is greatly too extensive, and instead of being exhausted the different departments of the subject are scarcely noticed– Not unnaturally perhaps an author regards* authors *as the first of beings—Historians—Metaphysicians—Poets—are mentioned and something is said of Science generally– The powers of mind are also divided into Invention, Judgement, Memory and Imagination– Now all this falls greatly—immeasureably short of the subject. The great* actors *in Life's Drama are left out—tho' surely more illustrious than those who could merely tell or celebrate the story of their effects– Hampden was greater than Hume—& the elder and younger Brutus than the Historians of their conduct– In short the* speculative *efforts of mind are adverted to but the higher efforts of*

Will *or voluntary energy are overlooked– Warriors, Statesmen, Navigators—*
Merchants, Inventors of Machinery (Archimedes excepted) who alleviate and
almost defeat the doom "in the sweat of thy face shalt thou eat bread" – It might
be lawful to forget the Saints—Apostles & Martyrs, Stoics, Essenes, Jansenists,
Calvinists &ca—but surely it was wrong to overlook the devotedness of your
profession in the cause of humanity encountering so many dangers, or the
landable wrestlings of men of my trade in order to evacuate the ill temper and
pockets of the Leiges– Mind is too wide a field for a poem—or for a book– In
treating such a subject it would be necessary to write de rebus omnibus et
quibusdam aliis—*from the worm to the Angel, aye and higher than the Angel.–*
Poetry is unsuitable for the discussion of a subject of such extent– Begin with
the question– What is mind—whence came it & what is its destiny? Then
consider its modifications—in animals—in nations & individuals– Its progress
historically– Its sympathies, hatreds &ca.– The compliment to Jeffrey, I fear,
renders it scarcely possible for him to review the poem favourably– In deed
there are too many moderns mentioned– Byron "the Mount Blanc of intellect"
Byron had great poetical talents, but he was a conceited profligate, destitute
of common sense– This is Gods truth of him and it is truly a melancholly
circumstance that it should be so– I was once dragged to hear "Irving" preach–
We passed three weary hours listening to an exhibition of Zealously—slowly &
pompously delivered nothingness.– Having said so much if you still bid me send
the Book to Jeffrey I will obey but I fear the result." ——
So far my friends letter, I have freely communicated his sentiments as you may
probably convey them to Miss Barrett– Perhaps my friend is fastidious as he
published himself a volume some years ago on "Moral Science"* after having
given much attention to the subject of Mind. It was published by Longman Hurst
& Rees in the year 1805.– Should Miss B. wish to see it and not be able to procure
it nearer than N. Castle I shall have great plea⟨s⟩ure in sending it– It ⟨is⟩ full of
original views.– / I am, Dear Sir, yours truly / John Ramsay. [In unidentified
hand.] * *"Principles of Moral Science" by Robert Forsyth – 1805 – 8vo.*   [ERM-B]

SD566]   [ca. November 1826]. A.L.s. Samuel Moulton-Barrett (brother) to
Henrietta Moulton-Barrett. *I have just arrived here in time . . .*   [ERM-B]

SD567]   16 November 1826. A.L.s. Angela Bayford to Henrietta Moulton-
Barrett. *. . . Albert Heseltine has been staying with us a few days, he is only just*
returned from the West-Indies. He is a nice, good natured Boy, full of fun, &
amuses us not a little by his frequent introduction, of sea-phrases in every thing
he says. He has taken great pains to explain the meaning of these terms, & we
have profited so much by his instruction that many parts of that pretty little Poem
Fawlkner's Ship-wreck, which Ba in her kindness gave to Emily, are now elucidated,
to our no small gratification. . . . I am charged with a long message from Emily
to Ba, the purpose of which is to beg her to write immediately an account of all
she has been doing, & saying during her late absence from Hope-End; she expects
to derive much entertainment from it. . . .   [Altham]

SD568]   18 November 1826. A.L.s. Samuel Moulton-Barrett (brother) to
Henrietta Moulton-Barrett. *. . . I am in great haste as I must write to Tippy every*
Saturday, or she will think that I have forgot her; tell Bro that if he does not write
to one of them to thank them they will [not] give him anything again. This is quite
a secret so do not tell any body but Bro and Ba. . . .   [Altham]

SD569]   29 November 1826. A.L.s. Samuel Moulton-Barrett (brother) to
Henrietta Moulton-Barrett. *. . . Mr Hartley asked me to send him Ba's Poem for*

he said he had heard so much about it in the city that he must see it, so I am going to send it to him tomorrow. . . . [Altham]

SD570] 2 December 1826. A.L.s. Samuel Moulton-Barrett (brother) to Henrietta Moulton-Barrett. [Altham]

SD571] 23 December 1826. A.L.s. James Fraser to Samuel Moulton-Barrett (uncle). [ERM-B]

SD572] [25 December 1826]. A.L.s. Mary Trepsack to Henrietta Moulton-Barrett. *Your Letter of Wednesday my dear Addles gave us . . .* [Altham]

SD573] 28 December 1826. Birthday Letter signed. George Goodin Moulton-Barrett to Charles John Moulton-Barrett. [Berg]

SD574] 28 December 1826. Birthday Letter signed. Henrietta Moulton-Barrett to Charles John Moulton-Barrett. [Berg]

SD575] [?28 December 1826]. Birthday Letter signed. Henry Moulton-Barrett to Charles John Moulton-Barrett. *I hope you are not so . . .* [Berg]

SD576] 19 [*sic* for 29] December 1826. Birthday Letter signed. Thomas Butler to Charles John Moulton-Barrett. [Berg]

SD577] 29 December 1826. Birthday Letter signed. Samuel Moulton-Barrett (brother) to Charles John Moulton-Barrett. [Berg]

SUPPORTING DOCUMENTS: INDEX OF CORRESPONDENTS

(References are to SD number, not page number.)

APPENDIX III

Autobiographical Essays by EBB

AMONG THE COPIOUS juvenilia that are extant, five autobiographical sketches have survived. They are published here to provide background to EBB's early correspondence.

1. MY OWN CHARACTER [1]

"Sure I am that all the light we can let in upon our own minds all the acquaintance we can make with our own understandings will not only be very pleasant but bring us great advantage in directing our thoughts in the search of other things" Locke[.] [2]

Under the authority of so great a man I proceed in the investigation of myself with no small anxiety[.] Hitherto I have forgotten myself I have thought niether of my few perfections nor of my many failings[.] I have endeavoured to extricate myself in the windings of other souls—of other characters[.] I have endeavoured (I may say) to seek truth with an ardent eye—a sincere heart—of that I can boast—but I have never even in imagination looked into my own breast– How few indeed know themselves! The investigation of oneself is an anxious employment[.] The heart may appear cor[r]upted by vanity exalted by pride soured by ill temper & then that brilliant phantom so dear to every soul self estimation fades for *ever*—& those shining clouds on which you have soared so often to fame sink under self debasement—but shall such weakness prevent us from looking into ourselves? No!–

I am not vain but I have some tincture of pride about me which I fear not to own on the contrary which I like to boast of– I am not at all insensible to flattery when in a proportionate degree but when outraged I am conscious of it– I prefer praise most when seasoned with censure as it then appears under the light of truth– I detest flattery when given by those whom I feel unworthy[.] I detest flattery when carried (as I said before) beyond just limits– I confess that I enjoy fame more than any worldly pleasure. I know it is transient & yet I worship it as such– I am fond of reading & of all literary oc[c]upations– I hate needlework & drawing because I never feel oc[c]upied whilst I work or draw– I know not why—but I always am

1. This item dates from June 1818. It was written in a notebook which bears the title "Memorandum Book Containting [*sic*] the Day & Night thoughts of Elizth Barrett," now at Wellesley College (see *Reconstruction*, D1410). It was published previously in *BIS*, 2, 119–121, with two other entries, not of an autobiographical nature, from a copy in the hand of EBB's mother. This publication is from EBB's original manuscript.

2. John Locke, *An Essay Concerning Human Understanding* (1690), Introduction. In a notebook recording EBB's reading during the period 1824–26, the lengthiest analysis is devoted to Locke's *Essay* (see *Reconstruction*, D1369).

fatigued– Dancing I consider as mere idleness– I abhor Music– I am told it is the trouble of learning that I dislike– It is not so– I have no desire to learn– I always feel weary—full of en[n]ui when at the piano– I sit down discontented & I rise disgusted[.] Homer I adore as more than human and I never read Popes fine translation without feeling exalted above my self–[3] I dread being despised as vain more than I can express–

I am not cowardly in the least on the contrary I can sometimes brave the greatest dangers without fear nothing can provoke me more than a tax of cowardice which I hate– I am not in the least obstinate but I am always decided in what I think right– I have a resolution to bear pain or to do any thing that I wish.

I am very passionate but impatience is my ruling passion– I can confess without shame I am willing to repent & I can forgive without malice but impatience leads me into more faults than I can repent—but I CAN restrain myself tho' it must be with a strong effort– Perhaps I have passed over many very many of my faults perhaps I have looked only at my best side– However this may be I know not but if it is considered that this is written with an earnest desire of improvement with an earnest desire of reaching the truth—perhaps I MAY be forgiven–

2. GLIMPSES INTO MY OWN LIFE AND LITERARY CHARACTER[4]

To be ones own chronicler is a task generally dictated by extreme vanity and often by that instinctive feeling which prompts the soul of man to snatch the records of his life from the dun and misty ocean of oblivion– Man is naturally enamoured of immortality, and tho the brazen trump of fame echoes his deeds when he sleeps[,] tho the cold sod is closed oer his corrupted form yet he shrinks from that deathlike that awful stillness, the dreadful attribute of the grave– Nothing can more plainly denote the souls eternity than the instinctive thirst for immortality which universally throbs in the heart of man– Would that benevolent Being whose kind spirit finds pleasure in the happiness of his Creatures have implanted in their bosoms such a feeling in vain? Is it consonant with divine mercy to tantalise us afar with the bright and heavenly fields of immortality and then closing at once the glorious prospect, forbid that endearing hope to console and allow the cold turf to moulder with our dust and the soul which once animated it fondly considered by us immortal, instead of those glorious & celestial plains to find its last sad assylum in the grave?– The sage midst sandy desserts or buried in the awful stillness of wooded vales boasts that he can forget the world and despise its greatness, but oh can he as sincerely desire to be forgotten by it[,] can he look unmoved on the damp and mournful tomb which his own hands have framed and where soon his wearied limbs shall

3. Alexander Pope translated *The Iliad* (1715–20) and *The Odyssey* (1725–26).
4. This essay, the most ambitious of the five, is undated. Its context clearly indicates that its composition did not take place all at one time. The first part, composed in 1820 when she was fourteen, was later expanded to include her fifteenth birthday the following year. It was first published in *HUP*, I, 3–28. (Forman also published a later incomplete draft copy of this essay in *HUP*, II, 4–8, the manuscript of which sold with Forman's library and has not been located—see *Reconstruction*, D1298.) It is printed here from the manuscript in the Huntington Library (*Reconstruction*, D1297), which bears a docket by RB: "Her own life & character to her 15th year."

lay and tho sensible that the world cannot "soothe the cold dull ear of death"[5] yet is not that silence awful even to him, is it not dreadful to descend into that damp grave unseen unmourned unwept for and forgotten?

But no feeling of this kind has influenced me or prompted me to write my own life, I am of too little consequence, perhaps even to gain a transient thought when the earth has closed over me save from those dear friends who have loved me in life– My days may pass away as the moonbeam from the ocean or as the little particle of sand which now glimmers in the evening ray and now is borne away in the evening breeze! Perhaps these pages may never meet a human eye—and therefore no EXCESSIVE vanity can dictate them tho a feeling akin to it SELF LOVE may have prompted my not unwilling pen.– In writing my own life[,] to be impartial is a difficult task and being so can only excuse such an attempt from one so young and inexperienced!

$$- \quad - \quad - \quad - \quad - \quad - \quad -$$

$$- \quad - \quad - \quad - \quad - \quad - \quad -$$

$$- \quad - \quad - \quad - \quad - \quad - \quad -$$

I was always of a determined and if thwarted violent disposition– My actions and temper were infinitely more inflexible at three years old than now at fourteen– At that early age I can perfectly remember reigning in the Nursery and being renowned amongst the servants for self love and excessive passion– When reproved I always considered myself as an injured martyr and bitter have been the tears I have shed over my supposed wrongs. At four and a half my great delight was poring over fairy phenomenons and the actions of necromancers—& the seven champions of Christendom in "Popular tales" has beguiled many a weary hour.[6] At five I supposed myself a heroine and in my day dreams of bliss I constantly imaged to myself a forlorn damsel in distress rescued by some noble knight and often have I laid awake hours in darkness, "THINKING," as I expressed myself; but which was nothing more than musing on these fairy castles in the air!

I perfectly remember the delight I felt when I attained my sixth birthday[;] I enjoyed my triumph to a great degree over the inhabitants of the nursery, there being no UPSTART to dispute my authority, as Henrietta was quite an infant and my dearest Bro tho my constant companion and a beloved participator in all my pleasures never allowed the urge for power to injure the endearing sweetness of his temper.

I might, tho perhaps with injustice to myself, impute my never changing affection to this ever dear Brother to his mild and gentle conduct at this period. But he and I have attained an age not merely childish, an age to which infantine pursuits are no longer agreeable, we have attained an age when reason is no longer the subject of childish frivolity!–[7] Still I believe that our affection for each other has become infinitely more enthusiastic and more rivetted– At four I first mounted Pegasus but at six I thought myself priviledged to show off feats of horsemanship–

5. Thomas Gray, "Elegy Written in a Country Church Yard" (1751), l. 44, slightly misquoted.

6. *The Famous Historie of the Seven Champions of Christendom* (1579), a romance by Richard Johnson, does not appear in Maria Edgeworth's *Popular Tales* (1804), but it was frequently reprinted (often in simplified versions for children) in the early nineteenth century.

7. At this point EBB wrote and then cancelled the following comment: "He tho not less mild has reached an age where it is becoming to be manly, firm and determined; and I trust that my violence of temper has considerably abated."

In my sixth year[8] for some lines on virtue which I had pen[n]ed with great care I received from Papa a ten shilling note enclosed in a letter which was addrest to *the Poet Laureat of Hope End*; I mention this because I received much, more pleasure from the word *Poet* than from the ten shilling note– I did not understand the meaning of the word laureat but it being explained to me by my dearest Mama, the idea first presented itself to me of celebrating our birthdays by my verse[.] *"Poet laureat of Hope End"* was too great a tittle [sic] to lose– Nothing could contribute so much to my amusement as a novel. A novel at six years old may appear ridiculous, but it was a real desire that I felt,—not to instruct myself, I felt no such wish, but to divert myself and to afford more scope to my nightly meditations . . and it is worthy of remark that in a novel I carefully past over all passages which described CHILDREN–

The Fops love and pursuit of the heroines mother in *"Temper"* delighted me, but the description of the infancy of Emma was past over[9]– At SEVEN I began to think of *"forming my taste"*—perhaps I did not express my thoughts in those refined words but I considered it time *"to see what was best to write about & read about"*! At 7 too I read the History of England and Rome—at 8 I perused the History of Greece and it was at this age that I first found real delight in poetry– "The Minstrel"[10] Popes "Illiad"[,] some parts of the "Odyssey" passages from "Paradise lost" selected by my dearest Mama and some of Shakespeares plays among which were, "The Tempest," "Othello" and a few historical dramatic pieces constituted my Studies!– I was enchanted with all these but I think the story interested me more that [sic] the poetry till "The Minstrel" met my sight– I was then too young to feel the loveliness of simple beauty, I required something dazling to strike my mind– The brilliant imagery[,] the fine metaphors and the flowing numbers of "the Minstrel" truly astonished me. Every stanza excited my ardent admiration nor can I now remember the delight which I felt on perusing those pages without enthusiasm–

At nine I felt much pleasure from the effusions of my imagination in the adorned drapery of versification but nothing could compensate for the regret I felt on laying down a book to take up a pen– The subject of my studies was Pope's Illiad some passages from Shakespeare & Novels which I enjoyed to their full extent. At this age works of imagination only afforded me gratification and I trod the delightful fields of fancy without any of those conscientious scruples which now always attends me when wasting time in frivolous pleasures–

At ten my poetry was entirely formed by the style of written authors and I read that I might write– Novels were still my most delightful study combined with the sweet notes of poetic inspiration! At eleven I wished to be considered an authoress. Novels were thrown aside. Poetry and Essays were my studies & I felt the most ardent desire to understand the learned languages– To comprehend even the Greek alphabet was delight inexpressible. Under the tuition of M.[r] M.[c]Swiney I attained that which I so fervently desired.[11] For 8 months during this year I never

8. It appears that EBB's memory is faulty, and that she was in her ninth year at the time of the event described here. See letter 11, note 2. EBB's chronology from this point forward is suspect.

9. Emma is the heroine and "the Fop" the villain of a three-volume novel by Amelia Opie, *Temper, or Domestic Scenes* (1812).

10. "The Minstrel" (1771–74), an incomplete poem by James Beattie about the education of a shepherd-poet.

11. Daniel McSwiney, dates unknown, was engaged in 1817 to instruct Bro in Latin. He left his position in 1820 but is frequently mentioned in supporting documents as being in the Barretts' company in London.

remember having directed my attentions to any other object than the ambition of gaining fame– Literature was the star which in prospect illuminated my future days[;] it was the spur which prompted me . . the aim . . the very soul of my being– I was determined (and as I before stated my determinations were not "airlike dispersable") I was determined to gain the very pinnacle of excellence and even when this childish & foolishly ambitious idea had fled not by the weight of the argument of a more experienced adviser but by my own reflections & conviction I yet looked with regret . . painful regret to the beacon of that distinguished fame I had sighed for so long . . & so ardently!

I never felt more real anguish than when I was undecieved on this point. I am not vain naturally & I have still less of the pedant in my composition than self conceit but I confess that during these eight months I never felt myself of more consequence and never had a better opinion of my own talents– In short I was in infinite danger of being as vain as I was inexperienced! During this dangerous period I was from home & the fever of a heated imagination was perhaps increased by the intoxicating gai[e]ties of a watering place Ramsgate where we then were and where I commenced my poem "The Battle of Marathon" now in print!![12] When we came home one day after having written a page of poetry which I considered models of beauty I ran down stairs to the library to seek Popes Homer in order to compare them that I might enjoy my OWN SUPERIORITY–[13] I can never think of this instance of the intoxication of vanity without smiling at my childish folly & ridiculous vanity– I brought Homer up in triumph & read first my own Poem & afterwards began to compare– I read fifty lines from the glorious Father of the lyre— It was enough . . I felt the whole extent of my own immense & mortifying inferiority–

My first impulse was to throw with mingled feelings of contempt & anguish my composition on the floor—my next to burst into tears! & I wept for an hour and then returned to reason and humility– Since then I have not felt MANY twitches of vanity and my mind has never since been intoxicated by any ridiculous dreams of greatness!!– From this period for a twelvemonth I could find no pleasure in any book but Homer. I read & longed to read again and tho I nearly had it by heart I still found new beauties & fresh enchantments—

At twelve I enjoyed a literary life in all it's pleasures. Metaphysics were my highest delights and after having read a page from Locke my mind not only felt edified but exalted– At this age I was in great danger of becoming the founder of a religion of my own. I revolted at the idea of an established religion—my faith was sincere but my religion was founded solely on the imagination. It was not the deep persuasion of the mild Christian but the wild visions of an enthusiast. I worshipped God heart and soul but I forgot that my prayers should be pure & simple as the Father I adored[.] They were composed extempore & full of figurative & florid apostrophes.

I shall always look back to this time as the happiest of my life[;] my mind was above the frivolous sorrows of childhood when I trusted with enthusiastic faith to His mercy "who only chasteneth whom he loveth"–

12. From supporting documents we conjecture that EBB did not go to Ramsgate until May 1817 at the earliest and was back in Hope End in late September—perhaps four or five months in all. *The Battle of Marathon,* a Homeric epic, was completed in late 1819 and was privately printed at the expense of EBB's father in March of the following year. See *Reconstruction,* pp. 213–215.

13. Last word underscored three times.

One day I omitted a prayer wholly thro' forgetfulness but having afterwards remembered the neglect I was so imprest with the idea of having offended the God of my salvation that I hardly hoped for pardon. My whole mind was tortured & my prayers that night bespoke the anguish of my heart– It was not the humility of a sinner suing for pardon at the throne of mercy but the violent intreaties extorted by despair from my heart. The next morning I renewed with tenfold ardour my agonising prayers– My God My God why hast thou forsaken me I repeated in a tone of anguish. The morning was dark and a dingy mist floated in the mid air when on a sudden a flood of light rushing from the benignant sun thro that veil of loneliness beamed on my prostrate form & seemed to smile upon my prayers! My imagination took fire & I believed that my God had forgiven me. I felt as much awe[,] as much gratitude[,] as if the Deity himself had vouchsafed to comfort me and recieve me again unto his bosom. So great was the strength of my imagination which is now often too powerful for my controul. This year I read Milton for the first time *thro* together with Shakespeare & Pope's Homer– In perusing these glorious models of Poetic excellence I have often felt my soul kindled with the might of such sublime genius & glow with the enthusiasm of admiration!! I now read to gain idea's not to indulge my fancy and I studied the works of those critics whose attention was directed to my favorite authors. I had now attained my thirteenth birthday! I had taught myself "to throw away ambition" and to feel that pride & self conceit can only bring in self degradation on awaking from the splendid dream of vanity & folly! No incidents in my past life had contributed to stir up the embers of that pride & that determination of character which had now so considerably abated. My days had glided like the light bark on the summer sea undisturbed by any gale of adversity or sorrow! And yet my mind since the first year of my birth has ever been in commotion not proceeding from external causes but from those internal reflections & internal passions which are such powerful attributes of my character and which I trust it has been my study to subdue! My religious enthusiasm had subsided and I took upon myself to advocate the cause of the church of England![14] This was a curious change but I was borne away from all reason by the power, the fatal power, of my imagination– I finished my poem which I shall always consider a[s] a memorable epoch in my life– I was repaid for all my labours .. the book was printed!

At this period I perused all modern authors who have any claim to superior merit & poetic excellence. I was familiar with Shakespeare Milton Homer and Virgil Locke Hooker Pope–[15] I read Homer in the original with delight inexpressible together with Virgil. I now tasted those glorious rewards which I had sought so earnestly and with all my faults all my weaknesses I now felt certain that if I could not subdue them I might in time at least keep them under some controul & tho' I could not reach the splendid beacon of fame I might perhaps enjoy the benevolent beams of that literature which I had loved from my earliest infancy– The mists which cowered oer that haven of joy were partly dispersed and perhaps the gale of perseverence and application may waft my little bark near enough to that immortal fame to appreciate duly the magnificence of those soaring genius's who seek the pinacle of excellence tho I must not pursue! I am now fourteen and since those

14. EBB amended her 1813 edition of *The Book of Common Prayer* (*Reconstruction*, A277) to read "Church in England."
15. EBB has deleted "& the best authors in our language."

days of my tenderest infancy my character has not changed– It is still as proud as wilful as impatient of controul as impetuous but thanks be to God it is restrained. I have acquired a command of my self which has become so habitual that my disposition appears to my friends to have undergone a revolution– But to myself it is well known that the same violent inclinations are in my inmost heart and that altho habitual restraint has become almost a part of myself yet were I once to loose the rigid rein I might again be hurled with Phaeton far from every thing human . . every thing reasonable! My mind has and ever will be a turmoil of conflicting passions not so much influenced by exterior causes as by internal reflection and impetuosity– I have always some end in view which requires exertion for if that exertion be wanting I should indeed appear to myself a dreary void! The energy or perhaps impetuosity of my character allows me not to be tranquil and I look upon that tranquillity which I cannot enjoy with a feeling rather like contempt as precluding in great measure the intellectual faculties of the human mind!

My religion is I fear not so ardent but perhaps more reasonable than formerly and yet I must ever regret those enthusiastic visions of what may be called fanaticism which exalted my soul on the wings of fancy to the contemplation of the Deity– My admiration of literature especially of poetic literature can never be subdued nor can it be extinguished but with life. If there be any innate principle it is that with which the soul contemplates superior excellence in whatever form it may soar–!!!.–

After the glowing page of poetic fancy metaphysical knowledge must rank highest in my admiration– It exalts it improves it elevates the soul above any worldly views but what is yet better it convinces it– In accompan[y]ing Locke thro his complex reasoning & glorious subjects my mind seems more enlarged more cultivated & more enlightened! I am neither vain decietful or vindictive but I am proud impetuous & wilful! I am not irreligious but religion has not always the same power over my heart! I am capable of great application but I fear that capacity is not often exerted! Emulation forms a strong feature in my character– Either neglect or anger or even hatred I can bear with proper tranquillity but any thing like contempt my nature spurns at. It is not easy to lose but difficult to gain my entire esteem for it is founded on the good qualities of my friends but one ungenerous sentiment would lose it for ever!

I feel uncontroulable contempt for any littleness of mind, or mean[n]ess of soul & I feel that I can never love those whom I do not admire respect & venerate! I trust that I am Liberal for bigotry & prejudice I detest tho some of my friends assure me that I am mistaken on this point. I am neither envious or obstinate—but am easily irritated & easily appeased– My disposition is haughty impatient and fiery but I trust that my heart is good– I am confident it is grateful.

I understand little of Theology but am fond of listening to disputations on that subject.

I am capable of patriotism enthusiastic & sincere. At this period when the base & servile aristocracy of my beloved country overwhelm with insults our magnanimous and unfortunate Queen[16] I cannot restrain my indignation I cannot controul my enthusiasm– The dearest wish of my heart would [be] to serve her . . to serve the glorious Queen of my native ilse [sic]– I am too insignificant to aid her but by prayer & whilst I bow my heart in humble supplication to the throne of

16. Queen Caroline (1768–1821). See letter 109, note 1.

divine mercy may I hope that he who listeth to [the] voice of the unhappy will grant to the prayers of England the security and glory of her Queen?—

.   .   .   .   .

About this time my beloved Bro left us for school[17] .. If I ever loved any human being I love this dear Brother .. the Partner of my pleasures of my literary toils. My attachment to him is literally devoted! If to save him from anxiety from mental vexation any effort of mine could suffice Heaven knows my heart that I would unhesitatingly buy his happiness with my own misery!— But oh if there is a bitterness that is worse than death[,] if there is any pang which surpasses human wretchedness in agony it would be that with which I should behold him were he ever to stray from the path of honorable rectitude! Thou who from thy pure Heaven beholdest me while I trace these characters if ever that day is to come[,] that hour of unutterable grief[,] grant that ere that morning breaketh I may sleep in peace the cold sod reposing on my breast & deaf to the call of misery!

Grant my Father that ere I behold my beloved Brother! my valued friend whose upright and pure principles my soul now glories in[,] deviating from honor[,] I may have breathed my last sigh and preserve the ideal vision of his virtues to my grave!—

And you my own dearest Bro if these pages ever meet your eye, when the laugh of dissipation assails you—when the mercenary bribe is proffered you—when you ever feel tempted to turn from the once adored image of honor[,] remember that the happiness of one at least hangs on your conduct!— Oh remember her words who loves you[,] who venerates you even to fondness and spare that heart which your degradation would break!——

But while the tear swells in my eye should I not remember that those principles of honor and probity are too deeply rivetted in your breast to be shaken? Oh Yes! You whom I depend on as on myself will never disgrace those principles which animate this breast with such delight! I feel I know you never will——!!!

Perhaps there is too much of sentiment in my disposition and too little rational reflection! I have beheld silently the pure and wide expanse of Ocean. I have remembered the littleness of Man when compared to the Majesty of God and my heart has throbbed almost wildly with a strange and undefined feeling!— I have gazed on the fleeting clouds which rolled their light columns over a dark blue sky and wept while I felt that such was the futility of life—!

My feelings are acute in the extreme but as nothing is so odious in my eyes as a damsel famed in story for a superabundance of sensibility they are carefully restrained! I have so habituated myself to this sort of continued restraint, that I often appear to my dearest friends to lack common feeling!— I do not blame them! They know me not and I feel a sort of mysterious pleasure in their mistake!—

It is pleasing to all minds to feel that they are judged harshly—it robs Conscience of half her arrows——

I remember when very young—before I had passed the first years of infancy [——]being told by a servant whom I had offended "that I was cold and unfeeling and that every one thought so whatever they might say"— I heard this declaration with the greatest pretended calmness—tho my head perfectly seemed to swim so violent was my indignation, but pride unconquerable pride sealed my lips!— I only

17. Bro left Hope End for London in the early months of 1820, residing with his grandmother Elizabeth Moulton until entering Charterhouse. He advanced from the ninth form in 1820 to the third in 1826.

smiled[—]a contemptuous smile I meant it to be[—]and walked away! And yet I was not angry, only astonished unspeakably astonished!– That whole day my usual calmness sat on my brow, it was remarked that I was more silent than I was accustomed to be—! No! I could not preserve buoyant spirits when the bitterness of death was at my heart! I was young very young then to govern myself—but I did to it and I gloried in that self command, but when the shades of night descended[,] when I was left alone to hold solitary converse with my pillow[,] feelings so long repressed rushed like a cataract to my heart, and tears gushed wildly forth!——

My views of every subject are naturally cheerful and light as the first young visions of aerial hope but there have been moments, nay hours when contemplation has been arrayed in sorrows dusky robe, when Man has appeared to me black as night and happiness but a name!– And yet I have not felt miserable even then and I cannot entirely agree with our great Bard!

> The mind is its own place & of itself
> Can make a hell of Heaven & Heaven of Hell!–[18]

I must ever believe that misery is influenced by external events. There is a kind of pensive melancholy which is the consequence of meditation, but misery must rack the soul influenced by more violent reverses!

My mind is naturally independant and spurns that subserviency of opinion which is generally considered necessary to feminine softness! But this is a subject on which I must always feel strongly for I feel within me an almost proud consciousness of independance which prompts me to defend my opinions & to yield them only to conviction!!!!!!!

My friends may differ from me; the world may accuse me but this I am determined never to retract!!

Better oh how much better to be the ridicule of mankind, the scoff of society[,] than lose that self respect which tho' this heart [were] bursting yet would elevate me above misery—above wretchedness & above abasement!!! These principles are irrevocable! It is not I feel it is not vanity that dictates them! it is not[—]I know it is not an encroachment on masculine prerogative but it is a proud sentiment which will never never allow me to be humbled in my own eyes!!!

To be a good linguist is the height of my ambition & I do not believe that I can ever cease desiring to attain this!! The wish appears to be innate and rooted in my very nature!! It is actuated by two motives[.] In primo . . to be sincere vanity has not a little to do with it!! The second perhaps cannot be so easily defined but whenever I am employed in any literary undertaking which requires much depth of thought & learned reference I cannot help feeling uneasy & imagining that if I were conversant with such languages I might perhaps come to descision at once on a point which now occupies days in conjecture!!

This is tormenting & sometimes agitates me to a painful & almost nervous degree. I well remember three years ago ere I had the advantage of M.r M.cSwineys instruction & having found myself entangled in one of these perplexities crying very heartily for half an hour because I did not understand Greek!!!–

It was then I made a secret vow never to pause at undertaking any literary difficulty if convinced of its final utility, but manfully to wade thro the waves of learning stopping my ears against the enchanted voice of the Syren and unmindful of either the rocks of disappointment or the waves of labour. I believe I have

18. Milton, *Paradise Lost* (1667) I, 254–255, misquoted.

resolution enough to abide by my determination for if life be spent in the steep ascent towards the bright pin[n]acle of learning it is a life well employed and tho it be a life of labour & anxiety yet it is not a monotonous one! There is variety in it at least!!! Oh monotony! monotony if there is a Demon to whom Beelzebub is a seraph[,] thou art he! If there is one more tedious, more teazing more agonizing to an author! thou art he. Yes take the Palm & for Heaven's sake never let me behold thy face again!!!

My attachment to my friends can scarcely be defined! It is a sentiment at once sincere enthusiastic devoted & melancholy!– I really believe I am disinterested! At least I feel as if I moved & breathed not for myself!! Perhaps this is from romance of disposition, but I always imagine that I was sent on the earth for some purpose! To suffer! to die! to defend! To save by my death my country or some very very dear friends! To suffer in the cause of freedom!! I know, I understand not how this is but I feel it to my heart core & so strong is this feeling that it amounts almost to presentiment! But this is only sometimes. Sometimes when my mood is melancholy & mysterious, I do not pretend to more sentiment than my neighbours (tho I sincerely believe I possess too much) for it is only at times that I feel this extraordinary depression of spirits, enthusiasm of disposition & mysterious feelings!! In society I am pretty nearly the same as other people only much more awkward much more wild & much more mad!! These moments I may call lucid intervals tho they are not always very sane—! It is only when I am sola that the fits come on & before they are over I generally vent my feelings in tears!

And now the scene must close! I have carried up the tragic Comedy to the epoch when I have reached my fifteenth year & most stupid dramatis personæ they have been! Pray Readers (if I have the good fortune to have any) do not believe I think myself a fool! To tell you the simple truth I do not! only rather mad or thereabouts! But I have done with egotism & if all my gentle auditors understand me as well as I do myself I shall be happy!!!

My life has been chequered by my own feelings not from external causes, & like Rosalind I have "laughed & wept in the same breath"–[19] My past days now appear as a bright star glimmering far far away & I feel almost agony to turn from it for ever! Before a darkness there are miseries—there may be joys which await me!! but I know not!! My destiny lies in the hands of God!![20]

And you my most patient auditors[,] as it may be requisite for dramatic effect to give you a little advice before the Curtain falls let me begs [sic] you if you wish to keep up your spirits never to write your own life.

---

19. "That laughs, and weeps, and all but with a breath" (Shakespeare, "Venus and Adonis" [1593], l. 414). The line is not found in *As You Like It*, as EBB's reference to Rosalind suggests.

20. EBB's serious illness of 1821–22 began soon after her fifteenth birthday and probably accounts for the tone of this penultimate paragraph.

3. MY CHARACTER AND BRO'S COMPARED![21]

Hope End, 1821 Feb.

To compare different characters, to distinguish with exactness the different shades by which the minds of different individuals are marked in a stronger or lesser degree perhaps requires more nicety & delicacy of judgement than I possess!– To be perfectly conversant with ones own mind & understanding & sentiments is a most difficult task! For what says Locke "The understanding like the eye whilst it makes us see & perceive all other things, takes no notice of itself." This observation is worthy of the great Metaphysician and at once determines the judgement & siezes on the imagination!—— If any vanity be discussed in the following pages it must be forgiven as I would lay open my own heart with sincerity; unrestrained by that false delicacy which might prompt me to appear in the eyes of my friends with more humility than I really possess. I would wish to be frank– I may think better of my own talents than they deserve .. my opinion cannot exalt them as I feel it is founded on that self partiality which is natural to almost every mind– I believe that we each are blessed with abilities—my dear Bro's are more solid & more profound—mine are more refined & dazzling. I prefer in the sweet plains of literature Poetry Metaphysics & fanciful philosophy. He delights in the sober reasoning of the Historian! He feels greater interest in the noble Sallust while I have remained entranced over a page of the divine & animated Cicero! When we read I have remarked that the Authors errors are always foremost in his mind while mine is almost intoxicated with his beauties!– I may be an enthusiastic admirer of any noble work but Bro will always be the better critic! If Locke is correct when he declares that "Ecstasy is dreaming with the eyes open" I have certainly been in a continued reverie since my birth while my dear Bro wide awake has had full leasure to look about him & to reflect!——

We each are fiery in politics but Bro's patriotism is dictated by reason, justice & a proper portion of moderation, mine is more ardent & more enthusiastic! I know that we each would sacrifice our happiness our lives for our beloved country but when Bro laid his head on the block feelings of conscious honor of conscious rectitude would at once soothe & exalt his noble soul while mine would be swelling with pride indignation and the hope of glory!–

I have read more than Bro but I have not reflected so much! He cannot be superficial in any branch of literature or learning because he is particularly acute in his powers of reasoning while I may be so in every thing!– I am ambitious & proud in the extreme he does not possess enough of emulation or pride!

I am not content till I excel; but Bro is satisfied with mediocrity–! He possesses too much humility to soar and therefore generally stoops lower than is necessary[.] I am much too proud to stoop at all for any thing or for any body but would stand for ever on the tiptoe of expectation admiring the empty bubbles of that fame so far beyond my reach!– Our dispositions are perhaps similar for tho I am much more fiery yet we both easily forgive!– Independance we each glory in and rather than give up our opinions if founded on conscience I believe we would willingly descend into the grave–! My imagination is perhaps more exalted & more glowing

21. EBB wrote this hitherto unpublished essay in one of her workbooks. Several months after its composition she asked Henrietta to "tear the whole article out and keep it" (see letter 137 and *Reconstruction*, D1324). The original is now in the Armstrong Browning Library.

than my dear Bro's but in judgement he infinitely surpasses me! From our infancy it has been for me to excite him to energy while he has not disdained to be my Mentor, my adviser & my friend!– Thus has our friendship been cemented by the strongest of all possible ties! Our minds our souls are united by the same opinions, the same interests! Together have we conversed, read, studied—together have we fagged at the grammar, wept over the torn dictionary—triumphed over classical difficulties & reaped the glorious reward of perseverance—success! If there be any tie stronger than these, I know not of it! Let the cold reasoner scoff but let those who have perused together the Roman & Greek Classics, and who have together resisted difficulties of style & language decide whether or not our attachment be founded on folly–!

My beloved Bro and I have parted on the plain of life–![22] The last farewell is agony, for alas! our pursuits will now no longer be the same!– Where beneath this Heaven shall I again find a friend so disinterested, so generous, so attached? I may ascend the delightful hill of classical learning but he who added pleasure to every cherished object is no longer with me!– I may strike again the melodious chords of the lyre but the echo will die away in melancholy stillness thro the silent scales for the once prized tone greets his ear no more!– I am convinced that my brightest hours are faded for ever—but I possess fortitude—it shall be exercised—I possess energy & it shall not sleep–! I do not, I will not complain tho I turn from the memory of past days with painful regret, and the pen which traces this page of sadness shall never recur to the subject again!– Then farewell my beloved Bro! Brother of my affections, friend of my soul! We shall often meet but we shall be no longer as we have been! We shall no longer be partners in the same labours—pleasures—studies, but we may yet love each other fondly, sincerely and whilst your image is entwined with every delightful every cherished recollection, may mine still cling around your heart, not less esteemed, & not less beloved!

---

4. UNTITLED ESSAY[23]

Hope End.
Feby 4.th 1827. Sunday.

I have thought of writing down some pleasant passages of my life which it is for the interest & my happiness to bear in remembrance. It will do me more good to write down some of the bitter passages; for remembrance is very apt to send bitter things away thro' the ivory gate like dreams. And remembrance is apt to do this, tho' without prudence. For to remember evil in the happy day, will occasion thanksgiving,—while to remember evil in the evil day will occasion consolation. As we *have* arisen from sorrow & rejoiced, so we *may* arise from sorrow & rejoice.

I had a great deal of pain yesterday evening. For some months I have been employed on my work respecting the development of genius, the subject of which

---

22. A year earlier, in 1820, Bro was sent to Charterhouse, London, for his formal education.

23. Extracts of these discouraging remarks by EBB's father were first printed in Sotheran's Catalogue 737 (1913), item 327, with a facsimile page. H.B. Forman reprinted these extracts in *HUP*, II, 75–78. The manuscript is printed here in full, for the first time, from the original at Scripps College.

has been approved by Mr. Price,[24]—the execution of which has been hurried by him. Some months ago, I read a part of what I had written to Papa, who professed to have heard nothing from the weakness of my voice. I was not discouraged by this, but much disappointed. I worked on in my solitude, without the advantage of his advice, feeling alternately sanguine & out of heart, about my poetical prospects. Having got my work in a sufficient state of forwardness I wrote out part of it & took down to Papa, yesterday evening, eight sheets.[25] I said to him "I have copied for you something which I should be much obliged to you to look at, when you have time." "Is it *prose* or *English*"—"*English*, but not *prose*". Papa smiled at his mistake, & seemed in a very good humour & not over critical. I gave him the sheets. He complained first of my illegibility, then of my obscurity. "You can never please people [with] this want of explicitness. I told you so in the case of your Essay on Mind. He then complained of my involved style & obsolete words. "Where did this word come from?" "From Spenser". "I wish you had never read Spenser". "Your harmony is defective—*you* who write so much about measure— (alluding to my correspondance with Mr Price)—I told you by writing on that subject you would destroy your style." "The lines you complain of, Papa, were written before I wrote on that subject at all".

He expressed his disapprobation strongly with regard to my conception of Theon's character. "He is a madman, & the most disagreable man I ever heard of"–

When Papa had read three sheets & part of a fourth, in a very hesitating & ridiculing manner, constantly mistaking the words, hardly waiting for my correction, & almost entirely missing the final pause of every line, he gave me my dismissal in words it is good for me to remember.

"There is precisely the same fault here as what you have been condemning in "*Almaché*["]– There is no variety!– You ring changes on one idea all through. You might give the character you would entertain us with in a page & a half. The broodings of your hero are the broodings of a madman—& his egotism is insufferable. Lord Byron lets you look into his melancholy mind, but by glimpses only. There never *was* such a character as Theon's. Neither is your bad conception of a general plan redeemed by your poetry, which has less harmony than any thing you ever wrote. Indeed the whole production is most *wretched!* I *must* tell you so—& I think it quite lamentable that you should have passed so much time to such an effect. You see the subject is *beyond your grasp*—& you must be content *with what you can reach*. I cannot read any more– I would not read over again what I *have* read, for fifty pounds—really not for *ten*. I advise you to burn the wretched thing."

Thus was I dismissed after months of anxious solitary thought, after months of apprehension mingled with rejoicing expectation. I did not say a word: it was harder to prevent myself from shedding a tear. I took my papers, & when I went to bed, had a marble heaviness at my heart. How will this end?–

It seems to me a little hard that half an hour of patient attention should not be vouchsafed to my half year's patient composition, but I have no business to complain of this. I have recieved much more gratification from the approbation my writings have met with, than they or I had a right to expect. Mr. Price's friendship has given me more continued happiness than any single circumstance ever did—& I pray for *him*, as the grateful pray.

24. See letter 236.
25. Probably the manuscript described in *Reconstruction*, D732.

I have also experienced much mortification at different times about my compositions. They have cost me almost as many tears as smiles—but perhaps tears do me good. I have hardly ever been mortified as I was mortified last night—but perhaps this also will do me good. I was growing a little too exalting in myself, a little too full of myself, & it is right that I should be made apprehensive about myself. Papa's expression "that my subject was beyond my grasp" lets me see at once how limited he considers my talents. I believe I did not think my talents so limited, & I certainly did not know that *he* thought so. The knowledge is worth something, but it is very very bitter to receive at first.

I shall get over this in time, & in the meanwhile will fag harder than I have yet fagged. I cannot give up completing the poem I was advised to burn, but I shall revise & I hope improve it. [26] How happy I should be *now*, if I had not shewn it to Papa last night!– *Now* I am disturbed, humbled,—& feel every instant . . as I did not feel yesterday.

> These little cares are great to little *me*
> & I cast them on Him who careth for me!

I am even now rather more comfortable from emptying my heart on paper–
Dearest Papa would be sorry to think how much he grieved me!

---

5. UNTITLED ESSAY[27]

Beth has a kind smile, I think, for a child of ten years, but still she thought too much of her own agency in every good act meditated towards others. Her eyes were bright with selfwill,—& the long lashes could scarcely soften them. What she would do hereafter, was her reigning thought. She hated conventions of every sort,—because she felt them to be inimical to the development of her selfwill. She loved herself in the love of truth—perhaps (I fear) she loved herself in her love of love. She had a bitter scorn of all things that were not spontaneous,—because her own impulses were sufficient for her own life. Once her father met her on the stairs in the morning. Beth smiled at him for she loved him. [']'Not a word" said he– 'No.' she said—[']I have nothing to say'. 'Will you not ask me if I am well–' [']No—If you had been ill, you w.^d have told me.['] Her father was angry & led her by the hand into the breakfastroom.

["]Here is a little girl who thinks it too much trouble to ask her father how he is.["]

---

26. Yet the poem remained unpublished until after EBB's death, first appearing in *HUP*, II, 99–133.

27. This document is undated and the paper bears no watermark. The hand, however compares to other manuscripts written in the early 1840's, and perhaps was composed to amuse her young cousin Lizzie Barrett. It appears that EBB's composition was interrupted. At the bottom of the final page, which is only half full, is a list of sixteen animals. Extracts appeared in Sotheran's Catalogue 737 (1913), item 293, with a facsimile page. It is printed here in full from the original manuscript at Scripps College. The references to Moses the pony, and to riding on the Malvern Hills, confirm that "Beth" was EBB herself.

Beth blushed & was sorry, but she knew in her heart that she did not think it too much trouble, but too much falsehood.

Again, she fell across her uncle's foot or in some headlong child's trick inconvenienced him. He said to her, 'Beth, why do you not beg my pardon'– [']'Because I did not mean to do it. It was an accident. Why sh^d I beg your pardon?" Her uncle was not pleased with her—& Beth was proud again.

It was by slow degrees that Beth became reconciled to the conventions of life—the signs which have succeeded the substances. She was loth to admit that she lived in a land of shadows.

Beth desired to be beautiful. She stood sometimes before a pier glass in her mother's room. She stood on her tiptoes, & multiplied by three every feature in her face. When she had done, she smiled & thought that perhaps, when her hair was grown down to her feet as she meant it to do, she might be almost as pretty, as Peggy, the cottager's daughter in the lane. That might happen when she was fifteen—& that was the age when all the princesses in the fairy tales were fallen in love with.

Beth intended to be very much in love when she was fifteen,—but she did not mean to go so far as to be married, even at sixteen. She meant however to be in love, & she settled that her lover's name sh^d be Henry;—if it were not Ld Byron. Her lover was to be a poet in any case—and Beth was inclined to believe that he w^d be Ld Byron.

But Beth was a poet herself—& there was the reigning thought– No woman was ever before such a poet as she w^d be. As Homer was among men, so w^d she be among women—she w^d be the feminine of Homer. Many persons w^d be obliged to say that she was a little taller than Homer if anything. When she grew up she w^d wear men's clothes, & live in a Greek island, the sea melting into turquoises all around it. She w^d teach the islanders the ancient Greek, & they should all talk there of the old glories in the real Greek sunshine, with the right ais & ois– Or she w^d live in a cave on Parnassus mount, and feed upon cresses & Helicon water, & Beth might have said Grace after the sweet diet of that dream.

Beth was also a warrior. When she was fifteen she w^d arm herself in complete steel (Beth always thought of a suit of armour & never of a red coat) & ride on a steed, along the banks of the Danube, every where by her chanted songs, .. for she was to sing her own poetry all the way she went .. attracting to her side many warriors—so that by the time she reached Stambol, Beth w^d be the chief of a battalion & she w^d destroy the Turkish empire, & deliver 'Greece the glorious'– And the flashing of swords was bright in the eyes of Beth. And when Greece was finally delivered, she was directly to begin to talk old Greek again, with the right ais & ois.

Poor Beth had one great misfortune. She was born a woman. Now she despised nearly all the women in the world except Ma^{dme} de Stael– She could not abide their littlenesses called delicacies, their pretty headaches, & soft mincing voices, their nerves & affectations. She thought to herself that no man was vain of being weaker than another man, but rather ashamed. She thought that a woman's weakness, she sh^d not be vain of therefore, but ashamed. One word Beth hated in her soul .. & the word was "feminine". Beth thanked her gods that she was not & never w^d be feminine. Beth could run rapidly & leap high,—and though her hands were miserably little to be sure, she had very strong wrists. When the colour came into Beths cheeks she c^d hold up against anyone of her size, with her little wrists– She c^d climb too pretty well up trees—but, although she never told, she was apt to be frightened when she had to turn & come down. She could slide too, .. with a little room for a run. And she liked fishing, though she did not often catch anything. And best of all, though she cared for bows & arrows, & squirts & popguns—best of all, did she like riding .. gallopping till the trees raced past her & the clouds were shot over her head like horizontal arrows from a giant's bow—gallopping till she felt the still air to gather against her face & chest like a wind—leaping over ditches—feeling the live creature beneath her, swerve and bound with its own force like a ball in its course, running races till the goal in sight vanished in the rapidity of reaching it. These were great joys for Beth. Her poney, Moses, had a tail longer by nine times than the patriarch's beard—& when she tied the end of it with a ribbon, the bow to a short one touched the ground– A black poney with a ragged mane. To dress it out with ribbons of many colours, like Joseph's coat, was a great joy to Beth. Sometimes Moses was upon the hills, & rejoicing in his liberty, refused to be caught. In vain, did Beth entreat with silver speech all the little boys in the world away from the keeping of sheep to the catching of Moses. The patriarch w^{dnt} be caught. Beth filled her bonnet with corn, & extended it wistfully—'Moses, good Moses—come, & let me ride you'. Moses w^d as soon be entreated of Pharoah's daughter—sometimes indeed he w^d come—and sometimes he was driven into the angle of a hedge, & seized on by the forelock .. as if he were Time himself. But sometimes poor Beth having cheered on the little boys in vain, & run in her own person until her heart beat & she heard it with her ears, and her cheeks burnt to scarlet, had to go home with the tears running down them, disappointed of the hope of her ride, & thinking bitter things of Moses. At other times, great was the joy thereof. Moses was a mountain poney—very little & fleet & black as a coal,—when Beth rode in the Malvern hills, she w^d leave the rein loose, & Moses w^d climb the long steeps, surefootedly as a goat. He never forgot the traditions of his Shetland.

Beth was fond too of a dog called Havannah—a poodle which used to be half shaved in poodle fashion. 'Vannah' as she called him, understood for the most part only french—& Beth's first French was murmured in his ear. The venez ici—& 'coucher', were next to the 'baisez moi' which she climbed upon her father's bed to wake him withal– It was a large white bed, & a Mont Blanc to Beth for climbing upon. And then, between little gasps of breath, & low childish laughters, that 'Baisez moi' was lisped against the pillow. She liked this sort of French much better than the French put into verbs, which appeared to her a most atrocious invention—& probably Boney's own.

List of Absent Letters

DURING THE COURSE of our research in editing the Brownings' correspondence, brief references have been found, principally in sale catalogues, to additional letters. All attempts to locate these documents have failed. In addition, some letters are in known locations, but access to them has been denied. Following is a list of letters which, for such reasons, are absent from this volume. Those that are located and become available will be presented in a supplementary volume.

[July 1822]. EBB to [?Henry Colburn]. Offered for sale by AAA, 14 March 1921, lot 67. To a critic who has discouraged her from publishing "The Enchantress," but has praised other poems, EBB states that she "is only sixteen."

[ca. 1823]. EBB to Edward Moulton-Barrett & Samuel Moulton-Barrett (brothers). Offered for sale by Sotheby's, 12 May 1953, lot 295. 1 p., 8vo. The letter, in Latin, signed "Tua Soror dilectissima," was previously owned by Dorothy Hewlett. On page 32 of her *Elizabeth Barrett Browning* (London, 1953), the address is quoted as follows: "Puero eruditissimo et elegantissimo Bro a manu stultissimi Sam de puella impudentissima– / 'Scribimus docti indoctique' / Horace / 'O tempora o mores' / Cicero."

June 1826. EBB to Uvedale Price. In the private collection of Aurelia Brooks Harlan.

List of Collections

(References are to letter number, not page number.)

List of Correspondents

Index

Index

(For frequently-mentioned persons not covered by the biographical sketches in Appendix I, the main identifying reference is italicized.)

Burke, Edmund, 276
Burns, Mr., 241
Bussier, Mrs., 137
Butler, Miss, 25
Butler, Arabella Sarah (EBB's cousin), 21, 144, 228
Butler, Charlotte (*née* Graham-Clarke) ("Lotte"), (EBB's aunt), 197, 198, 199n, 221
  biographical sketch, 298
  see also Clarke, Charlotte Graham-
Butler, Charlotte Mary ("Arlette"), (EBB's cousin), 222n
Butler, Frances (*née* Graham-Clarke) ("Fannie"), (EBB's aunt), 8, 9n, 21, 25
  biographical sketch, 298–299
Butler, George (EBB's uncle), 21
Butler, Louisa Charlotte (EBB's cousin), 225, 228
Butler, Richard Pierce (EBB's cousin), 21
Butler, Richard Pierce (EBB's uncle), 144, 145n, 198, 199n
Butler, Samuel
  quotation from, 112
Butler, Thomas (EBB's uncle), 14, 21, 144, 198
Button (dog), 16
Byron, Lord, 218, 231, 240
  Childe Harold's Pilgrimage, 67, 182
  quotations from, 108, 181
  "Stanzas on the Death of," xlviii, 198, 206n, 242n
  The Corsair, 45

Cæsar, Julius, 122
Calliope, 57, 99
Cambridge, 172
Campbell, Thomas, 107n, 160, 237
  Gertrude of Wyoming, 223
  letters from, 164, 169
  letters to, 104, 164, 180
  The Pleasures of Hope, 182
  Theodric, 209
Canning, George, 97, 98n, 176, 181
Carden, I., 134, 221
Carlow, 144
Carlton, 13
Caroline, 32, 33
Caroline, Queen, 95n, 97, *98n*, 118, 139
Cassandra, 107
Castalian Spring, 189
Castlereagh, Lord, 97, 113, 202
Castor, 116
Catalani, Angelica, 145
  "On Hearing Catalani Sing," 146n

Catholics, Roman, 177
  The Catholic question, 177n
Cecchi, Giovan Maria
  quotation from, 110
Celestina, 147
Cenis, Mt., 137
Chamberlayne, William
  quotation from, 280
Chances Pitch, 220
Chapman, William Herbert, 176
Character and Circumstances of Nations, 66
Charitie, An Excelente Balade of, 280
Charles the Second, 233
Charlotte, Princess, 47
  "Oh Charlotte hope of Britains," 47n
Charterhouse, 103 and n, 149, 155, 163, 168, 172, 174, 178, 179, 180, 185, 188, 195, 196 and n, 203, 204, 206, 208n, 230, 269, 274, 275, 277, 278, 279
  deaths of scholars/pensioners, 175, 176, 204
  fagging at, 194–195 and n
  founding of, 176n
  houses at, 175n
  punishment at, 166, 175, 176n, 192n, 195n
Chatterton, Thomas
  quotations from, 280
Chaucer, Geoffrey, 248, 249, 253, 254, 266, 269
  quotations from, 249, 253, 259, 266
  "The Knight's Tale," 249n, 259
Cheltenham, 7, 8, 63, 66n, 137, 192, 203, 223, 233
  EBB at, 65, 199n, 200, 201, 202n
Chesterfield, Lord, 226
Childe Harold's Pilgrimage, 67, 182
Chiron, 219
Churton, Edward, 174, 195
Cicero, Marcus Tullius, 114, 174, 181, 261
  quotation from, 111
Circe, 44
Clarke, Miss, 237, 238
Clarke, Arabella Graham- ("Bell"/ "Bummy"), (EBB's aunt), 1, 3, 5, 10, 14, 16, 25, 26, 27, 53, 116, 144, 162, 169, 198, 199, 228, 233
  at Hope End, 87
  biographical sketch, 297–298
  letter from, 143
  letters to, 20, 54, 87, 143